Table of Contents

UNIT 6 The World in Uncertain Times, 1950–the Present 252–322

Pretest

The following pretest is an actual New York State Regents Examination that was given in January 1990. Taking this exam and checking your results will help you identify your strengths and weaknesses. This process will help you focus your review in United States History and Government on those subject areas you need to study most.

On the day you take the Regents Examination, you will fill in an Answer Sheet with your answers to Part I and write your answers to Part II essay questions on separate sheets of paper. In this book, you will circle the answers to Part I and answer essay questions on separate sheets of paper.

Complete this exam and then correct it using the answers directly following it. As you proceed to read the Test-Taking Strategies section of this book, you will find more information that will help you succeed on the Regents Examination in United States History and Government.

Part I (55 credits)

Answer all 48 questions in this part.

Directions (1–48): For each statement or question, write on the separate answer sheet the *number* of the word or expression that, of those given, best completes the statement or answers the question.

1 The Bill of Rights of the United States Constitution includes a guarantee of the right to
  1 assemble peacefully
  2 have a job
  3 strike against an employer
  4 vote in elections

Base your answers to questions 2 and 3 on the passage below and on your knowledge of social studies.

  "To take a single step beyond these specific [Constitutional] limits to the powers of Congress is to grasp unlimited power.

  "The power to create a [national] bank has not, in my opinion, been delegated to Congress by the Constitution. Supporters of the Bank Bill argue that a [national] bank would be a great convenience in collecting taxes. Even if this argument were true, the Constitution allows only for laws which are 'necessary,' not those which are merely 'convenient' for carrying out delegated powers."

2 The author of this passage is most concerned about the
  1 use of public funds to create a national bank
  2 problem of collecting Federal taxes
  3 increase in the powers of state governments
  4 possible abuse of congressional power

3 The speaker is basing his argument mainly on a strict interpretation of which provision of the Federal Constitution?
  1 Preamble
  2 elastic clause
  3 judicial review
  4 apportionment of Representatives

4 The United States Supreme Court has the power to
  1 appoint its own members
  2 interpret Federal law
  3 preside over hearings to approve a treaty
  4 vote to end a filibuster

5 The idea expressed in the quotation "All just government derives its authority from the consent of the governed" is most directly found in
  1 the Magna Carta
  2 the English Bill of Rights
  3 the United States Declaration of Independence
  4 Washington's Farewell Address

6 A primary aim of the writers of the United States Constitution was to
  1 strengthen the power of the central government
  2 change from a government based on division of powers to one based on a single power
  3 develop a governmental system based on the principle of supremacy of the states
  4 weaken the power of the executive

7 Under the provisions of the original United States Constitution, the most democratically selected body was the
  1 Senate
  2 Cabinet
  3 Supreme Court
  4 House of Representatives

8 The due process clause of the 14th amendment to the United States Constitution most nearly means that
  1 all labor-management contracts must be reviewed by a commission of the Federal Government
  2 members of minority groups must be given preferential treatment in employment
  3 the selection of the President and Vice President must follow a prescribed set of steps
  4 a standard set of procedures must be followed before any action is taken to punish persons accused of breaking the law

9 In an outline, one of these entries is a main topic and three are subtopics. Which is the main topic?
   1 Alexander Hamilton's Economic Program
   2 The Rise of National Political Parties
   3 The Constitution's First Tests
   4 John Adams' Stormy Presidency

10 During most of the 19th century, the United States had an open immigration policy mainly because
   1 there was no organized opposition to immigration
   2 there was a great demand for labor in the United States
   3 the natural population growth of the United States was small
   4 very few people were interested in coming to live in the United States

11 A major feature of the Reconstruction period was that
   1 new legislation and constitutional amendments attempted to provide equal rights and opportunities for blacks
   2 the South rapidly developed into the nation's major industrial center
   3 a spirit of cooperation existed between the executive and legislative branches
   4 new state governments in the South concentrated on ending corruption and enforcing Reconstruction plans

12 One similarity between the Knights of Labor and the American Federation of Labor is that both
   1 were limited to skilled workers
   2 nominated candidates for national political office
   3 were organized on a nationwide basis
   4 were advocates of economic and social revolution

13 Between 1876 and 1900, the economic policies of the United States Government were most favorable to the interests of
   1 urban industrial workers
   2 northern businesses
   3 western farmers
   4 southern sharecroppers and tenant farmers

14 Which statement best explains why some United States Supreme Court decisions are reversals of earlier decisions?
   1 Court decisions reflect changing social, political, and economic conditions.
   2 Presidents elected by a clear majority often demand that the Court implement their policies.
   3 Supreme Court Justices are often pressured by Congress to reflect the views of Congress.
   4 According to the Constitution, Justices have a specific responsibility to correct errors of past decisions.

15 Political machines flourished in United States cities at the turn of the century mainly because
   1 the machines maintained high standards of honesty in government
   2 Americans were too preoccupied with foreign affairs to deal with domestic political affairs
   3 reform movements concentrated on social problems and ignored political issues
   4 the machines provided jobs and services to the immigrants and the poor

16 A basic economic goal of labor unions of the late 19th-century was to achieve
   1 government ownership of industry
   2 a shorter workday and higher wages
   3 increased fringe benefits and medical coverage
   4 equal pay for equal work

17 In United States history, third political parties have had the greatest influence on the nation when
   1 they controlled the committees of Congress
   2 they won control of state governments
   3 the major parties adopted their ideas
   4 several such parties formed coalitions to win national elections

18 Which factor contributed most directly to the settlement and development of the Great Plains after the Civil War?
   1 freeing of slaves in the Southern States
   2 construction of railroads west of the Mississippi River
   3 influx of immigrants from eastern and southern Europe
   4 hospitality of the Indian tribes inhabiting the region

19 Which two philosophies dominated the thinking of most political and business leaders during the late 19th century in the United States?
1 social Darwinism and laissez faire
2 utopian socialism and the social gospel
3 populism and pragmatism
4 communism and anarchism

20 A major goal of the Progressive movement was to
1 increase the influence of corporations on government
2 reduce the surpluses produced by farmers
3 encourage the growth of labor unions
4 eliminate unfair business practices

21 Which characteristic was common to most of the new immigrants who entered the United States between 1890 and the mid-1920's?
1 They came from northern and western Europe.
2 They received economic assistance from government welfare programs.
3 They tended to settle in urban areas.
4 They became disillusioned and returned to their native countries.

22 The War Industries Board, the War Labor Board, and the Food Administration were all created as part of the United States war effort in World War I. Their creation demonstrates that in time of war
1 individual freedoms are suspended
2 government becomes more involved in directing the economy
3 the United States adopts a socialist economy
4 farming is given an equal status with industry

23 Which is the most valid statement concerning the social welfare programs of the New Deal period?
1 Charitable causes received little private financial support.
2 Health care costs were greater in rural areas than in urban areas.
3 Government assumed responsibility for functions previously performed by other institutions.
4 State governments refused to participate in programs for the poor.

24 The writings of muckrakers of the late 19th-century had the most direct impact on
1 efforts to increase public education in the South
2 the struggle for women's rights
3 reform in the area of factory working conditions
4 elimination of segregation in the South

25 At the outbreak of World War I in 1914, most Americans believed that
1 their country should stay out of the war
2 sending direct aid to Russia was necessary and desirable
3 the government should immediately declare war against Germany
4 the government should be more concerned with conditions in the Far East than with events in Europe

26 A major weakness in the prosperity of the 1920's was that it was
1 confined to the industrial states of the Northeast
2 accompanied by runaway inflation
3 based on large Federal expenditures
4 unevenly distributed through the population

27 Which aspect of life during the 1920's most likely caused the decade to be labeled the "Roaring Twenties"?
1 technological improvement
2 social change
3 political reform
4 territorial expansion

28 Which legislation best illustrates that laws must be accepted by a large portion of the population or they become impossible to enforce?
1 establishment of immigration quotas
2 placement of high tariffs on imports
3 passage of Prohibition
4 banning of prayer in public schools

29 In the period between World War I and World War II, which group made the greatest gains in political rights?
1 blacks
2 women
3 new immigrants
4 Native American Indians

Base your answers to questions 30 and 31 on the cartoon below and on your knowledge of social studies.

"WE TOLD YOU IT WOULDN'T WORK!"

30 Which statement best expresses the main idea of the cartoon?

1 The failure of the United States to join the League crippled the League's effectiveness.
2 Public opinion in the United States strongly supported the League.
3 Even after the United States joined, the League failed to work.
4 Most people in the United States wanted the League to fail.

31 The situation portrayed in the cartoon helped lead the United States to adopt which policy in the period after World War II?

1 neutrality
2 support of the formation of the United Nations
3 isolationism
4 military aid to Poland and other Eastern European nations

32 In World War II, the United States was allied with the Soviet Union, but that alliance became a rivalry shortly after the end of the war. Which statement most accurately explains this change?

1 Alliances tend to last only as long as the nations involved see a mutual self-interest.
2 Historically, alliances made by countries with differing economic systems seldom last more than a few years.
3 The Soviet Union stood in the way of United States territorial expansion.
4 The United States refused Soviet requests for a long-term commitment to supply them with arms.

33 An economic impact of United States entry into World War II was that the United States

1 became a debtor nation
2 became nearly bankrupt
3 accelerated its recovery from the Great Depression
4 was forced to accept government ownership of most major industries

34 In the 1930's, the United States responded to the rise of totalitarian powers in Europe by

1 rapidly expanding its military power
2 joining other democracies in a system of collective security
3 signing nonaggression pacts with the totalitarian nations
4 adopting a series of neutrality laws

35 The primary purpose of the Marshall Plan was to help bring about the

1 formation of military alliances
2 economic recovery of Europe
3 unification of Germany
4 invasion of Eastern Europe

36 Which action has the United States Supreme Court found to be a violation of the principle of separation of church and state?

1 election of a member of the clergy to public office
2 appointment of chaplains to the armed services
3 granting of tax-exempt status to churches
4 recitation of prayers in public schools

Base your answer to question 37 on the graphs below and on your knowledge of social studies.

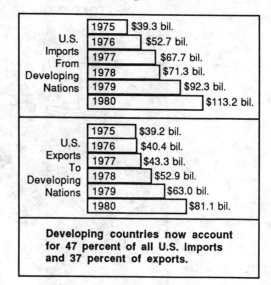

U.S. Imports From Developing Nations	
1975	$39.3 bil.
1976	$52.7 bil.
1977	$67.7 bil.
1978	$71.3 bil.
1979	$92.3 bil.
1980	$113.2 bil.

U.S. Exports To Developing Nations	
1975	$39.2 bil.
1976	$40.4 bil.
1977	$43.3 bil.
1978	$52.9 bil.
1979	$63.0 bil.
1980	$81.1 bil.

Developing countries now account for 47 percent of all U.S. imports and 37 percent of exports.

37 A valid conclusion based on the graphs is that

1 by 1980 more than half of all United States imports came from developing countries
2 the United States places no tariffs on imports from developing countries
3 the United States has consistently had a trade deficit with developing nations
4 the gap between exports and imports narrowed steadily between 1975 and 1980

38 The War Powers Act (1973) was passed mainly in response to a concern that Presidents of the United States

1 had the power to make treaties without informing the Senate
2 could involve the nation's armed forces in combat without congressional approval
3 had failed to control harmful antiwar protests
4 had refused to present proposed military budgets to Congress

39 Since World War II, the integration of United States public schools has been most significantly stimulated by

1 decisions of Federal and state courts
2 passage of constitutional amendments
3 leadership of school boards in the South
4 actions of state legislatures

Base your answer to question 40 on the cartoon below and on your knowledge of social studies.

40 Which statement best summarizes the main idea of the cartoon?
  1 Congress does not have the power to deal with major problems facing the nation.
  2 Most members of Congress feel defense is more important than social programs.
  3 Congress has to make difficult choices concerning the funding of social programs and of defense.
  4 Defense and social programs receive an equal share of the Federal budget.

41 Former Chief Justice Warren Burger has stated that on the Supreme Court a whisper can become a shout. This statement most likely refers to the idea that
  1 decisions of the Court have far-reaching effects
  2 dissenting opinions among the Justices often create deadlocks on the Court
  3 the great majority of cases deal with the principle of freedom of speech
  4 Court decisions sometimes represent reversals of previous decisions

42 Which is a common criticism that management has made of labor unions?
  1 Unions fail to protect their members from swings in the economic cycle.
  2 Recessions could be avoided if unions would accept contracts that cover more than one year.
  3 Participation in a union requires time taken away from the worker's job.
  4 Excessive wage demands lead to price hikes that result in inflation.

Base your answers to questions 43 and 44 on the cartoon below and on your knowledge of social studies.

43 This cartoon dealt with United States foreign policy toward
   1 Eastern Europe   3 Latin America
   2 the Far East   4 Africa

44 The author of this cartoon suggested that the United States should
   1 attempt to overthrow foreign governments
   2 submit international disputes to the United Nations for binding arbitration
   3 provide foreign nations with military aid
   4 not interfere in the internal affairs of other nations

45 Since the Great Depression of the 1930's, which action has the Federal Government most often taken to lower the unemployment rate?
   1 increased government spending
   2 raised individual and corporate taxes
   3 raised the retirement age
   4 increased the minimum wage

46 The "yellow journalism" of the Spanish-American War and television coverage of the Vietnam War both illustrate that
   1 government can limit freedom of the press in times of national crisis
   2 the news media can be trusted to portray events accurately
   3 the American people, on the basis of the information they receive, can influence government policy
   4 public opinion is rarely affected by the news media

47 Which statement is most accurate about government in the United States during the 20th century?

1 The two-party political system has been replaced by a multiparty system.
2 There have been no serious conflicts between branches of the Federal Government.
3 The judicial branch has less and less influence on society.
4 The Federal Government has assumed powers formerly exercised by the states.

48 Which aspect of the United States political process has been developed through custom and gradual change rather than by constitutional amendment?

1 selection of Presidential candidates
2 extension of the right to vote
3 filling vacancies in the office of Vice President
4 direct election of Senators

Answers to the following questions are to be written on paper provided by the school.

Students Please Note:

In developing your answers to Parts II and III, be sure to

(1) include specific factual information and evidence whenever possible
(2) keep to the questions asked; do not go off on tangents
(3) avoid overgeneralizations or sweeping statements without sufficient proof; do not overstate your case
(4) keep these general definitions in mind:

   (a) <u>discuss</u> means "to make observations about something using facts, reasoning, and argument; to present in some detail"
   (b) <u>describe</u> means "to illustrate something in words or tell about it"
   (c) <u>show</u> means "to point out; to set forth clearly a position or idea by stating it and giving data which support it"
   (d) <u>explain</u> means "to make plain or understandable; to give reasons for or causes of; to show the logical development or relationships of"

Part II

ANSWER ONE QUESTION FROM THIS PART. [15]

1 Throughout United States history, certain enduring issues have been reflected in cases brought before the Supreme Court.

Enduring Constitutional Issues — Supreme Court Cases

Representation in government — *Baker* v. *Carr* (1962)
Relationship between the Federal and state governments —
   McCulloch v. *Maryland* (1819)
Role of the judiciary — *Marbury* v. *Madison* (1803)
Protection of civil liberties — *Korematsu* v. *United States* (1944)
Rights of the accused — *Miranda* v. *Arizona* (1966)
Equality before the law — *Brown* v. *Board of Education* (1954)
Rights of women — *Roe* v. *Wade* (1973)

Select *three* of the issues listed above and for *each* one chosen:

- Describe the specific issue in the Supreme Court case cited
- Discuss the Court's decision in the case
- Show how that decision affected the enduring constitutional issue [5,5,5]

2 The illustration below shows some of the principles of the Federal Constitution that promote and protect freedom in the United States.

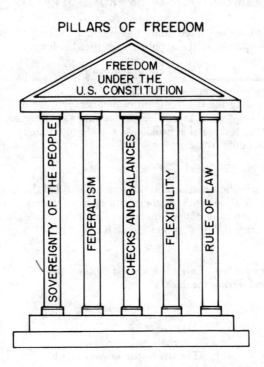

PILLARS OF FREEDOM

FREEDOM
UNDER THE
U.S. CONSTITUTION

SOVEREIGNTY OF THE PEOPLE · FEDERALISM · CHECKS AND BALANCES · FLEXIBILITY · RULE OF LAW

Choose *three* of the principles of government represented by the pillars in the illustration. For *each* one chosen:

- Define that principle of government
- Using specific information, show how that principle has promoted freedom under the Constitution   [5,5,5]

Part III

ANSWER TWO QUESTIONS FROM THIS PART. [30]

3 Throughout its history, the United States has pursued a variety of policies in its relations with other countries. Some of these policies are listed below.

United States Foreign Policies

Supporting disarmament
Promoting the development of democracy
Improving social or economic conditions in other countries
Seeking territorial expansion of the United States
Responding to aggression

Select *three* of the policies listed. For *each* one chosen:

- Describe a specific situation and time period that led the United States to use the policy in its relations with another country or countries
- Describe an action or actions taken by the United States to carry out this policy [You must use a different action for each policy.] [5,5,5]

4 Many of the major problems facing the United States during the 1980's will continue to challenge the nation during the 1990's.

Problems

AIDS epidemic
International terrorism
Threats to the environment
Drug epidemic
Homelessness

Choose *three* of the problems from the list above. For *each* one chosen:

- Describe the nature of the problem
- Discuss its effect on United States society as a whole
- Explain why solutions to the problem are difficult to achieve [5,5,5]

5 Throughout United States history, courageous men and women have sought to improve society by participating in reform movements such as those listed below.

Reform Movements

Women's rights
Organized labor
International peace
Civil rights
Educational reform
Consumer protection
Native American Indian rights

Select *three* of these reform movements and for *each* one chosen:

- Identify *one* person or *one* specific group associated with the movement and describe that person's or group's influence on the movement
- Discuss the extent to which the movement has improved society in the United States [5,5,5]

6 In a recent survey, historians graded United States Presidents on characteristics such as leadership qualities, accomplishments, crisis management, political skills, and integrity. Some Presidents and their grade levels are listed below.

High Grades	Low Grades
Abraham Lincoln	Andrew Johnson
Theodore Roosevelt	Ulysses S. Grant
Woodrow Wilson	Warren Harding
Franklin D. Roosevelt	Richard Nixon

  a Select *one* President from each group. For *each* President selected, discuss to what extent you agree or disagree with the historians' rating of that President. Use specific historical information to support your position.   [5,5]

  b Identify any President *not* listed above and state whether you would give that President a high or a low grade. Support your position by using specific historical information.   [5]

7 Economic problems have been a major concern in the United States in various periods since the Civil War. Some of these problems are listed below.

Economic Problems

Rise of monopolies
Farm bankruptcies
Bank failures
Inflation
Trade gap
Budget deficit

Choose *three* of the economic problems listed and for *each* one chosen:

  • Show how the problem has been a major concern during a specific period since the Civil War
  • Discuss a major cause of the problem
  • Discuss *one* action taken by the United States Government to deal with the problem   [5,5,5]

PRETEST ANSWERS

Part I (55 credits)

1. **1**	13. **2**	25. **1**	37. **3**
2. **4**	14. **1**	26. **4**	38. **2**
3. **2**	15. **4**	27. **1**	39. **1**
4. **2**	16. **2**	28. **3**	40. **3**
5. **3**	17. **3**	29. **2**	41. **1**
6. **1**	18. **2**	30. **1**	42. **4**
7. **4**	19. **1**	31. **2**	43. **3**
8. **4**	20. **4**	32. **1**	44. **4**
9. **3**	21. **3**	33. **3**	45. **1**
10. **2**	22. **2**	34. **4**	46. **3**
11. **1**	23. **3**	35. **2**	47. **4**
12. **3**	24. **3**	36. **4**	48. **1**

Part II (45 credits)

Refer to the Test-Taking Strategies section that follows for review of how to best organize and answer essay questions. Instruction is given on blocking essays, and specific essays from the Pretest are used as examples.

Test-Taking Strategies: How to Take a Regents Exam in Social Studies _____

This section of the book is intended to help you prepare to take the Regents Examination itself. Other parts of the book review the contents of the course you have studied. This section includes hints about preparing for and actually taking the examination based on test-taking skills you have probably been developing for years in social studies classes. Read and think carefully about all parts of this section as you prepare for the examination.

PREPARING TO TAKE THE REGENTS EXAMINATION

1. If review sessions are offered by your teacher or school, *attend* them. You will probably be reminded of something you studied earlier in the year and have not thought of since then. Review sessions also help you bring together the main ideas of the whole course.

2. Two heads can be better than one. Try to review with a friend or a family member who can give you the chance to explain various parts of this course. You will have a better chance of remembering details if you have already explained them correctly to someone else. It has been said that the best way to learn something is to teach it to someone.

3. Be sure you know the correct time and place of the examination. Arriving half an hour late can make the difference between passing and failing. Be sure someone else at your house has a schedule of your exams.

4. As important as it is to review carefully and over a period of time for your exams, do not make the mistake of "over studying." This could leave you exhausted and unable to think clearly during the exam itself. This exam is important enough for you to ask your employer for time off right before the exam.

5. Come to the exam prepared to stay for the entire three hours. Do not tell someone to pick you up in two hours—you will need all the time allowed. Don't sacrifice a year's worth of work to get outside faster on a nice day.

6. Bring several dark ink pens and pencils.

7. Eat something before the exam so your energy level stays high.

8. If at all possible, wear a watch. You will need to pay close attention to the time during the exam, and you might be seated where you cannot see a clock.

TAKING THE EXAMINATION

1. Use a reliable method of getting to school so you can arrive early in the exam room. This will allow you to get your mind on the task at hand.

2. If you are allowed to select your own seat, be sure to choose one with the least distraction. Choose one away from doors or windows.

3. Dress comfortably for sitting in one place for a long period of time.

4. *Listen* carefully to all directions given by the proctor(s).

5. Read all directions written on the test booklet as you take the exam. If you have reviewed well you will be familiar with the terms "discuss," "explain," "show," and "describe."

Nonetheless, take the time to read carefully the instructions given to you on the test.

6. Become a participant in the exam, not a spectator. You may write on the exam. Underline key ideas. You may write in the margins as you think about the questions. The idea is for you to interact with the exam. Other hints are given as you review the multiple-choice questions from the practice examination.

7. **DON'T leave blanks**. No credit can be given for a blank on either multiple-choice or essay questions. Write something. Write anything, but *never* leave an answer blank.

THE MULTIPLE-CHOICE SECTION

Part I of the Regents Examination is made up of questions worth 55 points. The conversion table on the short-answer page is for your teacher's use in calculating your score on the multiple-choice questions. Part I usually has anywhere from 47 to 49 questions. It does not really matter how many questions there are. Just be certain to answer *all* of them.

Multiple-choice questions tend to fall into certain categories you can identify as you take an examination. The following is about identifying these categories and improving your ability to answer certain categories of questions. Samples of these questions come from the January 1990 practice exam.

Data-Based Questions

Data-based questions are those in which you use specific information provided to you in the examination to answer a question or questions. You will probably not be able to answer the question(s) without this information; you will also need to know some social studies background to help interpret the information. There are several types of data-based questions. Some of these appear in the practice exam.

READING PASSAGES Questions like 2 and 3 on the practice exam are based on a selected reading passage. Such questions often require an ability to recognize opinions expressed in a passage.

If there are words you are unsure of in the selection, try to find a root word you know. Be sure to look for dates or other historical references to help you. You may write notes in the margin near the selection.

Question 2 The correct answer is choice 4. The first sentence is really the place to find the answer.

Question 3 The correct answer is choice 2. The phrase "laws which are 'necessary'" near the end of the reading passage should help you make an association with the elastic clause or "*necessary* and proper" clause. As you read this book, you will find key vocabulary and social studies phrases highlighted throughout.

GRAPHS Graphs may appear in several forms—bar graphs, line graphs, or pie graphs. Graph questions can be some of the easiest on the exam if you go slowly and use the information you are given.

On the practice test see question 37. Note that the graph compares imports and exports for the same years, 1975 to 1980.

When answering graph questions (and many other data-based questions), study the choices carefully to see if each choice can really be determined from the data given. In question 37, choice 2 mentions tariffs, but no data on tariffs is included on the graphs. Choice 3 is the correct answer, but to reach it you must compare the imports and exports for each year given.

POLITICAL CARTOONS The practice examination has three cartoons accounting for five multiple-choice questions. When analyzing a political cartoon, follow these steps:

1. Study the caption.

2. Look for a date.

3. Read all words in the cartoon. Look closely for any small print written on figures or objects in the cartoon.

4. Identify the symbolism used by a cartoonist. Some common symbols include a bear for the Soviet Union, and an eagle or the figure of Uncle Sam for the United States.

Question 30 The man with the tall hat is Uncle Sam, who represents the United States. He is responsible for disabling the League of Nations, represented by the fire truck. Notice in the upper-right corner "Europe" and "Poland" are written so small that it would be easy to miss them. Question 30 asks about the significance of Uncle Sam sitting on the front ·wheel labeled "U.S. League of Membership." The best answer is choice 1.

Question 31 Note that in question 32 the time period asked about is not the years after World War I, when the United States refused to join the League of Nations, but the years after World War II. Remember that the United States supported the formation of the United Nations after World War II. The correct answer has to be 2.

Question 40 Notice that the door is labeled Congress and two large figures marked Social Programs and Defense are struggling to get through that door. The figure representing Congress behind the door looks puzzled about how to deal with both figures. The best answer is choice 3, because both needs must be considered by Congress.

Question 43 In this case be sure to read all of the cartoonist's words. Note that the size of the gun is out of proportion to the size of the Contra. In question 43 you may need to know from your study that the word "Contra" is associated with Latin America, or you may be able to guess based on the facial characteristics drawn by the cartoonist.

Question 44 In question 44 you must interpret the written message of the cartoonist. You should recognize that the cartoonist's use of ads encouraging financial support of poor children in developing nations as a model is ironic. The cartoonist's real message is that the United States should not interfere in the internal affairs of other countries, which is choice 4.

OUTLINES Some Regents questions ask you to complete a hypothetical outline. In question 9, you are simply asked to determine the main topic. In this type of question, look for the most general answer. Recognize that the other choices would be subheads on the outline under the main topic. The right choice is 3 because 1, 2, and 4 are examples of the Constitution's first tests.

QUOTATION   INTERPRETATION QUESTIONS This type of question asks you to explain the idea of a given quotation. Sometimes the author and/or the time period of the quotation is given. This is not the case in question 5.

The key phrase in question 5 is "consent of the governed." This concept is frequently tested. You need to remember that the Declaration of Independence marked the beginning of a new concept of government in that it justified the participation of citizens in decision making.

Types of Data-Based Questions Not on this Practice Exam

There are other types of data-based questions that do not appear on the practice exam. Strategies for dealing with these questions are given below.

MAPS When maps are given, be sure to look for the following:

- a key explaining any symbols used
- dates
- specific place locations
- compass point for directions

TABLES OF INFORMATION Tables are frequently used in questions that require you to draw conclusions. Be *very* careful to base your conclusions *only* on the information in the table unless the question specifically asks you to do otherwise. Be sure to note the source and date of the information given in the table.

SPEAKER QUESTIONS Speaker questions present different reading passages by different people on the same topic. The questions can be very difficult. When answering speaker questions follow these steps:

- Determine the theme or topic which all of the speakers are addressing.
- Read the questions before you study the speakers' statements too closely; often you do not have to read each speaker's viewpoint to answer a question.
- Be sure you are reading the correct speaker when answering each question.
- Take your time when answering speaker questions. You will probably need to go back and forth among the readings as you analyze the differences between speakers.

TIMELINES A timeline is a graphic way of showing relationships among events over time. Questions dealing with timelines often ask you to draw a conclusion about a series of events. When answering timeline questions, be careful to focus on the time period shown; do not jump to a different era to answer the question.

Other Multiple-Choice Questions

Many other types of multiple-choice questions appear on Regents Examinations.

RECALL QUESTIONS These are questions that require you to know specific information about people, events, topics, and concepts studied in the course. Throughout this review book you will find the 15 concepts drawn to your attention in the Making Connections column. Important people, terms, and events, are highlighted in **bold** type. You can also find a glossary of social studies terms and concepts at the back of the book. Some of the recall questions that appear on the practice exam are discussed below.

Question 1 This question requires specific knowledge of the Bill of Rights. However, you can also use process of elimination here. You should know that some people are always unemployed at any given time and that strikes are forbidden in some types of jobs; you can thus eliminate choices 2 and 3. Choice 4 would be called the "distractor" because it looks good at first. However, you should remember that some groups of Americans—women, blacks, and Indians—did not get the right to vote until long after the Bill of Rights was ratified.

Question 4 Here you must identify a power of the Supreme Court. The key word in answering this question is "interpret." If you have learned the following about the three branches of government, you will have no trouble.

Legislative	Executive	Judicial
Makes	*Enforces*	*Interprets*

THE LAWS

Question 11 This question is about a specific event—Reconstruction. Multiple-choice questions are written carefully. The words used in them provide clues to the correct answers. In choice 1, notice the word "attempted." That word makes 1 the correct answer because this is a good example of a question where legislation and amendments did *try* to provide equal rights (they just weren't always successful). In choice 2, the word "rapidly" points out a wrong choice because, as you know, it took the South a long time to recover from the Civil War. In choice 3, "spirit of cooperation" shows that this is a wrong choice. Choice 4 describes the opposite of what actually happened.

Question 38 This question requires you to know specific information about an event—the passage of the War Powers Act. The date of the act should help you to connect its passage with the conclusion of the war in Vietnam. You need to know that the war in Vietnam, which cost thousands of American lives, was the nation's longest war. Yet it was fought without a formal declaration of war by Congress. This war marked a failure of the system of checks and balances, and passage of the War Powers Act was an attempt to correct it. The correct answer is number 2.

Examples of other questions from this category on the practice exam are 5, 8, 11, 22, 25, 26, 36.

CAUSE-AND-EFFECT QUESTIONS

These questions test your understanding of the concepts of cause and effect. A cause is an event or action that brings about another event or action—an effect. Your study of history should have revealed that almost everything is either the cause or result of some event. These questions can ask about either causes or effects. They may also be asking the goal(s) of a particular event or action.

Question 18 The words cause and effect are not used here, but the question tests your knowledge of the cause of settlement on the Great Plains in a particular time period—after the Civil War. The use of the newly developed railroad as transportation was key to the western development (choice 2). Choice 1 is wrong because the freed slaves did not move West, and 3 is wrong because those immigrants generally stayed in urban areas to work in factories. Note the word "hospitality" in choice 4. Few of the Indian tribes welcomed the arrival of the settlers on the plains.

Question 20 The Progressives were organized for the reason implied by their name—to make "progress." This progress or improvement was directed at improving the lives of the consumer and the average working person. Choice 4 is the only choice that describes a condition that would improve the lives of working people.

Other cause-and-effect questions on the practice exam are 16, 17, 28, 32, 34, and 35.

TIME REFERENCE OR CHRONOLOGY QUESTIONS

These are questions that make reference to a particular time period. You rarely need to identify specific dates on Regents exams.

However, you often do need to know the *time sequence* or *order of events*.

Question 29   With a question like this, it is a good idea to write the dates of the period above the question so that you can focus on that specific time. Remember, a condition that was true in one time period may change or cease to exist in another time period. When answering question 29, you should remember that the 19th amendment granting women the right to vote was passed in 1920 (between the wars). Not until well *after* World War II did the other groups make great gains in their political rights.

Other time reference questions are 21, 25, 27, and 39.

GENERALIZATIONS   These questions require you to make a general statement about a particular event, time period, or body of information. You are really being asked to draw a conclusion.

Question 6   You are being asked to explain why the Constitution was written. To do so, you need to recall the problems of the Articles of Confederation. Choice 1 is correct because the Constitution does establish a strong central government.

Question 23   This question asks you to recall the purpose of the social welfare programs of the New Deal and to recognize that the power of the federal government expanded during this time period. "Valid" is a word frequently used on tests, and it means "true." Choice 3 is a true statement about the growth of the federal government during the New Deal.

Question 34   This is an interesting question for several reasons.

- It has a time reference (1930s).
- It asks for a result.
- It includes a specific Need to Know vocabulary word—totalitarian.

You need to recall that the foreign policy goal of the United States during this time period was to stay out of wars. Choice 4, about adopting neutrality laws, is correct.

Other questions from the practice exam using generalizations are 7, 10, 13, 14, 15, 21, and 27.

Types of Multiple-Choice Questions Not on the Practice Exam

FACT AND OPINION   These questions require you to find a statement that is clearly either fact or opinion. If you keep in mind that certain words such as *largest, most important, most significant,* and *greatest contribution* signal opinions, you should have no trouble with this type of question. It is difficult to make true statements that include the words *always, never, all,* or *none*.

SOURCES AND REFERENCES   Some questions test your ability to identify a valid source of information. A primary source is one written or told by someone who was present at an event. These sources can be biased, but they can also give a special insight into an event. Secondary sources are those that are written after an event, such as a textbook.

QUESTIONS ABOUT SOCIAL SCIENTISTS   Some questions ask about the jobs of certain types of social scientists. These might include the following:

Historians: People who study the past and make judgments on why events happened and how they affected other events.

Economists: People who study the monetary systems of countries or cultures. The work of economists is important to our understanding of events such as the Great Depression.

Political Scientists: People who study the workings of government and politics. For example, political scientists analyze the results of elections to determine trends in voting patterns.

CONTENT SUMMARY OF MULTIPLE-CHOICE QUESTIONS:

The following is a summary of the content that appeared on the multiple-choice section of the practice exam. The unit with which the content is most associated appears in parentheses. Notice that some units tend to be tested more heavily than others.

Bill of Rights   (1)

Strict interpretation of the Constitution   (1)

Preamble to the Constitution   (1)

elastic clause   (1)

judicial review   (1)

apportionment of representatives   (1)

delegated powers   (1)

limits on the powers of Congress   (1)

powers of the Supreme Court   (1)

filibuster   (1)

Magna Carta   (1, and Global Studies)

English Bill of Rights   (1, and Global Studies)

Washington's Farewell Address   (1)

U.S. Constitution   (1)

Senate   (1)

Cabinet   (1)

House of Representatives   (1)

due process clause of the 14th Amendment   (2)

Alexander Hamilton's economic program   (1)

rise of national political parties   (1)

John Adams's Presidency   (1)

19th-century immigration policy   (2)

Reconstruction   (2)

Knights of Labor   (2)

American Federation of Labor   (2)

sharecroppers and tenant farmers   (2)

Supreme Court decisions   (all units)

political machines   (2)

third parties   (1, 3)

Great Plains   (2)

Civil War   (1, 2)

Social Darwinism   (2)

laissez faire   (2)

utopian socialism   (2)

social gospel   (2)

populism   (2, 3)

communism   (4, 5)

Progressive movement   (3)

immigration 1890–1920   (2, 3)

War Industries Board   (4)

War Labor Board   (4)

Food Administration   (4)

World War I   (4)

New Deal   (4)

muckrakers   (3)

prosperity of the 1920s   (4)

prohibition   (3)

League of Nations   (4)

World War II   (5)

totalitarianism   (5)

collective security   (5)

neutrality laws   (5)

nonaggression pact   (5)

Marshall Plan   (5)

prayer in public schools   (6)

U.S. imports/exports   (6)

War Powers Act   (6)

integration of public schools (5, 6)

congressional spending (6)

labor unions (6)

Burger Court (6)

Contras in Latin America (6)

Great Depression (4)

Spanish American War and "yellow journalism" (3)

Vietnam War (6)

government in the 20th century (4, 5, 6)

THE ESSAY SECTION

The format of the written section of the United States History and Government Regents Examination differs from that of the Global Studies Regents Examination you probably have already taken. The essay portion of the United States History and Government examination is divided into Part II and Part III.

The general directions for the essays appear before the Part II questions. Be sure to read these directions carefully. They appear in this review book in the practice test sections.

Part II includes two questions about government, politics, the Constitution, and law-related issues. You must do *one* of these two questions. Do *not* do more than one of these questions, but be sure to do all parts of the one you choose. Study these two questions, and compare the kinds of information you need to know to answer each of them. Then you can chose the one you know more about.

Part III includes five questions about any part of the course. You will need to answer all parts of *two* of these questions.

Blocking Essay Answers

Blocking an essay is a way of organizing your ideas before you write your answer. Organizing your thoughts before writing will help you earn more points on the essays and avoid leaving out parts of the essays. Experts in helping students prepare for tests know that the more involved you become with a test the better you will do on it.

Read essay question 1 of Part II of the practice exam carefully. Note that the question directs you to select issues from a list and discuss three aspects of each issue. The numbers in brackets at the end of the question tell you how much each part of your answer is worth. After reading the question, you should next block out your answers, following the steps below.

STEPS IN BLOCKING AN ESSAY

1. Underline the words that tell you what you need to do: *discuss, describe, explain*, etc.
2. Study the directions next to each "•" (bullet).
3. Use those directions to form headings for your block.
4. Under each section of your block, write facts to help you answer that part of the question.
5. It is also helpful to write the points each part of the question is worth in the appropriate section of your blocks. This will help you focus on enough details to earn all the points allotted for each part of the question.
6. When you have arranged all your facts in the section of a block, check to see if you have left any sections empty. If you cannot completely block the entire question, you may decide to try another question.

The block below for Part II, Question 1 has been drawn up following these steps. One section of the block has been completed for you. Try to complete all the other sections.

When you review this and other practice essay questions in this book, try to do *all* parts of each essay question, not just the number of sections that the directions require. Doing this will help you review more material on each topic.

Essay Block for Part II, Question 1

Select three issues	Describe the specific issue in the case chosen	Discuss the Court's decision	How did the decision affect the enduring issue?
Equality before the law	Linda Brown wanted to go to the local public school, but she was prevented due to a policy of segregation.	Court ruled that separate but equal is not OK, which had been the precedent set by *Plessy* v. *Ferguson* in 1896.	Equality before the law was guaranteed by integration of public schools. [5]
			[5]
			[5]

Blocks for each of the essays in the practice exam are done for you below. They are models for you to study as you develop your own blocks for practice essays throughout this book.

Essay Block for Part II, Question 2

Choose three principles	Define the principle	Show how the principle has encouraged freedom
checks and balances	This prevents any one of the three branches of government from becoming too powerful; it lets each branch stop the actions of the other branches.	The Supreme Court can declare laws unconstitutional; in *Brown*, the Court reversed an earlier decision (*Plessy*) to increase freedoms and equality. [5]
		[5]
		[5]

Essay Block for Part III, Question 3

Select three policies	Describe a specific situation	Identify time period of the situation	Describe an action taken by the United States to carry out the policy
territorial expansion	U.S. had a chance to buy Louisiana Territory.	1803	President Thomas Jefferson bought the Louisiana Territory from France, which needed money for Napoleon's European campaigns. Jefferson used this opportunity to expand the United States. [5]
			[5]
			[5]

Essay Block for Part III, Question 4

Choose three problems	Describe the nature of the problem	Discuss effects on United States society	Why are solutions difficult?
drug epidemic	Large quantities of illegal drugs are easily available in U.S. Law enforcement to control drug use is costly.	Drug use has led to higher crime rates. Young children are exposed to drugs.	Costs of stopping drugs at the nation's borders are high. Drug users don't want to stop using. [5]
			[5]
			[5]

Essay Block for Part III, Question 5

Select three reform movements	Identify person or group associated with movement	Discuss the influence of person or group	Describe the extent to which the movement improved United States society
women's rights	Susan B. Anthony	She lead the 19th-century movement for women's right to vote; organized Seneca Falls Convention.	The 19th Amendment in 1920 gave women the right to vote, and is referred to as the Susan B. Anthony amendment. [5]
			[5]
			[5]

Essay Block for Part III, Question 6

Note: This is the only essay question on this examination that requires you to use a different kind of block. This question is divided into parts *a* and *b*. Remember, with this type of question you must do *both* parts to get full credit.

a Two Presidents	Discuss whether you agree or disagree with ratings using historical information
High Grades: Franklin Roosevelt	Agree: He was President during two national crises: New Deal and World War II; he increased executive power; he created "alphabet agencies": AAA, WPA, FDIC, SEC; he acted as Commander in Chief in World War II. [5]
Low Grades: Richard Nixon	Agree: Watergate affair showed abuse of presidential power; he was first President to resign in the face of probable impeachment [5]
b President of your choice. High or low grades?	George Washington: high grades, because as first President he set precedents such as the Cabinet and the two-term presidency. He also established neutrality policy in foreign affairs to keep the young country out of war. [5]

Essay Block for Part III, Question 7

Choose three economic problems	Show how the problem was a major concern	Give time period	Discuss *major* cause of problem	Discuss one action of U.S. government
bank failures	Americans had put their life savings in banks that made bad investments and then failed; thousands of citizens lost everything.	Great Depression of the 1930s	Banks risked money on unsafe investments and then went bankrupt.	Federal Deposit Insurance Corporation was formed to protect depositors. [5]
				[5]
				[5]

UNIT 1

Constitutional Foundations of the U.S. Democratic Republic

MAKING CONNECTIONS

As you review each unit, you will find additional information in this column: key ideas, important social studies concepts, Enduring Constitutional Issues, test-taking tips, and questions to reinforce your reading. These items are closely tied to the Regents examination. Read this material carefully, and jot down any other facts that you need to remember in the column's blank spaces. Using this column will *add to your success on the Regents exam.*

The course you have been taking all year is called United States History and Government. Therefore, the Regents examination you will be taking will test what you know not only about our nation's history but about our government as well. How much of the Regents will be about United States government varies from test to test. In Part I of the examination, which is made up of multiple-choice questions worth 55 points, between 23 and 33 percent of the questions deal with United States government and constitutional history up to 1865. In Part II, you always have a choice of one of two 15-point essays on government; this represents 33 percent of the essay portion of the examination. In Part III, which is worth 30 points, you must select two of five essays that may include such government topics as the United States Presidents.

Based on this structure, you will need to know the answers to the following questions about United States government and our constitutional history through 1865 in order to pass the Regents examination:

1. What are the roots of the U.S. Constitution and Bill of Rights?
2. What opinions about government were discussed and debated by the Framers and what compromises did they reach in order to create the Constitution and get it approved by the states?
3. What is the structure of the United States Constitution, and how does the government it describes operate?
4. What are the Thirteen Enduring Constitutional Issues? Why were they important when the Constitution was written, and why have they remained critical questions throughout U.S. history?
5. What conflicting opinions about government were discussed and debated in the early years of our nation after the Constitution went into effect?
6. How did sectionalism and slavery bring on a constitutional crisis that led the nation to the Civil War?

The Roots of the U.S. Constitution and the Bill of Rights

A **constitution** is a nation's plan of government. Before we examine the United States Constitution and the features that make it unique, we must ask what were the roots of the ideas in that document. To do that, we must look at the historical origins of the United States of America.

What was to become the nation known as the United States of America began with the settlement of Virginia in 1607. Between that event and the settling of Georgia in 1732, a total of 13 English colonies were established along the Atlantic coast of North America.

The settlers of these colonies included Africans brought against their will, Scotch-Irish from northern Ireland, Germans, Portuguese, Jews, Swedes, Dutch, French, Welsh, Irish, Scots, and Swiss. A majority of the population of each colony, however, was English. This fact would greatly affect the nature of the government that developed in the United States. That government would have been quite different if the 13 colonies had been colonies of France or Spain rather than of England.

The governments of the 13 colonies differed, but, because of this common English origin, their similarities were greater than their differences. The government of each colony reflected ideas about government that came from the heritage of Western civilization. Those ideas were then modified by centuries of English thought and practice and by the American colonial experience.

MAJOR HISTORICAL INFLUENCES ON AMERICAN GOVERNMENT

Some key concepts of government had their roots in ancient times.

Greece

The concept of **democracy**, or government by the people, began in the city-state of Athens in what is now Greece between 750 B.C. and 550 B.C. Athens had a **direct democracy**, one in which all eligible citizens participated in government.

Rome

The concept of **republican government** was established by the ancient Romans in 509 B.C. In a **republic**, voters elect **representatives**

MAKING CONNECTIONS

Ethnic Groups in Colonial America, 1775

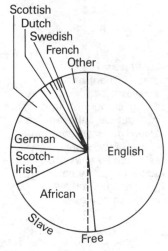

Regents Tip Some regents examination questions require you to read and interpret graphs. Study the graph on colonial population, then answer the following questions. For what year does the graph show the different ethnic qroups that made up the colonial population?

What was the second largest ethnic group in that year?

Key Ideas Many ancient Greek and Roman political ideas were adopted by the English and altered by them over several centuries.

MAKING CONNECTIONS

Common Law is law that developed from traditional and court decisions in England. It became the basis of English and then American law.

Key Ideas The establishment of rule by law was the first principle of English government. The English thus believed in a *limited government*, one whose powers are restricted by laws. In dictatorships by contrast, governments have unlimited power.

who speak and act for a number of other citizens in the business of government. These representatives are supposed to work for the common good. This form of government is sometimes called **representative democracy**. The writers of the Constitution defined a representative government working for the common good as a government committed to protecting individual rights.

Other basic concepts of constitutional government and of **common law** were established in England before or during the colonial period in America.

Magna Carta

In 1215 King John of England was forced to sign the **Magna Carta**, or Great Charter, a document that placed limits on his power to rule. For example, this document guaranteed the nobles—but not the rest of the people—a jury trial.

Petition of Right

In 1628 the English **Parliament**, or lawmaking body, forced King Charles I to sign the **Petition of Right**. This document clearly stated in writing some basic rights of the people.

English Bill of Rights

In 1689 Parliament again forced English monarchs to agree to another document—the **English Bill of Rights**. This document again listed the rights of the people and set other limits on the ruler, including the fact that everyone—even the ruler—must obey the law. The rights of Parliament were clearly established. For example, the ruler could collect taxes only with the consent of Parliament.

Another influence on the Framers of the Constitution was the European **Enlightenment**. This eighteenth-century intellectual movement held that social progress could be achieved through reliance on reason and experience. The Framers looked to several Enlightenment philosophers when drafting the Constitution.

John Locke

Locke's ideas influenced the Declaration of Independence, state constitutions, and the United States Constitution. Locke believed that people are born free with certain **natural rights**, including the rights to life, liberty, and property. Such rights predate any government and exist in the ''state of nature.'' Locke also wrote about the **social contract** theory. This theory holds that people agree to form a state and grant to its government the powers necessary to protect their natural rights. When a government fails to protect these rights, the contract has been broken and the people are free to change or even to replace that government. This means that governments exist with the **consent of the governed**.

The Baron de Montesquieu

This French philosopher wrote admiringly of the British system of republican government. Montesquieu believed that the British system was successful because the power to govern was divided among the monarch and the two houses of Parliament. Montesquieu said that the division helped keep political power balanced among the branches, so that no one branch had too much power. You see this concept in our Constitution's provisions for **separation of powers** and **checks and balances**.

Jean Jacques Rousseau

Rousseau, another French philosopher, developed further the idea of a social contract. His arguments in support of government by the consent of the governed influenced our Declaration of Independence.

THE COLONIAL EXPERIENCE

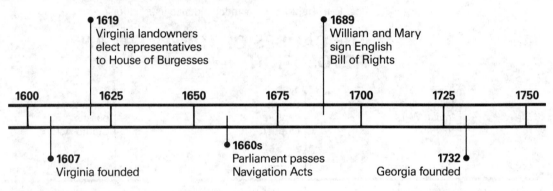

1619 Virginia landowners elect representatives to House of Burgesses

1689 William and Mary sign English Bill of Rights

1600 — 1625 — 1650 — 1675 — 1700 — 1725 — 1750

1607 Virginia founded

1660s Parliament passes Navigation Acts

1732 Georgia founded

In the nearly 170 years between the founding of the first English colony and the American Declaration of Independence from Great Britain (1776), two forces helped shape an American way of life: (1) the colonies' English roots, and (2) the colonists' experience on the edge of a wilderness thousands of miles from their home country. Some key facts about colonial experiences and understandings of government are listed below:

- The colonists believed in limits on the power of government—limits imposed by English laws and traditions. However, they also recognized the need for local governments, especially in lands far removed from the home country.

- The colonists wrote laws based on the principle that government existed to protect people's natural rights.

- In 1619 Virginia colonists took a major step toward republican government when they instituted the colonies' first representative lawmaking body, the **House of Burgesses**. Because members of this legislature were elected—in this case by male property owners—the colonists also were exercising their right to vote. In New England, **town meetings** provided another early opportunity for citizens to vote. At these gatherings, however, the people governed themselves through direct democracy.

MAKING CONNECTIONS

Background Life on the *frontier* was an important part of the colonial experience. The frontier was the constantly changing line between the areas settled and not yet settled by colonists.

MAKING CONNECTIONS

- In 1620, before landing at Plymouth in present-day Massachusetts, the Pilgrims signed the **Mayflower Compact**. This compact was a contract in which colonists gave their consent to be governed.

- Every colony except Pennsylvania established a **bicameral**, or two-house, **legislature** modeled after the two-house English Parliament.

- A system of separation of powers developed in the colonies, with government divided into three branches—the legislative, the executive, and the judicial. However, since colonial governors were often appointed by the king and the judges by the governors, it was primarily through the colonial legislatures, elected by the people, that the colonists received their training in self-government.

If, in fact, these features of democratic government existed in the English colonies, why did the colonies wage war against England and decide to fight for their independence as a nation?

THE CAUSES OF THE AMERICAN REVOLUTION

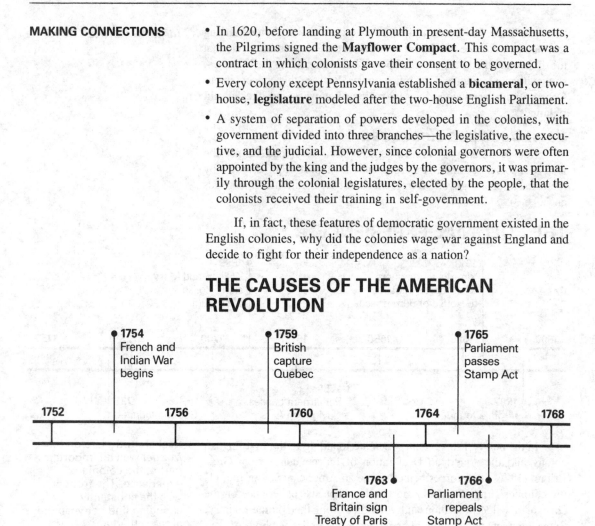

1754 French and Indian War begins

1759 British capture Quebec

1765 Parliament passes Stamp Act

1752   1756   1760   1764   1768

1763 France and Britain sign Treaty of Paris

1766 Parliament repeals Stamp Act

For almost a century before the outbreak of the American Revolution in 1775, England and France had been involved in a rivalry for power, not only in Europe, but wherever the two nations had colonies. Preoccupied with France, England governed the colonies for most of this period up to 1763 under a policy known as **salutary neglect**, or a healthy ignoring of the colonies. Thus, the colonies had many years in which to exercise their belief in self-government.

By 1763, a relationship had developed between England and its North American colonies similar to the federal form of government later set down in the United States Constitution. The colonists saw themselves as living under two governments much as you live under both a state and a national government in our federal system. The government in England controlled foreign affairs and foreign trade, while the colonists exercised self-government in what they considered to be local matters.

After the Treaty of Paris of 1763, which marked England's victory over France in the Seven Years' (or French and Indian) War, English policy changed. Just 12 years later, economic, political, and social disagreements led to the American Revolution.

North America in 1753

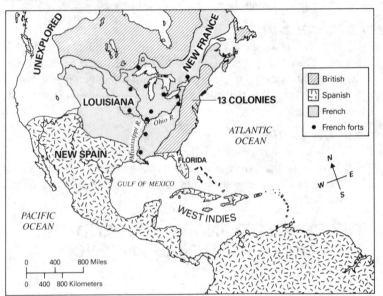

North America in 1763

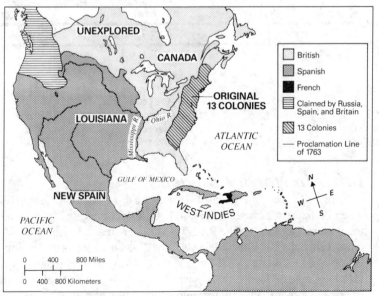

MAKING CONNECTIONS

Key Ideas Revolution and political change in England also affected the development of an independence movement in the North American colonies.

Regents Tip On some exams, you may be asked to compare two maps or charts. For example, compare this map with the map of North America in 1763. Then answer the following question.
What European nation lost the greatest amount of territory in North America between 1753 and 1763?

Economic Causes

After 1763, Parliament took tighter control of trade. It began to enforce the policy of **mercantilism**. This policy held that colonies exist to provide raw materials and markets for the economic benefit of the home country. Parliament also passed the **Sugar Act** in 1764 and the **Stamp Act** in 1765, primarily to raise **revenue**, or money, to support an army to defend the frontiers of the colonies.

Political Causes

The colonists reacted to the new taxes with **boycotts** and other protests. They charged that England had violated their natural rights. They insisted on the principle of "no taxation without representation." Colonists claimed that only their colonial legislatures, not Parliament, could tax them.

Social Causes

The British government failed to understand the colonists' fears of the power of that government and the extent to which the colonists had developed an independent political life and a sense of themselves as Americans.

THE REVOLUTIONARY WAR AND THE DECLARATION OF INDEPENDENCE

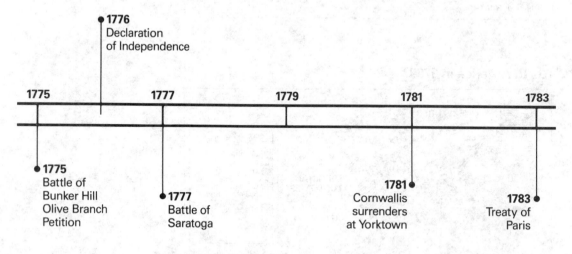

1776 Declaration of Independence

1775 — 1777 — 1779 — 1781 — 1783

1775 Battle of Bunker Hill Olive Branch Petition

1777 Battle of Saratoga

1781 Cornwallis surrenders at Yorktown

1783 Treaty of Paris

Crisis in North America

In 1773 the issue of taxation without representation rose again when Parliament passed the **Tea Act**. Colonists protested by holding the **Boston Tea Party**. The British government reacted with what colonists called the **"Intolerable Acts"** of 1774. These acts aimed at punishing Massachusetts by closing the port of Boston, forbidding town meetings, and reducing the powers of the legislature. More British troops were sent to occupy the colony and enforce the acts.

Colonial Efforts at Union

In the fall of 1774, twelve of the colonies sent representatives to Philadelphia to plan a response to the British actions in Massachusetts. This meeting became known as the **First Continental Congress**. After the start of the American Revolution in 1775, a **Second Continental Congress** met and took charge of the war effort. This successful cooperation among the colonies differed sharply from the attempt of Benjamin Franklin to get the colonies to agree to the **Albany Plan of Union** against the French in 1754. That plan was rejected by the colonies because they feared loss of self-government.

After 1776 and the decision to fight for independence as a nation, the Second Continental Congress became the first government of this nation. The Congress had no constitutional basis but was an **ad hoc** organization, created in a crisis and supported by popular opinion. It remained the national government until 1781.

Decision for Independence

In June 1776 Richard Henry Lee of Virginia presented a resolution to the Congress calling for independence from Great Britain. The Congress appointed a committee to draft a formal declaration. The resulting **Declaration of Independence** was almost entirely the work of Thomas Jefferson, a Virginia-born scholar, statesman, architect, and scientist. On July 4, delegates signed the Declaration of Independence. This date marks the birth of the United States of America. Each year on July 4, we celebrate that birthday. You need to know the following key facts about this major document in American history:

MAKING CONNECTIONS

Background An *ad hoc* organization is one set up for a specific, limited purpose.

The Declaration of Independence

The PURPOSE of the Declaration:	The Declaration's KEY IDEAS OF GOVERNMENT:
• To announce to the world that the colonies were now a new, independent nation • To explain and justify the reasons that the united colonies had decided to become the United States of America	• People have natural rights, including the rights to "Life, Liberty, and the pursuit of Happiness." • Governments receive their power to govern "from the consent of the governed" by social contract or compact in which the government agrees to protect the people's natural rights. • When a government fails to protect and respect those rights, it is the "Right of the People to alter or to abolish" that government.
The THREE PARTS of the Declaration:	
• A theory of government • A list of grievances against the King • A formal resolution declaring independence	

The last sentence of the Declaration shows how much the delegates were willing to risk in support of the revolution and its ideals. In all, 56 delegates signed the Declaration, pledging "to each other our Lives, our Fortunes and our Sacred Honor."

MAKING CONNECTIONS

Key Ideas The Declaration of Independence set high ideals and goals that are yet to be fully attained.

The ideals of the Declaration of Independence are still a goal for our nation. They have also served to inspire people in other nations and at other times—during the French Revolution of the late 1700s, the South American independence movement in the early 1800s, and even twentieth-century independence movements in Africa and Asia.

THE ARTICLES OF CONFEDERATION, 1781–1789

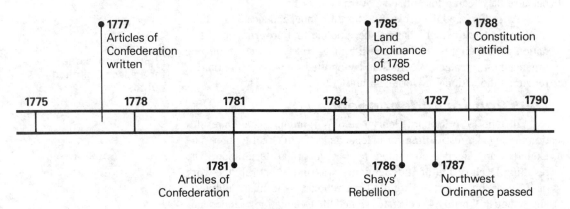

The first constitution of the United States was the **Articles of Confederation**. This constitution was proposed by the Second Continental Congress in 1777 and went into effect in 1781 after each of the 13 states had **ratified**, or approved, it. The Articles reflected the colonists' fears of a strong central government. These fears were based on their experiences with Great Britain and the desires of the individual states to protect their powers. As a result, the Articles created a weak national government.

An Alliance of Independent States

The Articles set up a confederation, or "firm league of friendship," among the 13 states. The Articles seemed more like a treaty among the states rather than a plan of centralized government. By definition, a **confederation** is an alliance of independent states in which the parts (in this case, the states) give what power they choose to the central government, but remain **sovereign**, keeping the greater part of the power to rule. An earlier model of a confederation in the history of our nation is that of the **Haudenosaunee**, or the **League of the Iroquois**. This League of first five and then six Iroquois nations was at the peak of its power between 1644 and 1700. The League of Iroquois influenced Franklin's Albany Plan of Union.

Achievements of the Confederation Government

The government under the Articles of Confederation had major powers. These included the powers to make treaties, declare war, and receive ambassadors. The Confederation also had some notable achievements to its credit:

- Successful conclusion of the American Revolution
- Negotiation of the Treaty of Paris of 1783, ending the war and setting the western border of the new nation at the Mississippi River
- Passage of the Land Ordinance of 1785 and of the Northwest Ordinance of 1787, which (a) set the pattern by which new states could join the nation on a basis of equality with the 13 original states and (b) prohibited slavery in the Northwest Territory.

North America in 1783

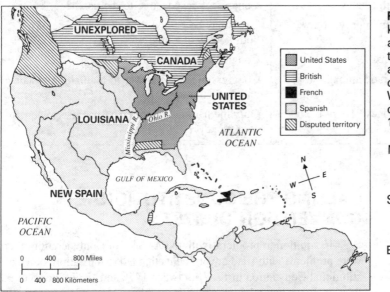

Regents Tip Read map keys carefully before answering questions. Study the accompanying map and answer the following question.
What were the boundaries of the new United States in 1783?

North

South

East

West

Weaknesses of the Confederation Government

Because of the fears noted earlier, however, the Confederation government proved too weak to deal with the problems of what has been called the Critical Period of 1781–1789. The Congress had no power to raise money. There was no single national currency because the states could also coin money. The Congress could not tax the people directly but had to ask the states for funds. It lacked an executive, or president, to direct the operations of government. Also, the Congress could raise an army only with the consent of the states. The new nation soon found itself with severe economic problems and unable to command respect at home or abroad. But all 13 states had to agree before the Articles could be changed, so it was nearly impossible to make improvements to this constitution.

Not surprisingly then, when the Constitutional Convention met in 1787, delegates soon decided to write a new plan of government. The chart on page 38 shows how the delegates tried to correct the weaknesses of the Articles of Confederation.

Key Ideas The delegates to the Constitutional Convention created a federal system, which is a compromise between a confederation and a unitary system of government

Governments of the United States: 1781 and 1789

How the Weaknesses of the Articles of Confederation Were Corrected by the Constitution	
Articles of Confederation	**Constitution of the United States**
States have most of the power. The national government has little.	States have some power, but most power is given to the national government.
No executive officer to carry out the laws of Congress.	A President heads the executive branch of the government.
No national courts. Only state courts exist.	Both national and state courts exist.
Congress is responsible to the states.	Congress is responsible to the people.
Nine out of 13 states have to approve a law before it can go into effect.	Laws may be passed by a majority vote of both houses of Congress.
Congress has no power to tax.	Congress given the power to tax.
Congress can not regulate trade among the states.	Congress given the power to regulate interstate and foreign trade.
Each state coins its own money. There is no national currency.	Only the national government has the power to coin money.

MAKING CONNECTIONS

CALLING THE CONSTITUTIONAL CONVENTION OF 1787

In addition to problems with the Articles of Confederation, there were problems with state governments that led to the calling of a Constitutional Convention in 1787. Between 1776 and 1787, eleven of the thirteen states had adopted new constitutions. Most of these constitutions reflected American fears of a strong executive. The states resisted putting too much power into the hands of a single person such as a governor. Instead, they gave most of the power to the legislatures. In some cases, the legislature elected the governor so that there was no real separation of powers. By the middle of the 1780s many of the nation's leaders were concerned about these new state governments. The laws of the states changed as quickly as did the group holding power. In the view of some leaders, the state legislatures had too much power; there was too much freedom and not enough order or stability.

In 1786 a group of debt-stricken farmers in Massachusetts turned to violence. Though short-lived, **Shays' Rebellion** fueled fears of spreading national collapse and mob rule. Meanwhile, the new government faced increasing difficulty in regulating interstate and foreign trade and dealing with the nation's debt. These problems led to a call for a Constitutional Convention in Philadelphia in May 1787 for ''the sole and express purpose of amending the Articles of Confederation.''

Regents Questions for Practice _____

Review the Test-Taking Strategies section of this book. Then answer the following questions, drawn from actual Regents examinations. Circle the *number* of the word or expression that best completes the statement or answers the question. Write your answers to essay questions on a separate piece of paper. Hints on good ways to approach these questions are provided in the margins.

MAKING CONNECTIONS

1. In writing the Declaration of Independence, Thomas Jefferson based his argument for American independence on the idea that
   1 people have natural rights as human beings
   2 the British refused to import colonial raw materials
   3 monarchy was evil by nature
   4 Britain was too far away to rule the Colonies effectively

Test Hint   Before answering a multiple-choice question, underline the key words in the question.

2. The primary purpose of the United States Declaration of Independence is to
   1 establish the basic law of the land in the United States
   2 explain and justify why the American colonists revolted against their mother country
   3 provide a clear plan for a meaningful and effective political system
   4 guarantee human rights for all Americans

3. Which quotation from the Declaration of Independence describes the fundamental principle of government in the United States?
   1 "imposing taxes on us without our consent"
   2 "governments long established should not be changed for light and transient causes"
   3 "depriving us, in many cases, of the benefits of trial by jury"
   4 "deriving their just powers from the consent of the governed"

4. The most essential feature of democratic government is
   1 a bicameral legislature
   2 a free and open election process
   3 a written constitution
   4 separate branches of government

Test Hint   Note that questions 4, 5, and 6 all ask about your understanding of *democracy*. Which two questions are testing the same concept?

5. Which has generally been associated with the needs of democracy as found in the United States?
   1 universal military training
   2 a system of public education
   3 an unchanging interpretation of the Constitution
   4 government ownership of industry

MAKING CONNECTIONS

Test Hint Remember to read all the choices before you select an answer.

6. "If a nation expects to be ignorant and free, in a state of civilization, it expects what never was and never will be." Which idea is most strongly supported by this statement?

1 compulsory education   3 a strong central government
2 universal suffrage   4 government's right to tax

7. The ideals of the Athenian State, Roman law, and the Mayflower Compact contributed most significantly to the growth of the principles of
1 government under law and the consent of the governed
2 religious freedom and women's suffrage
3 checks and balances and separation of powers
4 racial equality and equal treatment under law

8. Which feature of government was developed most fully during the colonial era?

1 separation of church and   3 universal suffrage
  state   4 representative assemblies
2 an independent court
  system

9. In the 18th century, the British colonies in North America were most similar to Great Britain in their
1 common law legal system
2 countrywide established church
3 opportunities for social mobility
4 dependence upon manufacturing as the economic base

10. Which was most influential in making the idea of separation of church and state a part of the United States political tradition?
1 the democratic heritage of ancient Athens
2 the Roman Republic's principles of religious freedom
3 practices of European colonial governments
4 the diversity of the new nation's population

11. An important aim of mercantilism as practiced by European countries during the 17th and 18th centuries was to
1 attain national self-sufficiency
2 acquire naval bases
3 destroy the Italian trade monopoly
4 achieve free trade

12. American colonial documents include such phrases as:
"We do mutually convenant and combine ourselves to enact, constitute, and frame such just and equal laws."
"We do enter into combination and confederation together."
Which principle in the United States Constitution can trace its origins to such colonial experiences as are indicated by these quotations?
1 checks and balances
2 division of powers
3 judicial review
4 consent of the governed

13. The major objection that British colonists in North America had to English rule was that they were
1 denied the right to arm themselves for defense
2 denied the rights of citizens who lived in England
3 forced to settle wilderness areas
4 forced to farm crops ordered by England

Writing and Ratifying the United States Constitution, 1787–1789

Fifty-five delegates, representing all the states except Rhode Island, met in Independence Hall in Philadelphia in May 1787 at the Constitutional Convention. These men would have been considered outstanding citizens in any period of history. They were young, but most had experience in government. Thirty-nine had been members of the Continental Congress. Eight had signed the Declaration of Independence. Thirty had served in the Continental Army. Thirty-one had attended college at a time when only a very few among the population ever did so. The delegates were wealthy lawyers, planters, and merchants at a time when most of the population were small farmers.

The most famous delegate was **George Washington**, who had commanded the Continental Army and was now elected president of the Convention. Another well-known figure was **James Madison**, whom some consider to have had the most influence on the Constitution. Also attending were **Benjamin Franklin** and **Alexander Hamilton**, a strong nationalist from New York.

Some famous Americans from the Revolution were noticeably absent. Thomas Jefferson and John Adams were serving the country as diplomats in Europe. A few patriots, such as **Patrick Henry**, refused to attend because they suspected that the Convention would try to create a strong national government, which they opposed. Still others were not selected by their states.

Also missing from the Convention were women, Native Americans, black Americans, and poorer white men. At that time in our history, these groups had limited political and legal rights.

KEY COMPROMISES AT THE CONVENTION

Early in the Convention, the delegates made two crucial decisions. First, they agreed that discussions would be kept secret in order to debate freely without outside pressure. They also decided to ignore the original aim of the meeting—the revision of the Articles of Confederation—and instead write a new constitution.

Most of what we know about the Convention comes to us from Madison's notes. It can be said that the debates, which lasted from May into September, involved both much conflict and much compromise. In fact, the United States Constitution has been called a "bundle of compromises." Four key compromises made the constitution possible:

Regents Tip Jot down key phrases to help you remember the positions of the different sides in major compromises at the Convention.

MAKING CONNECTIONS

Great Compromise

Virginia's position:

New Jersey's position:

Three-fifths Compromise

North's position:

South's position:

Commerce Compromise

North's position:

South's position:

Compromise of the Presidency

Pro strong national government:

Pro states' rights:

The Great Compromise

The first issue to be resolved was that of **representation**. The plan offered by Virginia delegates called for a bicameral, or two-house, legislature. A state's representation in each house would be based on its population. Larger states, of course, supported this plan.

The smaller states favored the **New Jersey Plan**. This plan called for a one-house, or unicameral, legislature in which each state had equal representation.

The **Virginia Plan** served as the basis for much of the new constitution. However, the matter of representation had to be settled by what is known as the **Great Compromise**, which gave something to both large and small states. The compromise created a bicameral legislature, our **Congress**. The states had equal representation in the upper house, or the **Senate**. In the lower house, or the **House of Representatives**, representation was based on population. In addition, all bills dealing with money would have to start in the House, but would need the approval of the Senate.

The Three-Fifths Compromise

This compromise grew out of a bitter debate over slavery and power. Southerners wanted their slaves counted for purposes of deciding representation in the House but not for purposes of determining taxes. The compromise reached was that three-fifths of the slaves in a state were counted for both representation and taxation.

The Commerce Compromise

Slavery figured in this compromise, too. Northerners wanted a government that could regulate trade. However, Southerners feared that the importing of slaves would be prohibited and that their agricultural exports would be taxed. The delegates agreed that no export duties could be passed by Congress and that Congress could not prohibit the slave trade for 20 years.

Compromise of the Presidency

The delegates favoring a strong national government wanted a President elected directly by the people, while those favoring states' rights wanted state legislatures to select the President. The resulting compromise was the indirect election of the President through the electoral college system.

RATIFICATION OF THE CONSTITUTION

After months of debate in Philadelphia, delegates approved the Constitution of the United States. It is now the oldest written national constitution in the world. In 1787, however, it was new, different, untested—and the subject of much controversy.

On September 17, 1787, thirty-nine of the delegates remaining in Philadelphia signed the Constitution. The fact that three, including **George Mason**, author of the Virginia Bill of Rights, refused to sign gives an indication of the coming debate. The Framers had written that 9 of the 13 states must approve the Constitution for it to go into effect. Approval would be done through special conventions called in each state rather than through the state legislatures.

MAKING CONNECTIONS

The Great Debate

Two groups formed in each state: the **Federalists**, who favored **ratification**, or approval, and the **Anti-Federalists**, who opposed it.

The Federalist Arguments:	The Anti-Federalist Arguments:
• Wanted a strong national government to provide order and protect rights of people.	• Wanted a weak national government so that it would not threaten the rights of the people or the powers of the states.
• Claimed that a bill of rights was unnecessary because the new government's powers were limited by the Constitution.	• Wanted to add a bill of rights to protect the people against abuses of power.

Ratification

The first five states ratified the Constitution within a few months. Then the fight became more bitter. Massachusetts approved it in February with the suggestion that amendments be added to protect citizens' rights. Other states also took this course of action, and by June 1788 nine states had given their approval—enough for ratification. But these did not include the states of Virginia and New York. The success of the new government depended upon acceptance of the Constitution by these two key states.

In Virginia, James Madison led the fight for ratification against the opposition of George Mason and Patrick Henry. Virginia approved the Constitution by 10 votes but with amendments suggested. New York was the next battleground. Here **The Federalist**—a series of pro-ratification essays by Alexander Hamilton, John Jay, and James Madison—helped turn the tide against the Anti-Federalists led by Governor George Clinton. Ratification was by a margin of three votes. **The Federalist** remains one of the finest statements on government and the Constitution ever written.

When the new government took office in 1789, one of the first acts of Congress was to act on the suggestions of the states and propose the first 10 amendments to the Constitution. James Madison prepared the first draft of these amendments, known as the **Bill of Rights**. The states soon ratified them.

Key Ideas People who live in a democracy like the United States have many rights and freedoms such as those listed in the Bill of Rights. However, these rights are accompanied by many responsibilities. It is the balance of rights and responsibilities that makes the system work.

Regents Questions for Practice _____

MAKING CONNECTIONS

Review the Test-Taking Strategies section of this book. Then answer the following questions, drawn from actual Regents examinations. Circle the *number* of the word or expression that best completes the statement or answers the question. Write your answers to essay questions on a separate piece of paper. Hints on good ways to approach these questions are provided in the margins.

1. "We should consider we are providing a constitution for future generations of Americans, and not merely for the particular circumstances of the moment."
    —Delegate at the Constitutional Convention of 1787
    The writers of the Constitution best reflected this idea when they provided that
    1 Senators should be elected directly by the people
    2 three-fifths of the slaves should be counted as part of the total population
    3 Congress shall make all laws necessary and proper to carry out its constitutional powers
    4 political parties should be established to represent various viewpoints

2. At the Constitutional Convention of 1787, the Great Compromise was concerned mainly with
    1 representation of the states in Congress
    2 the powers of the executive
    3 the question of slavery
    4 control of interstate commerce

3. Which quotation from the United States Constitution best illustrates the balance between order and liberty?
    1 "The Congress shall have the power . . . to borrow money on the credit of the United States."
    2 "The privilege of the writ of habeas corpus shall not be suspended, unless when in cases of rebellion or invasion the public safety may require it."
    3 "The President shall be Commander-in-Chief of the Army and Navy of the United States, and of the militia of the several states, when called into the actual service of the United States."
    4 "The judicial power of the United States shall be vested in one Supreme Court and in such inferior courts as the Congress may from time to time ordain and establish."

4. A democratic society tries to maintain a balance between personal freedom and restraint which may make law enforcement more difficult. Which situation best illustrates the main idea of this statement?

1 Passports are required for United States citizens traveling abroad.
2 Many States require automobile owners to carry liability insurance.
3 Information obtained by wiretapping is not admissible as evidence in a criminal trial.
4 In a military trial, the accused waives the right to have the case reviewed by a grand jury.

5. A major objection to the United States Constitution when it was presented for ratification in 1787 was that the Constitution

1 reserved too much power to the states
2 contained too many compromises
3 required the approval of all the states to ratify it
4 provided insufficient guarantees of civil liberties

6. In the later 1780s, some key states were persuaded to ratify the Constitution by the promise that provision would be made for

1 low taxes
2 a bill of rights
3 a national court system
4 national assumption of state debts

7. Which was the basic reason that the Bill of Rights was added to the original United States Constitution?

1 Local governments demanded a listing of their powers.
2 There was a need for a strong central authority.
3 Individuals needed protection from possible abuses of Government powers.
4 The powers of Congress were not sufficiently defined in the original Constitution.

Four statements dealing with formation of a new government are given below. Base your answers to questions 8 and 9 on these statements and on your knowledge of social studies.

Statement A: Each person must be able to voice his or her concerns on all issues that involve this new nation and bear the responsibility for the decisions made.

Statement B: The power of this new nation must rest in a strong, stable group that makes important decisions with the approval, but not the participation, of all.

Statement C: There must be several governments within one nation to ensure adequate voice and responsibility to all.

Statement D: Individuals must not allow their freedoms to be swallowed by an all-powerful government.

MAKING CONNECTIONS

Test Hint Key words in this question are "balance" and "make law enforcement *more* difficult."

Test Hint Note that questions 5, 6, and 7 are all concerned in different ways with the Bill of Rights.

Test Hint Note that questions 8 and 9 are both based on the same four statements about the formation of a new government. As you read the statements look for differences in points of view about government.

8. Which statement best shows the desire for safeguards such as those in the Bill of Rights?
(1) A   (2) B
(3) C   (4) D

9. Which statement best represents the ideas of federalism?
(1) A   (2) B
(3) C   (4) D

10. Which is characteristic of both democracy and capitalism?
1 guarantees of a high standard of living
2 equality among people
3 very limited competition
4 considerable individual choice

11. Any nation having a republican form of government must provide for
1 a written constitution
2 guaranteed civil liberties
3 election of representatives
4 division of authority among three levels of government

Essay Questions

Following are essay questions about the unit you have been reviewing. Before answering each, apply the lessons you learned in the Test-Taking Strategies section by blocking each essay. The first block has been organized for you to help you get started with the prewriting that is so necessary in preparing a good Regents answer.

1. Commenting about the period preceding the Constitutional Convention, historian Thomas Bailey wrote:
". . . although the Confederation was praiseworthy as confederations went, the troubled times demanded not a loose confederation but a tightly knit federation."

a Discuss one way in which government under the Articles of Confederation was praiseworthy.   [3]

b Government under the Articles of Confederation could not deal effectively with many issues that arose during the 1780's. Some of these issues involved:
Currency
Commerce
National security
Domestic order
National leadership

Choose two of these issues and for each once chosen:
• Discuss why government under the Articles of Confederation was ineffective in dealing with the issue
• Explain how the United States Constitution attempted to address the issue.   [6, 6]

ESSAY 1
PART A

Why the Articles were praiseworthy
[3]

PART B

Issue	Why the Articles were ineffective	How the Constitution tried to correct the problem
National security	States could make treaties with other nations; no direction on who could declare war.	The Senate must approve all treaties which can only be made by the federal government; only Congress can declare war. [6]
		[6]

2. In reference to the Declaration of Independence and the United States Constitution, it has been said that 1776 gave us liberty, but 1787 gave us order.
   a Discuss the extent to which you agree with the statement above. In your discussion, include three specific points of evidence that support your position. [9]
   b Discuss how either liberty or order was fostered by the adoption of the Bill of Rights in 1791. Cite two specific references to the Bill of Rights to support your position. [6]

MAKING CONNECTIONS

Enduring Issues

In this section you will be introduced to the Thirteen Enduring Constitutional Issues. These are the basic constitutional principles which have developed over the nation's history and which continue to challenge our nation today. Throughout the rest of the book, a special symbol in this column will alert you that the text is discussing how a key constitutional principle developed over the nation's history. The questions that follow the first appearance of each issue will help you think about ways these issues continue to be important.

Enduring Issues

National Power— Limits and Potential

The national government is one of limited powers. But has it become too powerful or does it need even more power to handle crises in the modern world?

The United States Constitution is not simply a group of laws. It is a fundamental plan, or framework, clearly defining and limiting the powers of government. Our Constitution has served as a model for plans of government in many other nations.

In the **Preamble**, or introduction, to the Constitution, the Framers set down the reasons they wrote the document:

- To create a better, stronger national government
- To ensure a system of justice
- To provide for peace at home
- To provide for the defense of the nation
- To promote the well-being of the people
- To secure liberty to the people and to future generations

BASIC PRINCIPLES OF THE CONSTITUTION

The Preamble opens with the words "We the people." The first phrase of the Constitution thus demonstrates one of six basic principles on which the document is based. These principles and their meanings are listed below.

Popular Sovereignty

"Popular" means "of or by the people." "Sovereignty" means "supreme power." Our Constitution is based on the idea that the source of all power or authority to govern is the people. This type of government is **democracy**, or government by the consent of the governed.

Limited Government

The powers of the government are defined by the Constitution. In this way, our government is limited by law. The Constitution places limits on both the state and national governments and on the officials of these governments as well.

Federalism

The Constitution divides the power to govern between the states and the national government. This division of power between levels of government creates a **federal system** of government. This means that

- Both national and state governments have powers to govern in certain areas.
- Both national and state governments govern the people directly.
- Both national and state governments must agree to changes in how the Constitution divides the powers of government.
- Disputes over power between the national and state governments are settled by the courts. However, the **Supremacy Clause** in Article VI of the Constitution makes the Constitution, federal laws, and treaties superior to state laws.

Separation of Powers

The Constitution divides the power to govern among the **legislative**, **executive**, and **judiciary** branches within the national government. This division ensures that no one branch can dominate the government. Each branch takes its power directly from the Constitution, not from another branch. Each branch has its own officials, who are selected in different ways and who serve different terms of office.

MAKING CONNECTIONS

Enduring Issues

The Separation of Powers and the Capacity to Govern

Have the separation of powers and checks and balances kept one branch of government from dominating the others?

Separation of Powers

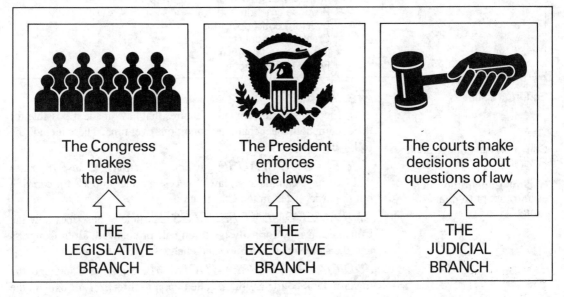

The Congress makes the laws

THE LEGISLATIVE BRANCH

The President enforces the laws

THE EXECUTIVE BRANCH

The courts make decisions about questions of law

THE JUDICIAL BRANCH

Checks and Balances

Related to the separation of powers is the constitutional system of **checks and balances**. This system gives each branch of the national government ways to check, or control, the other branches. This prevents too much power from falling into the hands of any one part of the government.

The Checks and Balances System

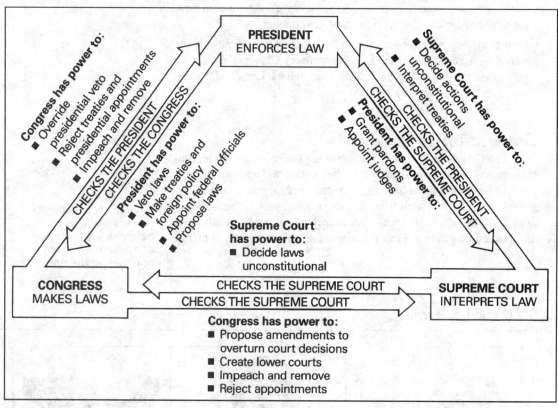

PRESIDENT
ENFORCES LAW

Congress has power to:
■ Override presidential veto
■ Reject treaties and presidential appointments
■ Impeach and remove

CHECKS THE PRESIDENT
CHECKS THE CONGRESS

President has power to:
■ Veto laws
■ Make treaties and foreign policy
■ Appoint federal officials
■ Propose laws

Supreme Court has power to:
■ Decide actions unconstitutional
■ Interpret treaties

CHECKS THE PRESIDENT
CHECKS THE SUPREME COURT

President has power to:
■ Grant pardons
■ Appoint judges

Supreme Court has power to:
■ Decide laws unconstitutional

CONGRESS
MAKES LAWS

CHECKS THE SUPREME COURT
CHECKS THE SUPREME COURT

SUPREME COURT
INTERPRETS LAW

Congress has power to:
■ Propose amendments to overturn court decisions
■ Create lower courts
■ Impeach and remove
■ Reject appointments

Constitutional Change and Flexibility

Has the Constitution been able to adapt to changing times?

Flexibility

The Constitution contains features that have made it possible for the document to meet changing conditions over time. These include the following.

THE ELASTIC CLAUSE   Article 1, Section 8, Clause 18, states that Congress can make all laws "necessary and proper" for carrying out the tasks listed in the Constitution.

THE AMENDMENT PROCESS   Article V describes how the Constitution may formally be **amended**, or changed. Both Congress and the states must agree to such changes.

JUDICIAL INTERPRETATION   The Supreme Court and the lower federal courts are often called upon to **interpret**, or explain the meaning of, the Constitution and federal laws.

FEDERALISM IN THE CONSTITUTION

The principle of federalism is so important to our government that it merits more discussion.

Types of Governments

A federal government differs from both unitary and confederation governments. In a **unitary government**, political power is in the hands of a central government that directly governs the people. Any subdivisions of government are created by the central government in order to put laws into effect more efficiently. A **confederation** is an alliance created by the member states. The states keep most of the power, and the states, not the central government, act directly on the people.

Types of Governments

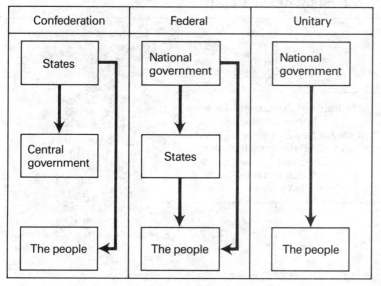

Dividing the Powers of Government

The Constitution divides the power to govern between the national and the state governments in the following way:

DELEGATED POWERS Certain powers of the national government are spelled out in the Constitution. Most of these **delegated** or **enumerated** powers are listed in Article I, Section 8. One example is the power of the national government to declare war.

IMPLIED POWERS Certain powers of the national government are not stated in writing. Their existence is implied by Article I, Section 8, Clause 18—known as the **elastic clause**. One example of an **implied power** is the regulation of child labor; this power is implied by the delegated power to regulate interstate commerce.

MAKING CONNECTIONS

Enduring Issues

Federalism— The Balance Between Nation and State

Is power in the federal system still balanced between the national government and the states? Should it be?

Remember the following definitions when thinking about the powers of government:
Delegated means "specifically assigned or given to."
Implied means "included as a necessary part or effect of some statement or action."
Concurrent means "existing side by side."
Reserved means "kept back."

MAKING CONNECTIONS

DENIED POWERS   Certain powers are denied to the national government—for example, the power to pass an export tax. Other powers are denied to the states—for example, the power to print money. Still other powers are denied to both national and state governments—for example, the power to deny the right to vote because of sex or race.

CONCURRENT POWER   Certain powers belong to both national and state governments. One example of such a **concurrent power** is the right to tax.

RESERVED POWERS   Certain powers remain with the states. These **reserved powers** are neither delegated to the national government nor denied to the states. One example is the power to make divorce laws.

System of Federalism

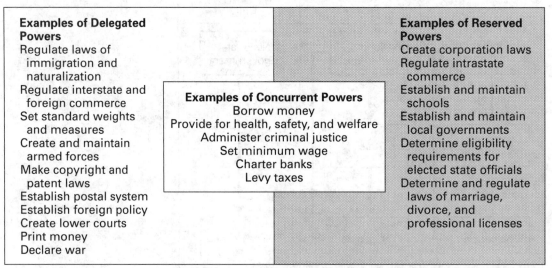

Examples of Delegated Powers
Regulate laws of immigration and naturalization
Regulate interstate and foreign commerce
Set standard weights and measures
Create and maintain armed forces
Make copyright and patent laws
Establish postal system
Establish foreign policy
Create lower courts
Print money
Declare war

Examples of Concurrent Powers
Borrow money
Provide for health, safety, and welfare
Administer criminal justice
Set minimum wage
Charter banks
Levy taxes

Examples of Reserved Powers
Create corporation laws
Regulate intrastate commerce
Establish and maintain schools
Establish and maintain local governments
Determine eligibility requirements for elected state officials
Determine and regulate laws of marriage, divorce, and professional licenses

The Constitution spells out other aspects of federalism in Article IV. This article describes relations among the states and lists guarantees that the national government makes to the states. Article VII, which describes ratification of the Constitution, serves as a reminder that the new national government had to be approved by the individual states.

The Basic Organization and Functions of Government Under the Constitution

The first three articles of the Constitution describe and define the powers of the legislative, executive, and judicial branches of the national government. These articles detail the separation of powers, while showing how each branch can check and balance the others.

The first three articles also give the terms of office and qualifications for some positions in the national government. The election process for the presidency is the only one described in detail. In the original Constitution, only members of the House of Representatives were elected directly by the people. Today the people also directly elect United States Senators. The President is still elected indirectly, under the electoral college system. Federal judges continue to be appointed, not elected.

MAKING CONNECTIONS

Federal Officeholders

Office	Number	Term	Selection	Requirements
Representative	At least 1 per state; based on state population	2 years	Elected by voters of congressional district	Age 25 or over Citizen for 7 years Resident of state in which elected
Senator	2 per state	6 years	Original Constitution— elected by state legislature Amendment 17— elected by voters	Age 30 or over Citizen for 9 years Resident of state in which elected
President and Vice-President	1	4 years	Elected by electoral college	Age 35 or over Natural-born citizen Resident of U.S. for 14 years
Supreme Court judge	9	Life	Appointed by President	No requirements in Constitution

ARTICLE I: THE LEGISLATIVE BRANCH

Article I establishes the United States Congress with its two houses—the Senate and the House of Representatives. Congress is the legislative, or lawmaking branch of government. Article I gives the qualifications for election to Congress, the rights and privileges of members of Congress, and some basic operating procedures of both houses. The Article also lists the powers delegated, or given, to Congress.

Regents Tip Remember that some Regents examination questions require you to read and interpret charts. Study the accompanying chart and answer the question that follows.
How does the term of a Supreme Court justice differ from those of other federal officeholders shown on the chart?

MAKING CONNECTIONS

Background Note that the chart is arranged by *type* of power. The numbers represent the clauses of Section 8 of the Constitution that grant the powers to Congress.

Enduring Issues

Property Rights and Economic Policy

What powers granted Congress show that the writers of the Constitution intended the federal government to play a role in shaping the nation's economic policy? Does the federal government have too much power in this area today?

The Powers of Congress as Stated (by Articles) in the United States Constitution

Expressed Powers
Peace Powers

1. To lay taxes
   a. Direct (not used since the War Between the States, except income tax)
   b. Indirect (customs [tariffs], excise for internal revenue)
2. To borrow money
3. To regulate foreign and interstate commerce
4. To establish naturalization and bankruptcy laws
5. To coin money and regulate its value; to regulate weights and measures
6. To punish counterfeiters of federal money and securities
7. To establish post offices and post roads
8. To grant patents and copyrights
9. To create courts inferior to the Supreme Court
10. To define and punish piracies and felonies on the high seas; to define and punish offenses against the law of nations
17. To exercise exclusive jurisdiction over the District of Columbia; to exercise exclusive jurisdiction over forts, dockyards, national parks, federal buildings, and the like

War Powers
11. To declare war; to grant letters of marque and reprisal; to make rules concerning captures on land and water 12. To raise and support armies 13. To provide and maintain a navy 14. To make laws governing land and naval forces 15. To provide for calling forth the militia to execute federal laws, suppress insurrections, and repel invasions 16. To provide for organizing, arming, and disciplining the militia, and for its governing when in the service of the Union
Implied Powers
18. To make all laws necessary and proper for carrying into execution the foregoing powers, such as: To define and provide punishment for federal crimes To establish the Federal Reserve System To improve rivers, canals, harbors, and other waterways To fix minimum wages, maximum hours of work

Each house of Congress also has special duties that it alone can perform.

Special Powers of the House and Senate

House	Senate
• To select the President if no candidate receives a majority of the electoral vote • To bring impeachment charges • To originate all revenue (money) bills	• To select the Vice President if no candidate has a majority of the electoral vote • To act as jury in cases of impeachment • To ratify treaties (by a two-thirds vote) • To approve presidential appointments (by a majority vote)

Article I briefly outlines how a bill becomes a federal law. This process requires the approval of each house and of the President. A presidential **veto**, or rejection, of a bill can be overridden by a two-thirds vote of each house. As the diagram, ''How a Bill Becomes a Law'' shows, the process today is quite complex, and a bill must pass through numerous committees before becoming a law.

ARTICLE II: THE EXECUTIVE BRANCH

Article II outlines the workings of the **executive branch**, including the method of electing the President as well as the powers and duties of the office.

Electing the President

Article II describes the process by which the President is elected. Amendments 12, 20, 22, and 25 have changed this process.

As noted in Section 2, a key compromise of the Constitutional Convention involved the method of electing the president. Under the resulting electoral college system, voters cast their ballots for electors. Those electors cast the actual votes for President and Vice President. Each state was granted as many presidential electors as it had senators plus representatives.

In addition to Constitutional requirements, customs and precedents developed that influenced how the President is elected. After Washington's two terms, the formation of political parties forced changes in the election process. No longer did electors exercise their own judgments. Rather, they pledged in advance to vote for the presidential candidate of their party. Today, while the names of the presidential candidates appear on the ballot, voters are actually casting their ballots for a slate of electors chosen by each candidate's party.

By 1832, national conventions had become the method of selecting party candidates. Today more than half the delegates to such

MAKING CONNECTIONS

Background Customs and traditional practices can become precedents. A **precedent** is an action or decision which serves as the basis for a later action or decision.

How a Bill Becomes a Law

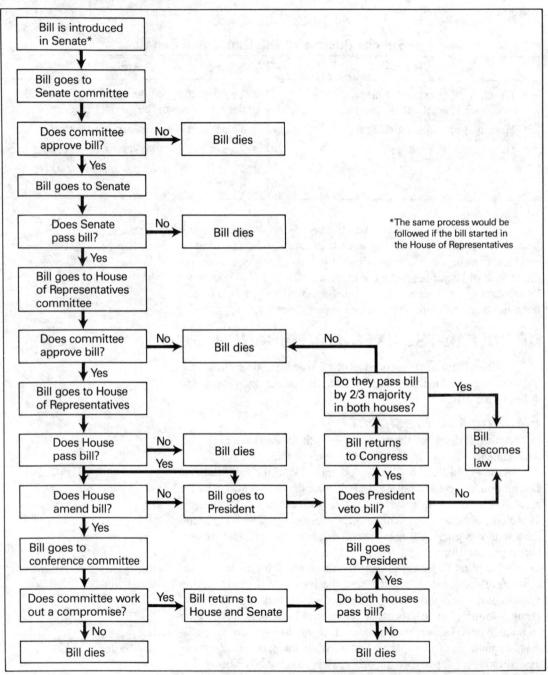

Bill is introduced in Senate*

Bill goes to Senate committee

Does committee approve bill? — No → Bill dies

Yes

Bill goes to Senate

Does Senate pass bill? — No → Bill dies

*The same process would be followed if the bill started in the House of Representatives

Yes

Bill goes to House of Representatives committee

Does committee approve bill? — No → Bill dies

Yes

Bill goes to House of Representatives

Does House pass bill? — No → Bill dies

Yes

Does House amend bill? — No → Bill goes to President

Yes

Bill goes to conference committee

Does committee work out a compromise? — Yes → Bill returns to House and Senate

No

Bill dies

Do both houses pass bill?

No → Bill dies

Yes

Bill goes to President

Yes

Does President veto bill? — No → Bill becomes law

Yes

Bill returns to Congress

Do they pass bill by 2/3 majority in both houses? — Yes → Bill becomes law

No → Bill dies

national conventions are selected through party presidential primaries. Such primaries are only one step in today's complex path to the presidency. The accompanying chart summarizes key steps along that path.

The Path to the Presidency

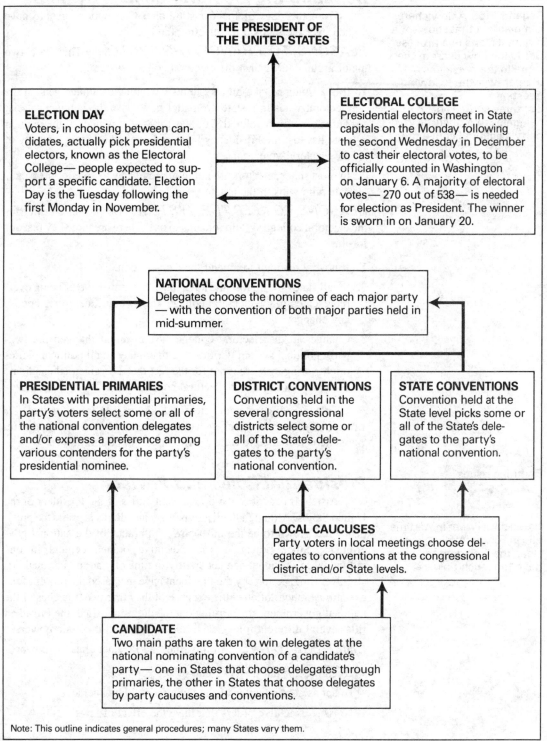

THE PRESIDENT OF THE UNITED STATES

ELECTION DAY
Voters, in choosing between candidates, actually pick presidential electors, known as the Electoral College— people expected to support a specific candidate. Election Day is the Tuesday following the first Monday in November.

ELECTORAL COLLEGE
Presidential electors meet in State capitals on the Monday following the second Wednesday in December to cast their electoral votes, to be officially counted in Washington on January 6. A majority of electoral votes— 270 out of 538— is needed for election as President. The winner is sworn in on January 20.

NATIONAL CONVENTIONS
Delegates choose the nominee of each major party — with the convention of both major parties held in mid-summer.

PRESIDENTIAL PRIMARIES
In States with presidential primaries, party's voters select some or all of the national convention delegates and/or express a preference among various contenders for the party's presidential nominee.

DISTRICT CONVENTIONS
Conventions held in the several congressional districts select some or all of the State's delegates to the party's national convention.

STATE CONVENTIONS
Convention held at the State level picks some or all of the State's delegates to the party's national convention.

LOCAL CAUCUSES
Party voters in local meetings choose delegates to conventions at the congressional district and/or State levels.

CANDIDATE
Two main paths are taken to win delegates at the national nominating convention of a candidate's party— one in States that choose delegates through primaries, the other in States that choose delegates by party caucuses and conventions.

Note: This outline indicates general procedures; many States vary them.

MAKING CONNECTIONS

Regents Tip A flow chart is a diagram that shows the different steps in a process. Study the flow chart of the route to the presidency, then answer the following question.
List three sources of delegates to a political party's national convention.

1.

2.

3.

Debating the Electoral College System

From the days of the Constitutional Convention, people have argued over the method of selecting the President.

REASONS TO CHANGE THE SYSTEM There are two major arguments against the electoral college system.

1. It is a "winner-take-all" system. A winning candidate gets all the electoral votes in a state no matter how close the popular vote is. Three times—in 1824, 1876, and 1888—the winner of the popular vote has lost the Presidency because he failed to win a majority of the electoral vote.

2. In most states, electors are not required by law to vote for the candidate who wins in their state.

REASONS TO KEEP THE SYSTEM Despite such criticisms the electoral college system remains in use. There are three key reasons for this.

1. It is very difficult to amend the Constitution.

2. Small states would lose the advantage they now have of being over-represented in the electoral college; they would, therefore, oppose any change.

3. Changes in the electoral college system might threaten the two-party political system. Critics fear that many small political parties might spring up were it not for the fact that a presidential candidate needs a majority of the electoral college vote.

This map illustrates the electoral vote in the states for the 1996 presidential election. After each census, the number of electoral votes per state can change to reflect any changes in population.

Enduring Issues

Presidential Power in Wartime and in Foreign Affairs
Does the President today have too much power?

Presidential Roles and Powers

Article II describes the powers and duties of the President of the United States. Although the list of powers and duties is brief, the presidency has grown to be the most powerful branch of the national government. Since power in the executive branch centers in one individual, a President can act swiftly in time of war and national crisis. Over time, actions by the President have increased the power of the executive branch, often at the expense of the other two branches of the national government. In carrying out the duties of office, the President fills several different roles. Each role carries with it certain powers.

CHIEF EXECUTIVE In this role, the President has the power

• To enforce or put the laws into effect

• To act as administrator of the huge federal bureaucracy

• To issue executive orders that have the effect of laws

Electoral Vote of Each State—1996

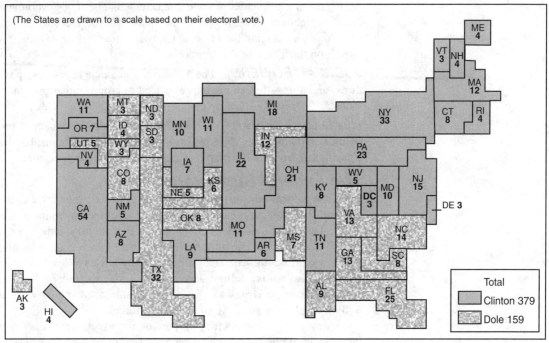

(The States are drawn to a scale based on their electoral vote.)

Total	
▨	Clinton 379
▨	Dole 159

- To appoint judges, diplomats, cabinet officers, and other high government officials—some with the consent of the Senate and others without this approval
- To remove appointed government officials within the executive branch

CHIEF DIPLOMAT   In this role, the President has the power

- To make treaties
- To make executive agreements with nations without the approval of the Senate
- To extend diplomatic recognition to a nation or withdraw such recognition

COMMANDER IN CHIEF   In this role, the President has broad military powers that are shared with Congress. In times of war, these powers are even stronger.

CHIEF LEGISLATOR   In this role of lawmaker, the President has the power

- To recommend legislation to Congress
- To veto potential laws

MAKING CONNECTIONS

Continuing Issues:
From time to time, historians and political scientists rate the performance of the Presidents. The most highly rated tend to be those who have used their powers most broadly.
Great Presidents: George Washington, Thomas Jefferson, Abraham Lincoln, Franklin D. Roosevelt
Near-great Presidents: Andrew Jackson, Theodore Roosevelt, Woodrow Wilson, Harry Truman

MAKING CONNECTIONS

CHIEF OF STATE   In addition to being head of the government, the President is also **chief of state**, the ceremonial head of government and the symbol of all the people of the nation. He fills this role in such ceremonies as lighting the national Christmas tree and the laying of a wreath on the Tomb of the Unknowns.

JUDICIAL POWERS   The President can grant **reprieves**, **pardons**, and **amnesties**, or pardons extended to groups rather than individuals.

HEAD OF THE PARTY   The President is also the leader of the political party in power. The duties of this role are not mentioned in the Constitution because the party system developed through custom.

The Federal Bureaucracy

The **federal bureaucracy** is made up of the administrative agencies and staff that put the decisions or policies of the government into effect. The Constitution does not mention a bureaucracy, although the presidential power of appointment implied that a bureaucratic administration would be needed. Such a bureaucracy has developed through legislation, executive action, and custom. Today the federal bureaucracy is the single largest employer in the nation, with nearly three million employees exclusive of the armed forces.

Most of the bureaucracy is part of the executive branch and includes the White House staff, which works directly for the president, and the 14 executive departments, which are headed by Cabinet officers. In addition, the bureaucracy includes independent executive agencies, such as NASA, that are not part of the 14 departments; government corporations, such as the Federal Deposit Insurance Corporation; and independent regulatory agencies, such as the Federal Communications Commission. The independent regulatory agencies enforce the laws governing our economy. They are largely free of presidential control because of the laws concerning conditions and terms of appointment and removal of agency members.

Enduring Issues

The Judiciary— Interpreter of the Constitution or Shaper of Public Policy?

What has the role of the federal courts been in the past and what *should* that role be?

ARTICLE III: THE JUDICIAL BRANCH

Article III of the Constitution creates the Supreme Court and gives Congress the power to create other, lower federal courts. The role of this **judicial branch** is to interpret the law. In addition to this national court system, each of the 50 states has its own court system. This dual national/state court structure is another example of federalism.

Jurisdiction

In setting up a national court system independent of the states, the Framers of the Constitution recognized and corrected a weakness of the Articles of Confederation. With two court systems—federal and

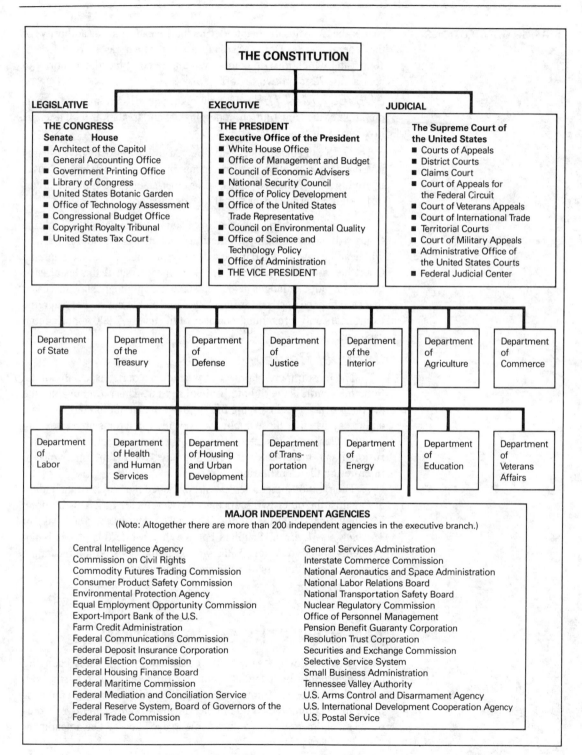

THE CONSTITUTION

LEGISLATIVE

THE CONGRESS
Senate   House
- Architect of the Capitol
- General Accounting Office
- Government Printing Office
- Library of Congress
- United States Botanic Garden
- Office of Technology Assessment
- Congressional Budget Office
- Copyright Royalty Tribunal
- United States Tax Court

EXECUTIVE

THE PRESIDENT
Executive Office of the President
- White House Office
- Office of Management and Budget
- Council of Economic Advisers
- National Security Council
- Office of Policy Development
- Office of the United States
  Trade Representative
- Council on Environmental Quality
- Office of Science and
  Technology Policy
- Office of Administration
- **THE VICE PRESIDENT**

JUDICIAL

**The Supreme Court of
the United States**
- Courts of Appeals
- District Courts
- Claims Court
- Court of Appeals for
  the Federal Circuit
- Court of Veterans Appeals
- Court of International Trade
- Territorial Courts
- Court of Military Appeals
- Administrative Office of
  the United States Courts
- Federal Judicial Center

| Department of State | Department of the Treasury | Department of Defense | Department of Justice | Department of the Interior | Department of Agriculture | Department of Commerce |

| Department of Labor | Department of Health and Human Services | Department of Housing and Urban Development | Department of Transportation | Department of Energy | Department of Education | Department of Veterans Affairs |

MAJOR INDEPENDENT AGENCIES
(Note: Altogether there are more than 200 independent agencies in the executive branch.)

Central Intelligence Agency
Commission on Civil Rights
Commodity Futures Trading Commission
Consumer Product Safety Commission
Environmental Protection Agency
Equal Employment Opportunity Commission
Export-Import Bank of the U.S.
Farm Credit Administration
Federal Communications Commission
Federal Deposit Insurance Corporation
Federal Election Commission
Federal Housing Finance Board
Federal Maritime Commission
Federal Mediation and Conciliation Service
Federal Reserve System, Board of Governors of the
Federal Trade Commission

General Services Administration
Interstate Commerce Commission
National Aeronautics and Space Administration
National Labor Relations Board
National Transportation Safety Board
Nuclear Regulatory Commission
Office of Personnel Management
Pension Benefit Guaranty Corporation
Resolution Trust Corporation
Securities and Exchange Commission
Selective Service System
Small Business Administration
Tennessee Valley Authority
U.S. Arms Control and Disarmament Agency
U.S. International Development Cooperation Agency
U.S. Postal Service

state—the Constitution had to define the **jurisdiction**, or authority, of the federal courts. Doing so made it clear which cases go to federal courts and which to state courts. Whether a court has the authority to hear a case rests on two factors:

SUBJECT MATTER   Federal courts hear cases involving interpretation of the Constitution, federal laws, and treaties as well as cases involving maritime law.

PARTIES   Federal courts are directed to have jurisdiction if cases involve certain **parties**, or participants in a case. For example, cases involving U.S. officials, states suing other states, and representatives of foreign governments are tried in federal courts.

The Constitution states that in certain types of cases the Supreme Court will have **original jurisdiction**. This means the Supreme Court will hear the case first and make a decision. In most cases, the Supreme Court has **appellate jurisdiction**. This means that if the losing side believes a judge or judges made a mistake in applying the law in a case, that case may be appealed from a lower to a higher court. The Supreme Court hears only a few hundred cases of the nearly 5,000 appealed to it each year.

Judicial Review

The most important power of the federal courts, especially of the Supreme Court, is the right to **judicial review**. This power enables the courts to hear cases involving the application and interpretation of law and to say whether those applications or interpretations are in keeping with the Constitution's intent. Laws that are not are declared **unconstitutional** and, therefore, void. The Supreme Court is the final voice in interpreting the Constitution.

The right of judicial review strengthened the power of the judiciary against the other two branches of government. Chief Justice John Marshall first stated the right of judicial review in the 1803 case of *Marbury* v. *Madison*. Scholars believe that, while this power is not explicitly stated in Article 3, the writers of the Constitution meant the Supreme Court in particular to have this power.

AMENDING THE CONSTITUTION

Article 5 describes methods of **amending**, or formally changing the Constitution. In accordance with the principle of federalism, both national and state governments are involved in the amendment process. In the most common method of amendment, Congress approves a proposed amendment by a two-thirds vote in each house. The amendment

The Federal Court System

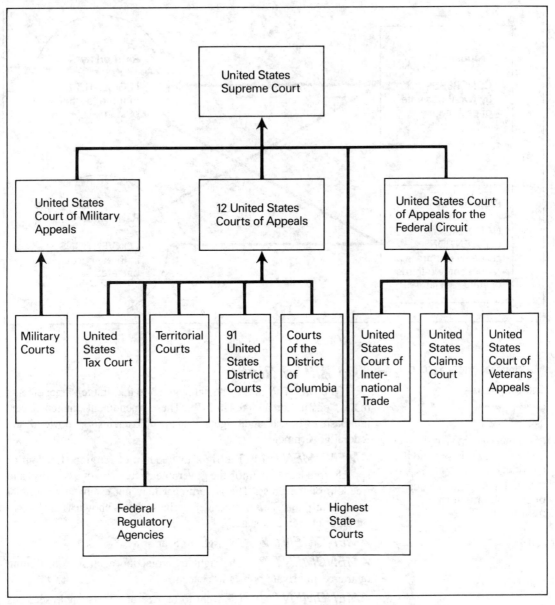

then goes to the legislatures of the states. If three-quarters of them ratify it, the amendment becomes part of the Constitution. Twenty-six amendments have been adopted by this method. To date, only the 21st Amendment has been ratified by special conventions called in the states.

Regents Tip This is another example of a flow chart. Which federal court hears cases appealed from the highest state courts?

Methods of Amending the Constitution

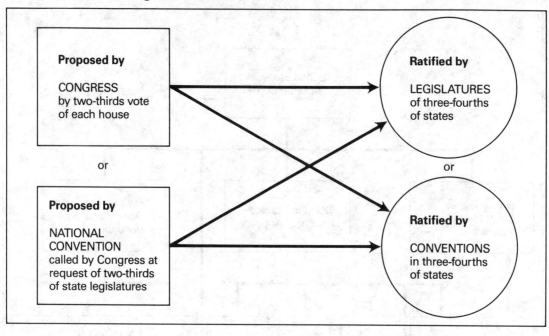

MAKING CONNECTIONS

Enduring Issues

Civil Liberties—The Balance Between Government and the Individual

What civil liberties issues pose problems for the nation today?

The Bill of Rights

The **Bill of Rights** is the name given to the first ten amendments to the Constitution adopted in 1791. These amendments guarantee certain basic or fundamental rights of the people against the power of the federal government.

AMENDMENT 1   The right to freedom of religion, freedom of speech, freedom to petition the government, freedom of assembly, and freedom of the press. The government may not establish an official national religion. This amendment defines what is known as the "separation of church and state."

AMENDMENT 2   The right to bear arms.

AMENDMENT 3   The right to protection against troops being quartered in private homes in peacetime.

AMENDMENT 4   The right to be free of unreasonable searches and seizures; warrants for searches can be issued only "upon probable cause."

AMENDMENT 5   The right, if accused of a crime,

- To be accused formally by a **grand jury**.
- Not to be tried twice for the same crime, a practice known as **double jeopardy**.

- Not to to be forced to give evidence against oneself.
- To receive a fair trial and protection by all proper legal procedures, a guarantee known as **due process of law**.
- To receive fair compensation if the government takes private property for public purposes.

AMENDMENT 6   The right, if accused of a crime,

- To be told the charges.
- To receive a "speedy and public trial" with an "impartial" jury.
- To face the prosecution witnesses.
- To have the services of a defense lawyer.
- To force, through the legal process, defense witnesses to testify in court.

AMENDMENT 7   The right to a jury trial in many types of non-criminal cases.

AMENDMENT 8   The right to protection against "excessive" bail and fines and "cruel and unusual punishment."

AMENDMENT 9   The guarantee that other rights not listed in the Constitution are also protected.

AMENDMENT 10   The guarantee that the people or the states have all powers not given to the national government or denied to the states; these are reserved powers.

Extending Constitutional Protections

In the 200 years since the Bill of Rights was added to the Constitution, the rights of the people have been expanded by court decisions and by other amendments. The 14th Amendment contains the **equal protection clause**. Court interpretations have held that this amendment extends the protections of most of the Bill of Rights against the states as well as the national government.

The Courts have held that the civil rights of people, defined in the Bill of Rights and other amendments, are **relative**, not absolute. The courts have thus tried to balance an individual's rights against the rights of society and the rights of other individuals. Sometimes basic civil rights conflict with each other. For example, the accused's 5th Amendment right to confront witnesses might clash with a reporter's 1st Amendment, freedom-of-the-press right to protect news sources. In such conflicts, the courts must decide the issue.

Additional Constitutional Amendments

The accompanying chart lists constitutional amendments passed between 1795 and 1992. Note that the 13th, 14th, and 15th amendments were passed after the Civil War to free the former slaves, to make them citizens, and to give them the right to vote.

MAKING CONNECTIONS

Enduring Issues

Criminal Penalties: Rights of the Accused and Protection of the Community

Which amendments specifically deal with this issue? To which other Enduring Issue is it most closely related?

Enduring Issues

Equality— Its Definition as a Constitutional Value

How far does the 14th Amendment permit the legislature and the courts to go in extending equal protection under the law?

MAKING CONNECTIONS

Enduring Issues

The Rights of Women Under the Constitution

The Rights of Ethnic and Racial Groups Under the Constitution

What amendments extend rights to women and ethnic and racial groups? Do their rights receive adequate protection today?

Amendments to the Constitution

Amendments	Subject	Year Adopted
1st–10th	The Bill of Rights	1791
11th	Immunity of States from certain suits	1795
12th	Changes in Electoral College procedure	1804
13th	Prohibition of slavery	1865
14th	Citizenship, due process, and equal protection	1868
15th	No denial of vote because of race, color or previous condition of servitude	1870
16th	Power of Congress to tax incomes	1913
17th	Direct election of U.S. Senators	1913
18th	National (liquor) prohibition	1919
19th	Woman Suffrage	1920
20th	Changes of dates for congressional and presidential terms	1933
21st	Repeal of the 18th Amendment	1933
22nd	Limit on presidential tenure	1951
23rd	District of Columbia electoral vote	1961
24th	Prohibition of tax payment as a qualification to vote in federal elections	1964
25th	Procedures for determining presidential disability and succession, and for filling a vice presidential vacancy	1967
26th	Sets the minimum age for voting in all elections at 18	1971
27th	Bans mid-term congressional pay raises	1992

The accompanying chart illustrates how the right to vote has expanded since the Constitution went into effect in 1789.

The Right to Vote

Year	People Allowed to Vote
1789	White men over age 21 who meet property requirements (state laws)
Early 1800s–1850s	All white men over age 21 (state laws)
1870	Black men (Amendment 15)
1920	Women (Amendment 19)
1961	People in the District of Columbia in presidential elections (Amendment 23)
1971	People over age 18 (Amendment 26)

MAKING CONNECTIONS

Enduring Issues

Avenues of Representation

The right to vote has expanded, but is our government today more or less representative of "we the people"?

NEW YORK STATE GOVERNMENT COMPARED TO THE FEDERAL GOVERNMENT

Like the United States, New York has a constitution and a Bill of Rights. Like the federal government, the New York government has three branches. The governor heads the executive branch. The bicameral legislature is made up of a Senate and an Assembly. The highest court in the judicial branch is the Court of Appeals.

THE UNITED STATES GOVERNMENT COMPARED TO OTHER TYPES OF GOVERNMENTS

The United States government differs significantly from the parliamentary democracy of Great Britain and the nondemocratic government of the former Soviet Union. The chart on the next page gives some of the major differences among these three governments. Drastic changes have taken place in the former Soviet Union, altering the differences shown on the chart. In August 1991, a group of Communist Party leaders, desiring a return to a hard-line Communist government, placed Soviet President Mikhail Gorbachev under arrest. When the Soviet public heard of the attempted coup, protestors took to the streets, popularly elected office holders denounced Gorbachev's arrest, and the coup failed.

On January 1, 1992, the Soviet Union was officially dissolved, and the Commonwealth of Independent States was formed. The new commonwealth is a federation of 12 of the 15 former Soviet republics, each of which retains sovereignty usually associated with an independent country.

Comparative Political Systems

United States Democratic Republic	Great Britain Parliamentary Democracy	The Former Soviet Union Socialist Republic
Congress consists of Senate and House of Representatives; President elected by the people	Parliament consists of House of Commons (elected) and House of Lords (hereditary); chooses Prime Minister	Congress of People's Deputies and Supreme Soviet; President of the USSR (and General Secretary of Communist Party of the Soviet Union) headed the government
Written constitution as fundamental law	No single written document delegating power; any act of Parliament constitutional	Written constitution, was not in fact a fundamental law
System of checks and balances controls executive, legislative and judicial branches of government	No system of checks and balances; Prime Minister must have majority support in Parliament	No system of checks and balances; Communist Party dominated the political process

Regents Questions for Practice _____

MAKING CONNECTIONS

Review the Test-Taking Strategies section of this book. Then answer the following questions, drawn from actual Regents examinations. Circle the *number* of the word or expression that best completes the statement or answers the question. Write your answers to essay questions on a separate piece of paper. Hints on good ways to approach these questions are provided in the margins.

Test Hint The principle of federalism is often tested. Remember the "Dynamic Duo," with power divided in TWO between national and state governments.

1. The principle of federalism as established by the United States Constitution provides for the
   1. separation of powers of the three branches of government
   2. placement of ultimate sovereignty in the hands of the state governments
   3. divisions of power between the state governments and the national government
   4. creation of a republican form of government

2. Which best illustrates the concept of federalism as it is reflected in the United States Government structure?
   1. The constitutional system of checks and balances tends to concentrate power in the judicial branch.
   2. The Constitution assigns some responsibilities to the Federal Government and some to the States, while others are shared by both Federal and State governments.

3 According to the Constitution, economic power is divided among the Federal Government, union leaders, and business officials.

4 Authority to make, implement, and enforce decisions is derived from a written constitution.

3. Which action best exemplifies the principle of checks and balances in the United States Constitution?

1 The President negotiates a treaty.

2 The House of Representatives initiates a revenue bill.

3 The Vice President presides over a Senate meeting.

4 The Senate ratifies a Presidential appointment.

4. The statement in the United States Constitution that the President ". . . shall nominate, and by and with the advice and consent of the Senate, shall appoint . . . judges of the Supreme Court" illustrates which governmental principle?

1 judicial review   3 checks and balances

2 executive privilege   4 minority rights

5. United States Supreme Court decisions in cases involving the first amendment to the Federal Constitution generally reflect the principle that

1 if an action is based on a religious belief, it must be allowed

2 only demonstrations that support the beliefs of the majority may be held

3 freedoms of speech and religion are absolute

4 individual rights must be balanced against the needs of society at the time

6. The fact that there are libel laws in the United States demonstrates that

1 this nation is not a democracy

2 Government officials consider themselves above the law

3 the Federal Government is seeking powers of censorship

4 the freedoms guaranteed by the first amendment are limited

7. An analysis of the federal-state relationship in United States history indicates that these levels of government have

1 cooperated fully in applying national law

2 generally agreed on the assumption of more powers by the states

3 often disagreed over how state and federal powers are to be balanced

4 both willingly given up power in times of national crisis

8. An advantage of a federal system of government is that it

1 ensures speedy decisions

2 guarantees the most democratic approach to government

3 permits both national and local approaches to problems

4 is the least costly form of government

MAKING CONNECTIONS

Test Hint Questions 3 and 4 are about a different division of power, this time WITHIN the national government. They deal with the division of the national government's powers into three branches—executive, legislative, and judicial. These two pie graphs show the different divisions of power. Don't confuse the two.

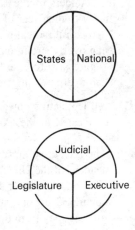

Test Hint Questions 5 and 6 show how the same idea can be tested in different ways.

9. The fact that the United States Constitution provided for federalism and a system of checks and balances suggests that
   1 the original thirteen states sought to dominate the national government
   2 its writers desired the national government to rule over the states
   3 its writers feared a concentration of political power
   4 the American people of that time supported a military government

10. The system of federalism was adopted by the founders of the United States due primarily to their fear of
    1 powerful radical groups
    2 an overly strong national judiciary
    3 aggressive foreign leaders
    4 an overpowering central government

11. "All legislative power herein granted shall be invested in the Congress of the United States."
    "The Executive power shall be vested in a President of the United States."
    "The Judicial power shall be vested in one Supreme Court and such inferior courts as Congress may from time to time ordain and establish."
    These opening sentences of the first three articles of the United States Constitution most clearly express which of its major principles?
    1 separation of powers
    2 popular sovereignty
    3 federalism
    4 judicial review

Base your answers to questions 12 through 15 on the following selections from the United States Constitution and on your knowledge of social studies.

Selection A: "All legislative powers herein granted shall be vested in a Congress of the United States, which shall consist of a Senate and House of Representatives."

Selection B: "The Congress shall have power . . . to make all laws which shall be necessary and proper for carrying into execution the foregoing powers. . . ."

Selection C: "The Congress shall have power . . . to regulate commerce with foreign nations, and among the several states. . . ."

Selection D: The Congress, whenever two-thirds of both houses shall deem it necessary, shall propose amendments to this Constitution. . . ."

Selection E: "Congress shall make no law respecting an establishment of religion, or prohibiting the free exercise thereof; or abridging the freedom of speech, or of the press; or the right of the people peaceably to assemble, and to petition the government for a redress of grievances."

Selection F: "The Congress shall have power . . . to declare war. . . ."

12. To settle a controversy at the Constitutional Convention, a compromise concerning representation was reached which resulted in Selection
    (1) A (2) B (3) C (4) D

13. After the Supreme Court has declared a law unconstitutional, Congress may enact a similar law by applying the provisions of Selection
    (1) A (2) B (3) C (4) D

14. A reason for a basic difference between Congress and the President concerning the conduct of foreign policy is best indicated by Selection
    (1) A (2) B (3) C (4) F

15. Much of the railroad and antitrust legislation of the late 19th century was enacted by Congress under the provisions of Selection
    (1) A (2) B (3) C (4) D

16. The principle of separation of powers with a corresponding system of checks and balances is best illustrated by the power of the
   1 President to send troops to Vietnam
   2 Congress to establish post offices
   3 Supreme Court to review laws of Congress
   4 states to regulate educational systems

17. The United States Constitution provides for a system of checks and balances between branches of government, but at different times one branch has appeared more powerful than the others. This situation has occurred mainly because
   1 amendments to the Constitution have altered the balance between the branches
   2 certain events have required one branch temporarily to take more forceful approaches and actions
   3 the states have assumed more power relative to the power of the Federal Government
   4 the Constitution provides for a systematic rotation of power between the branches

18. Which headline refers to an action that may be justified under the elastic (necessary and proper) clause of the United States Constitution?
   1 President Vetoes Act of Congress
   2 Congress Passes Minimum-Wage Law
   3 President Appoints Ambassador to United Nations
   4 Unites States Senate Ratifies Treaty

19. According to the United States Constitution, a nationwide census is conducted every ten years in order to
   1 establish trends of enrollment in the major political parties
   2 determine the allocation of Federal monies for revenue sharing
   3 determine the number of Representatives each state will have in Congress
   4 study changes in social customs

20. The electoral college system was included in the United States Constitution as originally written primarily because the authors of the Constitution believed that
   1 political parties needed to be restrained
   2 the powers of the Presidency should be limited
   3 the general population lacked the knowledge to elect a President
   4 it would promote cooperation between Congress and the President

21. In the United States, the electoral college system affects the campaigns of major-party Presidential candidates by influencing candidates to
   1 concentrate upon the states with large populations
   2 place more emphasis on controversial issues than on personality
   3 focus upon the states where winning by a large plurality is likely
   4 appeal to the electoral college members rather than to the general public

22. A Presidential veto of a bill passed by Congress is an example of the President's use of
   1 the elastic clause of the Constitution
   2 an ex-post-facto law
   3 executive privilege
   4 the system of checks and balances

23. Which is the most important reason why the office of President of the United States became increasingly powerful after World War II?
   1 a greater involvement of the United States in world affairs
   2 a trend toward industrialization in the United States
   3 greater coverage of world affairs by the news media in the United States
   4 increased restrictions on rights of individual United States citizens to participate in government

24. Which area has historically involved a conflict between the power of the President as Commander in Chief and the power of the Congress to declare war?
1 diplomatic recognition of nations
2 intervention in other nations
3 appointment of ambassadors
4 domestic law enforcement

25. Much of the authority of the United States Supreme Court is based on its power to
1 propose legislation to Congress
2 change the distribution of powers as outlined in the Federal Constitution
3 amend state and federal constitutions
4 interpret the Federal Constitution

26. The power of the Supreme Court to decide whether or not a law violates the Constitution is known as
1 constitutional limitation
2 original jurisdiction
3 appellate jurisdiction
4 judicial review

27. Which is the most valid statement regarding the United States Supreme Court?
1 Supreme Court rulings generally reflect current social attitudes and values.
2 The Supreme Court is expected to review the legislative program of each Presidential administration.
3 Organized labor has consistently been the beneficiary of favorable Supreme Court decisions.
4 The power of the Supreme Court has significantly declined during the past 50 years.

28. "The legislature protects the rights of the majority while the courts protect the rights of minorities."
This statement can best be substantiated by a study of reforms in the
1 electoral college
2 criminal justice system
3 organization of businesses
4 labor movement

29. The purpose of amendments to the United States Constitution has generally been to
1 restrict the powers of the President
2 advance democratic ideals
3 prevent social change
4 limit the right to protest government actions

30. Which provision of the United States Constitution makes it possible to meet the needs of a changing society?
1 Congress, by a simple majority, can amend the Constitution.
2 Congress can pass all laws necessary and proper for carrying out its delegated powers.
3 Powers not delegated to the national government are reserved for the states.
4 Powers are separated among the three branches of government.

31. In the United States, which action would present the greatest threat to individual liberties?
1 eliminating the President's power to veto acts of Congress
2 abolishing the electoral college
3 suspending the Bill of Rights
4 limiting the number of immigrants to the United States

32. "The right of citizens of the United States, who are eighteen years of age or older, to vote shall not be denied or abridged by the United States or by any State on account of age."
This amendment to the United States Constitution restricted the
1 reserved powers of the States
2 delegated powers of Congress
3 powers assumed by the Supreme Court
4 powers retained by the people

Essay Questions

Following are essay questions about the unit you have been reviewing. Before answering each, apply the lessons you learned in the Test-Taking Strategies section by blocking each essay. The first block has been organized for you to help you get started with the prewriting that is so necessary in preparing a good Regents essay answer.

1. In 1787, the framers of the United States Constitution established a federal system which delegated some governmental powers to the National government, reserved other powers to the State governments, and assigned some powers to both levels.

   The delegated and reserved powers include the power to:
   * Coin money
   * Control education
   * Control interstate commerce
   * Take care of the poor and needy
   * Declare war
   * Determine voter qualifications
   * Establish local governments

   a From the list above, identify one power that was delegated to the National Government and one power that was reserved to the State governments. For each power selected, discuss why the framers of the Constitution either delegated that power to the National Government or reserved it to the State governments. [8]

   b Identify two governmental powers originally reserved to the States. Explain how and why the Federal Government has increased its role with regard to each of these powers. [You may use any of the reserved powers that are listed above or any other reserved powers.] [7]

PART A

	Description of power	Why delegated
National government	To coin money	Under the Articles, every state issued its own money; a single form of money for the whole nation would aid trade and commerce. [4]
State governments		[4]

PART B

Power reserved to the states	How and why the federal government has increased its role
Voter qualifications	Amendments and laws brought the vote to those who had been denied it such as 18-year-olds and blacks in the South.
	[Part B–Total 7]

2. The authors of the United States Constitution had to make decisions in each of the following areas:
   - Creating a Constitution adaptable to changing conditions
   - Resolving disputes over the meaning of the law
   - Avoiding the concentration of power
   - Conducting relations with other nations
   - Enforcing laws

   a Choose three of the areas listed above. For each one chosen, describe an issue related to that area and explain how the United States Constitution dealt with the issue. [9]

   b These issues have continued to challenge the United States ever since the Constitution was ratified. Choose one area from the list above. Identify a specific situation in United States history in which that issue arose again and explain how it was resolved. [6]

3. Since the United States Constitution was written, many generalizations have been made about it. Some of these generalizations are:
   - The Constitution is basically an economic document
   - The Constitution is a "bundle of compromises"
   - The Constitution has both divided and limited the powers of government
   - The strength of the Constitution rests on its flexibility
   - The Constitution combines European tradition and American colonial experiences

   Choose three of the generalizations listed above. For each one chosen, discuss the extent to which the generalization is accurate and use two specific examples to support your position. [5, 5, 5]

4. The Constitution provides both basic principles of government and means for adapting to changing times.

a Choose one of the governmental principles listed below. Define the principle and discuss how it operates in the United States.

> *PRINCIPLES*
> Checks and balances
> Federalism   [5]

b The Constitution provides for meeting the needs of changing times through such means as:
- The amending process
- The elastic clause (implied powers)
- Supreme Court decisions

Choose two of these means and, for each one chosen, discuss a specific example of how this means was used to help the United States respond to a need of society during a particular time period in United States history.   [5, 5]

5. The government of the United States today is, in many ways, quite different from the government established by the framers of the original United States Constitution. Different methods have been used to change the government established in the original Constitution. Among these methods are:
- Congressional action
- Presidential leadership
- Supreme Court decisions
- Constitution amendments

Select three of the methods listed above. For each one chosen, describe a specific governmental change brought about by the use of that method and explain how the change reflected the needs of society at the time.   [5, 5, 5]

6. Since the United States Constitution was written, certain topics treated by the Constitution have been the basis for controversy. Some of these topics are:
- Federal-State relations
- Church-State relations
- Rights of minorities
- Power of the Presidency
- Role of government in the economy
- Due process of law

Select three of the topics listed above. For each one chosen, discuss a controversy in United States history that arose in regard to this topic. Explain the relationship of the Constitution to the controversy. Include a specific time period and a description of the historical background in your response.   [5, 5, 5]

The Thirteen Enduring Constitutional Issues

WHAT ARE THE THIRTEEN ENDURING CONSTITUTIONAL ISSUES? WHY ARE THEY IMPORTANT?

As part of the celebration of the bicentennial of the United States Constitution in 1987, a group of well-respected historians and political scientists identified thirteen issues or questions that have endured throughout the 200-year history of the Constitution and continue to be of importance to this day in the development of our government and society. Because of their importance, these issues are tested on every Regents Examination, as the following chart demonstrates.

What You Need to Know About the Thirteen Enduring Constitutional Issues

The chart below explains the Thirteen Enduring Issues and the questions they raise for our nation. Under each issue is a list of related concepts that were tested on the Regents Examinations from June 1988 through June 1990. The letters **MC** followed by a number indicate the number of times the concept has been tested in a multiple-choice question. The letter **E** followed by a number indicates the number of times the concept has been tested in an essay question.

Issue One: National Power—Limits and Potential

The powers of the United States Government are limited: Those powers not delegated to the national government are reserved to the states or to the people. However, the powers of all three branches of the federal government have grown.

• Has the national government become too powerful?

or

• Do the limits placed on the national government make it incapable of dealing with the problems of the modern age?

CONCEPTS   **KEY: MC = multiple-choice; E = essay**

Loose vs. strict interpretation of Constitution   **MC** 2

Government of limited powers   **MC** 2

National leadership, improved by Constitution   **E** 1

Need for strong government; centralization of authority   **MC** 4

Conflict over slavery: at Constitutional Convention; 1820–1860   **MC** 2; **E** 1

Civil War, establishes federal supremacy over the states   **MC** 1

Government policy toward Native Americans   **MC** 2

Spanish-American War; acquiring overseas empire   **E** 1

Imperialism   **E** 2

Interstate Commerce Act, passage   **MC** 1

Sherman Antitrust Act, passage   **MC** 1

Antitrust movement   **MC** 1; **E** 1

CONCEPTS   KEY: MC = multiple-choice; E = essay

Theodore Roosevelt: Progressivism; New Nationalism   **MC** 1; **E** 1

Big business; industrialization; Progressivism **MC** 2; **E** 1

Commerce clause, used to regulate business   **MC** 1

Labor unions: Clayton Antitrust Act   **MC** 1

Woodrow Wilson: New Freedom   **MC** 1

Government mobilizes economy, World War I **MC** 1

Government assumes powers of states, twentieth century   **MC** 1

Presidential actions: expansion of government power **E** 1

New Deal, expands role of government   **MC** 6; **E** 1

Elastic Clause: Social Security; Pure Food and Drug Act   **MC** 1

New Deal: unemployment in 1930s   **E** 1

Great Society: demand for reform   **E** 1

Regulatory agencies, regulation of businesses   **MC** 1

New Federalism: demand for reform; less government involvement   **MC** 1; **E** 1

Role of government in everyday life   **E** 1

Issue Two: Federalism—The Balance Between the Nation and the States

The Constitution divided power between the states and the national government, reserving powers to the states and to the people but making the Constitution as well as the laws and treaties of the United States the supreme law of the land.

- Is the power still balanced, or has it tilted to the federal government?
- Has the shift of power to the federal government become greater since the New Deal, or did Reagan's New Federalism reverse this trend?

CONCEPTS   KEY: MC = multiple-choice; E = essay

Federalism: defined; advantages of; promotes freedom   **MC** 3; **E** 1

National leadership: improved by the Constitution **E** 1

Federal-state relationship: disagreements   **MC** 1

Federalism: *McCulloch* v. *Maryland*   **E** 1

Supreme Court cases: Federal v. state powers   **E** 1

John C. Calhoun: states' rights   **E** 1

Conflict over slavery: at Constitutional Convention; 1820–1860   **MC** 2; **E** 1

Civil War: federal supremacy over the states   **MC** 1

Reconstruction: amendments, legislation   **MC** 1

Greater federal supremacy: 13th, 14th, 15th Amendments   **MC** 4

Equal protection clause: 14th Amendment, purpose-effect   **MC** 1; **E** 1

Hayes election: federal troops withdrawn from South **MC** 1

Populists: reform movement; against banking and railroad interests   **MC** 2; **E** 1

Agrarian Protests, 1870–1900   **E** 1

TVA: federal intervention for regional needs   **MC** 1

Brown v. *Board of Education*   **MC** 3

Great Society, mid-1960s   **E** 1

New Federalism, 1980s   **E** 1

Issue Three: The Judiciary—Interpreter of the Constitution or Shaper of Public Policy

The Judiciary interprets the law and has the power to declare laws unconstitutional.

- Have the courts become lawmakers instead of law interpreters, acting when Congress has not acted?

- If the courts did not have the power to shape public policy, would our Bill of Rights and democracy itself be endangered?

CONCEPTS   KEY: MC = multiple-choice; E = essay

Authority of court, derived from power to interpret laws **MC** 2

Court as lawmaking body; "judicial activism" **MC** 3

Protection of rights of minorities, criminal justice system **MC** 1

Marshall Court: strengthened government and national unity **MC** 2

Judicial review: Constitution adapts to change **E** 1

Judicial review: strengthens judiciary **MC** 1

Marbury v. *Madison* **MC** 1; **E** 1

Judicial branch, 1803–1830: strong leadership **E** 1

Plessy v. *Ferguson* **MC** 1

Court decisions: far-reaching effects **MC** 1

Supreme Court: controversial social issues **MC** 1

Reversals of decisions, reflecting changing conditions **MC** 1

Brown v. *Board of Education*: school desegregation **MC** 2; **E** 1

"One man, one vote": court decisions **MC** 1; **E** 1

Abortion: court decisions **E** 2

Prayer in schools: separation of church and state; court decisions **MC** 1; **E** 3

Rights of accused persons: court decisions **MC** 1; **E** 2

Rights of minorities: court decisions **E** 2

Federal v. state powers: court decisions **E** 1

Checks and balances: court decisions **E** 1

Rights of individuals extended: court decisions **E** 1

Freedom of speech: court decisions **E** 1

Issue Four: Civil Liberties—The Balance Between Government and the Individual

A problem unique to a democratic government is how to balance the rights of the individual and the needs of society.

• In issues of order and security versus liberty, what is the role of the government?

• Should government protect the rights of the individual?

• Should government extend individual rights?

• Should government decide where the balance should be between individual and societal rights?

• What are the rights of the individual?

CONCEPTS   KEY: MC = multiple-choice; E = essay

Bill of Rights: liberties; furthered liberty and order **MC** 1; **E** 1

Due process of law, defined **MC** 2

Search and seizure: 4th Amendment **E** 1

Balance between individual rights and needs of society **MC** 2; **E** 1

Government: how to guarantee liberty and freedom to all citizens **E** 1

Conflict between two rights **MC** 1

Amendments and court decisions: expanded rights **MC** 1; **E** 1

Equal protection clause: 14th Amendment **MC** 1; **E** 1

"Clear and present danger": freedom of speech **MC** 1

World War I: increased nativism; cause **MC** 1; **E** 1

Relocation of Japanese-Americans; *Korematsu* v. *United States* **MC** 4; **E** 1

Red Scare, McCarthyism, fear of subversion, erosion of liberties **MC** 1

Cold War: extremism seen as un-American **MC** 1

Rights of accused: court decisions **MC** 1; **E** 2

Rights of minorities: court decisions **E** 2

Freedom of speech: court decisions **E** 1

Controversy: media censorship **E** 1

Controversy: students with AIDS attending public schools **E** 1

Controversy: testing for drug use **E** 1

Gun control **MC** 1

Rights of individual: effects of technology **E** 1

Issue Five: Criminal Penalties—Rights of the Accused and Protection of the Community

Again this is a question of balancing rights—in this case, the rights of individuals accused of crimes and those of citizens to be safe and secure.

- Why does an individual accused of a crime have rights?

- Are those rights easily defined?
- What are the rights of a victim of a crime?
- When do the rights of the accused interfere with society's ability to maintain law and order?

CONCEPTS   **KEY: MC = multiple-choice; E = essay**

Free press v. the rights of the accused   **MC** 1

Individual rights v. rights of society: death penalty
   E 1

Writ of habeas corpus: purpose   **MC** 1

Search and seizure: 4th Amendment   **E** 1

Due process of law, defined   **MC** 2

Rights of accused: court decisions   **MC** 1; **E** 1

Miranda v. *Arizona*: rights of accused   **E** 1

Need for reform: dealing with crime   **E** 1

Issue Six: Equality—Its Definition as a Constitutional Value

This issue involves questions of who is equal and in what ways.

- According to the Constitution, who is equal: men and women? all races? rich and poor? young and old?

- How are people equal: equal in opportunity? before the law? in entitlements?
- Does equality extend to economic and social opportunity?

CONCEPTS   **KEY: MC = multiple-choice; E = essay**

Conflict over slavery: at Constitutional Convention;
   1820–1860   **MC** 2; **E** 1

Equal protection clause: 14th Amendment   **MC** 1;
   E 1

Civil War: status of blacks in society   **E** 1

"Jim Crow" laws: legal basis for segregation
   MC 1

Passage of 14th and 15th Amendments   **MC** 3

Plessy v. *Ferguson*   **MC** 1

Women's suffrage movement   **MC** 3; **E** 1

Women's rights movement   **E** 2

New Deal: relief of human suffering; help for less
   fortunate   **MC** 2; **E** 1

Brown v. *Board of Education*   **MC** 2; **E** 1

Civil rights movement   **E** 1

Native American Movement   **E** 1

Great Society: help for less fortunate   **MC** 1

Affirmative action: court decisions   **E** 1

Need for reform: quality of education   **E** 1

Need for reform: adequate housing   **E** 1

Issue Seven: The Rights of Women Under the Constitution

Women are not mentioned in the Constitution except in the 19th Amendment, which protects their right to vote.

- Are federal laws and court rulings sufficiently protective of the rights of women?
- Was there a need for the defeated Equal Rights Amendment?

CONCEPTS   **KEY: MC = multiple-choice; E = essay**

Women's suffrage movement   **MC** 3; **E** 1

Elizabeth C. Stanton: women's rights   **E** 1

Women's Rights Movement   **E** 2

Effect of industrialization; role of women   **E** 1

Changing role of women   **E** 2

Abortion: court decisions   **E** 2

Affirmative action: court decisions   **E** 1

Issue Eight: The Rights of Ethnic and Racial Groups Under the Constitution

The Constitution has not always protected ethnic, racial, and other minority groups. At times, it has even protected the rights of groups such as slaveholders when they discriminated against minorities.

- Has the Constitution done a good job of protecting the rights of ethnic and racial minorities—blacks, immigrants, Native Americans, Japanese Americans, and other groups?

- Until this century, did the Constitution do a better job of protecting vested economic and political groups instead?

- Will the gains that minorities have made continue, or do such groups need more protection of their rights?

- How do we balance minority rights and rule by a majority?

CONCEPTS   **KEY: MC = multiple-choice; E = essay**

Conflict over slavery: at Constitutional Convention; 1820–1860   **MC** 2; **E** 1

Frederick Douglass: abolitionism   **E** 1

Civil War: effect on status of blacks in society   **E** 1

Reconstruction: expanded opportunities for blacks   **MC** 1

"Jim Crow" laws: legal basis for segregation   **MC** 1

Equal protection clause: 14th Amendment   **MC** 1; **E** 1

Passage of 14th and 15th Amendments   **MC** 3

Plessy v. *Ferguson*   **MC** 1

Brown v. *Board of Education*   **MC** 2; **E** 1

Rights of minorities: court decisions   **E** 2

Martin Luther King, Jr.: civil rights movement   **E** 1

Civil rights movement of 1960s   **MC** 2; **E** 2

Mixed attitudes toward immigration; resentment   **MC** 1; **E** 1

Nativism: cause and effects   **MC** 1; **E** 2

Restrictions on immigration   **MC** 2; **E** 1

Movement against immigration of Chinese and other Asians   **MC** 2

Relocation of Japanese-American; *Korematsu* v. *United States*   **MC** 4; **E** 1

Native Americans: rights guaranteed by treaties   **MC** 1

Native Americans: values and culture misunderstood by government   **MC** 1

Native American Movement   **E** 1

Issue Nine: Presidential Powers in Wartime and in Foreign Affairs

The powers of the President have grown since the early days of the United States government, and they are even greater in wartime.

- Does the President have too much power, particularly since the Civil War?

- Are broad presidential powers necessary to conduct war and foreign affairs?

CONCEPTS   **KEY: MC = multiple-choice; E = essay**

Presidents: most control over foreign policy   **MC** 1

Successful Presidents' use of popularity and power   **MC** 1

Presidential power as Commander in Chief   **MC** 1

U.S. involvement in world affairs: increase in power of presidency   **MC** 1

Growth in influence of White House staff   **MC** 1

Presidential power grown at expense of other branches   **E** 1

George Washington: expanded governmental powers   **E** 1

George Washington: Proclamation of Neutrality   **E** 1

Lincoln and F.D.R.: increased presidential powers in wartime   **MC** 1

Lincoln: Emancipation Proclamation   **E** 1

Lincoln: reasons for high rating as President   **E** 1

Lincoln: expanded governmental powers   **E** 1

T. Roosevelt: expanded governmental powers   **MC** 1

CONCEPTS	KEY: MC = multiple-choice; E = essay
T. Roosevelt and F.D.R.: strong Presidents **MC** 1	Korean and Vietnam wars: expanded presidential wartime powers **MC** 1
Roosevelt Corollary to Monroe Doctrine **MC** 2	
T. Roosevelt: reasons for high rating as President **MC** 1	Truman: decision to drop atomic bomb **MC** 1
	Truman: policies to oppose communism **MC** 1
Wilson: Treaty of Versailles **MC** 2	Kennedy: containment **MC** 1
Wilson: reasons for high rating as President **E** 1	Kennedy: Cuban missile crisis **E** 1
F.D.R.: strong executive leadership **MC** 1	L.B.J.: expanded governmental powers **E** 1
F.D.R.: Japanese-American relocation as military necessity **MC** 2	War Powers Act: check on presidential power **MC** 2
F.D.R.: reasons for high rating as President **E** 1	Reagan: policies to oppose communism **MC** 1
F.D.R.: expanded governmental powers **E** 1	Reagan: negotiates SALT **MC** 1

Issue Ten: The Separation of Powers and the Capacity to Govern

The Constitution's plan of government set up three branches with separate powers as well as a system of checks and balances among them.

- Has the system of separation of powers and of checks and balances been effective in preventing dominance by one branch?

- Is this system necessary, or has it resulted in a badly run government that is slow to respond to the needs of the people and the nation?

CONCEPTS	KEY: MC = multiple-choice; E = essay
Checks and balances: purpose; how promoted freedom **MC** 1; **E** 1	Judicial review: strengthened judiciary **MC** 1
Presidential veto: example of checks and balances **MC** 1	Checks and balances: Reconstruction **E** 1
	Checks and balances: Treaty of Versailles **E** 1
Growth of executive power in times of crisis **MC** 1	Franklin Roosevelt: Reorganizing the Supreme Court **MC** 3; **E** 1
Periods of strong leadership of each of the three branches **MC** 1; **E** 1	Check and balances: Vietnam War **MC** 1
Supreme Court as "lawmaking body"; judicial activism **MC** 2	War Powers Act: check on presidential power **MC** 2
Checks and balances: Supreme Court decisions **MC** 1	Watergate: government based on laws not on an individual **MC** 1

Issue Eleven: Avenues of Representation

Since the Constitution was written, there has been a continuing expansion of the right to vote and to be represented in our political system. However, while our system has become more democratic and, therefore, more reflective of majority rule, there has also been growth in the power of political parties and of special interest groups.

- Has our government become more or less representative of "we the people?"

CONCEPTS   KEY: MC = multiple-choice; E = essay

Great Compromise: representation in Congress
    MC 1; **E** 1

Electoral College: lack of trust in voter   **MC** 1

House of Representatives: direct election by people
    MC 1

Passage of 14th and 15th Amendments   **MC** 3

Populist and Granger movements: political coalition;
    purpose   **MC** 4; **E** 1

Farmers' support of free silver   **MC** 1

Women's suffrage movement   **MC** 3; **E** 1

Direct election of senators   **E** 1

Progressivism: reform movement; goals; muckrakers
    MC 6; **E** 1

Third parties   **MC** 4

One man, one vote: effect on representative
    government   **MC** 1; **E** 1

Candidates' loyalty to a few major contributors
    MC 1

Public funding of campaigns: check on influence of
    special interests   **MC** 1

Politics: effects of technology   **E** 1

Government's encouragement of greater participation
    in political process   **E** 1

Issue Twelve: Property Rights and Economic Policy

The Constitution gives the government responsibility
for "promoting the general welfare" and Congress the
power to regulate commerce and taxes.

• Has government balanced its roles as promoter of
capitalism and free enterprise and as protector of the
public from the abuses of business?

CONCEPTS   KEY: MC = multiple-choice; E = essay

Constitutional support of capitalism; debates over
    commerce powers   **MC** 1; **E** 1

Hamilton: government encouragement of business;
    national bank   **MC** 2

Government support of business, 1876–1900   **MC** 1

Government support of business against unions,
    1860–1900   **MC** 1

Government involvement in economy, nineteenth
    century   **E** 1

Government action: rise of monopolies; Sherman
    Antitrust Act   **MC** 2

Commerce clause, used to regulate business   **MC** 1

Mobilization of economy for World War I   **MC** 1

T. Roosevelt and Wilson: problems of
    industrialization   **MC** 1

Hoover: economic philosophy   **MC** 1

New Deal: expanding role of government   **MC** 6;
    E 1

Debate over government regulating business, 1930s
    MC 1

New Deal: farm policy   **MC** 1

New Deal: action to cut unemployment   **E** 1

Unions: rights to organize, 1930s   **MC** 1

Government farm price supports   **MC** 1

Increase in government spending to decrease
    unemployment   **MC** 1

Government action: low farm income; farm
    bankruptcies   **E** 1

Regulatory agencies: regulation of business   **MC** 1

Government action: bank failures   **MC** 1

Government action: inflation   **E** 2

Reduction in taxes to stimulate consumer spending
    MC 2

Reagan economic view on individual initiative: New
    Federalism   **MC** 1; **E** 1

Reagan budget deficits   **MC** 1; **E** 2

Trade deficit: balance-of-payments deficit   **MC** 1;
    E 1

Government action: environmental protection;
    problems   **MC** 2; **E** 1

Adjusting to service economy in 1980s; loss of manu-
    facturing jobs   **MC** 1; **E** 1

Issue Thirteen: Constitutional Change and Flexibility

Provisions built into the Constitution as well as customs and procedures that have developed over time permit the Constitution to adapt to changing circumstances.

• Has the Constitution proven adaptable to changing times?

• Should the Constitution be easier to change?

• Has the amendment process, combined with judicial interpretation and the implied powers of the executive and legislative branches, kept the Constitution up to date to meet the challenges of the modern world?

CONCEPTS   **KEY: MC = multiple-choice; E = essay**

Elastic clause: definition; use **MC** 2

Hamilton's Bank Plan: implied powers **MC** 1

Commerce clause: regulation of business **MC** 1

Constitution: adaptability; methods used **E** 1

Government action: meeting the changing needs of society **E** 1

Flexibility in Constitution: promoted freedom **E** 1

Amendments and court decisions: expanding rights **MC** 1; **E** 1

Amendments: adapting to change **E** 1

Reversals of court decisions: reflecting changing times **MC** 1

Selecting presidential candidates: changing customs **MC** 1

Cabinet and congressional committees: custom and precedent **MC** 1

Federal Reserve System: regulatory powers **MC** 2

Regulatory agencies: regulation of business **MC** 1

SECTION 5

The Constitution Goes Into Effect

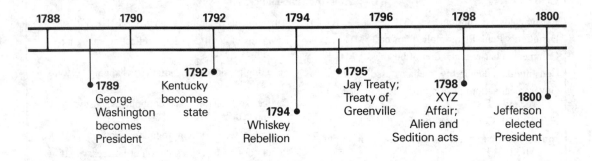

1788   1790   1792   1794   1796   1798   1800

1789
George
Washington
becomes
President

1792
Kentucky
becomes
state

1794
Whiskey
Rebellion

1795
Jay Treaty;
Treaty of
Greenville

1798
XYZ
Affair;
Alien and
Sedition acts

1800
Jefferson
elected
President

MAKING CONNECTIONS

Enduring Issues

Constitutional Change and
Flexibility

Earlier sections of this chapter examined the roots of the Constitution and how its plan of government operates. Now the focus will shift to how the Constitution was implemented, or put into effect, under the first Presidents. From now on, the column at the side will indicate which of the Enduring Issues defined in Section 4 is being discussed so that you can trace the way the Constitution developed.

Not all the events that shaped our government in these years grew out of the plan set down in the Constitution. From the time of our first Presidents—Washington, Adams, Jefferson, Madison, and Monroe—an **unwritten constitution** developed in response to changing times and circumstances. This unwritten constitution resulted from a combination of factors:

1. executive interpretations and actions
2. congressional interpretations and actions
3. court decisions, especially judicial review
4. customs and traditions
5. the actions of political parties

EXECUTIVE INTERPRETATION, ACTIONS, AND CUSTOM

Executive Decision-Making

George Washington sought advice from the heads of the executive departments. Consultation with these department heads, who were called the President's **Cabinet** became a common means of developing policy. Today, the **White House staff** also plays a major role in this

84

advisory process. After some controversy, it was determined that the President alone could dismiss heads of executive departments who were appointed with the consent of the Senate.

The early Presidents also consulted with Congressional leaders when developing policies. Such consultation is an informal, rather than a formal, procedure. Today, the Senate's official role often seems more "to consent" than "to advise" on Presidential decisions. This method of advising the President has become custom—part of the unwritten Constitution.

Developing a Financial Plan

Alexander Hamilton was the first Secretary of the Treasury. With Washington's support, he set out to put the government on a sound economic footing. His ideas for doing this were set out in a financial plan proposed to Congress. The plan included four key elements:

ASSUMPTION   Hamilton wanted the national government to pay off Revolutionary war debts run up by the Continental Congress. He also wanted it to **assume**, or take over and pay off, the wartime debts of the states as well. Hamilton believed that assuming the state debts and paying off government bonds at face value would establish the credit of the nation. Congress approved this plan.

A NATIONAL BANK   Hamilton wanted Congress to create a national bank. He believed a national banking system would win the government the support of the business community. Such a bank would also help the government in all its financial dealings. Congress chartered a national bank in 1791.

AN EXCISE TAX   Hamilton proposed that the government raise operating revenues through an **excise tax** on whiskey.

A PROTECTIVE TARIFF   Hamilton called for a **protective tariff** to shield products of the nation's infant industries from foreign competition. Congress rejected the protective tariff but passed tariffs to generate income for the government.

The Whiskey Rebellion

In 1794 western Pennsylvania farmers protested and refused to pay the excise tax—the internal tax on whiskey they made from grain. Washington called out state militias and put down this "**Whiskey Rebellion**." There is debate today over how serious a threat this rebellion was, but Washington's actions demonstrated that the new government intended to enforce federal law.

Foreign Policy

Washington exercised strong leadership in the area of foreign affairs. From 1789 to 1815, the French Revolution and the European wars that grew out of it put many pressures on our new, weak nation. Washington and the other Presidents of these years tried to protect the

MAKING CONNECTIONS

Enduring Issues

Property Rights and Economic Policy

Enduring Issues

Presidential Power

nation from such pressures. Washington, for example, supported the unpopular **Jay Treaty** with England because he realized the nation was in no position to go to war. With his **Proclamation of Neutrality** in 1793 and his **Farewell Address** in 1796, Washington set the pattern of United States foreign policy until well into this century. Washington believed economic ties with other nations were necessary, but he warned of the danger of "entangling" political alliances. Instead he urged the nation to take independent action in foreign affairs.

The Two-Term Presidency

Washington rejected a third term as President. In doing so, he established a tradition that was not broken until 1940 and 1944, when Franklin D. Roosevelt won a third and then a fourth term. Unhappiness over Roosevelt's break with tradition led to passage of the 22nd Amendment. The amendment made the custom of a President serving a maximum of two terms into an official part of the Constitution.

CONGRESSIONAL INTERPRETATION, ACTIONS, AND CUSTOM

Creating Structures of Government

The Constitution supplied few details of how the machinery of government would operate. In the nation's early years, Congressional actions helped set up that machinery. For example, the Constitution established only a Supreme Court. Congress, therefore, passed the **Judiciary Act of 1789**, creating the rest of the federal court system.

Congress also created the first five executive departments—Treasury, State, War (Defense), Attorney General (Justice), and Postmaster General. Today, through acts of Congress, there are 14 departments and over 200 independent agencies.

In 1789 Congress began the custom of assigning bills to committees. This developed into today's committee system, in which **standing committees** review all bills before sending them on to the full House or Senate. Congressional committees can also operate as **investigative committees**, gathering information in order to determine the need for new laws or to examine how current laws are working.

Lobbying

Enduring Issues

Avenues of Representation

Custom has also led to the development of **lobbying**, or actions by people representing special-interest groups for the purpose of influencing legislation. Such lobbying is protected by the 1st Amendment's "right to petition," although today it is regulated by federal law.

Today, lobbyists also direct their efforts at the executive and even the judicial branches. To achieve their aims, lobbyists attempt to rally interested citizens and the media to their cause. In addition to lobbying, special-interest groups, often known as **pressure groups**, may use other methods to influence legislation. For example, pressure groups currently fund over 4,000 **Political Action Committees** (PACs) through which they contribute to federal campaigns.

Strict vs. Loose Construction

Hamilton's proposal for a national bank started the first national debate between "strict" and "loose" constructionists. **Strict constructionists** favor a narrow interpretation of the Constitution, holding that government can do only those things the document spells out. **Loose constructionists** favor a freer reading of the Constitution that gives government more room to act.

Does the Constitution give the Congress and the President the power to create a national bank? Despite objections of such strict constructionists as Jefferson and Madison, Congress created such a bank using the implied powers of the elastic clause.

In 1803 Jefferson had the chance to double the size of the nation through the **Louisiana Purchase**. However, supporting the purchase meant adopting a "loose interpretation" of the Constitution. For the good of the nation, Jefferson changed his position and backed the Purchase. In addition to adding new lands, the Louisiana Purchase also gave the United States control of the vital Mississippi River.

MAKING CONNECTIONS

Key Ideas   In acquiring Louisiana, Jefferson sacrificed the principle of strict construction for the national good.

JUDICIAL INTERPRETATION OF THE CONSTITUTION

John Marshall

The nation's fourth Chief Justice, **John Marshall**, served from 1801 to 1835. Through a series of Supreme Court decisions, Marshall strengthened the power of the national government and made the judiciary a branch of government coequal with the legislative and executive branches. For example, Marshall's decision in *McCulloch* v. *Maryland*, 1819, protected the national bank from state control so that federal supremacy and national economic interests were strengthened.

Perhaps most critically, Marshall led the Court in the 1803 decision in *Marbury* v. *Madison*. This decision established the court's right of judicial review, its power to rule on the constitutionality of a law.

Enduring Issues

∞

The Judiciary

Activism vs. Restraint

Judicial review is a major part of the unwritten constitution. However, use of this power has led to an unresolved debate over its exercise. Those favoring **judicial activism** believe the Court should use this power to help make public policy, particularly when Congress has failed to act on pressing social problems. Those favoring **judicial restraint** believe that this power should be used only when there is an obvious violation of the Constitution. They feel that policy-making

Key Ideas   Court decisions have affected the separation of powers in the federal system.

MAKING CONNECTIONS

Enduring Issues

Avenues of Representation

Constitutional Change and Flexibility

should be left to the other two branches. As in the debate over "strict" versus "loose" construction, positions on this issue are affected by political considerations and by the particular law under discussion.

ACTIONS OF POLITICAL PARTIES

Political parties developed through custom and tradition. The debate between Federalists and Anti-Federalists over ratification revealed the existence of differences of opinion on government. These differences—also visible in debates over strict and loose construction and judicial activism and restraint—led to formation of the first two political parties—the **Federalists** and the **Democratic-Republicans**. The chart below summarizes the position of each party.

The First Political Parties

Federalists	Republicans
1. Led by A. Hamilton	1. Led by T. Jefferson
2. Wealthy and well-educated should lead nation	2. People should have political power
3. Strong central government	3. Strong state governments
4. Emphasis on manufacturing, shipping, and trade	4. Emphasis on agriculture
5. Loose interpretation of Constitution	5. Strict interpretation of Constitution
6. Pro-British	6. Pro-French
7. Favored national bank	7. Opposed national bank
8. Favored protective tariff	8. Opposed protective tariff

Key Ideas The peaceful transfer of political power from one party to another is an important feature of our democratic system.

The formation of political parties led to constitutional changes in the method of electing the President. Party politics also gave rise to nominating conventions and the pledging of electoral votes to a candidate.

In the first half of the nineteenth century, politics became more democratic as many more men had the right to vote. The campaign techniques and organization of political parties changed to appeal to this broader electorate.

While major political parties have changed infrequently, the nation has seen many influential "third parties." Such parties have offered criticisms and suggested reforms later adopted by the major parties when in power. You will review some of the actions of these parties later in this book.

GROWING NATIONALISM RAISES CONSTITUTIONAL ISSUES

War of 1812

From 1789 to 1815 events in Europe continued to influence domestic and foreign policies of the United States. American Presidents tried to stay out of European wars while still insisting on the United States' rights as a nation. The right to trade with European nations despite a blockade of the European coast was a major concern because America's economic well-being depended on such trade.

Despite American efforts to avoid conflict, Britain continued to violate American freedom of the seas, angering many Americans. Meanwhile, western "War Hawks" interested in expanding into British Canada and Spanish Florida also urged war. In 1812 Congress declared war on Britain. The war, however, did not have the support of all Americans and it provoked disputes among different sections of the nation. The war ended in a draw in 1814. Yet, the long-term result was to advance a growing sense of nationalism.

The American System

The new national spirit could be seen in a legislative program that Senator **Henry Clay** called the "**American System**." The program had benefits for the North, South, and West and included three key elements:

* A better national transportation system that would aid trade and national defense
* The first protective tariff to encourage manufacturing
* A second national bank

Foreign Policy

The new national self-confidence could also be seen in the diplomatic field. **John Quincy Adams**, Secretary of State for James Monroe, settled the border between the United States and Canada. He also acquired East Florida from Spain and reached agreement with that nation on the southern boundary of the Louisiana Purchase.

Adams was the chief adviser on the **Monroe Doctrine** of 1823. This doctrine became the foundation of United States foreign policy in the Western Hemisphere. The Monroe Doctrine contained the following key points:

* A call for an end to colonization in the Western Hemisphere by European nations
* An insistence on nonintervention by Europe in existing nations in this hemisphere
* A declaration that European interference was "dangerous to our peace and safety"
* A promise of noninterference by the United States in European affairs and European colonies

Key Ideas National self-interest—sometimes mixed with a desire to extend democratic ideals to other nations—provides the basis for the foreign policies of most democratic nations.

MAKING CONNECTIONS

In 1823 the United States lacked the military might to enforce this doctrine. However, Great Britain made known its willingness to support the United States if this policy were challenged. By the end of the nineteenth century, the United States was actively enforcing the policy on its own.

Regents Tip   Read questions carefully when answering data-base questions. Study the accompanying map, then answer the following question.
When did the United States acquire its first land bordering the Pacific Ocean?

Manifest Destiny

From 1803 to 1853, the United States expanded to its present continental boundaries. The greatest expansion came in the 1840s. This was the era of "**manifest destiny**." Manifest destiny was the name given to the belief that the United States had a divine mission to expand and to spread the ideals of freedom and democracy. What Americans saw as "manifest destiny" was viewed quite differently by the Native American and Mexican peoples affected by such expansion. Expansion increased national pride, but, by raising serious questions about slavery, contributed to growing sectional tensions.

Growth of the United States to 1853

TESTING THE CONSTITUTION: GROWING SECTIONALISM

Feelings of nationalism and sectionalism developed in the United States during the first half of the nineteenth century. These feelings grew stronger each decade, pulling the nation in opposite directions. The tensions led to the **Civil War** (1861–1865) which tested whether the nation and its Constitution would survive. As the three sections of the nation—North, South, and West—grew economically, differences developed among them, particularly between North and South. Before 1840, three major economic issues caused most disagreement.

The Internal Improvements Issue

Debate over the federal role in financing roads and canals continued through several decades of the early 1800s. Most opposition to federal funding came from the Southern states. Southerners protested that such internal improvements were to be paid for, in large part, through the protective tariff, which they also opposed.

The Tariff Issue

The accompanying chart illustrates how a protective tariff works. Southerners saw Northern industries as the chief beneficiaries of such tariffs. Meanwhile, the agricultural South, which manufactured few products, would pay higher prices for imported goods.

John C. Calhoun of South Carolina, a spokesman for states' rights, protested the **Tariff of 1828**. Calhoun argued that a state had the right to **nullify**, or declare void, any federal law that the state considered unconstitutional. This argument had first been advanced by Madison and Jefferson in the **Virginia and Kentucky Resolutions**. These measures had attacked the 1798 **Alien and Sedition Acts** as dangerous to civil liberties and representative government.

In 1832 a new tariff was passed. Although it was lower than that of 1828, South Carolina and Calhoun still protested. Calhoun resigned the vice presidency and led his state in nullifying the new tariff. President **Andrew Jackson** promptly denounced South Carolina's act as treason.

The crisis was resolved after Congress agreed to a gradual lowering of the tariff and passed a "**Force Bill**" authorizing the use of federal troops in South Carolina to collect the tariff. South Carolina then withdrew its nullification of the tariff. However, South Carolina then nullified the "Force Bill," indicating that the issue was not permanently settled.

The National Bank Issue

The **Second Bank of the United States** also provoked sectional differences. Most opposition to the Bank came from the South and the West. People from these regions wanted **cheap money**—a greater

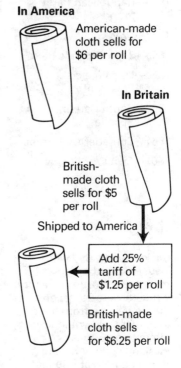

MAKING CONNECTIONS

EVENTS LEADING TO THE CIVIL WAR

1820—Missouri Compromise

1850—California Compromise

1854—Kansas-Nebraska Act

1854—Republican Party founded

1857—*Dred Scott* Case

1859—John Brown's Raid

1860—Lincoln elected President

1860—South Carolina Secedes

1861—Confederacy formed

1861—Civil War begins

Background By "wage slavery" Southerners meant that Northern factory workers were so dependent on the income from their jobs that they would accept almost any wages or working conditions and thus had no real freedom.

Enduring Issues

∞

Equality

supply of money in circulation. They also resented the control the national Bank had over state banking.

In 1832 Jackson used the power of the presidency and vetoed a bill to recharter the Bank. He then withdrew federal money from it, effectively killing the Bank. To Jackson and many of his followers, the Bank symbolized privilege and the power of special northern interests.

DEEPER DIFFERENCES TROUBLE THE NATION

The economic issues cited above were symptoms of much deeper economic, social, and political differences that increasingly divided the nation.

Economic Differences

In the 1800s, the North became a region with manufacturing, commercial, and urban centers. It developed a railroad system connecting it to western farmlands and markets. Its population grew rapidly, fed in part by an influx of immigrants who could find jobs in manufacturing.

In contrast, the South remained agricultural, with a plantation system dependent on slave labor. Its population grew more slowly because the region offered fewer jobs to immigrants. Its agricultural base made the South more economically dependent on the North both as a market for its crops and as a source of needed manufactured goods. Southern resentment toward the North grew.

Social Differences

Slavery lay at the root of the differences between ways of life in the North and the South. It influenced all aspects of Southern life. Southerners who at first called slavery a "necessary evil" later defended it as a "positive good." They attacked the Northern industrial economy for creating a system of "wage slavery" for factory workers.

While the intellectual energies of the South went into a defense of slavery, Northern ideas produced a burst of reform. Reformers called for free public education, the improvement of conditions for the mentally ill and the retarded, the prohibition of alcohol—or at least temperance in its use—rights for women, and **abolition**, or the ending of slavery. Women played a major role in all of these reforms.

Although such reforms aimed at improving society as a whole, they added to tensions within the nation. For example, because abolitionists attacked slavery as evil and immoral, their position offered no hope of compromise with the South.

Political Differences

Both the North and the South came to believe that the other region threatened its economic interests, civil liberties, and political rights. The South, for example, opposed protective tariffs and federal funding of internal improvements. If Congress legislated in these areas, what then was to prevent legislation against slavery? The **states' rights** philosophy was seen as one way of defending slavery against the federal government.

The North, on the other hand, feared the political power of the South. Until 1850 and the admission of California, there were an equal number of slave and free states in the Union. The South thus maintained a balance of power in the Senate. In the executive branch, meanwhile, slaveholders served as President for all but 22 years of the period between 1789 and 1861.

MAKING CONNECTIONS

Testing the Constitution: From Crisis to War

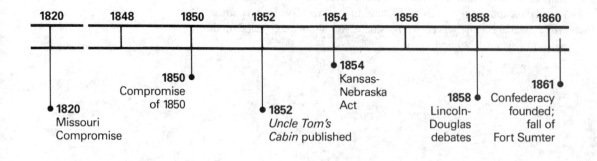

1820	1848	1850	1852	1854	1856	1858	1860

1854
Kansas-
Nebraska
Act

1850
Compromise
of 1850

1861
Confederacy
founded;
fall of
Fort Sumter

1820
Missouri
Compromise

1852
*Uncle Tom's
Cabin* published

1858
Lincoln-
Douglas
debates

MAKING CONNECTIONS

ANTI-SLAVERY
REFORM ⟷ TERRITORIAL
MOVEMENT EXPANSION

Enduring Issues

National Power— Limits and
Potential

SLAVERY AND EXPANSION

Differences between the North and the South over expansionism and abolition finally threatened the existence of the nation. The **Mexican War** of 1846 and the lands gained by it—the **Mexican Cession**—started a series of crises. The debate that followed on how slavery should be treated in those lands centered on constitutional issues.

In the Three-Fifths Compromise, the provision that Congress could not end the import of slaves before 1808, and in the fugitive slave clause, the Constitution had recognized and protected slavery. Such compromises had been seen as necessary to gain Southern agreement to the document. They were only removed when the Civil War led to the end of slavery itself.

Southern Views

Because of these earlier constitutional compromises, Southerners insisted that slavery be permitted in the new territories. Constitutional equality, they said, applied only to whites. Slavery in the territories, they claimed, was legal for the following reasons:

1. Congress did not have the authority to prevent the extension of slavery into the territories.
2. Congress had a constitutional duty to protect slavery in the South and in the territories.

94

Northern Views

Northerners who opposed slavery had a variety of positions.
1. Some wanted it abolished throughout the nation.
2. Some, for racist or economic reasons or both, did not want to compete with slave labor in the territories.
3. Some agreed with Abraham Lincoln: They condemned slavery as a "moral, social, and political evil" and would act to stop its spread to new territories, but felt that the Constitution protected slavery where it already existed.

These Northerners who sought to stop the spread of slavery used several arguments:
1. The Constitution gave Congress jurisdiction, or power, over the territories.
2. **Precedent**, or previous acts, justified congressional action. Precedents included
   • the **Northwest Ordinance**, by which the Confederation Congress had banned slavery in the territory north of the Ohio River.
   • the **Missouri Compromise** of 1820, which had banned slavery in that part of the Louisiana Purchase north of 36° 30′ latitude.

The Compromise of 1850

MAKING CONNECTIONS

The issue of slavery in the new territories was settled for a brief time by the **Compromise of 1850**, which included three key provisions:
1. California came into the Union as a free state.
2. The **Fugitive Slave Act** required that escaped slaves be returned to their owners.
3. **Popular sovereignty**, or a vote of the people living in the territory, would determine whether a territory in the Mexican Cession was to be slave or free.

Key Ideas Compromise postponed a clash between different sectional economic and social systems.

The Compromise of 1850 pleased almost no one. Northerners ignored the Fugitive Slave Act and often engaged in acts of civil disobedience to protest it. Popular sovereignty, meanwhile, left unanswered the question of when the vote to make a territory slave or free would be held. Would it be at the time the territory was settled or when it applied to become a state? This uncertainty set up the likelihood of clashes between pro- and anti-slavery advocates.

The Kansas-Nebraska Act

The issue of popular sovereignty lay behind a crisis in 1854. The Missouri Compromise had prohibited slavery in the lands that made up Kansas and Nebraska. Yet the **Kansas-Nebraska Act** of 1854 overturned the compromise by proposing that the question of slavery in those territories be decided by popular sovereignty. Violence followed when pro- and anti-slavery people rushed into Kansas to vote on the issue. In the fighting, over 200 died.

MAKING CONNECTIONS

First Party System
Democratic-
Republicans ⟷ Federalists

Second Party System
Democrats ⟷ Whigs

Third Party System
Democrats ⟷ Republicans

Enduring Issues

Equality

Reaction to the Kansas-Nebraska Act led to changes in the political party system. One major party, the **Whigs**, split into Northern and Southern wings and soon died out. The **Democrats** were seriously weakened in the North. A new party, the **Republicans**, was founded to oppose the spread of slavery. It was a sectional rather than a national party and proclaimed a platform of "Free Soil, Free Labor, Free Men."

The Dred Scott Case

In 1857 the Supreme Court gave its ruling on the question of slavery in the territories. In *Dred Scott* v. *Sanford*, Chief Justice **Roger Taney** made the following points:

1. No blacks, slave or free, were citizens. Blacks, therefore, were not entitled to constitutional protection.
2. The Missouri Compromise was unconstitutional because Congress could not deprive people of their right to property—slaves—by banning slavery in any territory.

Constitutional guarantees of rights would not be extended to black Americans until ratification of the 13th and 14th Amendments in 1865 and 1868.

Slavery in the Territories

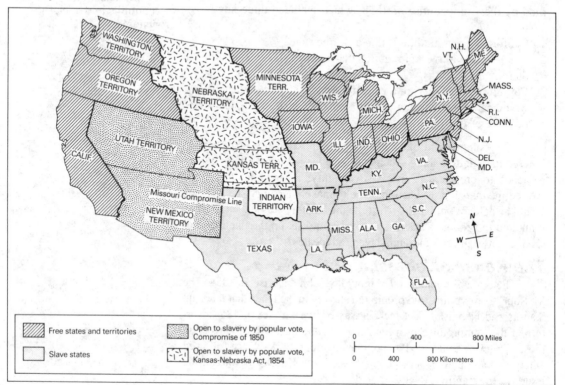

Free states and territories	Open to slavery by popular vote, Compromise of 1850
Slave states	Open to slavery by popular vote, Kansas-Nebraska Act, 1854

LINCOLN AND THE CIVIL WAR

The Dred Scott decision, the troubles in "Bleeding Kansas," and John Brown's raid raised tensions between the North and the South and made compromise more difficult.

Secession

The extent of the divisions in the nation became apparent in the election of 1860. Four parties fielded candidates in this election. The accompanying chart and graphs indicate that these candidates appealed to different sections. Lincoln, the first Republican to be elected President, received only 39 percent of the popular vote.

The election of a Northerner who opposed the extension of slavery drove some Southerners to action. Between the election and Lincoln's inauguration in March 1861, seven states **seceded**, or left the Union. Lame-duck President **James Buchanan** took no action to stop them. He stated that neither he nor Congress had the power to preserve the Union because it "rests upon public opinion and can never be cemented by the blood of its citizens shed in war."

Lincoln disagreed and denied that states could secede. In his **First Inaugural Address**, he stated that "in view of the Constitution and the law, the Union is unbroken."

Lincoln's policy was to oppose secession but not to take any military action against it until the South started the fighting. When the South fired on and seized **Fort Sumter** in Charleston harbor in South Carolina, Lincoln issued a call for troops to put down the rebellion, but four more Southern states seceded.

Lincoln's Aims and Actions

From the beginning of the secession crisis, Lincoln made it his goal to preserve the Union. He took bold executive action to achieve this aim.

- He ordered the arrest of Southern sympathizers in Maryland and Delaware to prevent secession of those states. Failure to act might have meant the encircling of the capital by Confederate states.

- He suspended the writ of **habeas corpus** in areas not in rebellion. He later won congressional approval for this step.

- He declared martial law, which led to the arrests of thousands for suspected disloyalty.

- He called out state militias, increased the size of the navy, ordered a naval blockade of the South, and approved funds for military expenses while Congress was not in session. Congress later gave its approval of these actions.

MAKING CONNECTIONS

Regents Tip Some questions may ask you to draw information from both a chart and a graph. Who was the Northern Democratic candidate in the election of 1860?

What percentage of the electoral vote did he receive?

Election of 1860

Candidate	Popular vote	Electoral vote
Lincoln	1,865,593	180
Douglas	1,382,713	12
Breckinridge	848,356	72
Bell	592,906	39

Party

	Republican
	Northern Democrat
	Southern Democrat
	Constitutional Union

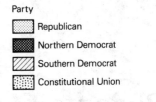

Percent popular vote

Percent electoral vote

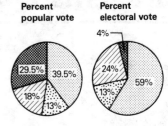

Background *Habeas corpus* is Latin for "you should have the body." A writ of *habeas corpus* requires an official holding a prisoner to explain to a court why that prisoner should not be released.

MAKING CONNECTIONS

Enduring Issues

Presidential Power

Enduring Issues

The Rights of Ethnic and
Racial Groups

Constitutional Questions

These and other actions by Lincoln broadened the power of the executive. They also raised troubling questions: Were such actions constitutional? Did they fall within the scope of the President's war powers, or were they dictatorial? Did the fact that some Northerners sympathized with the rebelling South justify the limiting of their civil rights? Did the intent of the President's actions affect their constitutionality? Did Lincoln set precedents for expanded executive action that later Presidents might use in more questionable circumstances?

Freeing the Slaves

Lincoln moved slowly on the issue of freeing the slaves, in part because his main objective was to preserve the Union. In 1862, however, Lincoln issued the **Emancipation Proclamation** to take effect on January 1, 1863. The proclamation freed slaves forever in those areas still in rebellion against the Union.

The Proclamation drew both criticism and praise. Some attacked it for freeing slaves only where the government could not enforce the decree while permitting slavery where it could act. On the other hand, the Proclamation lessened the chances of European aid to the South. Most of all, it added a new egalitarian and humanitarian objective to the war.

The Civil War ended in 1865 with the South devastated. The war left a legacy of bitterness and a host of new problems. It also left a total of 625,000 dead on both sides including Lincoln himself, assassinated within days of the war's end.

Regents Questions for Practice _____

Review the Test-Taking Strategies section of this book. Then answer the following questions, drawn from actual Regents examinations. Circle the *number* of the word or expression that best completes the statement or answers the question. Write your answers to essay questions on a separate piece of paper. Hints on good ways to approach these questions are provided in the margins.

Test Hint The first two questions test the same idea. What is that idea?

1. The Supreme Court under Chief Justice John Marshall influenced United States history in that the Court
   1 stimulated the States rights movement by supporting the idea that states could reject acts of Congress
   2 helped to create a sense of national unity by strengthening the Federal Government
   3 weakened the judiciary by refusing to deal with controversial issues
   4 became heavily involved in foreign affairs

2. Which is the most valid generalization about the United States Supreme Court under Chief Justice John Marshall?
1 It reduced the delegated powers of Congress.
2 It made decisions that strengthened the power of the National Government.
3 It usually supported the principle of States rights.
4 It followed a doctrine of strict interpretation of the Constitution.

3. A ''strict constructionist'' of the United States Constitution would favor which action?
1 the institution of programs for social reform
2 annexation of territory by the United States
3 bypassing constitutional restraints
4 limiting the power of the Federal Government

4. The most serious threat to democracy resulting from heavy election campaign costs is that, once elected, candidates frequently
1 owe money to friends and relatives
2 plan to use public funds to pay their debts
3 owe loyalty to a few major contributors
4 have little of their own savings left

5. In recent years, which measure has most often been proposed to reduce the influence of special interest groups on candidates running for political office?
1 increasing the length of political campaigns
2 increasing public funding of political campaigns
3 decreasing the number of elective offices
4 decreasing voter registration drives

6. During the period 1820–1860, the major concerns in the United States dealt with issues related to
1 determining the future of slavery
2 imposing immigration quotas
3 developing big business
4 acquiring an overseas empire

7. Which Presidential activity has been created by practice rather than by Constitution?
1 acting as Commander in Chief of the Armed Forces
2 acting as the leader of his political party
3 appointing ambassadors and consuls
4 acting upon bills passed by Congress

8. Which is a valid statement about the term of office of members of the cabinet of the President of the United States?
1 Their term of office is fixed by Congress.
2 They serve at the discretion of the President.
3 They have tenure for life.
4 Their term of office is limited by the Federal Constitution.

MAKING CONNECTIONS

Test Hint Regents questions often test your knowledge of important terms. Such terms appear in **bold** type throughout the text. What is a "strict constructionist"?

Test Hint Questions 4 and 5 are different ways of looking at cause and effect.

Test Hint Be aware of the time periods specified in questions. The answer to a question like this would be different if a different time period were given.

9. ''The United States Supreme Court has consistently sought to increase the power of the central government at the expense of the states.''

A historian attempting to support this idea would be most likely to cite Supreme Court decisions that have

1 expanded states rights
2 upheld laissez-faire economic principles
3 emphasized a loose interpretation of the Constitution
4 declared unconstitutional the practices of Federal regulatory agencies

10. Which issues were controversial in national politics during the period 1800–50?

1 racial prejudice, territorial expansion, immigration policy
2 tariff policy, nullification, rights of neutrals
3 regulation of railroads, overseas acquisitions, federal income tax policy
4 states' rights policy, control of the Northwest Territory, recognition of United States independence by France

11. Which best explains why candidates for President of the United States are nominated during national nominating conventions?

1 It is mandated by the Federal Constitution.
2 It is mandated by State Constitutions.
3 It is part of the United States political tradition.
4 It was instituted by an act of Congress.

12. In the United States, the Democratic and Republican parties have survived as the two major political parties mainly because each has been able to

1 eliminate differences among its members
2 gain the support of organized labor
3 represent a cross section of interest groups
4 achieve consistently the goals of its party platform

13. In the United States, third-party movements occur most often when

1 there is clear danger of foreign attack
2 the President is inconsistent in foreign policy
3 major political parties ignore vital public issues
4 interest in overseas trade and possessions intensifies

14. The best evidence that third or minor political parties have had a significant influence on United Stated history is that frequently

1 minor political parties have succeeded in dominating most state governments even though they could not control the Federal Government
2 the membership of Congress has been so divided among several political parties that Congress could take no effective action
3 many of the proposals of minor parties have been passed into law
4 a minor party has replaced one of the two major parties

15. The main purpose for proclaiming the Monroe Doctrine was to

1 exclude Portugal from Latin America
2 demand the protection of the Western Hemisphere by the British Navy
3 create a multilateral alliance of Latin American nations
4 safeguard the interests of the United States

16. During the 19th century, the United States followed a policy of manifest destiny. What effect did this have on United States relations with other nations?

1 Relations were strained because the policy led to a series of confrontations.
2 Relations were strained because the policy violated the Monroe Doctrine.
3 Relations were improved because the policy extended the benefits of democracy and advanced technology.
4 Relations were improved because the policy gave Latin Americans protection from invasion.

17. In the United States, the widespread disregard of the fugitive slave laws and of the Prohibition laws most clearly indicated that
    1 strongly held values are difficult to regulate
    2 the Federal Government is generally unable to enforce its own laws
    3 little respect is given to the legal system
    4 the judicial system is too lenient in its treatment of offenders

18. In the United States, the significant change represented by the Supreme Court's decisions concerning Dred Scott (1857) and *Brown* v. *Board of Education* (1954) best illustrates the
    1 ability of government to revise laws under the threat of civil war
    2 desire of all minority groups to be recognized
    3 disappearance of prejudice and discrimination
    4 continuing struggle of blacks to achieve equality

19. The executive branch of the United States Government has traditionally gained power during periods when
    1 the Presidency had been occupied by a high-ranking military officer
    2 the Republican Party was in the majority in Congress and the President was a Democrat
    3 there has been a serious domestic or international problem facing the United States
    4 the Supreme Court and Congress have been in conflict over constitutional issues

20. "Restriction of free thought and free speech is the most dangerous of all subversions. It is the one un-American act that could easily defeat us."
    In the the United States, the danger identified in this statement was the greatest during the

    1 Age of Jackson
    2 Civil War
    3 Spanish-American War
    4 New Deal Era in the 1930's

Base your answer to question 21 on the cartoon below and on your knowledge of social studies.

"King Andrew the First"

Library of Congress

21. The cartoonist is most clearly accusing President Jackson of which behavior?
    1 involving the United States in European wars
    2 exceeding the constitutional limits of his authority
    3 using government funds to support an extravagant lifestyle
    4 violating the Federal Constitution by granting titles of nobility

22. At the beginning of the Civil War, President Abraham Lincoln maintained that the war was being fought to
1 uphold national honor
2 prevent foreign involvement
3 free all slaves
4 preserve the Union

23. "Must a government of necessity be too strong for the liberties of its people, or too weak to maintain its own existence?"
—President Abraham Lincoln
In this quotation, President Lincoln was referring to the governmental dilemma of how to
1 provide for a military sufficient to defend the nation
2 develop adequate procedures for combating crime
3 balance the rights of the individual with the need for social control
4 maintain law and order in the South after the Civil War

Essay Questions

Following are essay questions about the unit you have been reviewing. Before answering each, apply the lesson you learned in the Test-Taking Strategies section by blocking each essay. The first block has been organized for you to help you get started with the prewriting that is so necessary in preparing a good Regents essay answer.

1. At various periods in United States history one of the three branches of the Federal Government has exercised strong leadership

BRANCHES/PERIODS
Executive/1933–1945
Judicial/1800–1830
Legislative/1865–1877

a Choose two of the branches listed above and show how each branch exercised strong leadership during the time period indicated. Use specific historical examples to support your answer. [5, 5]
b Some historians believe that since 1960 Presidential power has grown at the expense of the other two branches. Discuss the extent to which this statement is valid. Refer to two specific examples since 1960 to support your position. [5]

PART A

Strong leadership	Examples (minimum 2)
Executive 1933–1945 [5]	1 FDR proposed legislation to help end the depression—AAA, CCC, FDIC, Social Security, etc. 2 FDR met with other Allied leaders to plan the strategy during World War II.
     [5]	1 2

PART B

Growth of Presidential power since 1960	Examples
	1 Kennedy, Johnson, and Nixon conducted war in Vietnam without Congress declaring war.
   [5]	2

2. The United States Constitution has endured for 200 years in part because of its ability to adapt to changing times.

a One way in which the Constitution can be changed is through the use of the formal amending process. Below is an excerpt from the Constitution as originally written.

> SECTION 3. The Senate of the United States shall be composed of two Senators from each state, chosen by the Legislature thereof, for Six Years, and each Senator shall have one Vote.

Discuss how this provision has been changed by amendment. Your discussion must include a clear description of the change and reasons for the change.   [5]

b The Constitution has also been adapted to meet changing conditions through the use of the following methods:
- Judicial review
- Custom and usage
- Loose interpretation

Choose two of these methods. Discuss one way each method has been used to adapt the United States Constitution to meet changing conditions. In your response, describe the specific condition that required constitutional change and describe the specific change that resulted.   [5, 5]

3. The Constitution of the United States provides for a system of checks and balances among three equal branches of government—legislative, executive, and judicial. However, at different times in history, one branch has been viewed as being more powerful than the other two.

a Select two time periods for the list below and, for each one selected, explain why one specific branch of government was viewed as being more powerful at any time during that period. Use specific examples to support your answer.

TIME PERIODS
Jacksonian Era (1828–1840)
Civil War (1860–1865)
Reconstruction (1865–1876)
Post-World War I (1920–1929)
New Deal (1933–1939)
Nixon Era (1968–1974)   [5, 5]

b Choose one of the proposals listed below and discuss two effects that proposal might have on the system of checks and balances in the United States Government if that proposal were implemented.

PROPOSALS
- One Presidential term of 6 years
- Congressional override of Supreme Court decisions
- One-House legislature   [5]

4. The United States Constitution establishes a federal system of government. The nature of the system has been debated and refined throughout United States history.

a Explain the principle of federalism by using two examples of how the principle operates in the United States. [5]

b Choose two of the periods below. For each one chosen, discuss a specific disagreement that occurred concerning the principle of federalism.

PERIODS

- The Supreme Court under John Marshall (1801–1835)
- Reconstruction (1865–1876)
- Industrialization of the United States between 1876 and 1914
- The New Deal of President Franklin D. Roosevelt (1933–1941)
- The struggle for civil and political rights (1950–1970)
- The Administration of President Reagan (1981–present)

[5, 5]

5. United States Presidents have faced a number of challenges. In meeting those challenges, Presidents have often influenced the power of the Presidency. In the list below, challenges are paired with Presidents who dealt with them.

CHALLENGES/PRESIDENTS

- Economic problems facing the new nation/George Washington
- Disputes over national expansion/Thomas Jefferson
- Secession of the Southern States/Abraham Lincoln
- Problems of the industrialization of the United States/ Theodore Roosevelt
- Effects of the Great Depression/Franklin D. Roosevelt
- Communist expansion/Harry Truman
- Growth of international terrorism/Ronald Reagan

Select three pairs from the list above and for each one chosen:
- Describe the challenge faced by the President
- Discuss the President's response to the challenge
- Show how the President's response influenced the power of the Presidency [5, 5, 5]

UNIT 2

Industrialization of the United States

MAKING CONNECTIONS

The Civil War had torn the United States apart. With Union victory came the task of putting the nation back together. Yet the rebuilt nation would be a very different one. This unit reviews those changes that the Civil War brought to the United States. It also highlights how the shift from an agrarian to an industrial economy changed the United States and its people.

In the side columns of this Unit, you will see highlighted six of the Thirteen Enduring Constitutional Issues as described in Unit 1. Be sure you can explain how the main text in this Unit illustrates aspects of these Enduring Issues.

Next, review the social studies concepts listed on the chart, "The Fifteen Basic Concepts." From time to time you will find in the side column the heading Key Social Studies Concepts and beneath it several writing lines. On these lines list the social studies concepts that relate to the content in this main text.

Finally, keep in mind that you will need to know the answers to the following questions about this unit to pass the Regents examination:

Section 1: What social, political, and economic changes occurred as the nation sought to rebuild after the Civil War?

Section 2: What factors in the United States led to the shift from an agrarian to an industrial society and what were the results of this shift?

Section 3: How did patterns of immigration to the United States change in the nineteenth and early twentieth centuries and what did those changes mean for American society?

SECTION 1 — The Reconstructed Nation

The period immediately following the Civil War is known as **Reconstruction**. During these years from 1865 to 1877, the federal government focused on finding a way to bring the defeated Southern states back into the Union.

MAKING CONNECTIONS

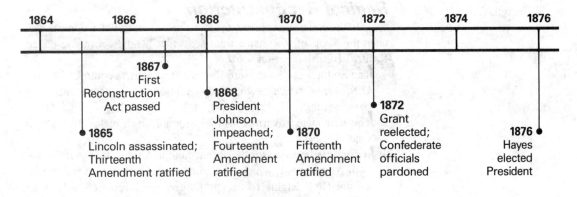

1864 — 1866 — 1868 — 1870 — 1872 — 1874 — 1876

1867 First Reconstruction Act passed

1865 Lincoln assassinated; Thirteenth Amendment ratified

1868 President Johnson impeached; Fourteenth Amendment ratified

1870 Fifteenth Amendment ratified

1872 Grant reelected; Confederate officials pardoned

1876 Hayes elected President

PLANS OF RECONSTRUCTION

Several different plans for Reconstruction emerged during and after the war. Much debate about differing plans centered on who would control Reconstruction, the President or Congress.

Lincoln's Plan

President Lincoln had begun to plan for the restoration of the South long before the end of the war. His plan of Reconstruction was based on the idea that the Southern states had never left the Union. It featured the following elements:

1. Pardons to Southerners who swore oaths of loyalty to the United States
2. Recognition of new Southern state governments when 10 percent of those who had voted in the 1860 election took these oaths and when the states adopted new constitutions abolishing slavery

Lincoln was open to suggestions from Congress for changes in his plan, but his assassination in April 1865 meant he would never carry out his program.

Enduring Issues

Federalism

MAKING CONNECTIONS

Enduring Issues

Separation of Powers

Continuing Issues Though Johnson was not found guilty, he was the only President actually impeached. In 1974 Richard Nixon resigned the presidency rather than face possible impeachment by Congress.

Key Social Studies Concepts:

Citizenship

Key Ideas Citizenship rights for Southern whites and former slaves were key controversies during Reconstruction.

Johnson's Plan

Vice President **Andrew Johnson** became head of the government after Lincoln's death. He intended to follow the broad outlines of Lincoln's plan. Johnson recognized four Southern state governments and prepared to readmit the others.

Radical Republicans, however, controlled Congress. They wanted harsher terms for Reconstruction. Johnson's failure to consider Congressional views on Reconstruction and his efforts to block Radical plans finally led Republicans in Congress to attempt impeachment. In 1868 the House charged him with ''high crimes and misdemeanors'' for violating the **Tenure of Office Act**. The Senate came within one vote of removing Johnson from office. Johnson's political power, however, was gone.

Radical Reconstruction

In the end of this period, the Republican-controlled Congress dictated the terms of Reconstruction. The chief features of this so-called **Radical Reconstruction** were:

1. The South was divided into five military districts controlled by the U.S. Army, while new state constitutions and governments were being set up.
2. The new state governments had to grant black males the right to vote.
3. Before readmission to the Union, Southern states had to ratify the 14th Amendment, which, in addition to addressing several fundamental Civil Rights issues, prohibited many former Confederate officers and government officials from voting.

State Governments During Reconstruction

Immediately after the Civil War ended, white Southerners who had served in leadership positions before and during the Civil War tried to reassert their control of state and local governments. They were especially concerned with limiting the freedom and movement of the former slaves.

When the Radical plan of Reconstruction took effect, most of the former Confederate leaders—largely Democrats—were barred from holding office and voting. Republicans headed the new state governments that emerged. Blacks, who had recently won the right to vote, overwhelmingly supported these Republican governments. In many cases, blacks themselves won election to office.

Many white southerners deeply resented these Reconstruction governments and the role of blacks in them. They branded the few white Southerners active in those governments as **scalawags** and the Republican Northerners who came South to take part in Reconstruction as **carpetbaggers**. White Southerners used terror and violence in efforts to keep blacks from taking part in government.

New Constitutional Amendments

During the Reconstruction period, the states ratified three amendments to the Constitution. The chief features of these amendments were:

- **13th Amendment** (1865): This amendment abolished slavery in the United States.
- **14th Amendment** (1868): This amendment (1) said all native-born or naturalized people, including blacks, were citizens; (2) forbade the states to make laws that "abridge the privileges . . . of citizens. . . ."; that "deprive any person of life, liberty, or property, without due process of law"; and that "deny to any person . . . the equal protection of the laws"; (3) limited the rights of former Confederate officers and government officials; and (4) promised to pay debts run up by the federal government during the Civil War but declared Confederate debts to be void.
- **15th Amendment** (1870): This amendment declared that states could not keep citizens from voting because of "race, color, or previous condition of servitude" (slavery).

President Grant

The first presidential election after the end of the Civil War took place in 1868. Union war hero General **Ulysses S. Grant** ran as a Republican and won. Grant's strengths, however, were those of a military leader, not those of a politician or government leader. Scandals and corruption damaged Grant's administration, as business owners in the booming post-war economy offered bribes to politicians who would do favors for them.

Among the most notorious scandals were:

- **The Credit Mobilier Scandal**: Railroad officials swindled stockholders, then bribed members of Congress to block any investigation.
- **The "Salary Grab"**: Congress voted itself a 50 percent pay raise and added two years of "back pay." Public outcry forced repeal of this act.
- **The "Whiskey Ring"**: Whiskey distillers paid graft to federal tax collectors rather than pay taxes on their liquor.

Political corruption was also common at state and local levels. Perhaps the most notorious figure was **William "Boss" Tweed**, who ran the Tammany Hall political machine in New York City in the 1860s and 1870s. The artist **Thomas Nast** attacked Tweed's behavior in a series of stinging cartoons that helped turn public opinion against Tweed.

MAKING CONNECTIONS

Key Ideas   The 14th Amendment caused the transfer of significant legislative power over civil rights from the states to the federal government. Due process of law is important.

Enduring Issues

Avenues of Representation

Key Social Studies Concepts:

Political System

Regents' Tip   Some Regents examination questions are based on cartoons. Study this cartoon of "Boss" Tweed by Thomas Nast. What symbolism does Nast use in the cartoon?
What opinion do you think Nast has of Tweed? Why?

October 21, 1871

THE END OF RECONSTRUCTION

Corruption in the Grant Administration weakened the political strength of the Republican party. In addition, by the early 1870s all but a handful of former Confederates could vote again. Most of these white Southern males now voted Democratic in reaction against Radical Republican Reconstruction, giving rise to the term "**Solid South**." For most of the next century, the Democratic party would dominate voting in the South.

The Election of 1876

The emergence of the Solid South gave the Democrats greater power in politics at the national level. In 1876 Democrats nominated **Samuel Tilden**, the governor of New York, to run for President against Republican **Rutherford B. Hayes**, the governor of Ohio.

Key Social Studies Concepts:

Political Systems

Tilden clearly won the popular vote, but the electoral vote was disputed. Four states sent in disputed election returns. Which votes were counted would determine the outcome of the election.

A special electoral commission was named to count the votes. The Republican majority on the commission gave all the disputed electoral votes to Hayes, thus guaranteeing his victory.

Democrats agreed to go along with the commission's decision in return for promises by Hayes to:

Continuing Issues Events surrounding the election of 1876 point out reasons people have called for reform of the electoral college system. Many people believe that a modern election with results like those of 1876, where the winner of the popular vote lost the electoral vote, would lead to such reform.

1. Withdraw federal troops from the South, thus ending Reconstruction
2. Name a Southerner to his Cabinet
3. Support federal spending on internal improvements in the South

White Control in the South

With the end of Reconstruction, white Southerners moved to eliminate any political advances blacks had made during the period. By 1900, the civil rights of Southern blacks had been sharply limited. White Southerners used various methods to curb black rights.

BLACK CODES These measures, passed in most Southern states immediately after the Civil War, were based on old slave codes and aimed at keeping blacks in conditions close to slavery. The **Black Codes** produced an angry reaction in the North that helped passage of the Radical Reconstruction program. Reconstruction governments in the South overturned these codes.

SECRET SOCIETIES White southerners originally formed groups like the **Ku Klux Klan** to try to frighten blacks and their supporters out of taking part in Reconstruction governments. The lawlessness and brutality these groups demonstrated led the federal government to use the Army against the societies. With the end of Reconstruction and the growth of white political power, the Klan and other similar groups played a less active role in the South. Such organizations, however, remain active to this day.

POLL TAXES Southern states imposed a tax on every voter. Many blacks were too poor to pay **poll taxes** and thus could not vote.

LITERACY TESTS Some states required people to demonstrate that they could read and write before they voted. Often **literacy tests** involved interpreting a difficult part of the Constitution. Since few blacks had received any schooling, few could pass these tests.

GRANDFATHER CLAUSES Poll taxes and literacy tests might have also kept poor and uneducated whites from voting. To prevent this, southern states added **grandfather clauses** to their constitutions. These clauses allowed the son or grandson of a man eligible to vote in 1867 to vote himself even if he could neither pay the tax nor pass the test. Since few blacks could vote in 1867, the clause benefited whites almost exclusively.

JIM CROW LAWS Southern states also passed laws establishing social **segregation**, or the separation of people on the basis of race. Such **Jim Crow laws** forbade blacks from riding in the same railroad cars as whites or drinking from the same water fountains.

The Supreme Court and Segregation

The legality of Jim Crow laws was the chief issue in a case that reached the Supreme Court in 1896. In the landmark case of *Plessy* v. *Ferguson*, the Court ruled segregation to be legal as long as blacks had access to "equal but separate" facilities.

The Court's ruling in this case set a precedent that justified segregation in all public facilities—schools, hospitals, passenger terminals, and more—until the 1950s. It was not until the landmark case of *Brown* v. *Board of Education of Topeka, Kansas*, 1954, that the Supreme Court reversed the finding in *Plessy* v. *Ferguson*. The decision stated that facilities separated solely on the basis of race were by their nature unequal.

MAKING CONNECTIONS

Key Ideas Despite constitutional amendments, attainment of equal opportunity for American blacks was difficult in the late nineteenth century.

Enduring Issues

The Judiciary

Regents Questions for Practice _____

Review the **Test-Taking Strategies** section of this book. Then answer the following questions, drawn from actual Regents examinations. Circle the *number* of the word or expression that best completes the statement or answers the question. Write your answers to essay questions on a separate piece of paper. Hints on good ways to approach these questions are provided in the margins.

1. The fourteenth amendment is important because, in addition to awarding citizenship to former slaves, it
   1 guarantees women the right to vote
   2 abolishes the poll tax
   3 guarantees equal protection under the law
   4 provides protection against illegal search and seizure

Test Hint Remember that it is important to know constitutional amendments by number.

MAKING CONNECTIONS

Test Hint   Remember that the next three multiple-choice questions are based on the statements by these speakers. Underline the key ideas in each statement to help you contrast the different points of view.

This discussion of constitutional amendments took place just after the Civil War. Base your answers to questions 2 through 4 on this discussion and on your knowledge of social studies.

Speaker A: Some slaves were freed after the Emancipation Proclamation; others were freed by an amendment to the Constitution. We all know that free men may vote, and we do not need further amendments to tell us that.

Speaker B: If we pass these amendments, we still do not ensure the rights of the freed people. In states where white people traditionally have run the government, freed people will find it difficult to exercise their rights.

Speaker C: As a member of the Republican Party, I want to see these amendments adopted to ensure the voting strength of our party in the South.

Speaker D: These amendments must be passed. The passage of these amendments will guarantee equal rights with no further governmental action required.

2. The constitutional amendments under discussion are the
   1 first and second
   2 fifth and tenth
   3 fourteenth and fifteenth
   4 twenty-first and twenty-second

3. Speaker C assumed that the Republican Party could count on the votes of the
   1 former slaves
   2 Western farmers
   3 urban factory workers
   4 former Confederate soldiers

4. Which speaker describes most clearly the political situation that actually occurred after Reconstruction?
   (1) A   (3) C
   (2) B   (4) D

5. Which provided the legal basis for segregation in late 19th century United States?
   1 Supreme Court decisions that excluded blacks from voting
   2 adoption of laws by the United States Congress
   3 passage of ''Jim Crow'' laws by state legislatures
   4 laws in northern states that prevented blacks from working in factories

6. The decision of the Supreme Court in the 1896 *Plessy* v. *Ferguson* case is important because it:
   1 upheld the legality of sharecropping
   2 denounced the violence of the Ku Klux Klan
   3 approved separate but equal facilities for black Americans
   4 declared slavery to be illegal

The Rise of American Business, Industry, and Labor—1865–1920

A CHANGING ECONOMIC STRUCTURE

Well before the Civil War broke out, the United States had taken its first steps toward industrialization. Developments in Europe, especially in Great Britain, prompted this change. The use of new technologies in manufacturing—particularly steam engines and machines to spin thread and weave cloth—gave rise to the **Industrial Revolution** in Great Britain during the 1700s.

By the late 1700s and early 1800s, these new technologies reached the United States and this nation's industrialization began. Abundant supplies of iron and coal and the many swiftly flowing rivers for water power in the North, especially in New England, attracted builders of mills and factories to that region. The development of transportation systems in the region—railroads and canals, such as the Erie Canal in New York State—also encouraged the growth of industry.

By the time of the Civil War, the factories of the North had entered a worldwide competition for markets. While agriculture, especially in its westernmost states, continued to be a major part of its economy, the region took on a new identity as a manufacturing area. The South, by contrast, remained primarily an agricultural region dependent chiefly on its cotton crop.

Economic Developments in the North

The Civil War stimulated economic growth in the North. The industrialization that had started before the war accelerated as Northern factories rushed to keep up with the Union's demand for guns, ammunition, uniforms, and other necessary products. Improvements in railroad systems helped speed troop movements. Since so many Northern farm workers entered the army, the farms themselves became more heavily mechanized so that fewer workers could produce more crops. Finally, fighting rarely took place in the North, and so the region was spared the destruction of war.

After the war, the growing Northern factories looked to overseas markets for their goods. Meanwhile, completion of the **transcontinental railroad** opened new markets in the West and brought products of

MAKING CONNECTIONS

Key Ideas In the development of industry, the United States had advantages such as abundant natural resources and excellent transportation potential.

The U.S. and the World: As you learned in your Global Studies course, Germany in the late 1800s was at about the same stage of industrial development, while Japan was just on the threshold of industrialization.

Key Social Studies Concepts:

Technology

MAKING CONNECTIONS

Key Ideas The problems
of the post-Civil War South
were, in many ways, similar
to those of underdeveloped
new nations after World
War II.

western farms and mines east. New waves of immigrants arrived in the
United States. Some sought farms in the West, but many found
employment in the booming industries of the North.

Economic Developments in the South

The Civil War ruined the South's economy. It ended slavery, thus
killing the plantation system on which Southern wealth was based.
During the fighting, plantations had been burned, railroads ripped up,
and the region's few factories destroyed.

After the war, many farmers and planters had to sell off parts of
their land to pay off debts or to start over. These land owners often
found themselves in debt to banks or merchants. Despite hardships,
Southern farmers again began to produce cotton. Tobacco, too,
became an important crop. Some Southern leaders, however, believed
that the South's economy should not rest simply on agriculture. They
wanted a "**New South**," and pushed to rebuild railroads, start textile
and steel mills, drill for oil, and mine coal.

Despite these changes, the South lagged behind the North in economic growth. Agriculture still produced the most jobs, and often poor
whites and blacks had to work as **sharecroppers**, farming a piece of
someone else's land not for wages, but for a share of the crop.

Beginning in the 1880s, blacks began a migration to the North in
search of better jobs. This migration accelerated during and after
World War I.

Key Ideas Advantages of
corporations included
greater efficiency, a
broader base of capital, and
increased legal protection.

BUSINESS DEVELOPMENTS
The Growth of Corporations

Before the Civil War, **sole proprietors**, or single owners, and
partnerships had controlled most American businesses. The mills and
factories that came with industrialization, however, usually required
greater **capital**, or money for investment, than one person or a few
partners could raise. To raise capital for expansion, many businesses
became **corporations**. A corporation is a business in which many
investors own shares, usually called **stocks**. In exchange for their
investment, each stockholder receives a **dividend**, or part of the corporation's profits.

Besides paying dividends, the corporations also limited investor
losses. If a corporation failed, an investor lost only his or her investment and was not responsible for the corporation's debts.

The money raised by corporations speeded the growth of American industry. Among the fastest growing industries were transportation
(railroads, urban transportation, and, later, automobiles), building
materials (steel), energy (coal, oil, and electricity), and communications (telegraph and telephone).

Other Forms of Business Organization

As the nation's economy boomed and industries grew larger in the late 1800s, other new forms of business organizations appeared. Often the aim of such business organizations was to eliminate competition and dominate a particular area of the economy.

MONOPOLY A company or small group of companies that has complete control over a particular field of business is a **monopoly**. One example of a monopoly in the late 1800s was the E. C. Knight Sugar Company.

Having a monopoly in a field would allow a company to raise prices to almost any level it desired. Such abuses led to federal legislation aimed at curbing monopolies. However, some monopolies are permitted today. Public utility companies that provide gas, water, and electricity are examples of private companies that have a monopoly in their field. Government agencies closely monitor the operations of such utilities.

CONGLOMERATE A corporation that owns a group of unrelated companies is a **conglomerate**. Such conglomerates are usually formed by **merger**, the process by which one company acquires legal control over another. Mergers and conglomerates are both legal and common today. The Beatrice Company, for example, is a conglomerate that has acquired many different divisions through mergers.

POOL Sometimes competing companies in one field would enter into agreements to fix prices and divide business. Such an agreement was a **pool**. Railroad companies in the late 1800s formed such pools, which were later outlawed.

TRUST A group of corporations in the same or related fields would sometimes agree to combine under a single board of trustees that controlled the actions of all the member corporations. This was a **trust**. Shareholders in the corporations received dividends from the trust, but lost any say in its operation. The Standard Oil Trust was one example of such a combination. Trusts were later outlawed.

Key Ideas Pools, trusts, and holding companies tended to produce monopolies and thereby threatened business competition.

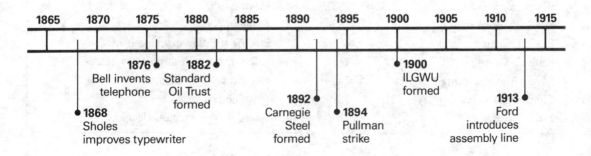

MAKING CONNECTIONS

HOLDING COMPANY   To get around the outlawing of trusts, corporations formed **holding companies**. The holding company bought controlling amounts of stock in different corporations rather than take operations over directly as a trust did. In time, holding companies were outlawed, too.

Innovation

While these new forms of business organization helped young industries to get started and to maximize profits, the ideas of inventors enabled industries to grow technologically and move into new markets. The following chart lists key inventors and inventions of the late 1800s. Study it and think of how these inventions would have affected the lives of Americans at that time. Which inventions are still in use in some form today?

A Time of Invention

Inventor	Date	Invention
Elisha Otis	1852	passenger elevator
Henry Bessemer	1856	perfected bessemer process for making steel
Gordon McKay	1858	machine for sewing shoe soles onto uppers
George Pullman	1864	railroad sleeping car
Thaddeus Lowe	1865	compression ice machine
George Westinghouse	1868	air brake
Thomas Alva Edison	1869	electric voting machine
Andrew S. Hallide	1871	cable streetcar
Stephen Dudley Field	1874	electric streetcar
Melville Bissell	1876	carpet sweeper
Alexander Graham Bell	1876	telephone
Thomas Alva Edison	1878	phonograph
Thomas Alva Edison	1879	first practical incandescent bulb
James Ritty	1879	cash register
Henry W. Seely	1882	electric iron
Lewis E. Waterman	1884	fountain pen
Elihu Thomas	1886	electric welding machine
King C. Gillette	1888	safety razor with throwaway blades
Singer Manufacturing Co.	1889	electric sewing machine
Charles and J. Frank Duryea	1893	gasoline-powered car
John Thurman	1899	motor-driven vacuum cleaner

Entrepreneurs

These new forms of business organization and new ideas from inventors helped American industry grow in the late 1800s and early 1900s. Yet without the business knowledge and daring of certain individuals that growth would have been much slower.

These individuals were **entrepreneurs**, the people who took responsibility for the organization and operation of a new business venture. The entrepreneurs often risked the initial money, or **venture capital**, in such a business. Their willingness and ability to risk large sums often earned the entrepreneurs enormous profits. The business decisions they made also had great impact on the lives of most Americans. Some of the key entrepreneurs of the late 1800s and early 1900s are listed below.

ANDREW CARNEGIE   An immigrant from Scotland, Carnegie started work in a textile factory at age 13. He worked his way up through a variety of jobs and invested his money shrewdly. At age 32, Carnegie entered the steel industry, which was booming due to the growth of railroads. Carnegie sought to control all aspects of steelmaking and built his company into the world's largest steelmaker.

Carnegie sold his company in 1901 for a half billion dollars. He believed the wealthy had a duty to society and gave millions to charities. He also underwrote the founding of free public libraries all across the country.

JOHN D. ROCKEFELLER   Rockefeller entered the oil-refining business during the Civil War. He believed competition was wasteful and used ruthless methods to eliminate competitors. By 1879, his Standard Oil Company controlled over 90 percent of American oil refining. In 1882 he formed the Standard Oil Trust to control more aspects of oil production. Rockefeller also gave away millions to charity.

J. PIERPONT MORGAN   Trained as a banker, Morgan profited by making loans to growing businesses. He took control of many bankrupt railroads in the late 1800s, reorganized them, and made a profit. He also controlled electrical, insurance, and shipping companies. Morgan bought Carnegie Steel in 1901, merged it with other companies, and created the United States Steel Corporation, the world's largest.

HENRY FORD   Ford revolutionized auto making in 1913 by using a **moving assembly line** that permitted the **mass production** of cars, significantly lowering the cost of production. Ford also paid workers higher wages, and set a standard that enabled laborers to afford such purchases. Ford amassed a huge fortune and donated much of it to charity.

Attitudes Toward Business

Industrialization and the changes associated with it caused changes in American attitudes toward business in the late 1800s. Tradi-

MAKING CONNECTIONS

Key Ideas   Venture capital is the life blood in the formation of new enterprises. The expectation of a return on their money is what leads investors to put their funds into such an enterprise.

tional attitudes, of course, still existed. They could be seen in books by the popular writer **Horatio Alger**. Alger's novels describe poor boys who become rich through hard work and luck.

Alger's novels illustrate what is known as the **Puritan work ethic**. This is the belief, brought with the Puritans to colonial New England, that hard work builds character and is its own reward.

The tremendous wealth some entrepreneurs gained during the late 1800s, as well as the cut-throat business methods they used, led some Americans to rethink their ideas on the meaning of business success. New philosophies tried to explain and justify both the accumulation of wealth and the practices used to achieve it.

LAISSEZ FAIRE   Many supporters of late 1800s business growth restated an older philosophy. This was the principle of **laissez faire**, or noninterference. Economist **Adam Smith**, in his 1776 book *The Wealth of Nations*, and many other writers had supported this principle which holds that government should not interfere in the economic workings of a nation. They believed that a **free-enterprise system** in which private individuals make the economic decisions is most efficient.

During the late 1800s, economists restated the importance of *laissez-faire* policies to economic growth. Government interference with business was minimal for much of this period, and entrepreneurs expanded their businesses and earned great wealth.

Background   The chief spokesperson for the ideas of Social Darwinism was Herbert Spencer.

SOCIAL DARWINISM   Laissez-faire capitalists found justification for their beliefs in new scientific theories being developed at that time. Naturalist **Charles Darwin** had developed a theory of evolution that described how animal species live or die by a process of natural selection. Other writers simplified Darwin's theories and created a philosophy called **Social Darwinism**.

Social Darwinists held that life was a struggle for the "survival of the fittest." Unregulated business competition would see weak businesses fail and healthy businesses thrive. Government action regulating business practices would interfere with the process of natural selection. Likewise, any government programs to aid the poor or workers would also violate natural "laws."

"ROBBER BARONS" OR PHILANTHROPISTS?   The philosophies described above and the growing gulf between rich and poor led some Americans to attack laissez-faire policies and those who profited from them. Instead of holding up wealthy entrepreneurs as Horatio Alger heroes, such critics condemned them as "**robber barons**" who gained their riches at the expense of the poor and the working class.

The lavish lifestyles of the wealthy at this time fed such criticism. During this so-called **Gilded Age**, the rich spent freely to show off their wealth, a practice known as **conspicuous consumption**.

Public criticism and a sense of social responsibility led some entrepreneurs to use a part of their wealth to aid society. People like

Carnegie and Rockefeller became **philanthropists**, donating vast sums of money to charities and such public works as schools, museums, libraries, and orchestras.

GOVERNMENT POLICIES TOWARD BUSINESS

The federal government held a laissez-faire attitude toward business for much of this period. Expanding industries and growing foreign trade seemed to justify such an attitude. In addition, many business leaders made financial contributions, legal and illegal, to the politicians who set federal policies.

Growing Government Involvement

Several factors led the government to take the first steps in the late 1800s toward regulating business:

* Intermittent lagging national economy
* Growing criticism of practices that saw big business profit at the expense of the poor and working class
* Increasing grassroots political pressure for change

Though government intervention at this time had limited impact, it did set the course for more federal actions in years to come.

MUNN v. ILLINOIS   During the late 1800s, railroads developed a number of policies that discriminated against farmers and small shippers. These groups pressured some states to pass laws regulating railroad practices. The railroads sued to have such laws overturned.

In 1877 the Supreme Court reached a decision in the landmark case of *Munn* v. *Illinois*. The Court, in upholding an Illinois law controlling railroad charges, said that the Constitution recognized a state's right to a "police power" that permitted regulation of private property "affected with a public interest." This set a major precedent for future court decisions and laws.

INTERSTATE COMMERCE COMMISSION   In 1887 public pressure for reform of railroad policies led Congress to pass the **Interstate Commerce Act.** The act set up the **Interstate Commerce Commission**, an agency charged with ending such railroad abuses as pools and **rebates**, discounts only available to special customers. Although court decisions kept the commission ineffective for several years, its establishment set a precedent for federal regulation of interstate commerce.

SHERMAN ANTITRUST ACT   By the late 1800s, some large corporations and trusts had eliminated most competition and won almost total monopolies in their fields. Politicians heeded the public protests over the resulting abuses. One result was the **Sherman Antitrust Act** of 1890. The act prohibited monopolies by declaring illegal any business combination or trust "in restraint of trade or commerce."

THE VULTURES' ROOST

Culver Pictures

Courts, however, refused to support strong enforcement of the act. In addition, corporations formed holding companies rather than trusts to get around the act. Once again, the precedent set by the act proved more important than the act itself.

LABOR ORGANIZATIONS

Business growth in the late 1800s brought generally higher wages to American workers. Yet periodic unemployment and poor working conditions remained a fact of life for workers. In addition, employers held enormous power over the lives of their workers and could lower wages and fire employees at will.

Key Ideas   Organized labor has often led movements for justice and human rights while seeking better working conditions for its members.

The Growth of Unions

To improve conditions, increasing numbers of American workers formed labor unions. The first unions had appeared in the 1820s, but as working conditions changed with industrialization, many more workers became interested in unions.

Americans had long understood the values of cooperation and association, and labor unions provided a means to put these values into action. **Collective bargaining**, in which union members representing workers negotiated labor issues with management, meant that, instead of each worker trying to achieve individual aims, a united group would put pressure on management. Several early unions helped advance the cause of labor.

Regents Tip   Practice your data-base skills by studying the graph and then checking off the period during which labor unions experienced their greatest rate of growth.

_____ 1898–1900
_____ 1902–1904
_____ 1904–1906

Growing Unions

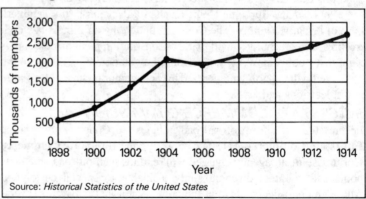

Source: *Historical Statistics of the United States*

KNIGHTS OF LABOR   Under the direction of **Terence Powderly**, the **Knights of Labor**, which had been formed in 1869, welcomed skilled and unskilled workers as well as women, blacks, and immigrants. The Knights opposed child labor and fought for an eight-hour day for workers. As a rule, they opposed strikes, but a successful strike against railroads in 1885 brought a flood of new members. A wave of antilabor feeling swept the nation after the Haymarket Riot in late 1886. The Knights declined in influence due to a series of unsuccessful strikes and competition from the American Federation of Labor with its concentration on bread-and-butter issues.

AMERICAN FEDERATION OF LABOR

In 1886 **Samuel Gompers** formed the **American Federation of Labor** (AFL). The AFL was a collection of many different **craft unions**, unions of skilled workers in similar trades. The AFL fought for immediate goals—an eight-hour day, better wages, and improved working conditions. The policy that the AFL followed is known as "**bread-and-butter unionism.**" It so appealed to workers that AFL membership reached more than a million by 1904, making the AFL the most powerful union in the nation.

INTERNATIONAL LADIES' GARMENT WORKERS UNION

Women made up the majority of workers in the garment industries. In 1910, the **International Ladies' Garment Workers Union** (ILGWU) was formed to represent the laborers who toiled in sweatshops. A successful strike in 1910 brought in many new members and the ILGWU soon became an important part of the AFL.

Labor Conflict

If collective bargaining failed, labor unions often used **strikes**, or work stoppages, to achieve their aims. Strikes sometimes ended in union victories; often, however, they led to violence as business owners sought state and even federal support to end walkouts. The strikes and labor-associated violence listed below sometimes advanced the cause of labor and sometimes set it back.

GREAT RAILWAY STRIKE

In 1877 a series of pay cuts for railroad workers led to a strike that spread across several states. At the request of state governors, President Hayes sent federal troops to help end the strike. The workers gained little benefit from the strike, and owners took a harder position against unions.

HAYMARKET RIOT

A labor rally called by Chicago anarchists in 1886 ended with a bomb blast and riot that left 18 people, including 8 police officers, dead. Although the Knights of Labor had no responsibility for the violence, some public opinion blamed them.

HOMESTEAD STRIKE

In 1892 union members at the Carnegie steel plant in Homestead, Pennsylvania, went on strike to protest a wage cut. Management brought in security guards to protect the plant. In the fighting that followed, 16 people were killed. The National Guard finally ended the fighting and the strike. Fewer than 25 percent of the striking workers got their jobs back. The strike brought the union movement in the steel industry to a halt for 20 years.

PULLMAN STRIKE

In 1894 a strike by railway car makers in Illinois spread and tied up other rail lines. President Cleveland

MAKING CONNECTIONS

Key Ideas More progress in labor–management relations has resulted from negotiation and mediation than from confrontation or violence.

Enduring Issues

National Power—Limits and Potentials

Key Ideas Government has played a crucial role in affecting the power balance between management and labor.

MAKING CONNECTIONS

obtained an **injunction**, or court order, against the strikers and sent in federal troops to end the strike. Cleveland's action confirmed the belief of many that government favored the interests of business over those of labor.

LAWRENCE TEXTILE STRIKE   The **Industrial Workers of the World** (IWW), a radical union of skilled and unskilled laborers, led a huge strike against the textile mills in Lawrence, Massachusetts, in 1912. The strike proved one of the greatest successes of that era, and workers won most of their demands.

Regents Questions for Practice _____

Review the **Test-Taking Strategies section of this book. Then answer the following questions, drawn from actual Regents examinations. Circle the *number* of the word or expression that best completes the statement or answers the question. Write your answers to essay questions on a separate piece of paper. Hints on good ways to approach these questions are provided in the margins.**

1. ''The merchants will manage commerce the better, the more they are left free to manage for themselves.''   —Thomas Jefferson
    Which theory is best described in this question?
    1 social Darwinism   3 socialism
    2 laissez-faire capitalism   4 mercantilism

Test Hint   Note that this is really a form of cause-and-effect question. It asks you to think about the relationship between monopolies (cause) and the way they influence the economy (effect).

2. One effect of monopolies on the United States economy is that they have tended to
    1 reduce business competition
    2 keep prices low
    3 give consumers a greater choice in goods and services
    4 lead to a greater variety in the price for a particular product or service

3. During the late 1800s a major purpose of pools, trusts and holding companies in the United States business practices was to
    1 reduce competition
    2 promote socialist policies
    3 share management skills
    4 lower corporate income taxes

4. A nation seeking to encourage development of its resources and industries would most likely adopt an economic policy which includes
    1 an increase in investments abroad
    2 high tariffs on imported goods
    3 reductions in government spending
    4 high taxes on industrial profits

5. Which was the direct result of the industrialization of the United States economy after 1840?
1 less emphasis on the formal education of workers
2 increased productivity per worker per hour
3 decrease in the population of urban areas
4 increase in the prices of consumer goods

6. Which was a major reason for the failure of early 19th century labor unions in the United States?
1 public disapproval of social and fraternal organizations
2 Congressional measures outlawing collective bargaining
3 oversupply of technical workers
4 the worker's fear of economic reprisals

7. Which is a valid statement about the economy of the United States during the period 1865 to 1900?
1 Business was strictly regulated by the federal government.
2 The gross national product steadily decreased.
3 Barriers to international trade were abolished.
4 There was a trend toward the growth of large businesses.

8. "Combinations in industry are the result of an . . . economic law which cannot be repealed by political legislation." The author of this quotation would probably favor which economic policy?
1 antitrust laws   3 mercantilism
2 laissez-faire capitalism   4 social security laws

MAKING CONNECTIONS

Test Hint Note that this is another cause-and-effect question. What happened after industrialization (cause)?

Test Hint To make sure you understand the time period under discussion, change the centuries to dates (in this case, 1800s) right on your test paper.

Test Hint Note that this question asks you to make a generalization about the nation's economy during the late 1800s. Remember that a generalization is a statement that applies in most, but not all instances. (*Valid* means true.)

---

9. According to the theory of laissez-faire economics prices should be determined chiefly by
1 government regulations
2 supply and demand
3 leaders of business and industry
4 negotiations between labor and management

10. Which would a laissez-faire economist most likely favor?
1 government support of basic industries
2 high protective tariffs on imports
3 minimal government regulation
4 unemployment insurance and workers' compensation programs

11. Which best describes the change in the economic base of the northeastern part of the United States between 1820 and 1890?
1 Ownership of major industries was transferred from private individuals to the federal government.

2 As agricultural productivity increased, the farmer became the leading economic figure.
3 Economic productivity declined as major industries moved to the South and West.
4 Large-scale manufacturing became a major economic activity.

12. An important change due to the growth of population that accompanied the Industrial Revolution in the 19th century was the
1 lessening of contrast between the wealthy and the poor
2 rapid development of an urbanized society
3 growth of self-sufficient farms
4 reversal in migration patterns

13. Which was the major reason for the slow growth of labor unions in the United States during the 19th century?
1 presence of language and cultural barriers among workers
2 lack of public and legal support for union activities
3 existence of adequate wages and good working conditions
4 rejection of unionization by skilled workers

14. The primary purpose of forming a corporation is to
1 gain control over a particular industry
2 force down the price of manufactured articles
3 allow for greater accumulation of investment
4 obtain higher wages for industrial workers

15. During the 19th century the United States government reacted to union attempts to organize labor by
1 taking a neutral position concerning unions
2 supporting industry in its efforts to suppress unions
3 limiting unions membership to unskilled workers
4 providing strikers with unemployment benefits

16. Which was a major obstacle to the formation of labor unions in the United States during the period 1860–1900?
1 prohibition of labor organizations by the Constitution
2 general government support of management
3 excellent working conditions in the United States factories of the time
4 status of factory workers as equal partners with management

17. "Ours is a country where people . . . can attain to the most elevated positions or acquire a large amount of personal wealth . . . according to their talents, prudence, and personal exertions." This quotation most clearly supports the idea that
1 the United States has a centrally controlled economic system
2 economic collectivism is part of American life
3 regulated capitalism restricts private initiative
4 upward social mobility and the work ethic are closely related

18. In the United States the homes of late 19th-century millionaires most strongly reflected their owners
1 concern for preserving the natural environment
2 emphasis on a lavish display of wealth
3 interest in reviving traditional United States architectural styles
4 preference for simple and modest lifestyles

19. Conspicuous consumption most nearly means the tendency to
1 impress others with one's material possessions
2 increase one's caloric intake
3 publicize one's products through advertising
4 donate huge sums to charitable organizations

20. The use of the term "Gilded Age" to describe the United States society during the latter part of the 19th century suggests that, at this time, the nation was concerned mainly with
1 materialistic goals
2 overseas expansion
3 social equality
4 literary and artistic advancement

American Society Adjusts to Industrialism

INDUSTRIALIZATION AND URBANIZATION

Industrialization and the growth of cities went hand in hand. Cities offered large numbers of workers for new factories. Cities provided transportation facilities for raw materials and finished goods. As more plants were built, more workers moved to cities seeking jobs. In 1880 less than a quarter of Americans lived in cities. By 1900, almost 40 percent did. By 1920, more than half of all Americans lived in cities. This shift from rural to urban life had both positive and negative effects.

MAKING CONNECTIONS

Key Ideas The growth of urban centers was stimulated by locations on key transportation routes. Improved transportation contributed to growing national economic interdependence.

Urban and Rural Population, 1850–1900

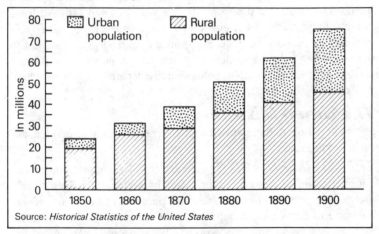

Source: *Historical Statistics of the United States*

Regents Tip Practice your data-base skills by answering the following questions about the graph. Approximately how many Americans lived in cities in 1850?

In 1900?

Negative Effects of City Growth

HOUSING Construction of decent housing often lagged behind the growth of city populations. Much city housing consisted of multi-family buildings called **tenements**. Immigrant and working-class families, who could pay little for rent, crowded into such buildings. These poorly maintained tenements deteriorated and whole neighborhoods became **slums**. Crime flourished in such poor, crowded neighborhoods.

HEALTH   Urban crowding helped spread disease. Water and sanitation facilities were often inadequate. Poor families could not afford proper diets and lacked knowledge of basic health procedures.

POLITICS   **Political "machines"** took control of many city governments. Corruption flourished, and money that could have been spent on public works often ended up in private pockets.

Positive Effects of City Growth

NEW TECHNOLOGIES   Builders turned to new technologies to meet the challenge posed by huge numbers of people living together. Subways, elevated trains, and streetcars provided mass transportation. Steel girders and elevators made possible high-rise "skyscrapers." Gas and electric lights brightened city streets and made them safer. Growing health problems forced officials to design and build new water and sewage systems.

CULTURAL ADVANCES   Public and private money funded new museums, concert halls, theaters, and parks. New printing presses turned out mass-circulation newspapers, magazines, and popular novels. Public schools educated more students than ever before and reforms started by people like **John Dewey** improved the quality of teaching.

COMMUNITY IMPROVEMENT   People formed groups intended to correct the problems of society. In Chicago **Jane Addams** of Hull House started a **settlement house movement** to provide education and services to the poor. Fair-minded political groups sought to unseat corrupt political machines and see that public money was spent on improved services such as police and fire departments and new hospitals, rather than on graft.

The Urban Mixture

The people of these growing cities generally could be divided into three broad groups.

THE WORKERS AND THE POOR   The largest group contained the workers and the poor. Most immigrants belonged to this group. Members of it lived in slums and poorer neighborhoods. Workers came to cities seeking jobs. Often wages were so low that entire families, including children, worked. These people often lacked the time and money to go to theaters or museums or use other resources that cities provided.

THE MIDDLE CLASS   Doctors, lawyers, office workers, and skilled laborers made up a growing middle class. Middle-class neighborhoods offered less crowded, better maintained housing. The middle-class people had both money and leisure time. They could afford to go to concerts, attend increasingly popular football, basketball, or baseball games, and save money for their children's higher education. They made up a large part of the market for popular publications, including the increasingly popular regional literature.

THE WEALTHY   Entrepreneurs and wealthy business people usually made the city their chief residence, though they often had summer estates outside it. The rich made up the smallest segment of urban society. They lived in large mansions or elegant apartment buildings. They often contributed to charities and cultural institutions such as opera companies and libraries. They could enjoy the broadest range of benefits of city life.

Changes in Women's Lives

Industrialization and urbanization brought changes to the lives of women in all the classes mentioned above. Many Americans had long held the view that the ideal woman was one who devoted herself to home and family, instilling in her husband and children high moral values. In fact, usually only wealthy women had been able to meet this ideal. In the late 1800s, changes in society meant that the ideal applied to even fewer women.

NEW EMPLOYMENT OPPORTUNITIES   Among the poor and working class, women often had to hold jobs outside the home. New inventions, such as the typewriter, telephone, and telegraph, created new jobs that women rushed to fill.

Middle- and upper-class women also sought jobs. Many of these women had long been active in reform movements, such as abolition and temperance, and had attended college in increasing numbers through the 1800s. They sought to apply their educations and social concerns in the job market. Women took jobs as teachers, social workers, doctors, and lawyers, often struggling against public disapproval.

Women thus became an ever-larger part of the work force. Between 1880 and 1910, the number of working women grew from 2.6 million to 8 million. Conditions they met in the workplace—hostility, laws that barred women from certain jobs, unequal pay—led more women to seek legal remedies. The right to vote—granted to black males by the 15th Amendment—gave women the political power to force change. The **women's suffrage movement** grew more active.

IMMIGRATION

From its beginnings, the United States had been a nation of immigrants. After the Civil War, however, industrializing America drew an even greater flood of immigrants to its shores. From 1865 to 1900, some 13.5 million people arrived from abroad. Not until the 1920s would the numbers begin to dwindle. Immigration to America can be divided into three stages.

MAKING CONNECTIONS

Key Social Studies Concepts:

Change

MAKING CONNECTIONS

The New Immigrants

Where they came from 1840–1860

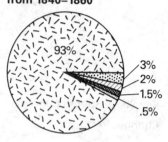

93%

3%
2%
1.5%
.5%

Where they came from 1880–1900

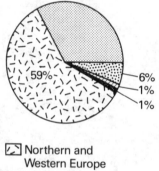

59%

6%
1%
1%

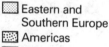

◺ Northern and
  Western Europe

▨ Eastern and
  Southern Europe

▦ Americas

▨ Asia

■ All others

Source: *Historical Statistics of the United States*

Key Ideas Migration of peoples to the United States was caused by circumstances abroad as well as by the promise of a better life in America.

Key Social Studies Concepts:

Culture, Diversity

Colonial Immigration

This period lasted from the arrival of the first English settlers through the Declaration of Independence. The following features characterize this period of immigration.

COLONIAL IMMIGRANTS Settlers from England made up the largest part of these immigrants. However, Scotch-Irish, German, Swedish, and Dutch settlers also came in significant numbers. Large numbers of Africans were also part of the colonial immigration.

REASONS FOR IMMIGRATION Some of these settlers came seeking political and religious freedom. Others sought to improve their economic standing and their way of life. The Africans came unwillingly, as slaves.

AREAS OF SETTLEMENT English settlement spread along the Atlantic Coast from Maine to Georgia and inland to the Appalachians. Within this area, ethnic populations concentrated in certain regions. For example, many Dutch settled in New York and New Jersey, many Germans in Pennsylvania, and many Scotch-Irish in the backcountry areas of North and South Carolina. Most Africans came at first to the Chesapeake region, then spread through the South.

DIFFICULTIES THEY FACED The immigrants came into conflict with the Native Americans. They also had to overcome the challenge of building homes, farms, and a new way of life in an unfamiliar wilderness region.

CONTRIBUTIONS The immigrants succeeded in establishing a culture much like the one they had left in Europe, yet heavily influenced by the geographic factors encountered in North America. In addition to their language, English settlers brought forms of government, religions, family and cultural traditions, and economic patterns from their home country. Other groups contributed customs from their home countries. All worked to build a successful economy in North America.

"Old" Immigration

The "Old Immigration" covered the years from the establishment of the United States through the Civil War. Most of the "old" immigrants came from northern and western Europe. Ireland, Germany, and Scandinavia were major sources of immigration.

REASONS FOR IMMIGRATION Massive famine caused by failure of the potato crop drove Irish immigrants to seek opportunity in the United States. Revolution in Germany caused many immigrants to seek peace and stability in America. Many people continued to arrive in search of better economic opportunity.

AREAS OF SETTLEMENT The Irish largely settled in cities in the Northeast. Some Germans also stayed in cities, but many moved west to start farms, as did a large number of Scandinavian immigrants.

DIFFICULTIES THEY FACED Irish and German Catholic immigrants often faced hostility on their arrival in the United States. Some Americans feared economic competition from the newcomers. Since at this time the nation was predominantly Protestant, resentment toward Catholics was also strong. A political party called the "**Know-Nothings**" agitated to restrict immigration.

CONTRIBUTIONS Irish workers helped build railroads and canals and labored in factories. Germans and Scandinavians brought, among other things, advanced farming techniques and new ideas on education such as kindergarten.

"New" Immigration

The "New" Immigration covered the time from after the Civil War to 1924. This period was marked by a shift in sources of immigration to southern and eastern Europe, especially the nations of Italy, Poland, Russia, and eastern Europe. In addition, substantial numbers of Japanese and Chinese arrived.

REASONS FOR IMMIGRATION Hope of greater economic opportunity prompted many of these immigrants to come to America. Some also came seeking political freedom. Other groups, such as Russian Jews, sought religious freedom.

AREAS OF SETTLEMENT Most of the "new" immigrants settled in cities, especially industrial centers and ports. Asian immigrants tended to settle on the west coast, usually in California.

DIFFICULTIES THEY FACED The growing numbers of new immigrants produced reactions of fear and hostility among many native-born Americans whose ancestors had come from very different backgrounds. Newcomers faced discrimination in jobs and housing. Meanwhile, popular pressure to limit immigration increased.

CONTRIBUTIONS The new immigrants found an abundance of jobs in the nation's expanding industries. Yet the steady stream of new workers to fill such jobs kept wages low. Young Italian and Jewish girls worked in the sweatshops of the garment industry. Poles and Slavs labored in the coal mines and steel mills of Pennsylvania and the Midwest. Chinese workers made major contributions to the building of the transcontinental railroad. These immigrants thus aided America's economic expansion. They also contributed to the nation's rich cultural diversity.

MAKING CONNECTIONS

Key Ideas Americans have held varying attitudes toward immigration. Empathy and a spirit of welcome have been mixed with prejudice and resistance.

Enduring Issues

Rights of Ethnic and Racial Groups

Reaction Against Immigration

The flood of immigration in the late 1800s brought with it a new wave of **nativism**. This was the belief that native-born Americans and their ways of life were superior to immigrants and their ways of life. In the late 1800s, descendants of the old immigrants were often among the nativists protesting the arrival of new immigrants.

Nativists believed that immigrant languages, religions, and traditions would have a negative impact on American society. Nativist workers believed that the many new immigrants competing for jobs kept wages low. A series of downturns in the economy added to fears that immigrants would take jobs from native-born Americans.

Immigrants thus often met with prejudice and discrimination. Jokes and stereotypes of the newcomers were common. Nativists also tried to use political clout to influence legislation against immigrants. Key developments in this area include the following.

Reaction Against Immigration

- **Know-Nothing Party**: The party's members worked during the 1850s to limit the voting strength of immigrants, keep Catholics out of public office, and require a lengthy residence before citizenship. Also known as the American Party, the Know-Nothing Party achieved none of these goals and died out by the late 1850s.

- **Chinese Exclusion Act of 1882**: Some native-born Americans labelled immigration from Asia a "**yellow peril**." Under pressure from California, which had already barred Chinese from owning property or working at certain jobs, Congress passed this law sharply limiting Chinese immigration.

- **"Gentlemen's Agreement"**: In 1907 President Roosevelt reached an informal agreement with Japan under which that nation halted the emigration of its people to the United States.

- **Literacy Tests**: In 1917 Congress enacted a law barring any immigrant who could not read or write.

- **Emergency Quota Act of 1921**: This law sharply limited the number of immigrants to the United States each year to about 350,000.

- **National Origins Quota Act of 1924**: This law further reduced immigration and biased it in favor of those from northern and western Europe.

- **National Origins Act of 1929**: This act further limited immigration to 150,000 people a year.

Immigrants and American Society

Over the years, sociologists and others who studied immigration developed different theories on how immigrants were absorbed into the larger society.

"MELTING-POT" THEORY   According to this theory, people from various cultures have met in the United States to form a "new American." The contributions of individual groups are not easily distinguished. The final "new" culture is more important than its parts.

ASSIMILATION   According to this theory, immigrants disappeared into an already established American culture. They gave up older languages and customs and became "**Americanized**," adopting the appearances and attitudes of the larger society in order to be accepted. Those like African and Asian Americans who were least similar had the hardest time assimilating.

PLURALISM   This theory recognizes that groups do not always lose their distinctive characters. They can live side by side, with each group contributing in different ways to society. This approach is sometimes called the "**salad-bowl**" **theory**, since groups, like different vegetables in a salad, remain identifiable but create a new, larger whole.

MAKING CONNECTIONS

Key Ideas   In a crisis of identity, immigrants often have to choose what cultural traditions to retain and what American behaviors to adopt.

THE AMERICAN WEST IN THE LATE 1800s

In 1893 **Frederick Jackson Turner** wrote in his paper "The Significance of the Frontier in American History" that the frontier "and the advance of American settlement westward, explain American development." Turner claimed life on the frontier had given rise to inventiveness, independence, and unique American customs. In 1890, just three years before Turner published his paper, a spokesperson for a government agency had announced that the frontier was closed. Industrialization had aided the settling of the West and speeded the end of the frontier.

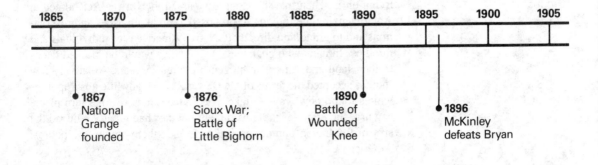

| 1865 | 1870 | 1875 | 1880 | 1885 | 1890 | 1895 | 1900 | 1905 |

1867
National
Grange
founded

1876
Sioux War;
Battle of
Little Bighorn

1890
Battle of
Wounded
Knee

1896
McKinley
defeats Bryan

Native Americans and Westward Expansion

The westward expansion of the late 1800s continued to create problems for the Native Americans who stood in its path. Ever since the first Europeans had arrived in North America, the newcomers and the Native Americans had come into conflict over possession of the land.

Enduring Issues

National Power— Limits and Potential

MAKING CONNECTIONS

INDIAN REMOVAL After the colonies became the United States, the federal government used a combination of treaties and force to move Indians ever farther west. Then in the 1830s, President Andrew Jackson began his policy of **Indian removal**, aimed at forcing all Native Americans onto lands west of the Mississippi. The forced movement of southern Indians, including the Cherokee and the Creek, over the **Trail of Tears** to the west was one result of this policy. A series of wars with the Seminoles of Florida was another.

By the 1840s, only scattered groups of Native Americans still lived in the East. Most lived west of the Mississippi on lands that few whites wanted. The California gold rush, the building of the transcontinental railroad, and the discovery of rich farmland in the Great Plains changed this situation. Now white settlers began to move onto Indian lands in the West.

Key Ideas The Indian wars were clashes between peoples of unequal numbers and technological skills and differing levels of organization, resulting in *genocide*.

INDIAN WARS The Indians fought back. From the 1850s to 1890, a series of Indian wars raged in the West. Some wars ended in treaties and new federal policies toward the Indians. Gradually the Indians were forced onto smaller and smaller areas of land called **reservations**. Though the Indians tried to resist, the greater numbers of whites, their superior technology, and divisions among Indian peoples that did not permit a unified resistance spelled defeat for Native Americans. The defeat of the Sioux at Wounded Knee, South Dakota, in 1890 is usually considered the end of the Indian Wars.

Enduring Issues

Rights of Ethnic and Racial Groups

CHANGING GOVERNMENT POLICIES In victory, the federal government continued to display little understanding or respect for Indian cultures and values. Indians were given reservation land that rarely could produce adequate crops or support game for the people living on it. Then in 1887 Congress passed the **Dawes Act**, aimed at Americanizing the Indians. It proposed to break up tribes and reservations and to grant land directly to Native Americans as individuals and families. Indians who abandoned tribal ways would be granted deeds to their land and American citizenship after 25 years. Relatively few Indians accepted the terms of the Dawes Act. Meanwhile unscrupulous whites found new ways to take over Indian lands. By the turn of the century, the effect of the government policies had greatly reduced the size of the Indian population and had made them among the poorest Americans.

The Economy of the West

New technologies helped settlers who moved onto Indian lands exploit the wealth of the West. Railroads brought settlers and carried western crops and products to eastern markets. Barbed wire aided the growth of both farming and ranching. Steel plows cut tough prairie soil. Windmills pulled water to the surface of dry western lands. Mechanical reapers and farm tools allowed a smaller number of workers to plant and harvest larger crops.

Key Ideas The challenge of using the raw materials of the Great Plains was met by technological ingenuity. The natural environment thus undergoes constant change as people interact with it.

The riches of the West took many forms. Miners dug millions of dollars in ore out of western mines, not just gold and silver, but also copper, lead, and zinc. Ranchers turned cattle raising into big business, as cowhands moved huge herds across the open ranges to rail lines. Farmers overcame heat, blizzards, droughts, insects, and occasional conflicts with ranchers to raise crops on the Great Plains. Many settled lands claimed under the Homestead Act and later built huge farms. By 1890, American farmers were raising enough to feed the nation and still export wheat and other crops.

Farmers, Populists, and Politics

THE GRANGE   Many farmers facing the hardships and isolation of rural life joined the **Grange**. This organization, founded in 1867, was originally meant to develop social ties. However, poor economic conditions made farmers aware that railroad companies, which often stored farmers' crops and carried them to market, had great control over their lives. To win back some of this control, the Grange began to press for political changes to limit the power of the railroads. Pressure from the Grange and other groups led to the state laws regulating railroads that were upheld in *Munn* v. *Illinois* and to the federal law creating the **Interstate Commerce Commission** (both mentioned in Section 2 of this Unit).

THE POPULIST PARTY   Farmers realized that the best hope of winning more reforms was the formation of a new political party. In 1891 they founded the **Populist Party**, which had among its goals a graduated income tax, direct election of United States senators, use of the secret ballot, and government ownership of railroads, telegraphs, and telephones. The new party had strong **grass-roots support**, or support directly from the people rather than established political figures. It soon made strong showings in elections for state legislatures and the United States Congress.

THE ELECTION OF 1896   The Populists made their strongest showing in the election of 1896, the first election to follow an economic depression that had begun in 1893. The chief Populist issue in the campaign was "**free silver**." This free coinage of silver would produce "**cheap money**," or currency inflated in value that would make it easier for farmers to pay off debts. **William Jennings Bryan**, who ran on both the Populist and Democratic tickets, argued tirelessly for this idea. Republican candidate **William McKinley** had the support of big business, which contributed heavily to his campaign. McKinley claimed the nation's economy was sound and opposed "free silver."

McKinley won the election by a huge margin. The nation's economy meanwhile improved and the Populists disappeared as a political party. Yet many of their ideas were later adopted by the other political parties and remain in use today.

The defeat of the Populists symbolized the great changes that had swept the nation since the Civil War. The economy had changed from agrarian to industrial. The United States was becoming a nation of cities rather than farms and villages. The frontier was closing and its

MAKING CONNECTIONS

influence coming to an end. New immigrants were creating a new, complex, pluralistic culture in America. By 1900, the United States was entering both a new century and a new Modern Age.

Regents Questions for Practice _____

Review the Test-Taking Strategies section of this book. Then answer the following questions, drawn from actual Regents examinations. Circle the *number* of the word or expression that best completes the statement or answers the question. Write your answers to essay questions on a separate piece of paper. Hints on good ways to approach these questions are provided in the margins.

1. An experience of the majority of immigrants to the United States was that they
   1 frequently met resentment
   2 settled in rural areas where cheap land was available
   3 were rapidly assimilated into the predominant lifestyle
   4 joined radical political parties to bring about economic reform

2. Which statement about immigration to the United States is most accurate?
   1 Industrial growth lead to decreased demand for cheap immigrant labor.
   2 The diversity of the immigrant population helped to create a pluralistic society.
   3 Organized labor generally favored unrestricted immigration.
   4 Most 19th century immigration acts were designed to prevent discrimination in immigration.

Test Hint Note important vocabulary, *social mobility* and the date.

3. From 1840 to 1900, each new group of immigrants to the United States contributed to the upward social mobility of the previous groups by
   1 filling the unskilled and semiskilled jobs
   2 creating a climate for social reform
   3 stimulating interest in free public education
   4 reinforcing the ethnic heritage of earlier groups

Test Hint Notice that this is a generalization about *all* the periods of immigration.

4. Most of the immigrants to the United States came in order to
   1 search for adventure
   2 attain economic advancement
   3 promote their political philosophy
   4 practice their religious beliefs openly

5. During the 19th century, discrimination against immigrants to the United States was based mainly on the belief that immigrants
   1 lowered "downtown" property values
   2 would have too great an influence on the enactment of legislation favorable to European nations
   3 lowered the scale of wages because they were willing to work for less money
   4 placed an undue burden on available social services

MAKING CONNECTIONS

6. The primary reason the United States did not limit immigration during the pre–Civil War period was that
   1 nativist protest groups such as the Know-Nothings had been outlawed
   2 internal expansion created appropriate conditions for a growing population
   3 the number of foreigners seeking entrance was very small
   4 the United States Constitution specifically prohibited placing barriers on immigration

Test Hint *Primary,* meaning the most important reason, is the key word here.

7. A major reason why people migrated to the western part of the United States during the 19th century was because that part of the country
   1 provided an abundance of cheap labor
   2 guaranteed protection from violence
   3 protected the right of landowners to own slaves
   4 offered increased opportunities for social mobility

8. "The United States is the child of the world, not of England alone." Which statement best supports this observation?
   1 The diverse origins of the people of the United States have led to a pluralistic society.
   2 The Anglo-Saxon tradition of the consent of the governed influenced colonial government.
   3 The ideas of European writers have become part of the basic political philosophy of the United States.
   4 African and Asian societies contributed more to the United States cultural development than did England.

Test Hint Try to rewrite the quotation in your own words before answering the question.

9. Which was a common complaint of nativist groups in the United States during the late 19th and early 20th centuries?
   1 Congress failed to protect domestic industries.
   2 The flow of immigration to the United States was too great.
   3 Too many national leaders were coming from rural backgrounds.
   4 Hiring for government jobs was too selective.

10. Most of the immigrants who came to the United States in the late 19th century were
1 middle class families with investment capital
2 educated persons well prepared to face the problems of resettlement
3 members of religious groups seeking to establish ideal religious communities
4 peasants and laborers seeking to better their lives

11. A major reason why the United States had a liberal immigration policy during the 19th century was that
1 most United States legislators were foreign born
2 the natural population growth of the United States was small
3 there was great demand for labor in the United States
4 favorable economic conditions in Europe kept immigration to the United States low

12. In the mid 1800s, the concept of nativism was evidenced in the national political platform of the Know-Nothing Party by a plank calling for
1 restoring as much land as possible to the Indians
2 extending the borders of the United States to the Pacific Ocean
3 eliminating slavery in the South
4 restricting immigration

13. Nineteenth and early twentieth century immigrants to the United States faced the least resistance when they
1 came from poor rural areas of Europe
2 kept their own unique customs
3 came during a period of labor shortage
4 came in search of religious freedom

Base your answers to questions 14 and 15 on the cartoon below and your knowledge of social studies.

— Thomas Nast, 1870

14. According to this 1870 cartoon, which statement about the time period is accurate?
1 Chinese laborers were welcomed to the United States with open arms.
2 The Know-Nothing Party was formed to help gain rights for minorities.
3 Very few Chinese were interested in coming to the United States.
4 A movement existed in the United States to prevent the immigration of Chinese.

15. At the time this cartoon was published, the majority of immigrants to the United States were coming from
1 Africa
2 Europe
3 Asia
4 South America

16. Europeans who came to the United States between 1880 and 1920 have been described as new immigrants mainly because they
    1 were considered physically and mentally superior to earlier immigrants
    2 arrived before the closing of the frontier and settled in farms in the West
    3 came generally from different countries than most earlier immigrants
    4 came chiefly from northern and western Europe

17. The Chinese Exclusion Act, the Gentlemen's Agreement, and the National Origins Act were reactions to earlier United States policies of
    1 requiring proof of literacy in order to be admitted
    2 permitting unlimited immigration
    3 restricting immigration to the middle and upper classes
    4 encouraging the immigration of scientists and intellectuals

18. The passage of the immigration acts of 1921 and 1924 indicated that the United States wished to
    1 restrict the flow of immigrants
    2 continue the immigration policies followed during most of the 19th century
    3 encourage cultural diversity
    4 play a larger role in international affairs

19. In the United States during the first half of the 19th century, reformers who advocated the rights of women also most often supported
    1 the abolition of slavery
    2 the provision of free land to new settlers
    3 increases in immigration
    4 territorial expansion into Mexico and Canada

20. In the United States economic opportunities for women expanded during the last quarter of the 19th century primarily because of the growth of

    1 opportunities to buy farms in the West
    2 industry and technology
    3 big-city political machines
    4 organized labor

21. "Many, if not most, of our Indian wars have had their origin in broken promises and acts of injustice on our part." The author of this statement would most likely agree that the history of the United States treatment of American Indians was primarily the result of
    1 prejudice toward Indian religions
    2 the desire for territorial expansion
    3 a refusal of Indians to negotiate treaties
    4 opposing economic and political systems

22. Which means for redressing grievances is applicable to American Indians but is usually not applicable to other minority groups?
    1 nonviolent marches to draw attention to injustices
    2 equal educational and employment opportunity laws
    3 economic boycott of all products manufactured in the United States
    4 collective lawsuits to recover ancestral lands

23. For American Indians, one effect of life on the reservations has been continued
    1 awareness of cultural identity
    2 increases in average lifespan
    3 opportunity for assimilation
    4 emphasis on materialism

24. The history of black Americans and American Indians is similar in that both
    1 were reluctant immigrants to the United States
    2 have had difficulty obtaining equal protection of the law
    3 have been fully assimilated into American life
    4 have settled mainly in the South

Base your answers to questions 27–29 on the quotation below and on your knowledge of social studies.

". . . American social development has been continually beginning over again on the frontier. This perennial rebirth, this fluidity of American life, this expansion westward with its new opportunities, its continuous touch with the simplicity of primitive society, furnished the forces dominating American character. The true point of view in the history of this nation is not the Atlantic Coast, it is the Great West. The frontier is the line of most rapid and effective Americanization. The wilderness masters the colonists."

—Frederick Jackson Turner, "The Significance of the Frontier in American History" 1893

25. According to Frederick Jackson Turner, the culture of the United States was primarily the result of the

1   dependence of each generation on its predecessors
2   western settlers experience in adjusting to new surroundings
3   pioneer's ability to maintain contact with the settled areas back east
4   influence of the frontier in making settlers more like Easterners

26. In this statement Turner describes the frontier not only as an area but also as a
1   process of developing culture
2   preserver of traditions
3   solution to European problems
4   developer of economic systems

27. Which characteristic of the West as described by Turner is most applicable to contemporary society in the United States?
1   simplicity of life
2   westward expansion
3   new opportunities
4   frontier environment

Essay Questions

Following are essay questions about the Unit you have been reviewing. Before answering each, apply the lessons you learned in the Test-Taking Strategies section by blocking each essay. The first block has been organized for you to help you get started with the prewriting that is so necessary in preparing a good Regents essay answer.

1. The growth of industry in 19th century United States had a major impact on the aspects of society that are listed below.

Aspects of Society
Role of Women
Urbanization
Rise of organized labor
Government involvement in the economy
Status of the farmer

Select three of the aspects of society listed. Using specific examples, show how the growth of industry in the 19th century had a major impact on each of the three aspects. [5, 5, 5]

Set up a block on your own paper using this format (you may also write directly in this space):

ASPECTS OF SOCIETY	EXAMPLES showing how the growth of industry had a MAJOR impact on each aspect
1 role of women [5]	1 women began to take jobs in factories and offices, spent less time at home and with families 2 women began to go to schools to learn professions such as medicine and law, previously held only by men
2 urbanization [5]	1 cities were the center for factories and workers crowded into them 2 cities became cultural centers for those who could afford the arts, theater, music, etc.
3 organized labor [5]	1 workers tried to organize to earn better wages, safer working conditions, and shorter hours 2 organized labor was sometimes involved in strikes and demonstrations that caused violence

2. In the United States, geographic differences have contributed to the development of specific regions, each with its own needs and concerns. Listed below are three geographic regions.

Regions
Northeast
South
West

a For each region listed, explain the impact of specific geographic factors on the economic and historic development of the region. [12]
b Show how technological development has lessened the influence of geographic factors on the United States. [3]

3. Many aspects of United States society have been greatly affected by technological changes. Choose three of the aspects of United States society listed below. Explain how each one chosen has been affected by a specific technological development. (Use a different development for each aspect.) [5, 5, 5]

Aspects of United States Society

Urbanization	Rights of the individual
Agriculture	Politics
Cultural homogeneity	Environment

UNIT
3

The Progressive Movement: Responses to Industrialization and Urbanization

Section 1 Reform in America
Section 2 America Reaching Out

In Unit 2 you reviewed how, between the end of the Civil War and the turn of the century (1865–1900), the United States became a more industrialized and urbanized nation. These changes, while bringing many benefits to society, created problems as well.

In Unit 3 you will review how Americans reacted to change, both at home and overseas, in the years from 1900 to 1920. This period is called the **Progressive Era**. The term comes from the word "progress" and indicates that Americans were reacting to problems by working for reform.

There are always questions on the United States History and Government Regents Exam about the Progressive Era and its Presidents, especially Theodore Roosevelt and Woodrow Wilson. As part of your review of this unit, check the Enduring Issues chart in Unit One and the charts about the Presidents and important people at the back of the book to see what has been tested about this period in our history.

Remember that you will need to know the answers to the following questions in order to pass the Regents examination:

Section 1: What were the causes of the Progressive Movement and how successful was it in meeting its goals? Who were the people who achieved these goals?

Section 2: What were the causes of increased international involvement of the United States from 1890 to 1920? What were the effects of this involvement on the United States and other peoples around the world?

In some periods of the nation's history, Americans were inclined to accept society as it was. At other times, they challenged society's values and practices, working to reform them. This shifting balance is as much a part of the American tradition as reform itself.

Reform in America

THE REFORM TRADITION

The reform tradition in the United States goes back to the beginning of our history.

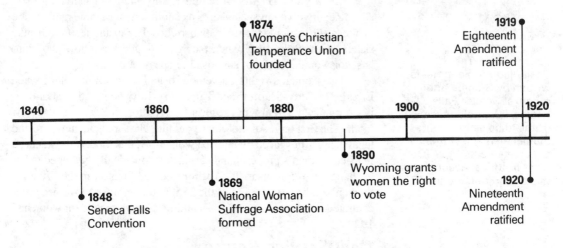

1874
Women's Christian Temperance Union founded

1919
Eighteenth Amendment ratified

1840   1860   1880   1900   1920

1890
Wyoming grants women the right to vote

1848
Seneca Falls Convention

1869
National Woman Suffrage Association formed

1920
Nineteenth Amendment ratified

The Revolutionary Era

The period before, during, and after the American Revolution, while mainly a time of governmental change, produced other reforms as well.

- After the Revolution, state governments adopted more democratic constitutions and reduced property requirements for voting.

- By 1800, most northern states had passed laws abolishing slavery. Some individuals in both the North and the South voluntarily freed their slaves.

- Recognizing the need for education if the people were to govern, some states in the early 1800s began supporting public elementary education. Educational opportunities for girls and young women also expanded.

141

MAKING CONNECTIONS

Enduring Issues

- Equality
- The Rights of Women

Background The Declaration of Sentiments, written by Stanton and others at Seneca Falls, begins, "We hold these truths to be self-evident: that all men and women are created equal. . . ." On what historical document is this declaration modeled?

Abolition

The movement to abolish slavery began before the American Revolution, when Quakers founded the first abolitionist societies, but did not gain strength until the early 1800s. The invention of the cotton gin in 1793 made cotton growing profitable, and slavery spread. Beginning in the 1830s, the abolition movement, organized by both black and white men and women, worked constantly for an end to slavery. The best known black abolitionists were **Frederick Douglass**, **Harriet Tubman**, and **Sojourner Truth**. Other famous abolitionists included **Angelina** and **Sarah Grimké** and **William Lloyd Garrison**. As you reviewed in Unit One, the Civil War put an end to slavery; it was formally abolished with the ratification of the 13th Amendment in 1865.

Women's Rights

The **women's rights**, or feminist, **movement** began in the 1830s, as women involved in such causes as abolitionism became more aware of the need to work for their own rights. For example, the Grimké sisters met with hostility when they tried to address fellow abolitionists, for women were not supposed to speak in public.

The women's rights movement began officially in 1848, when **Elizabeth Cady Stanton** and **Lucretia Mott**, both active abolitionists, organized a **Women's Rights Convention** in Seneca Falls, New York. The first target of this chiefly middle-class movement was to end legal inequalities faced by married women. At this time, for instance, a married woman's property and earnings automatically belonged to her husband. In 1853 **Susan B. Anthony** joined Stanton in the drive for women's rights. Beginning in the 1850s, the feminist movement concentrated on women's suffrage—gaining the right to vote for women in 1920.

Civil Service Reform

Civil service reform was an attempt to change the way people were hired for government jobs. Traditionally, these jobs went to people who had worked to help their political party win the election. Since the presidency of Andrew Jackson (1829–1837), this method was called the **spoils system**, from the saying "To the victor belong the spoils" (rewards). In 1881 President James Garfield was killed by a party worker who had failed to get a government job. People began to demand reform, and it was supported by the new president, Chester Arthur. The **Pendleton Act** of 1883 marked the beginning of civil service reform.

- It provided that competitive exams would be used to hire some government workers.
- It set up a commission to administer the tests.
- It banned the common practice of forcing government employees to give money to political parties.

Care of the Mentally Ill

The crusade to improve conditions for the mentally ill began with the work of one woman, **Dorothea Dix**. She first studied conditions in Massachusetts, where many of the insane were kept chained in prisons. In the 1840s her findings were reported to the state legislature, which authorized funds for state mental hospitals. Dix later worked with several other states that followed the example of Massachusetts.

REASONS FOR PROGRESSIVE REFORMS

In the late 1800s, the United States became a rich and powerful nation. With industrialization and urbanization came problems. The Progressive Movement was a reaction to such problems as:

- Powerful monopolies restricting competition
- An economic depression in the 1890s
- Labor unrest and violence
- Unhealthy and unsafe living and working conditions
- An increased gap between living standards of the rich and the poor
- Large numbers of "new immigrants" crowded into cities
- Urban poverty, crime, congestion, and poor sanitation
- Political corruption at all levels of government
- Abuse of the nation's natural resources

Who Were the Progressives?

The **Progressives** were Americans who set out to tackle the problems of their era. They did not form one single group. The Progressive Movement was made up of many different movements, and the Progressives were many different kinds of Americans. Their commitment and their success varied from person to person and from cause to cause. They did have some things in common, however.

CHARACTERISTICS The Progressives were influenced by the Populists, but differed from them. While the Populists lived in the country or in small towns, the Progressives were largely city dwellers. Most of the Populists were farmers, who focused on farm problems. The Progressives tended to be educated professionals—doctors, lawyers, social workers, clergy, and teachers—with a wide range of concerns.

BELIEFS AND GOALS Like all reformers, the Progressives were optimists. They believed that abuses of power by government and business could be ended. They believed that new developments in technology and science could be used to improve the basic institutions of American society—business, government, education, and family life. Progressives believed in capitalism, and were concerned about the

MAKING CONNECTIONS

Regents Tip Review social studies terms before taking the examination.
Define the following terms:
Industrialize:

Urbanize:

Regents Tip Remember that you may be asked to compare and contrast different groups.
List two key differences between Populists and Progressives.
1.

2.

MAKING CONNECTIONS
Enduring Issues

Avenues of Representation

growth of socialism as a more radical reaction to the effects of industrialization. Progressives wanted to bypass party politics, which they saw as corrupt, but had faith that a strong government could and should correct abuses and protect rights.

Not all Americans were Progressives or agreed with Progressive goals. Many business and political leaders opposed business regulation and accepted the Social Darwinists' view that the vast differences in wealth and power in American society were the result of scientific forces that could not be changed. Many workers and farmers did not benefit from Progressive reform, nor did most black Americans.

FACTORS AIDING THE MOVEMENT   Many Progressives acted through national voluntary organizations, which grew rapidly beginning in the 1890s. The fact that the movement was centered in cities at a time when more of the population was living in cities helped communication among Progressives. So did the expanding telephone and telegraph systems. The availability of inexpensive mass-circulation magazines and newspapers also helped spread Progressive ideas.

Key Ideas   Media has played an investigative role at various times in American history. By providing a different view, the media gives the public a balanced view compared to those of governments, corporations, or other sources of power.

The Muckrakers

The **muckrakers** were mainly journalists and writers, but also artists and photographers, who helped bring reform issues to the attention of the public. Muckrakers investigated and exposed corruption and injustice. Their articles were widely read in mass-circulation magazines. They also wrote novels dramatizing situations that demanded reform.

Muckraker	Book/Article	Subject of Exposé
Frank Norris	*The Octopus* (1901)	monopolistic railroad practices in California
Ida Tarbell	*History of the Standard Oil Company* (1903)	ruthless practices of Standard Oil
Lincoln Steffens	*The Shame of the Cities* (1904)	urban political corruption
Jacob Riis	*How the Other Half Lives* (1890)	life in New York's tenements
Upton Sinclair	*The Jungle* (1906)	dangerous conditions in meatpacking industry

That muckrakers were effective can be seen by the passage in 1906 of the **Pure Food and Drug Act** and the **Meat Inspection Act**—pioneering consumer protection legislation. The government passed these laws after it became clear that the dangerous conditions exposed by Sinclair's novel *The Jungle* were based on fact.

As time passed, the muckrakers' influence declined, partly because readers tired of their sensationalism. The tradition has continued to the present day, however.

Other Workers for Reform

Other people and groups also worked to bring Progressive reforms to American society.

CITIES AND SETTLEMENT HOUSES Attempts to end the poverty, crowding, and disease of American cities began before 1900. Once the germ theory of disease was accepted, cities put more effort into improving water and sewage systems. A well-known urban reformer was **Jacob Riis**, who used writings and photographs to show the need for better housing for the poor. Some Protestant church leaders became part of the **Social Gospel movement**, which worked to help poor city dwellers. One goal of urban reformers was building codes that would require safer, better-lighted, airier, and more sanitary tenements.

One early group of Progressive urban reformers were the settlement house workers. **Settlement houses,** located in working-class slums, offered people—especially immigrants— education, child care, social activities, and help in finding jobs. Well-known settlement houses included **Hull House**, founded by **Jane Addams** in Chicago, and the **Henry Street Settlement**, founded by **Lillian Wald** in New York City.

THE PEACE MOVEMENT Addams and Wald were among the Americans who led peace groups, such as the **Woman's Peace Party**, in the period before and during World War I. Support of **pacifism**—the policy of opposition to war and fighting—weakened with America's entry into World War I in 1917, but was later revived. Pacifist **Jeannette Rankin**, the first woman elected to Congress (1916), voted against United States entry into World War I (and World War II as well). For her pacifist efforts, Jane Addams won the Nobel Peace Prize in 1931.

TEMPERANCE AND PROHIBITION The **temperance movement**, which opposed the use of alcoholic beverages, began in the 1820s. Over the years, its chief goal became **prohibition**—outlawing the manufacture and sale of alcoholic beverages. Under the leadership of **Frances Willard**, the **Women's Christian Temperance Union (WCTU)**, founded in 1874, was a strong advocate of prohibition; its members included many Populists and Progressives. The temperance crusade led to national prohibition with the adoption of the **18th Amendment**, which banned the manufacture, sale, and transportation of alcoholic beverages in the United States as of 1920.

WOMEN'S RIGHTS Suffrage for women continued to be the main goal of the feminist movement in the Progressive Era. Women who had experienced success in other reform activities wanted to be

MAKING CONNECTIONS

Continuing Issues More recent examples of the muckraking tradition include the publication by *The New York Times* of the *Pentagon Papers*, which revealed government deception in its conduct of the Vietnam War, and the reporting on the Watergate scandal by the *Washington Post*'s Bob Woodward and Carl Bernstein that led to President Nixon's resignation.

Enduring Issues

- Avenues of Representation
- Change and Flexibility
- Equality

MAKING CONNECTIONS

Regents Tip Study all dates provided in a map key and on the map itself carefully.
Which region of the country was first to grant voting rights to women?

able to vote. And many suffragists thought that the women's vote would serve to correct various social problems.

In the 1860s the women's suffrage movement had split over the best way to achieve its goals. The more radical organization was led by Stanton and Anthony; the more moderate one was headed by **Lucy Stone** and her husband **Henry Blackwell**. In 1890 the groups merged to form the **National American Woman Suffrage Association (NAWSA)**.

In the 1900s, leadership of the campaign passed to **Carrie Chapman Catt** of NAWSA and to **Alice Paul**, who led the more militant Congressional Union. The highly visible activity of women during World War I brought them the final public support needed. In 1920 the **19th Amendment**, giving women the right to vote, was ratified.

Voting Rights of Women Before 1920

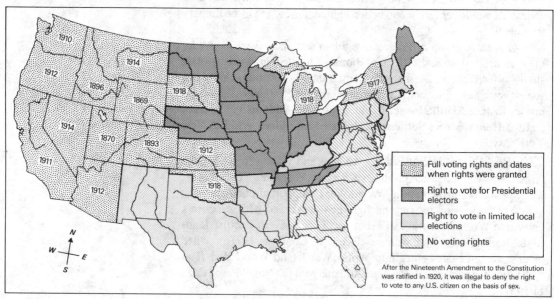

	Full voting rights and dates when rights were granted
	Right to vote for Presidential electors
	Right to vote in limited local elections
	No voting rights

After the Nineteenth Amendment to the Constitution was ratified in 1920, it was illegal to deny the right to vote to any U.S. citizen on the basis of sex.

Another sign of women's progress was the growth of educational opportunities. Among women's colleges founded in the late 1800s were **Vassar** (1861), **Wellesley** (1870), and **Smith** (1871). State universities set up under the **Morrill Act** of 1862 were coeducational. By the early 1900s, over 100,000 women were attending college.

A third aspect of the women's movement was family planning through birth control. This campaign was led by **Margaret Sanger**, who began her work as a nurse caring for poor immigrant women in New York City. The American Birth Control League founded by Sanger later became the **Planned Parenthood Federation**. Sanger's movement was controversial. She was arrested several times for sending information about contraception through the mail.

THE RIGHTS OF AFRICAN AMERICANS

The decades after the Civil War were a difficult time for African Americans. Laws prevented them from exercising their right to vote. The Supreme Court in *Plessy* v. *Ferguson*, 1896, ruled legal "Jim Crow" laws requiring segregated—"separate but equal"—public facilities for African Americans and whites.

Lynchings by white mobs took the lives of hundreds of African Americans. Key African American leaders who worked to secure their people's rights are described below.

- **Booker T. Washington**, a former slave and founder of Tuskegee Institute, urged African Americans to concentrate on learning a vocation in order to establish themselves economically. This strategy, he believed, would increase their own self-esteem and earn them respect from white society. Washington's policy, called **accommodation**, was expressed in an 1895 speech known as the **Atlanta Compromise**.

- **W.E.B. Du Bois**, a Harvard-educated professor, shared Washington's view of the importance of education, but rejected accommodation. He felt that African Americans should
  (a) protest unfair treatment and
  (b) receive a broad, liberal—rather than vocational—education. In 1905 Du Bois founded the **Niagara Movement** to work for equal rights. More successful was the **National Association for the Advancement of Colored People (NAACP)**, started in 1909 by a group of reformers that included Du Bois and Jane Addams. The NAACP successfully used lawsuits as a weapon on behalf of civil rights.

- **Marcus Garvey** founded in 1914 the **Universal Negro Improvement Association**, an African American nationalist and separatist group. The group wanted a separate black economy and urged African Americans to emigrate to Africa. Many of Garvey's ideas influenced the Black Power movement of the 1960s.

- **Ida B. Wells-Barnett** was a journalist who, in the 1890s, launched a national crusade against lynching. She was also a suffragist and one of the founders of the NAACP.

RIGHTS OF JEWISH AMERICANS

A Jewish service organization called **B'nai B'rith** ("Sons of the Covenant") had been founded in the 1840s. Progressive Era American Jews established an agency of B'nai B'rith, the **Anti-Defamation League**, in 1913. At first it worked mainly to combat **defamation**, or libels and slander, directed against Jews. Later its program was broadened to aim at securing the civil liberties of all Americans.

MAKING CONNECTIONS

Enduring Issues

- The Judiciary
- Equality
- Ethnic and Racial Groups
- Civil Liberties

MAKING CONNECTIONS

Enduring Issues

Avenues of Representation

33%

City Commissioner Plan

City Commissioners
- Water commissioner
- Sanitation commissioner
- Police commissioner
- Fire commissioner

Make laws and direct

City services
- Safe water
- Waste disposal
- Police protection
- Fire protection

City council makes laws and hires manager

City manager directs

City Manager Plan

PROGRESSIVISM AT THE CITY AND STATE LEVELS

During the Progressive Era, political reform took place at all levels of government—city, state, and national.

City Government

Given the Progressives' concern about urban problems, it is not surprising that they first concentrated their efforts on city government. As early as 1890, Americans interested in good government worked to elect reformist mayors. Success in doing so, however, did not always insure permanent improvement. Progressives had to change the way city government worked as well.

Two new types of city government are associated with the Progressive Movement. They were popular in small and medium-sized cities.

- **City Commissioner Plan** Instead of having a mayor and city council, the city is run by a group of commissioners. Each commissioner is in charge of one aspect of city government.

- **City Manager Plan** The city council hires a professional city manager, who runs the various departments.

State Government

Progressives also acted to limit the power of boss-controlled political machines and powerful business interests at the state level. Wisconsin, under Governor **Robert M. LaFollette**, was the model for Progressive reform. The state passed laws to regulate railroads, lobbying, and banking. It also started civil service reforms, shifted more of the tax burden to the wealthy and to corporations, required employers to compensate workers injured on the job, and provided for factory inspections.

Several other states passed laws like those of Wisconsin. Leading Progressive governors included **Hiram Johnson** of California, who reformed the railroad industry, **Woodrow Wilson** of New Jersey, and **Theodore Roosevelt** of New York.

Progressive reforms often proved difficult to enforce, meeting opposition from business interests and the courts. Thus changes in the way state governments worked were also part of the Progressive program. These changes, aimed at increasing citizen participation in government, included the following:

- The **secret, or Australian, ballot**, prevents party bosses (and anyone else) from knowing how people vote.

- The **initiative** is a system that allows voters to petition the legislature to consider a proposed law.

- In a **referendum**, voters decide whether a given bill or constitutional amendment should be passed.

- **Recall** is a form of petition used to force elected officials out of office.
- A **direct primary** allows voters, rather than party leaders, to select candidates to run for office.

Another Progressive reform that affected the national government as well as state governments was the ratification in 1913 of the **17th Amendment**. It provided for the direct election—election by the people—of United States senators. Up to this time senators had been elected by state legislatures, which were often controlled by corporations or political bosses.

Remember that the secret ballot, initiative, referendum, and direct election of senators were all parts of the Populist party program. Adoption of these reforms offers an example of how third parties can influence major parties.

MAKING CONNECTIONS

Regents Tip Labels in cartoons help you to understand the point the cartoonist is trying to make Who are the men at the desks?

Who do the large figures represent?

PROGRESSIVISM IN NATIONAL GOVERNMENT: ROOSEVELT

The first three Presidents of this century—Theodore Roosevelt, William Howard Taft, and Woodrow Wilson—are known as the Progressive Presidents. Roosevelt, elected Vice President in 1900, became President when President William McKinley was assassinated in 1901. He was elected in his own right in 1904.

Although basically conservative, Roosevelt did not hesitate to use the power of the presidency to deal directly with social and economic problems. For example, he influenced passage in 1906 of the Pure Food and Drug Act and the Meat Inspection Act. Roosevelt saw his job as one of **stewardship**—leading the nation in the public interest, like a manager or supervisor. He believed that the President had any powers not specifically denied to the executive in the Constitution.

Enduring Issues

- National Power
- Property/Economic Policy

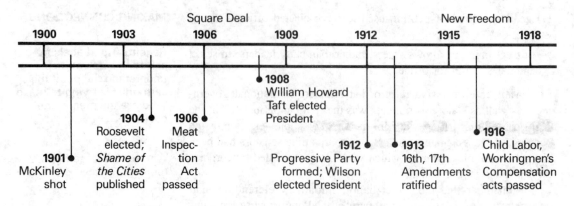

Square Deal   New Freedom

| 1900 | 1903 | 1906 | 1909 | 1912 | 1915 | 1918 |

1908
William Howard
Taft elected
President

1904
Roosevelt
elected;
*Shame of
the Cities*
published

1906
Meat
Inspec-
tion
Act
passed

1901
McKinley
shot

1912
Progressive Party
formed; Wilson
elected President

1913
16th, 17th
Amendments
ratified

1916
Child Labor,
Workingmen's
Compensation
acts passed

MAKING CONNECTIONS

Roosevelt's administration is often known as the **Square Deal**. His domestic reforms fall into three main categories—business regulation, labor conditions, and conservation.

Regulating Business

Roosevelt saw a difference between "good trusts," which were to be subject only to regulation, and "bad trusts," which were to be dissolved. The actions he took against big business earned him a reputation as a "**trust buster**."

Election of 1904

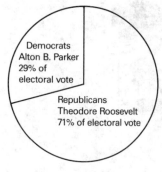

Democrats
Alton B. Parker
29% of
electoral vote

Republicans
Theodore Roosevelt
71% of electoral vote

Regents Tip Remember that the symbols a cartoonist uses give clues about the point he is trying to make.
How does the cartoonist represent trusts?

What does the cartoon say about Roosevelt's opinion of trusts?

THE NORTHERN SECURITIES CASE   Under the Sherman Antitrust Act, Roosevelt's Justice Department began prosecution of the Northern Securities Company in 1901. This holding company controlled the railroad system of the Pacific Northwest. The Supreme Court upheld the prosecution in *Northern Securities* v. *United States*, 1904, and ordered the holding company to be dissolved.

THE "BEEF TRUST"   Another government antitrust action was directed against a group of meatpackers known as the "beef trust." This prosecution, too, was upheld by the Supreme Court, in *Swift & Co.* v. *United States*, 1905.

STRENGTHENING THE ICC   In 1906 Congress passed the **Hepburn Act**, strengthening the Interstate Commerce Commission (ICC). It could now set railroad shipping rates. Also, its powers were expanded to include regulation of pipelines, ferries, bridges, and terminals.

Labor Conditions

THE ANTHRACITE COAL STRIKE   In 1902, when Pennsylvania coal mine owners refused to negotiate with striking workers, Roosevelt threatened to send the army to take over the mines. The mine owners then agreed to arbitration, and the United Mine Workers, under John Mitchell, won shorter hours and higher wages.

EMPLOYERS' LIABILITY   One Progressive goal was to make employers assume more **liability**, or responsibility for their workers. The **Employers Liability Act** of 1906 provided accident insurance for workers on interstate railroads and in Washington, D.C.

WORKING HOURS   Another Progressive goal was to limit workers' hours on the job. Mixed results occurred in cases that involved conflicts between the rights of individuals and the rights of businesses.

- In *Lochner* v. *New York*, 1905, the Supreme Court ruled that a New York law limiting bakers' hours was unconstitutional because it interfered with workers' rights.

- In *Muller* v. *Oregon,* 1908, the Court let stand an Oregon law limiting women to a ten-hour work day, ruling the law justified because it protected women's health. The effect of laws like this, however, was to keep women out of better-paying jobs.

Conservation

Being a naturalist, Theodore Roosevelt was interested in protecting the nation's environment and its wilderness lands. His policies were influenced by such conservationists as **John Muir**.

The **Newlands Reclamation Act** of 1902 set aside money from the sale of public lands to build dams and irrigation systems in the West. Roosevelt placed national forests under the control of the U.S. Forest Service, headed by conservationist **Gifford Pinchot**. A total of about 150 million acres of land in Alaska and the Northwest were added to land already under the protection of the federal government.

MAKING CONNECTIONS

Enduring Issues

- The Judiciary
- Property/Economic Policy

Key Social Studies Concepts:

Environment

MAKING CONNECTIONS

Election of 1908

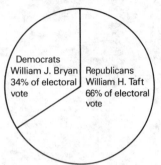

Democrats
William J. Bryan
34% of electoral
vote

Republicans
William H. Taft
66% of electoral
vote

Enduring Issues

- The Judiciary
- Property/Economic Policy

Regents Tip   Circle or "pie" graphs are particularly good at showing relations between parts and a whole. Which candidate in 1912 won the second largest share of the electoral vote?

Election of 1912

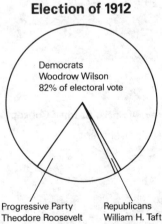

Democrats
Woodrow Wilson
82% of electoral vote

Progressive Party
Theodore Roosevelt
17% of electoral vote

Republicans
William H. Taft
1% of electoral
vote

PROGRESSIVISM IN NATIONAL GOVERNMENT: TAFT

Roosevelt had promised not to run for a third term, and was succeeded in office in 1909 by William Howard Taft. Taft began his presidency with the support of Roosevelt and the Progressive wing of the Republican party.

Reforms Under Taft

Under Taft, the Justice Department brought twice as many suits against big business as it had under Roosevelt. One of the most important cases involved the **Standard Oil Company**. In its decision in *Standard Oil Co. of New Jersey* v. *United States*, 1911, the Supreme Court ruled that the monopoly should be dissolved. But it also applied the so-called "rule of reason" to the Sherman Antitrust Act. There was a difference, said the Court, between "reasonable" and "unreasonable" business combinations. Size alone did not mean that a company was "unreasonable."

The Taft era witnessed other reforms, too. The **Mann-Elkins Act**, passed in 1910, gave the ICC the power to regulate communication by telephone and telegraph. In 1913 the **16th Amendment** was ratified, authorizing Congress to impose an income tax.

Problems for Taft

Taft was not as able a politician as Roosevelt, and he soon ran into problems. He wanted to lower the tariff, but Congress, in the **Payne-Aldrich Act** of 1909 set higher rather than lower rates. Taft angered Progressives by calling the law "the best bill that the Republican party ever passed." Taft ran into more trouble the following year. After a conflict between his Secretary of the Interior and Gifford Pinchot, Taft dismissed Pinchot—a favorite of Progressive conservationists—from the Forest Service. Such actions caused the Republican party to split into a Taft faction and a Progressive faction.

PROGRESSIVISM IN NATIONAL GOVERNMENT: WILSON

In 1912 Roosevelt challenged Taft for the Republican presidential nomination. When the nomination went to Taft, Roosevelt ran as the candidate of a third party, the **Progressive Party**. Woodrow Wilson was the Democratic candidate, and Eugene Debs ran on the Socialist ticket. Roosevelt offered what he called the **New Nationalism**, while Wilson called his program the **New Freedom**. Both were Progressive philosophies. Roosevelt, however, accepted social legislation and business regulation. The more traditional Wilson aimed for a return to competition in the marketplace with enforcement of antitrust laws. Wilson won the election of 1912, although he received only 41 percent of the popular vote. In 1916, he was reelected into office in an even closer race.

Progressive measures of the Wilson presidency fall into three main categories: financial reform, business regulation, and other reforms.

Financial Reform

In 1913 Wilson pressured Congress to pass the **Underwood Tariff Act**, which lowered the tariff for the first time since the Civil War. The law also provided for a **graduated income tax**—one that taxed larger incomes at a higher rate (6 percent) than it did lower ones (1 percent). This kind of tax, which takes a bigger share the higher the income, is known as a **progressive tax**.

Another financial reform of 1913 was the creation of the **Federal Reserve Board**. It heads a national banking system divided into 12 districts, each with a Federal Reserve bank. The federal government could now (1) issue a new, sound currency—Federal Reserve notes; (2) control the amount of money in circulation; and (3) shift money from one bank to another as needed.

Business Regulation

The **Federal Trade Commission Act** of 1914 aimed to prevent unfair competition. It created a commission to investigate such practices as false advertising and mislabeling.

The **Clayton Antitrust Act** of 1914 strengthened government's power to control business practices that threatened competition. Among other things, it prohibited companies from price fixing and from buying stocks in competing firms. The Clayton Act tried to end the practice of using antitrust laws against unions, but later Supreme Court decisions undercut this provision.

Other Reforms

* The **Adamson Act** of 1916 set an eight-hour day for workers on railroads in interstate commerce.

* The **Federal Farm Loan Act**, also passed in 1916, made low-interest loans available to farmers.

* A third 1916 bill, the **Keating-Owen Child Labor Act**, tried to outlaw child labor. But the Supreme Court ruled the law unconstitutional in the case of *Hammer* v. *Dagenhart*, 1918.

* Ratification of the **19th Amendment** in 1920 gave women the right to vote.

During World War I, American priorities shifted to the war effort, and the Progressive Era came to an end. The 1920s were a time when the trend shifted away from reform and toward acceptance of society as it was.

MAKING CONNECTIONS

Election of 1916

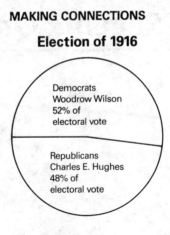

Democrats
Woodrow Wilson
52% of
electoral vote

Republicans
Charles E. Hughes
48% of
electoral vote

Enduring Issues

Change and Flexibility

Enduring Issues

* National Power
* Property/Economic Policy

Enduring Issues

* The Rights of Women
* Change and Flexibility

Regents Questions for Practice _____

Base your answers to question 1 on the quotations below and on your knowledge of social studies.

Test Hint Question 1 reviews how to deal with a "speaker" question. When answering this question, remember that Teddy Roosevelt was a *strong* President.

Quotation A: "It is the duty of the President to see that the laws of Congress are enforced. Legislative leadership should come from Congress, which is the source of national leadership."

Quotation B: "The President should be a strong leader. As the only person elected by all of the people, the President has the main responsibility to be the initiator of change."

Quotation C: "The President should have readily at hand experts from every field. As members of the Cabinet, these people should give expert advice to the President and the President should accept it."

Quotation D: "The real power of government should come from the state level. Authority should be vested with leaders who are knowledgeable about local situations."

Test Hint To answer Question 2, focus on the word "opponents" after reviewing the meaning of "imperial presidency."

1. Which quotation best reflects President Theodore Roosevelt's views of the powers of the President?
(1) A   (3) C
(2) B   (4) D

Test Hint Read these two questions about third parties. Question 3 asks you for a generalization about third parties. Question 4 also asks you for a generalization but gives you examples. You can conclude that all three of the parties named had influence. If you know about only *one* of these third parties you can answer the question.

2. Opponents of an "imperial presidency" would most likely agree with quotations.
(1) A and D   (3) B and D
(2) B and C   (4) A and B

3. "Third parties in the United States are not . . . especially important in their own right, but only in terms of their influence on the major parties."
Which is the most valid conclusion to be drawn from this quotation?

1 The contribution of third parties has been insignificant in American history.

2 The ideas of third parties have often been adopted by the two major parties.

3 Third-party leaders have often become the candidates of the major parties.

4 Third parties have failed to become important because they have been unable to develop new ideas.

MAKING CONNECTIONS

4. Which is the most valid conclusion to be drawn from a study of the role of the Populist, Progressive, and Prohibition Parties in United States history?

1 Coalition government is a practical idea for United States society.

2 Improvements for racial minorities are often initiated by third parties.

3 Third-party platforms are often important in helping to bring about change.

4 Voters are most greatly influenced by the religious beliefs they hold.

5. Which was the most characteristic of United States society at the end of the 19th century?

1 nationwide demand to grant civil rights to Southern blacks

2 a shift of emphasis in the economic system from large corporations to small businesses

3 a movement from rural, agrarian life to urban, industrial life

4 increasing involvement in political and social developments in Europe

Test Hint Note that the time period in a question often determines which answer is correct. In Question 5, "at the end of the 19th century" is the key phrase.

6. Which is the most accurate statement about the history of social reform in the United States?

1 Reform movements have often declined during times of war.

2 Most reform movements have sought to overthrow capitalism.

3 Politicians have played virtually no role in reform movements.

4 Reform movements have occurred mostly in the area of religion.

7. Jane Addams, Lillian Wald, and Jacob Riis are best known as

1 social reformers

2 leaders of industry

3 congressional leaders

4 inventors

8. Which is the main way that ethnic groups in the United States have helped to shape the national identity?

1 Most of the newer groups have blended in and adopted the ways of earlier immigrants.

2 Each group kept cultural characteristics that became part of the general culture.

3 Each group attempted to become the dominant force in society.

4 Ethnic groups made large financial contributions in support of the arts in the United States.

9. Which statement best describes a major experience of black Americans in Southern States during the period 1880–1930?
   1 They gained civil rights through a series of massive civil rights protests.
   2 They were denied civil rights as a result of changes in State laws and constitutions.
   3 They were granted more civil rights through a number of Supreme Court decisions.
   4 They were forced to return to Africa in large numbers.

10. The movement of blacks from the farms to the cities has been motivated chiefly by a desire for
    1 better economic participation
    2 better economic opportunity
    3 better housing
    4 improved educational opportunity

Base your answers to questions 11 and 12 on the speakers' statements below concerning women's rights and on your knowledge of social studies.

Speaker A: A woman's place is in the home.
Speaker B: The right to vote belongs to every qualified citizen, male or female.
Speaker C: Women are encouraged to work outside the home, but they should not expect to receive equal pay for equal work.
Speaker D: Equal educational opportunities should include equal athletic opportunities.

11. Which speaker expresses the most prevalent attitude toward women held by United States society during the 18th and 19th centuries?
    (1) A   (3) C
    (2) B   (4) D

12. Which speaker expresses one of the main objectives of the Seneca Falls Convention of 1848?
    (1) A   (3) C
    (2) B   (4) D

13. The quotation "The history of mankind is a history of repeated injuries and usurpations on the part of man toward woman" is from
    1 the Report and Resolutions of the Hartford Convention (1815)
    2 the Seneca Falls Declaration and Resolutions (1848)
    3 *The Impending Crisis* (1857)
    4 the Populist party Platform (1892)

14. Which resulted from the 19th century abolitionist and feminist movements in the United States?
    1 permanent solution of two of the most crucial problems of American society
    2 attitudes of hopelessness on the part of both groups
    3 losses in social prestige for both groups
    4 partial realization of the goals of both groups

15. The women's rights movement in the early 20th century focused its efforts primarily on securing
    1 a cabinet position for a woman
    2 reform of prisons
    3 civil rights for all minorities
    4 suffrage for women

16. Trust-busting, the suffragettes, and the Pure Food and Drug Act are associated with the
    1 New Deal
    2 Progressive Era
    3 return to "normalcy"
    4 Great Society

17. In the United States during the early part of the 20th century, reform writers helped to bring about passage of federal legislation designed to
    1 increase immigration
    2 protect the consumer
    3 encourage the growth of corporations
    4 sell public lands to private developers

18. In the United States, the term "muckraker" has been used to describe authors whose writings deal mainly with
    1 criticizing the government's social welfare policies
    2 publicizing constitutional issues relating to minorities' rights
    3 advancing the cause of socialism
    4 exposing social conditions in need of reform

19. Which action was hastened largely because public opinion was aroused by a contemporary novel?
    1 ratification of the 16th amendment
    2 establishment of the Interstate Commerce Commission
    3 passage of Social Security Act
    4 enactment of the Meat Inspection Act

20. During the late 19th and early 20th centuries in the United States, movements such as populism and progressivism suggested increased
    1 commitment by the federal government to big business
    2 public acceptance of corruption in government
    3 use of Federal Government power to correct social and economic problems
    4 effort to reduce discrimination against minority groups in public and private employment

21. The Progressives of 1900–1915 advocated
    1 an increase in the supply of money
    2 reforms extending democracy in government
    3 the laissez-faire policy
    4 government ownership of steel and textile industries

22. A basic feature of a progressive tax is that it takes into account the
    1 value of the programs on which the money will be spent
    2 amount of revenue generated by the tax
    3 costs of administering the tax collection procedures
    4 ability of people to pay the tax

23. The United States Federal Reserve System was established to
    1 serve as a source of loans for farmers
    2 solve the problems of the Great Depression
    3 balance the federal budget
    4 regulate the amount of money in circulation

Base your answers to questions 24 through 27 on the excerpt from the Progressive party platform of 1912 below and on your knowledge of United States history.

"We of the Progressive party here dedicate ourselves to the fulfillment of the duty laid upon us by our fathers to maintain the government of the people, by the people, and for the people whose foundations they laid. . . .

"To destroy this invisible government, to dissolve the unholy alliance between corrupt business and corrupt politics is the first task of the statesmanship of the day."

24. In 1912, the presidential candidate of the Progressive party was
    1 Woodrow Wilson 3 William H. Taft
    2 Eugene V. Debs   4 Theodore Roosevelt

25. The phrase "invisible government" refers to the power exerted by
    1 the President's Cabinet
    2 the Supreme Court
    3 pressure groups
    4 minority parties in Congress

26. The phrase "government of the people, by the people and for the people" has been previously stated in the
    1 Declaration of Independence
    2 Bill of Rights
    3 Preamble to the Constitution
    4 Gettysburg Address

27. The activity of the Progressive party in 1912 resulted in
    1 the election of its presidential candidate
    2 abolition of the seniority system in Congressional committees
    3 a Democratic victory
    4 the delay of Democratic reforms

2 America Reaching Out

Section 1 reviewed domestic highlights of the Progressive Era. Section 2 reviews **foreign policy**—relations between the United States and other nations—from the Civil War through the 1920s, a period that includes the Progressive Era. There are examples of three of the Enduring Issues in this section of Unit 3. As you will see, presidential power is the central issue.

BACKGROUND OF AMERICAN EXPANSION

In many ways American expansion overseas in the late 1800s and early 1900s was really a resumption of the expansionist drive that had been halted by the Civil War (1861–1865). The chart below will help you review American territorial growth up to 1867.

United States Expansion, 1803–1867

Date	Territory	How Acquired
1803	Louisiana Purchase	purchased from France
1819	Florida	occupation, followed by the treaty with Spain
1845	Texas	annexation
1846	Oregon Country	agreement with Great Britain
1848	Mexican Cession	Mexican War/treaty with Mexico
1853	Gadsden Purchase	purchase from Mexico
1867	Alaska	purchase from Russia
1867	Midway	occupation

Reasons for American Expansion

Several factors help explain United States expansion in the late 1800s.

MANIFEST DESTINY AND THE CLOSING OF THE FRONTIER As you have reviewed, American expansionists of the mid-1800s began speaking of the nation's "Manifest Destiny"—the idea that the United States was meant to spread out beyond its boundaries into both North and South America. This belief was fueled by the frontier thesis of historian Frederick Jackson Turner. In a famous essay of 1893, Turner argued that the existence of a frontier had been vital in shaping the American character. Added to Turner's thesis was another factor: in 1890 the Census Bureau had announced that the American frontier existed no longer. Some people interpreted these developments to mean that Americans needed new frontiers beyond their current borders.

SOCIAL DARWINISM   Closely tied to Manifest Destiny was the idea that the American way of life was so superior that the United States was obliged to carry its benefits to other peoples. (Few wondered whether these peoples wanted American "benefits," or recognized that this notion implied that other peoples and their ways of life were inferior.) The belief in American superiority was a form of **Social Darwinism**. In this case, the view was that, just as the law of nature results in the survival of superior people, so the same law leads to the survival of superior nations, which are meant to dominate inferior nations. Few questioned the fact that no scientific evidence supported this theory.

THE MISSIONARY SPIRIT   Another motive for expansion was the **missionary spirit**. It lay behind attempts to introduce Christianity and "civilization" to others, particularly in China where the movement was strongest. The missionary impulse did result in certain improvements, such as the building of schools and hospitals. But it also fostered a **paternalistic view**—one that saw the United States as a parent supervising weaker, less "developed" peoples. Underlying Manifest Destiny, Social Darwinism, and the missionary movement were racism, nationalism, and a strong sense of cultural superiority.

ECONOMIC FACTORS   Economics linked the domestic and foreign policy goals of the United States. Business leaders wanted raw materials from abroad. Both business leaders and farmers also wanted overseas markets; this need became especially important in the 1890s, when domestic consumption could not absorb the nation's output. At the same time, international competition increased as European nations, Japan, and the United States sought raw materials and markets.

NEW TECHNOLOGY   Technological improvements in transportation and communication shortened distances around the world at the same time that other inventions speeded industrial growth. Railroads connected factories and farms to Atlantic and Pacific ports, from which steamships carried goods to Europe, Latin America, and Asia. Communication was faster and easier thanks to the telegraph, telephone, and transatlantic cable.

MAKING CONNECTIONS

Key Ideas   As America became an industrial power in the late 19th century, it turned to overseas expansion as a means of expanding markets and providing raw materials.

American Foreign Trade, 1865–1915

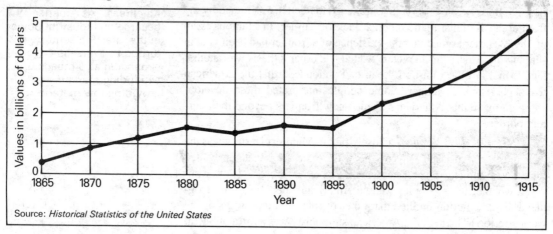

Source: *Historical Statistics of the United States*

MAKING CONNECTIONS

Regents Tip   Line graphs can help you trace trends over a period of time. What was the value of American foreign trade in 1865?

in 1900?

in 1915?

Continuing Issues   Debate goes on over whether free trade or protectionism is better for national and global economies. High costs of production in the United States often mean that foreign producers can sell their goods for less than American goods. In the 1980s the United States developed a trade deficit, meaning the value of imports exceeded the value of exports.

The U.S. navy began to expand in the 1880s, building steel-hulled warships with steam engines and the latest in weapons. Behind this growth was the urging of expansionists like Alfred T. Mahan, who argued that, as foreign trade grew, a nation needed a strong navy to protect shipping routes. The navy in turn needed bases at which to fuel.

THE ROLE OF TARIFFS   **Protective tariffs**, an expression of economic nationalism, are high taxes placed on imports in order to protect a nation's industry, agriculture, and work force from foreign competition. **Protectionism**, the practice of placing restrictions like tariffs on importers, is opposed by backers of free trade, who want low tariffs. Believers in free trade argue that protective tariffs lead to tariff wars: when tariffs rise, nations that are hurt economically raise their own tariffs in retaliation. Free trade, its supporters say, increases world trade in an era of economic interdependence. It also forces a nation's less competitive industries to improve.

• In 1890 a tariff gave American sugar cane producers an incentive that encouraged the native industry. This meant that the many American sugar plantation owners in Hawaii—at the time an independent country—could not receive as much for their crop as did sugar growers in the United States. American planters then carried out a successful revolution against the Hawaiian ruler, and Hawaii was soon annexed to the United States. This move meant that American growers in the islands could get as much for their sugar as growers on the mainland.

• The Wilson-Gorman Tariff of 1894 placed a 40 percent tax on Cuban sugar, which had previously entered the United States duty-free. Growers in Cuba lost millions because their sugar was no longer competitively priced. The result was economic chaos, which, combined with resentment of Spanish rule, set off a Cuban revolution against Spain in 1895.

THE SPANISH-AMERICAN WAR

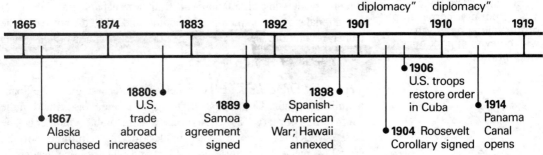

"Big stick diplomacy"   "Dollar diplomacy"

1865   1874   1883   1892   1901   1910   1919

1867
Alaska purchased

1880s
U.S. trade abroad increases

1889
Samoa agreement signed

1898
Spanish-American War; Hawaii annexed

1904 Roosevelt Corollary signed

1906
U.S. troops restore order in Cuba

1914
Panama Canal opens

As the chart on the next page makes clear, the United States added many new territories beginning in 1898. This growth made the United States a world power. Most of its territorial gains resulted from the Spanish-American War of 1898. This conflict

- led to the acquisition of many former Spanish territories that formed the basis of an American empire.

- set off a national debate among imperialists and anti-imperialists.

- led to increased American involvement in Latin America and Asia as the nation sought to protect its new lands.

Basic Causes of the War

There were several underlying causes for the war between Spain and the United States.

ECONOMIC   U.S. business interests had invested $50 million in Cuba. The Cuban revolution that broke out against Spain in 1895 endangered these investments, as well as trade.

HUMANITARIAN   Americans sympathized with the Cuban revolution and were appalled by the tactics of the Spanish military commander, Valeriano Weyler. He imprisoned hundreds of thousands of Cuban civilians in camps, where about 25 percent of them died from disease and starvation.

EXPANSIONIST   American expansionists—who included Theodore Roosevelt, Senator Henry Cabot Lodge, and Secretary of State John Hay—recognized that war offered an opportunity to seize territory from Spain, a weak nation.

Immediate Causes of the War

Added to the basic causes of the Spanish-American War were several immediate events that aroused Americans' emotions. These fed a growing **jingoism**—an aggressive, threatening patriotism—that created a warlike mood.

MAKING CONNECTIONS

Regents Tip Regents questions often deal with the causes of events. What is the difference between the *basic* and the *immediate* causes of a historical event?

YELLOW JOURNALISM   In the late 1890s, two of the most famous American publishers, **William Randolph Hearst** of the *New York World* and **Joseph Pulitzer** of the *New York Journal*, were battling for readers in a circulation war. Both newspapers printed the most sensational stories and pictures they could find about the horrors of the Cuban revolution. The stories often exaggerated and distorted events for emotional effect. This kind of sensationalism is called "**yellow journalism**."

THE DE LÔME LETTER   A personal letter written by the Spanish minister to the United States, Dupuy de Lôme, was printed in the Journal in February 1898. De Lôme's unfavorable comments—he called McKinley "weak and a bidder for the admiration of the crowd"—made it hard for the President and other political leaders to withstand demands for war.

SINKING OF THE MAINE   Less than a week after publication of the de Lôme letter, the United States battleship *Maine* exploded and sank in the harbor of Havana, Cuba, killing 266 Americans. The public blamed Spain, although a later investigation was never able to determine responsibility for the event.

The War and Its Results

In April 1898, despite Spain's agreement to an armistice with Cuba, McKinley asked Congress to declare war. Congress complied. It also approved the **Teller Amendment**, which promised that the United States would not annex Cuba.

The war lasted four months, with fighting in both the Caribbean Sea and the Pacific Ocean. The United States won an easy victory. Of the 5,000 Americans who lost their lives, fewer than 400 were killed in combat; the rest died from infection and disease. In December 1898 the **Treaty of Paris**

• granted Cuba its independence,

• gave the United States the Philippines, in return for $20 million,

• ceded Puerto Rico and Guam to the United States. (Hawaii, Samoa, and Wake Island were annexed in 1898 and 1899.)

The American Empire During the Progressive Era, 1898–1917

Date	Territory	How Acquired
1898	Hawaii	annexation after 1893 revolution
1898	Puerto Rico	gained from Spain after war
1898	Guam	gained from Spain after war
1898	Philippines	gained from Spain after war

The American Empire (cont'd.)

1899	Samoa	treaty with Great Britain
1899	Wake Island	annexation
1903	Panama Canal Zone	treaty with Panama
1917	Virgin Islands	purchase from Denmark

Acquiring an Empire

The issue of ratifying the Treaty of Paris set off a debate across the United States. As with all treaties, it had to be approved by a two-thirds vote of the Senate. The fundamental question was whether the United States should pursue **imperialism**—the policy of expanding a nation's power by foreign acquisitions.

DEBATING IMPERIALISM   Members of both political parties could be found on either side of the debate, as could Americans from all parts of the nation and all social classes. Progressives were also divided. Imperialists included Theodore Roosevelt, Senator Henry Cabot Lodge, and Alfred T. Mahan. Among the anti-imperialists were Andrew Carnegie, Mark Twain, Jane Addams, William Jennings Bryan, Booker T. Washington, and former Presidents Grover Cleveland and Benjamin Harrison. The chart summarizes the arguments of the two groups.

MAKING CONNECTIONS

Background   Imperialism is the attempt by a nation to control another, less developed nation or region economically, politically, and/or militarily. British, French, and Spanish domination of North America from the 1500s to the early 1800s is one example of imperialism.

Enduring Issues

Presidential Power

Imperialists	Anti-Imperialists
The United States needs colonies to compete economically.	Supporting an empire would be a financial burden.
To be a true world power, the United States needs colonies and naval bases.	The United States should concentrate its energies on solving problems at home.
It is the American destiny to expand, and its duty to care for poor, weak peoples.	Nonwhite people cannot be assimilated into American society.
To abandon territories makes the United States appear cowardly before the world.	An empire would involve the United States in more wars.
It is only honorable to keep land that Americans lost their lives to obtain.	It is a violation of democratic principles to annex land and not offer its people the same rights as those of U.S. citizens.

The Senate approved the Treaty of Paris by a small margin. A key factor was an uprising of Filipinos, led by **Emilio Aguinaldo**, against American rule. The bitter war ended only in 1901, with the capture of

MAKING CONNECTIONS

Key Social Studies Concepts:
Choice

Aguinaldo. Over 4,000 Americans were killed in the Philippine insurrection; 16,000 Filipinos died in combat.

GOVERNING THE TERRITORIES   The imperialist view was supported by the Supreme Court in 1901, with decisions in the **Insular Cases**. The Court ruled that people in annexed territories did not automatically have the rights of U.S. citizens. In some instances, however, the United States did try to balance what it saw as its own self-interest against the preference of people in the territories. Thus imperialism as practiced by the United States is sometimes referred to as ''hesitant colonialism.'' For example:

* Hawaii was made a territory in 1903, its first step on the way to statehood.

* In 1934 the Philippines was promised independence in ten years. This promise was delayed because of World War II, but was honored in 1946.

* The **Foraker Act** of 1900 provided for a Puerto Rican legislature elected by the people (with a governor and council appointed by the American President). Puerto Ricans received U.S. citizenship in 1917. In 1948 the island received commonwealth status.

AMERICA AS A WORLD POWER: LATIN AMERICA

Key Ideas   The overseas expansion of the United States came at the same time European nations were entering a new period of imperialism.

Having acquired an empire, the United States found itself increasingly involved around the globe as it protected both its new lands and its new status. The two regions of most concern to the United States were Latin America and Asia. Here again the operation of cause and effect is at work: (a) An expanded navy was needed to defend overseas colonies and markets in both the Western and Eastern hemispheres; (b) a canal linking the Atlantic and Pacific oceans was seen as necessary in order to move navy and commercial ships more quickly between the two oceans; (c) acquiring and then defending the Panama Canal and American possessions in the Caribbean involved the United States more deeply in affairs overseas.

The Panama Canal

As early as 1850, the United States had signed a treaty with Great Britain pledging that the two nations would jointly build a canal across the **isthmus**, or narrow piece of land, connecting North and South America. In 1901 the United States, through negotiations, gained the sole right to build and control such a canal as long as it would be open to all nations.

Under Theodore Roosevelt, the United States settled on a route across Panama (which belonged to Colombia). When Colombia

Territory Acquired by the United States, 1857–1899

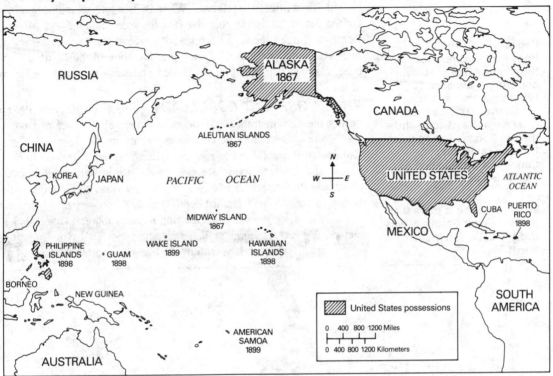

seemed reluctant to agree to financial terms, Roosevelt encouraged Panamanians to declare their independence, which they did. Americans then negotiated a treaty with the new nation of Panama, which gave the United States a strip of land six miles wide across Panama. The Panama Canal, dug across this **Panama Canal Zone**, opened to traffic in 1914. The Caribbean Sea now became a sort of ''American lake,'' because the United States controlled so much land around its borders.

Expanding the Monroe Doctrine

The Monroe Doctrine of 1823 warned foreign powers to stay out of the Western Hemisphere. For several decades, the relatively weak United States seldom referred to the doctrine. It was used, however, to support the American annexation of Texas as well as the Mexican War. It was used again, at the end of the Civil War, against France. The French had set up a puppet government in Mexico and refused to give in to American demands to withdraw. They gave in only after the United States massed troops along the Mexican border.

THE VENEZUELAN BOUNDARY DISPUTE
In 1895 the United States had an opportunity to restate and expand the Monroe Doctrine. Britain and Venezuela were involved in a quarrel over the

MAKING CONNECTIONS

Regents Tip Careful reading of maps can give insight into the United States relations with other nations.
What American territory was closest to Japan?

MAKING CONNECTIONS

Regents Tip Teddy Roosevelt was famous for the motto, "Speak softly and carry a big stick." What does the "big stick" represent in this cartoon? How does the cartoon show that, to Roosevelt and the United States, the Caribbean was viewed as an "American Lake"?

What evidence is there that the Roosevelt Corollary was used in Latin America in the 1980s?

boundary between Venezuela and British Guiana (now Guyana). The United States offered to arbitrate. When Britain refused arbitration, the United States, claiming that the British were violating the Monroe Doctrine, forced them to negotiate by threatening war. Secretary of State Richard Olney, in the Olney Interpretation of the Monroe Doctrine, claimed that "Today, the United States is practically sovereign of this continent. . . ."

THE ROOSEVELT COROLLARY Events of the early 1900s, during the administration of Theodore Roosevelt, further reinforced the Monroe Doctrine. Economic problems in Venezuela and the Dominican Republic led to threats of European intervention. In both cases, the United States stepped in to restore order. Roosevelt explained the American policy in a 1904 message to Congress. If a nation in the Western Hemisphere is guilty of consistently behaving wrongly he said, the Monroe Doctrine requires that the United States step in and act "as an international police power." This policy is known as the **Roosevelt Corollary to the Monroe Doctrine**.

A Series of Interventions

With the Monroe Doctrine as its justification, the United States intervened often in Latin American affairs in the 1900s. These actions left a heritage of distrust that persists today.

CUBA U.S. troops remained in Cuba until 1902. Cuban independence was limited by the **Platt Amendment** (1901), which remained part of the Cuban constitution until 1934. The amendment

- required that the United States approve treaties between Cuba and other nations
- gave the United States the right to lease naval bases in Cuba
- allowed the United States to intervene in Cuba to preserve order or peace (American troops were sent to Cuba twice between 1902 and 1922.)

THE USE OF ARMED FORCE The United States occupied Nicaragua with troops from 1912 until 1933. It also maintained a military occupation of Haiti (1915–1934) and the Dominican Republic (1916–1924).

ECONOMIC SUPERVISION The Dominican Republic had trouble paying its debts to European nations. When the Europeans threatened force, the United States took over Dominican finances, supervising them between 1905 and 1941.

DOLLAR DIPLOMACY President Taft favored "**dollar diplomacy**"— the federal government's encouragement of American investment overseas. Such investment tended to increase American intervention in foreign affairs.

MEXICO Early in 1913, Victoriano Huerta overthrew the president of Mexico and had him murdered. President Woodrow Wilson refused to recognize Huerta's government. He acted out of his belief in **moral diplomacy**—conducting foreign affairs in terms of judgments about right and wrong—and to protect American investments. In 1914 the U.S. Navy seized the Mexican port of Vera Cruz in order to prevent a German ship from landing its cargo of arms for Huerta. War seemed near, but Huerta resigned.

Trouble broke out again when **Pancho Villa** rebelled against the new Mexican president. Villa's 1916 border raid into New Mexico led to American deaths. Wilson sent 15,000 troops to the southwest under General John Pershing, but they failed to find Villa. Pershing's force was soon withdrawn, for world war was threatening to involve the United States.

THE GOOD NEIGHBOR POLICY Only under Herbert Hoover (1929–1933) and Franklin D. Roosevelt (1933–1945) did the United States try to improve its relations with Latin America. Roosevelt backed what came to be called the "**good neighbor policy**." This meant less emphasis on intervention and more on Pan-American cooperation. American economic dominance of the region continued, however.

MAKING CONNECTIONS

Regents Tip It is important to be aware of changes in American foreign policy.
Write a brief description of U.S. foreign policy in Latin America for each of the Presidents listed here.
Taft:

Wilson:

Franklin Roosevelt:

MAKING CONNECTIONS

THE UNITED STATES AS A WORLD POWER: ASIA

Just as acquiring an empire in the Western Hemisphere resulted in ever greater U.S. involvement in that area, acquiring Hawaii, Pacific bases, and the Philippines lead to an expanded American role in Asia.

China

The U.S. and the World
Actions by European nations in China provide another example of the renewed imperialism of the late 1800s.

American trade with China began in the 1780s through the port of Canton. By the late 1800s, however, Americans were afraid that their economic opportunities in China might be limited. Throughout the century, China had been subjected to imperialistic demands by Japan, Germany, Russia, Britain, and France. Each nation gained a **sphere of influence**—a region in which it had exclusive trade, mining, or other economic rights.

In 1899, Secretary of State John Hay tried to assure economic opportunity for the United States by asking the other powers to issue statements favoring equal trading rights for all. Although Hay received few definite replies, he went ahead and proclaimed the adoption of his program—called the **Open Door Policy**.

In 1900 antiforeign, patriotic Chinese attacked missionaries, diplomats, and other foreigners in China in what is known as the **Boxer Rebellion**. The colonial powers, including the United States, sent troops to restore order. Fearing that rival nations would take even more Chinese land, Hay expanded the Open Door Policy to mean that the "territorial integrity"—current boundaries—of China be preserved.

Japan

From 1900 to 1941, a key aim of American policy in Asia was to restrict Japanese growth and power. Japan had developed into a major economic power since 1854, the year **Commodore Matthew Perry** ended Japan's isolation by negotiating a treaty opening two Japanese ports to U.S. ships. Unlike China, Japan carried out a far-reaching modernization program making it a major economic power by 1900.

Japan displayed its growing strength by defeating Russia in the Russo-Japanese War of 1904–1905. The Japanese asked Theodore Roosevelt to mediate the peace treaty. The Americans and Japanese also arranged settlements between their two nations. One, the so-called **Gentlemen's Agreement**, restricted Japanese immigration to the United States. In 1908 the two nations also entered into the **Root-Takahira Agreement**. Both countries agreed to maintain the **status quo**—that is, to keep things as they were—in Asia. This meant upholding the Open Door Policy and supporting China's "independence and integrity."

THE UNITED STATES AND WORLD WAR I

MAKING CONNECTIONS

Regents Tip For each of these causes of World War I give an example:
Nationalism

World War I began in Europe in 1914 and lasted until 1918. The United States did not enter the war until 1917. The financial and human costs of this devastating conflict were enormous.

Causes of the War

There were several factors that led to the outbreak of war in Europe.

NATIONALISM Strong nationalistic competition had developed among France, Britain, Russia, Austria-Hungary, and Germany, especially after the unification of Germany in 1871. There was also national unrest within nations. For instance, the Czechs and Slovaks wanted to free themselves from Austro-Hungarian control.

Industrialism

IMPERIALISM Several nations were involved in keen competition for markets and colonies throughout the world.

Imperialism

THE ALLIANCE SYSTEM As national and imperial goals conflicted, two groups of nations organized against each other in an effort to maintain a **balance of power**. (1) The **Triple Alliance** consisted of Germany, Austria-Hungary, and Italy. (2) The **Triple Entente** was made up of France, Russia, and Great Britain. If fighting were to break out, members of either alliance were pledged to help each other.

Alliances

MILITARISM The early 1900s witnessed a continual buildup of armies and navies. Germany, for instance, tripled naval construction in order to challenge Britain's control of the seas.

Militarism

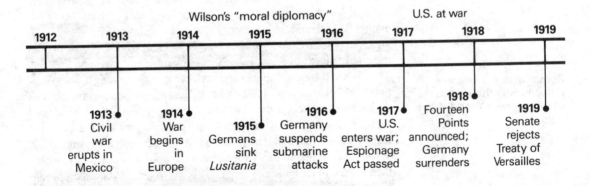

Wilson's "moral diplomacy" | U.S. at war

1912 | 1913 | 1914 | 1915 | 1916 | 1917 | 1918 | 1919

1913 Civil war erupts in Mexico

1914 War begins in Europe

1915 Germans sink *Lusitania*

1916 Germany suspends submarine attacks

1917 U.S. enters war; Espionage Act passed

1918 Fourteen Points announced; Germany surrenders

1919 Senate rejects Treaty of Versailles

Reasons for American Participation

War broke out in Europe in August 1914, after the heir to the Austro-Hungarian throne was assassinated. Because of the alliance system, most major European nations soon joined the conflict. The United States was officially neutral. In 1917, however, Americans were drawn into the war. There were several reasons for this.

MAKING CONNECTIONS

Enduring Issues

Presidential Power

Summarize Give three reasons why the United States entered World War I.

CULTURAL LINKS
Few Americans were truly neutral. Some sympathized with the **Central Powers** (dominated by Germany and Austria-Hungary)—German-Americans because of ties to Germany and Irish-Americans because of anti-British feeling. The majority of Americans, however, favored the **Allies** (the Triple Entente nations). Americans had long-standing cultural ties with Britain. They also felt loyalty to their first ally, France.

ECONOMIC TIES
United States links to the Allies were economic as well as cultural. A British blockade of the North Sea effectively ended American exports to Germany, which dropped in value from about $345 million in 1914 to $29 million in 1916. Meanwhile, the value of trade with the Allies increased sevenfold. American business and agriculture benefited from this trade, much of it financed by U.S. government loans to the Allies, totaling over $2 billion by 1917.

Most Americans did not believe that trade with or loans to the Allies violated the nation's neutrality. In fact, Wilson and his closest advisers were pro-Ally. But, even in the 1916 election for President, Wilson continued to proclaim American neutrality, campaigning on the slogan "He Kept Us Out Of War."

PROPAGANDA
Aided by their control of the transatlantic cable, the Allies conducted an effective propaganda campaign in the United States. They pictured the war as one of civilized, democratic nations against the barbaric monarchy of Germany.

GERMAN SUBMARINE WARFARE
The submarine was a new German weapon in World War I. A submarine was very vulnerable when surfaced. Thus, submarine commanders often ignored international law that required that a warship stop, identify itself, board the enemy vessel and remove its crew before sinking it. Germany's attempt to destroy the British blockade by attacking Allied ships was the single most important reason for American entrance into the war.

When a German submarine sank the British passenger liner *Lusitania* in 1915, almost 1,200 persons lost their lives, including 128 Americans. Although the ship was carrying ammunition, the United States was outraged by the attack on civilians. In 1916 the Germans torpedoed a French steamer, the *Sussex*, with injury to Americans. Wilson threatened to break diplomatic relations with Germany, which then agreed to the **Sussex Pledge**. This stated that (1) Germany would no longer sink passenger or merchant ships without warning; and (2) the Allies would no longer violate international law with their blockade. Wilson accepted the first part of the pledge but ignored the second.

EVENTS OF 1917
A series of events early in 1917 finally lead to America's entry into World War I.

- On February 1 Germany announced a policy of **unrestricted submarine warfare**. It warned it would attack without warning all vessels headed for Allied ports. The main reason for Germany's decision was that the war was at a stalemate. Germany decided to gamble that, although its move would probably bring the United States into the war, its U-boats could break the blockade and defeat the Allies before the United States could get troops to the battlefields.

- Two days later, the United States broke diplomatic relations with Germany. Tension and suspicion increased with the **Zimmermann note** of March 1. This was a message from the German foreign secretary, Arthur Zimmermann, to the German minister in Mexico. It urged a German military alliance with the Mexicans, promising them support in regaining their "lost territories" in the southwestern United States. When the message was made public, Americans reacted angrily.
- Four U.S. merchant ships were sunk by the Germans in March.
- Also in March, the Russian Revolution overthrew the czar. It appeared that more democratic forces would take control in Russia, so that if the United States went to war, it would be joining an alliance of democratic nations.

Mobilizing for War

The United States entered World War I on the side of the Allies in April 1917. The nation was poorly prepared for war, but it geared up for the conflict with patriotic enthusiasm.

THE ARMED FORCES Passage of the National Defense Act and the Navy Act, both in 1916, began the expansion of the armed forces. In May 1917 Congress passed the Selective Service Act, providing for a draft. Eventually all males between eighteen and forty-five had to register. The constitutionality of the draft was challenged but upheld by the Supreme Court.

By the end of the war, 4.8 million Americans had served in the armed forces, 2.8 million of them draftees. About 18 percent were foreign-born. Some 400,000 African-American troops served in the war. They had to serve in segregated units, and experienced other forms of discrimination as well. Many women served overseas with the Red Cross and the Salvation Army.

Over 2 million Americans served in France in a separate command, the **American Expeditionary Force**, led by General John J. Pershing. Their effort tipped the scale in favor of the Allies. The United States lost about 51,000 men.

THE ECONOMY Mobilizing the nation's economy for war led to the centralization and concentration of economic operations through a series of government agencies. Relying on the broad wartime powers of the President, Wilson used the **Council of National Defense** to oversee agencies such as these:

MAKING CONNECTIONS

Regents Tip Picture graphs show statistics in the form of pictures. Approximately how many casualties did Russia suffer in the war?

Approximately how much money did the United States spend on the war?

Costs of the War for the Allies

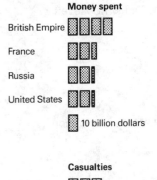

Money spent

British Empire

France

Russia

United States

![10 billion dollars] 10 billion dollars

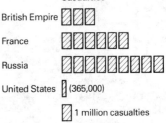

Casualties

British Empire

France

Russia

United States ⌇ (365,000)

![1 million casualties] 1 million casualties

Source: V.J. Esposito, *A Concise History of World War I*

Agency	Head	Responsibility
War Industries Board	Bernard Baruch	Decided what to produce, fixed prices, standardized products, assigned supplies
Food Administration	Herbert Hoover	Distributed food to soldiers and civilians, stimulated increased production, fixed prices
U.S. Railroad Administration	William McAdoo	Coordinated transportation facilities
National War Labor Board	Frank Walsh and William Howard Taft	Mediated labor issues to help prevent strikes

MAKING CONNECTIONS
Regents Tip For each of the following Presidents, give an example of an action that shows how much power a President can assume in wartime or in foreign affairs.

1. Teddy Roosevelt

2. Woodrow Wilson

Government control over the American economy increased vastly during World War I. For the first time, the government entered such fields as housing and labor relations. It also supervised various public utilities, including the telephone and telegraph.

World War I was financed by higher taxes, raised through the 1917 War Revenue Act, and by four Liberty Bond drives.

THE LABOR FORCE About 16 percent of male workers went into the military, so other groups took their place.

- Women went to work in some male-dominated fields, such as munitions factories. Most, however, worked in traditionally female jobs, for which there was an increased demand. Only about 5 percent of the women entering the wartime work force were new to work outside the home. At war's end, with the return of male workers, women were expected to quit their jobs. Between 1910 and 1920, only 500,000 more women were added to the work force.

- African Americans in great numbers moved from the South to the North (where most factories were located). This so-called "**great migration**," which lasted into the 1940s, brought 300,000 blacks north between 1910 and 1920. Although they were usually able to improve their economic situation, they were still faced with discrimination

The number of strikes dropped sharply during World War I, mainly because the Wilson government supported collective bargaining in return for a no-strike pledge. Membership in the American Federation of Labor grew by almost a million, and wages for war industry employees rose sharply.

WILSON'S MORAL DIPLOMACY To Wilson, World War I was a crusade. The Allies were fighting the "war to end all wars," a war "to make the world safe for democracy." These idealistic goals helped make Wilson the Allies' moral leader. They also helped mobilize the American people to support the first conflict the United States had ever fought outside the Western Hemisphere.

A propaganda campaign organized by the **Committee on Public Information** encouraged patriotism. Songs, posters, and pamphlets attacked Germany, urged the purchase of Liberty Bonds, and publicized conservation of resources. Patriotism was accompanied by an outbreak of anti-German hysteria. Americans burned German books, banned the teaching of German in some schools, and renamed sauerkraut "liberty cabbage."

WARTIME CONSTITUTIONAL ISSUES This social climate led to actions that compromised civil rights, usually in the name of national security. The **Espionage Act of 1917** made it a crime to interfere with the draft and allowed the postmaster general to bar "treasonous" materials from the mail. The **Sedition Act of 1918** made it a crime to speak or publish anything "disloyal, profane . . . or abusive" about the government, Constitution, flag, or military services of the United States.

Under these acts, the government prosecuted over 2,000 Americans and sent 1,500 to jail. Pacifists, socialists, and others seen as extremists suffered the most. **Eugene V. Debs**, the socialist presidential candidate in 1916, was sentenced to 10 years in prison for an antiwar speech. A special target was the **Industrial Workers of the World** (IWW), a radical union active in the West. Its leaders were arrested, its strikes broken up, and many of its members interned.

The Supreme Court ruled that free speech could be restricted in wartime in *Schenck* v. *United States*, 1919. In a unanimous decision, Justice Oliver Wendell Holmes wrote, "Free speech would not protect a man falsely shouting fire in a theater and causing panic. . ." Holmes went on to say that Congress has the right to prevent words that would cause "a clear and present danger." That same year, the Court upheld the Sedition Act.

WILSON AND THE TREATY OF VERSAILLES

World War I ended with an Allied victory in November 1918. President Wilson played a major role in the peacemaking process. He had first suggested his own peace proposals in January 1918. These **Fourteen Points** included the following:

- Open, not secret, diplomacy
- Freedom of the seas
- Removal of trade barriers

MAKING CONNECTIONS

Enduring Issues

Civil Liberties

Key Ideas Although the amount of opposition has varied from war to war, there has been opposition to every war in which the United States has fought.

MAKING CONNECTIONS

- Arms reduction
- Self-determination of peoples—that is, letting various national groups determine their own territorial boundaries
- An "association of nations" to guarantee political independence and territorial integrity

Key Social Studies Concepts:

Power

The Versailles Conference

The Fourteen Points became the basis for the peace negotiations held at Versailles, France, beginning in January 1919. Wilson led the American delegation, thus becoming the first American President to leave U.S. soil while in office. Other Allied leaders included Georges Clemenceau of France, David Lloyd George of Britain, and Vittorio Orlando of Italy.

European nations that had suffered far more than the United States were cool to Wilson's plans. They wanted to be repaid for some of their losses and some had made secret wartime deals involving territorial changes and money settlements that contradicted provisions of the Fourteen Points.

The most important agreement reached at Versailles was the treaty with Germany, the **Treaty of Versailles**. According to its provisions, Germany had to (1) accept complete responsibility for causing the war; (2) pay huge reparations to the Allies; (3) give up its military forces; (4) cede lands to the new nations of Poland and Czechoslovakia; and (5) give up its overseas colonies.

Wilson opposed many of the settlements of the Versailles Treaty and treaties with the other Central Powers. But the President was willing to compromise because the treaties provided for a new world organization, the **League of Nations**. The League, Wilson believed, would correct any problems caused by the peace treaties.

U.S. Rejection of the Treaty

The U.S. Senate had to approve the Versailles Treaty, and there Wilson ran into a great deal of opposition.

- Wilson had angered Republicans by excluding them from the American delegation to the Versailles Conference. Yet Republicans had a majority of seats in the Senate. The chairman of its foreign relations committee, Henry Cabot Lodge, distrusted and disliked Wilson. The feeling was mutual.
- Some features of the League of Nations worried Americans. They feared, for instance, that the United States might be obligated to furnish troops to defend member nations.

Key Ideas In periods of war, civil liberties have been limited because they are seen as less important than national security. How was this an issue in the Civil War as well as World War I?

- Wilson stubbornly refused to allow any but the most minor changes in the Treaty of Versailles.
- When Wilson went on a speaking tour to gain popular support for the treaty, he collapsed and then suffered a stroke. His illness thereafter prevented him from playing an active role.

The Senate voted several times on the Treaty of Versailles, but always defeated it. The United States made a separate peace with the Central Powers, and it never did join the League. Fundamentally, the nation had voted to retain its traditional foreign policy of preferring nonintervention and of acting alone when it did choose to play a role.

x

MAKING CONNECTIONS

Regents Tip Maps can be arranged in pairs to show changes over time. What nations were gone from the map of Europe by the end of the war?

Europe During the War

Europe After the War

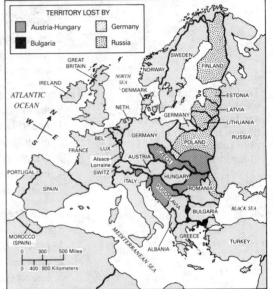

Regents Questions for Practice ___

Review the Test-Taking Strategies section of this book. Then answer the following questions, drawn from actual Regents examinations. Circle the *number* of the word or expression that best completes the statement or answers the question. Write your answers to essay questions on a separate piece of paper. Hints on good ways to approach these questions are provided in the margins.

MAKING CONNECTIONS

Test Hint Questions 1 and 2 deal in different ways with the causes of American expansion in the late 1800s.

1. In the late 1800s, which reason led the United States to give greater attention to the world beyond its borders?
   1 fear of revolution in Latin America
   2 fear of Russian expansion in Alaska
   3 interest in finding places to settle surplus population
   4 interest in obtaining markets for surplus goods

MAKING CONNECTIONS

2. Which pair of terms represent two major causes of imperialism in the 19th century?
1 industrialism and communism
2 communism and fascism
3 nationalism and industrialism
4 collectivism and missionary zeal

3. During the late 19th century, some United States newspapers printed exaggerated accounts of Spanish cruelty in Cuba. These reports helped to bring about the Spanish-American War primarily by
1 arousing public opinion against Spain
2 provoking the anger of the business community
3 alienating the Spanish government
4 encouraging the formation of Spanish revolutionary groups

Test Hint   Since both treaties were similar, if you are familiar with the terms of one treaty you should be able to answer the question.

4. The peace treaties ending the Mexican War of 1846 and the Spanish-American War of 1898 were similar in that both
1 ceded land to the United States
2 created a mutual defense pact
3 addressed the question of neutrality rights on the high seas
4 established a strong union of friendship between the countries involved in the treaty

5. A direct result of the Spanish-American War was that the United States
1 purchased the Virgin Islands
2 annexed Cuba
3 leased islands off the coast of Nicaragua
4 acquired areas in the Pacific and West Indies

Test Hint   Underline key words or phrases in each speaker's statement. For practice in summarizing, write a single word in the margin next to each statement that explains from what point of view the speaker is approaching the subject. For example, "military," "economic," "political," etc.

Speakers A, B, C, D, and E are discussing the Philippine Islands. Base your answers to questions 6 through 8 on their statements and on your knowledge of social studies.

Speaker A: "These poor, uncivilized, unchristianized people need our assistance if they are to be uplifted from their ignorance to a point at least approaching our level of civilization and accomplishment. The Philippines must be ours."

Speaker B: "These islands would certainly make excellent coaling stations for our great naval fleet which is growing each year as Congress approves additional funds for the construction of new ships."

Speaker C: "The shipping interests really find the Philippines to be excellent trading centers. Furthermore, they can be used to develop our commerce with China and Japan. We can use the islands as stopover and storage points for our merchant fleets."

Speaker D: "We have no alternative but to accept the Philippines as our own. God would not forgive us if we rejected his obvious faith and trust in our nation. Democracy must be carried to the four corners of the globe."

Speaker E: "Were our economic rivals to obtain the Philippines, it would be a commercial disaster for our nation. We entered the race late, but we must not fall behind now."

---

6. Each statement made by the speakers could be used to justify
   1 imperialism   3 coexistence
   2 containment   4 genocide

7. Which speaker's views are most in accord with an economic interpretation of history?
   (1) A   (3) C
   (2) B   (4) E

8. Speaker A's views are most similar to those of Speaker
   (1) E   (3) C
   (2) B   (4) D

9. Which statement reflects a foreign policy view held by both President James Monroe and President Theodore Roosevelt?
   1 Revolutionary movements in western Europe must be opposed.
   2 Close economic ties with Asia must be maintained.
   3 Noninvolvement in world affairs is the wisest policy for the United States.
   4 United States influence in Latin America must be accepted by other countries.

10. Which was a corollary to the original Monroe Doctrine?
   1 The Western Hemisphere is closed to further colonization.
   2 The United States may intervene in Latin America.
   3 The United States will not intervene in the affairs of Europe.
   4 The United States will respect European colonies already established in the New World.

11. In the late 19th and early 20th centuries, United States intervention in Latin America was motivated mainly by the United States desire to
   1 suppress Latin American movements for national independence
   2 reduce the influence of communism
   3 ensure the safety of its growing investments in the area
   4 counteract Spain's economic domination of the area

12. The early 20th-century policy of dollar diplomacy indicated a United States desire to
   1 institute the dollar as an international currency
   2 give generous amounts of foreign aid to less developed countries
   3 interact with foreign countries in ways profitable to United States corporations
   4 give trade preferences to nations that follow a capitalist system

13. A primary aim of the United States Open Door Policy was to
   1 encourage the Chinese to emigrate to other nations
   2 prevent European powers from dividing up China
   3 develop China's industrial capacity
   4 introduce democratic government into China

14. A cause basic to our entry into World War I was also basic to our entry into the
   1 Revolutionary War
   2 War of 1812
   3 Mexican War
   4 Civil War

15. President Woodrow Wilson's ideals were best represented in the Treaty of Versailles in its provisions calling for the
1 division of German colonies among the Allies
2 acceptance by Germany of full responsibility for World War I
3 establishment of a general association of the world's nations
4 payment of reparations to the Allies by Germany

16. "Why, by interweaving our destiny with that of any part of Europe, entangle our peace and prosperity in the toils of European ambition, rivalship, interest, humor or caprice?" Which action by the United States best reflects the philosophy expressed in this quotation?

1 passage of legislation restricting immigration
2 rejection of the Treaty of Versailles
3 enactment of the Lend-Lease Act
4 approval of the United Nations Charter

17. The United States Senate rejected United States membership in the League of Nations after World War I mainly because its Senate opponents
1 feared that membership would infringe upon United States national sovereignty
2 believed that membership would end United States participation in military alliances
3 did not wish to give financial aid to an international organization
4 were more concerned about the domestic problems created by the Great Depression

Essay Questions

Following are essay questions about the Unit that you have been reviewing. Before answering each, apply the lessons you have learned in the Test-Taking Strategies by blocking each essay. The first block has been organized for you to help you get started with the pre-writing that is so necessary in preparing a good Regents essay answer.

1. The United States has experienced periodic outbursts of reform. Some of these major reforms are listed below.

Civil service reform
Antitrust movement
Women's suffrage
Protection of the consumer
Temperance movement

Choose *three* reform movements from the list and for *each* one chosen:
• Discuss conditions that led to the need for reform
• Describe tactics used by supporters of the reform movement
• Discuss the extent to which the reform movement was successful in achieving its goals   [5, 5, 5]

Reform movement	Conditions that led to need for reform	Tactics of reformers	Success of movement
1. Women's suffrage	Women wanted the right to vote; women were working outside the home and were better educated.	protest marches, speeches, demonstrations	eventually very successful with passage of 19th amendment [5]
2.			[5]
3.			[5]

2. Reform movements have affected different aspects of United States society. Some of these aspects are:

Public education
Family life
Working Conditions
Equal Opportunity
Participation in government
Public welfare

Choose *three* aspects of United States society listed above. For *each* aspect chosen, describe a reform movement which affected that aspect of life and discuss the conditions which the reform movement was attempting to change [You must use a different reform movement for each aspect.]   [5, 5, 5]

3. Leadership is an essential ingredient for the success of any movement in history. Listed below are leaders paired with the movements they led.

Leaders/Movements
John C. Calhoun/ States rights
Elizabeth Cady Stanton/Women's rights
Frederick Douglass/Abolitionism
Samuel Gompers/Organized labor
William Jennings Bryan/Populism
Theodore Roosevelt/Progressivism
Eleanor Roosevelt/Human rights
Martin Luther King, Jr./Civil rights
Ralph Nader/Consumerism

Select *three* of the pairs listed above. For *each* pair selected, evaluate the success of the leader and movement by discussing
* The role of the leader in the movement
* Tactics used by the government
* The effect of the leader and the movement on United States history   [5, 5, 5]

4. Throughout history minority groups have experienced discrimination. At various times minority groups have been
* Unfairly taxed
* Forced to abandon their culture
* Denied an education
* Forced to live in certain areas
* Denied political and legal rights
* Imprisoned and/or exterminated

Select *three* of the methods of discrimination listed above. For *each* method chosen, describe a specific example of its use during any time period at any place in the world *and* discuss a significant effect of this form of discrimination on the minority group selected. Use a different minority group for each method of discrimination chosen.   [5, 5, 5]

5. In history, certain books and essays have had a significant impact on American society. Some of these works are:

Books and Essays
Thomas Paine—"Common Sense"
Adam Smith—*Wealth of Nations*
Harriet Beecher Stowe—*Uncle Tom's Cabin*
Upton Sinclair—*The Jungle*
Martin Luther King, Jr.—*Letters from the Birmingham Jail*
Betty Friedan—*The Feminine Mystique*

Choose *three* of the works listed above. For *each* one chosen
* Describe a main idea of the work
* Discuss the impact of the work on society   [5, 5, 5]

6. Some historians view the history of United States foreign policy as a sequence consisting of the stages listed below.

Time Period/Stage
1776–1823/Protecting National Independence
1824–1897/Fulfilling Manifest Destiny
1898–1918/Entering the World Scene
1919–1940/Limiting International Involvement
1941 to present/Accepting World Leadership

Choose *three* of the time periods listed above. For *each* one chosen, identify a specific United States foreign policy development. Explain how this development was consistent with the foreign policy stage of that time period and show how this development reflected a domestic need of the United States at the time.[5, 5, 5]

7. At various times, the foreign policy of the United States has been changed in response to new conditions. Below are listed several past United States foreign policies.

Foreign Policies
Monroe Doctrine (1823)
Open Door Policy (1899–1900)
Refusal to join the League of Nations (1919)
Nonrecognition of the Soviet Union (1917–1933)
Truman Doctrine (1947)
Nonrecognition of the People's Republic of China (1949–1978)

a Select *three* of the foreign policies listed above and for *each* one chosen, describe conditions that led the United States to adopt the policy. [9]

b For *two* of the policies selected in answer to a, describe specific circumstances that brought about a modification in that policy. [6]

8. Presidential decisions have had an important effect on the United States and the world. Listed below are headlines representing important presidential decisions.

Headlines
''McKinley Asks for War with Spain''
''Wilson Proposes the Fourteen Points''
''Truman Orders Dropping of Bomb on Hiroshima''
''Kennedy Orders Blockade of Cuba''
''Johnson Increases Military Forces in Vietnam''
''Carter Signs Camp David Accords with Sadat and Begin''

Select *three* of the decisions above. For *each* one selected, describe the circumstances which led to the decision and discuss two major results of that decision. [5, 5, 5]

UNIT 4

At Home and Abroad: Prosperity and Depression, 1917–1940

In Unit 3 you reviewed how Americans reacted to change, both in the United States and overseas, during the Progressive Era (1900–1920). In this unit you will review the major events of the twenty years after the Progressive period. During these two decades, the United States completed the transition to a modern, urban, industrial nation. The Enduring Constitutional Issue of Civil Liberties: The Balance Between Government and the Individual is an especially important one for the 1920s.

At the end of that decade, the nation plunged into a severe economic depression. President Franklin D. Roosevelt's New Deal programs in the 1930s attempted to overcome the effects of this Great Depression. Roosevelt and his programs are heavily tested on Regents examinations. Be alert to the Enduring Issue of National Power: Limits and Potentials, particularly as it relates to the federal government's power over economy, while you read the section on the Great Depression.

You will need to know the answers to the following questions in order to pass the Regents examination:

Section 1: What tensions developed between traditional rural culture and the new, urban-based values in the 1920s?

Section 2: What were the causes of the Great Depression and how did that event affect the American people and their institutions?

SECTION 1 — The Twenties

The 1920s were a time of many changes in the United States, especially in economic and social aspects of the nation's life.

MAKING CONNECTIONS

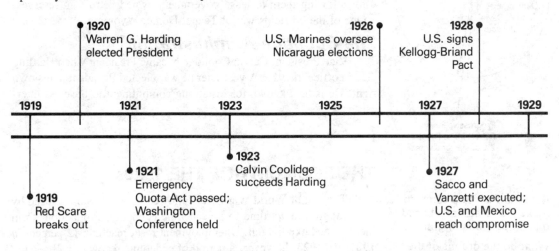

1920
Warren G. Harding elected President

1926
U.S. Marines oversee Nicaragua elections

1928
U.S. signs Kellogg-Briand Pact

1919   1921   1923   1925   1927   1929

1919
Red Scare breaks out

1921
Emergency Quota Act passed; Washington Conference held

1923
Calvin Coolidge succeeds Harding

1927
Sacco and Vanzetti executed; U.S. and Mexico reach compromise

THE POLITICS OF THE 1920s

The 1920 landslide election of Warren G. Harding and Calvin Coolidge represented a desire of many Americans to remove themselves from the pressures of world politics and the idealistic goals of the Progressives. Disillusioned, many Americans wanted to return to the traditional foreign policy of isolationism and to a less hectic social and political life for our nation. Harding responded to this national mood when he said that "America's present need . . . is normalcy."

The Harding Administration

Harding was an Ohio newspaper publisher, who had little experience or interest in politics. To his credit, he (a) pardoned socialist Eugene Debs, serving a prison term for opposing the war, and (b) supported antilynching legislation. Personally, Harding was an honest man. He appointed some talented, dedicated people to office, including Charles Evans Hughes as Secretary of State. But the President also

Election of 1920

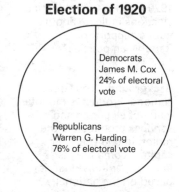

Democrats
James M. Cox
24% of electoral vote

Republicans
Warren G. Harding
76% of electoral vote

Regents Tip Examination questions sometimes ask you to make interpretations based on data in graphs.

How does this pie graph support the statement that the election of 1920 was a landslide?

MAKING CONNECTIONS

Election of 1924

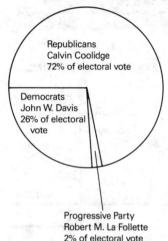

Republicans
Calvin Coolidge
72% of electoral vote

Democrats
John W. Davis
26% of electoral
vote

Progressive Party
Robert M. La Follette
2% of electoral vote

Regents Tip   You can also make interpretations based on comparisons of graphs.

What do the graphs of the 1920 and 1924 presidential elections indicate about public support for Republican policies?

Background   The Gross National Product is the total value of all goods and services produced in the nation in one year. Per capita income means income per individual; it is based on the national income divided by the population.

gave political jobs to members of the so-called **Ohio Gang**, corrupt associates who took advantage of him. After Harding's death in 1923, the public learned of several scandals during his administration. These included:

• Theft in the Veterans Bureau. Its head, who sold hospital supplies for his own profit, was imprisoned and fined.

• Fraud by the Alien Property Custodian. He was imprisoned for selling former German property for private profit.

• The **Teapot Dome Scandal**. Secretary of the Interior Albert Fall was convicted of accepting bribes from two oil executives in exchange for allowing them to lease government-owned petroleum reserves. One of the oil fields was at Teapot Dome, Wyoming.

The Coolidge Administration

Vice President Calvin Coolidge became President when Harding died in office in 1923. A year later he was elected President in his own right. He is best known for his strong commitment to business interests.

THE ECONOMY OF THE 1920s

The end of World War I was followed by a recession, caused by the shift from a wartime to a peacetime economy. Production, farm income, and exports fell. Unemployment rose, reaching 12 percent in 1921. By 1923, however, a period of economic recovery had begun.

Coolidge Prosperity

Coolidge retained the financier Andrew Mellon as Secretary of the Treasury. Mellon continued to act on the philosophy that government's role was to serve business.

The years between 1923 and 1929 were seen as a time of booming business. The Gross National Product (GNP) rose 40 percent. Per capita income went up 30 percent. Since there was little inflation, actual purchasing power, and therefore the standard of living, also increased. Yet when the stock market crashed in 1929 people questioned this "Coolidge prosperity."

Were the 1920s a Time of Business Boom or False Prosperity?

In order to answer that question, let us look at various aspects of the economy.

GOVERNMENT ECONOMIC POLICIES   The government's major economic policies helped only certain groups and often hurt the economy in the long term. Some groups, especially big corporations and the wealthy, benefited greatly from Coolidge prosperity.

- Businesses and the most wealthy were helped by tax laws which reduced personal income tax rates, particularly for upper income groups, removed most excise taxes, and lowered corporate income taxes.

- Reducing the national debt and balancing the budget were carried out by raising tariffs and demanding repayment of war debts.

- Tariff rates were raised in a return to protectionism. While Republicans argued that higher tariffs would limit foreign imports, thus helping both industry and agriculture, the actual effect was to weaken the world economy.

- Regulatory agencies such as the Federal Reserve Board, the Federal Trade Commission, and the Interstate Commerce Commission were staffed with people who saw their role as helping business rather than regulating it.

- A relaxed attitude toward corporate mergers was supported by the executive branch and by the Supreme Court, which continued to apply the 1911 "rule of reason." By 1929 about 1,300 corporations produced three-fourths of all American manufactured goods, and 200 companies owned half the nation's wealth.

GROUPS LEFT OUT Coolidge prosperity was not for everyone. Important segments of the population failed to share in the general rise in living standards:

LABOR Strikes in the steel, mining, and railroad industries failed. These failures were due in part to the government's use of troops and to **injunctions**, court orders that prohibit specified actions. The Supreme Court also ruled against child labor laws and against minimum wages for women and children.

Membership in labor unions fell from a high of about 5 million in 1921 to under 3.5 million in 1929. Unemployment remained at about 7 percent throughout the 1920s. In general, real wages for workers increased only slightly during this period.

FARMERS The only farmers to benefit from Coolidge prosperity were those involved in large commercial operations. Small farmers were hurt by a combination of factors.

- Farmers expanded production during World War I in response to rising prices and the demand for food. They added to their acreage and bought more farm machinery.

- New machinery and new farm techniques increased the farmers' yield per acre.

- After the war, when European farms began producing again, American farmers were growing too much. With overproduction, the prices of both farm products and farm land decreased dramatically. Farm income fell, and many farmers lost their land when they could not meet their mortgage payments.

MAKING CONNECTIONS

MAKING CONNECTIONS

Net farm income fell 50 percent during the 1920s. As a result, the number of farmers declined, too. By 1930 only about 20 percent of the labor force made a living by farming.

FLAWS IN THE STOCK MARKET   There were flaws in the structure of the great stock market boom of the 1920s as well. In large part, stocks were traded **on margin**. This meant that buyers could purchase stocks by making only small down payments in cash—sometimes as low as 5 percent of the value of the stocks. They borrowed the rest from brokers, and counted on their profits to repay the loans.

FOREIGN POLICY

In 1914 the United States was a **debtor nation**, meaning that it owed more money to foreign nations than they owed to the United States. In the 1920s the United States became the world's leading **creditor nation**, meaning that other countries owed more to the United States than it owed them. The nation was also the world's leading industrial producer, exporter, and financier. These changes were due in large part to money from the payment of war debts owed this nation by the former Allies.

The United States and Its Possessions, 1920

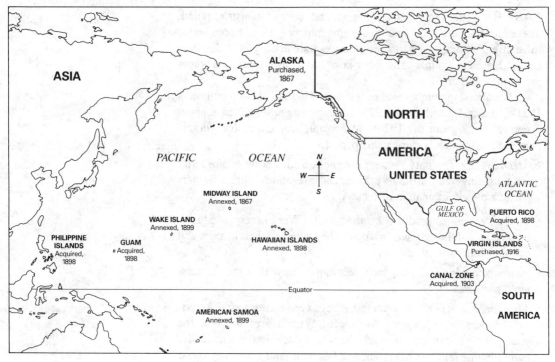

The War Debt Controversy

During World War I, as you reviewed in Unit 3, the European Allies borrowed a great deal of money from the United States in order to buy war supplies from American manufacturers. After the war, these debts became a source of conflict. European nations argued that their debts should be canceled because, while the United States had contributed money, Europe had paid a heavy price in lives. But the United States insisted on repayment.

A factor that made repayment difficult was U.S. protectionist policy. High American tariffs limited European trade with the United States, and thus reduced earnings that might have been used to pay off war debts. These tariffs also led to retaliation by 26 nations which raised their own tariff rates.

One step aimed at making repayment easier was the **Dawes Plan**, adopted in 1924. Under this plan, the United States lent funds to Germany so that it could make war reparations—money payments it owed to the European Allies. The Allies would in turn use the funds to make payments on the war debts they owed the United States.

The Search for Peace and Arms Control

Although the United States failed to join the League of Nations, it was still concerned with keeping the peace.

- In 1921 President Harding hosted the **Washington Naval Conference**. The United States, Britain, France, Italy, and Japan agreed to set limits on the number of warships each nation could build. They also pledged to keep the peace in Asia and to protect the independence of China. The conference, however, failed to establish any means of enforcement.

- In 1928, 15 nations met in Paris to sign the **Kellogg-Briand Pact**, which outlawed war except in self-defense. Enforcement provisions were missing from the pact which 60 nations eventually signed.

THE ROARING TWENTIES

The name "Roaring Twenties" refers to the struggle with social change in the United States as it became an urban, industrial nation. Changes in lifestyle, values, morals, and manners increased tension and conflict. The nation turned inward. Wealth, possessions, having fun, and sexual freedom influenced by Sigmund Freud's psychology were the new values.

Technology

Technology, combined with new marketing strategies, best explains the transformation of American society in the 1920s. Led by Henry Ford and the automobile industry, **mass production** with its moving **assembly line** resulted in uniform products produced at lower

MAKING CONNECTIONS

Regents Tip
Understanding the workings of cause and effect is an important part of Regents exams.

Higher U.S. tariffs =
Fewer foreign goods sold =
Less foreign money available =
1. Fewer U.S. goods sold
2. Fewer payments to U.S. for war debts
3. Higher foreign tariffs in retaliation

U.S. loans $ to Germany

Germany pays reparations to Allies

Allies pay war debts to U.S.

THE ROARING TWENTIES—a time of change. "To roar" means to make a loud noise or to cry out in excitement or pain. How does this definition reflect both the excitement and the tension of the 1920s?

MAKING CONNECTIONS

costs. It made possible a consumer-oriented economy, one in which more goods were available to more Americans.

The new technology also made American culture more uniform. Americans from one coast to the other tended to use the same products, wear the same styles, see the same movies, and listen to the same music. Regional and class differences were blurred, and individualism became less important than conformity.

New Industries and Their Effects on American Life

Background In the 1920s
- 15 million cars were sold
- 80 percent were bought on credit
- a Model T Ford cost $290 in 1920
- 20 percent of U.S. homes had electricity by the end of the 1920s
- 10 million families owned radios by 1929

The Automobile Industry:

1. stimulated steel, rubber, paint, glass, and oil industries
2. set off a real-estate boom in suburbs
3. led to an increase in highways and a decline in railroad construction and use
4. caused tractors to replace horses on farms
5. increased social equality as low prices made cars available to Americans at almost all income levels
6. stimulated installment buying
7. contributed to growing sophistication of advertising techniques

The Electrical Industry:

1. changed homes, businesses, and cities through electric lights
2. helped double business productivity through electric power
3. transformed life and leisure with electric-powered durable goods such as washing machines, stoves, vacuum cleaners, refrigerators, and irons
4. stimulated installment buying

Radio and Motion Pictures:

1. helped erase regional differences and homogenize American culture
2. increased people's expectations, often unrealistically
3. helped end rural isolation
4. helped popularize ragtime and jazz
5. provided an outlet for advertising
6. increased interest in politics and spectator sports

Urban-Suburban Growth

Background In 1900 there were 52 metropolitan centers of at least 100,000 people; by 1930 there were 30 such centers.

With more than half the population living in places with populations over 2,500, America in the 1920s was, for the first time in its history, an **urban** rather than a **rural** nation. Only the depression ended the building boom that was part of this growth. **Suburbs** grew even faster than cities. These new suburban political units drew people from the cities. The ultimate result was the present day conflict between urban and suburban needs, priorities, and values.

Shifting Cultural Values

The Roaring Twenties saw a revolution in American lifestyle. With a shorter work week and with more paid vacation, Americans had more leisure time in which to pursue pleasure.

LEISURE   Movies such as **The Ten Commandments** and the first talking picture, **The Jazz Singer**, drew 100 million people a week to theaters. Americans idolized movie stars like Charlie Chaplin. They also admired such sports figures as Babe Ruth and Red Grange.

Popular Heroes of the Twenties

Aviation	Charles Lindbergh, first solo flight across Atlantic
Baseball	George Herman (''Babe'') Ruth
Boxing	Jack Dempsey, Gene Tunney
Football	Harold (''Red'') Grange
Golf	Bobby Jones
Jazz	Louis Armstrong, Duke Ellington, Bessie Smith
Movies	Clara Bow, Theda Bara, Charlie Chaplin, Gloria Swanson, Rudolf Valentino
Swimming	Gertrude Ederle, first woman to swim English Channel
Tennis	William (''Big Bill'') Tilden

Americans eager for a good time enjoyed jazz and blues, styles created in the South by black musicians but soon carried all over the country and abroad. This distinctively American music—to which people danced such daring new steps as the Charleston—became so popular that the period of the twenties is often called the **Jazz Age**. The twenties were also a time when fads swept the country. These included bridge, crossword puzzles, and the board game of mah-jongg.

LITERATURE   The conflict created by changing American values saw expression in literature as well as in music and the movies. American writers of the twenties created many enduring works of literature. Several writers protested the effects of technology and mass consumption. They criticized the business mentality, the conformity of the times, and Americans' preoccupation with material things. Some, called **expatriates**, even left the United States to settle in Europe.

MAKING CONNECTIONS

Leading Writers of the Twenties

T.S. Eliot	poet	*The Waste Land*
William Faulkner	novelist	*The Sound and the Fury*
F. Scott Fitzgerald	novelist	*The Great Gatsby*
Ernest Hemingway	novelist	*A Farewell to Arms*
Langston Hughes	poet, novelist	*The Weary Blues*
Sinclair Lewis	novelist	*Main Street, Babbitt*
H.L. Mencken	journalist	*Prejudices, The American Language*
Eugene O'Neill	playwright	*Desire Under the Elms*
Ezra Pound	poet	*Cantos*
Edith Wharton	novelist	*The Age of Innocence*

Regents Tip Many Regents questions are based on your understanding of quotations on key topics. "We younger Negro artists who create now intend to express our individual dark-skinned selves without fear or shame. . . . We build our temples for tomorrow, strong as we know how, and we stand on top of the mountain, free within ourselves." Langston Hughes, *The Big Sea*

How does this quotation express the ideas of the Harlem Renaissance?

HARLEM RENAISSANCE One of the most important cultural movements of the 1920s was the **Harlem Renaissance**. It was led by a group of black writers, artists, musicians, and dancers in the New York City neighborhood of Harlem. These creative intellectual figures—mainly well-educated members of the middle class—felt alienated from the society of the twenties. In their works they called for action against bigotry and expressed pride in black culture and black identity. Outstanding figures of the Harlem Renaissance included W. E. B. Du Bois, Langston Hughes, and Alain Locke. Their works attracted renewed interest during the civil rights movement of the 1960s.

Women's Changing Roles

The conflict between modern and traditional values, so much a part of the twenties, is particularly clear when the contradictory roles of women are examined.

THE WORKFORCE Women lost many job opportunities when World War I ended in 1918. Even so, the number of women in the work force increased throughout the 1920s. By 1930, 10.5 million women were working outside the home. They made up 22 percent of the work force; this figure, however, represented an increase of only 1.4 percent of the total work force.

The influence of tradition can be seen in many aspects of women's working lives. Most working women were single, widowed, or divorced. While more married women worked than ever before, most Americans still believed that married women belonged at home, and that is where 90 percent of them were to be found. When working women married, they usually quit or were dismissed from their jobs.

Most women who did work continued to hold jobs in traditionally female—and traditionally low-paying, low-status, and low-mobility—occupations such as teaching, clerical work, and retail sales. Fewer than 20 percent worked in better-paying factory jobs. The number of female doctors and scientists actually decreased, at a time when almost a third of graduate degrees were earned by women.

One important gain for working women was the creation in 1920 of the **Women's Bureau**, part of the Department of Labor. It tried to improve conditions by working inside the government for women workers, and also provided data about them.

POLITICS In 1920 women voted in a national election for the first time. But their vote had little effect on the outcome. Women did not vote in large numbers, nor did they vote as a bloc. To encourage women to play a larger part in politics, the National American Woman Suffrage Association reorganized itself as the nonpartisan **League of Women Voters**.

The divisions of the 1920s were reflected in the fate of two different pieces of legislation. Encouraged by women reformers, Congress passed the **Sheppard-Towner Act** in 1921. With the aim of reducing infant mortality rates, the law provided for public health centers where women could learn about nutrition and health care. The program came to an end in 1929, largely because of opposition from physicians. An **Equal Rights Amendment** to the Constitution, proposed in 1923, led to bitter disagreement among women. Many feminists supported it. But others opposed it because they believed it would do away with special laws protecting women workers.

DAILY LIFE The "new woman" of the 1920s was the **flapper**—young and pretty, with bobbed hair and short skirts. She drank, she smoked, she was independent-minded, and she took advantage of women's new freedom. Economic, political, and social limits still restricted even flappers, however, and the image itself meant little to farm and factory workers, to minorities, and to the poor.

In some ways, technology made life easier in the 1920s. With electric washing machines, vacuum cleaners, stoves, and refrigerators, household chores did not require so much time, and there was less need for servants. On the other hand, the typical homemaker now had to handle almost all the household tasks.

Families changed during this period. There was a freer sexual climate, so that both divorce and family planning became more acceptable. Family size decreased; only 20 percent of women who married during the 1920s had five or more children. The family, which in earlier times had been a producing unit—growing and processing much of its food—was now a consuming unit. Marketing and advertising appeals flooded the media, appealing to consumers to buy more goods.

MAKING CONNECTIONS

Regents Tip In spite of changes, women's roles in society were still limited. To help you understand this point, list one example of a limit on women in the 1920s for each of the areas listed below.

1. Social:

2. Political:

3. Economic:

MAKING CONNECTIONS

Enduring Issues

Civil Liberties

Continuing Issues
Remember that fear of foreigners has been an issue that has arisen at many times throughout the nation's history.
1840s   Nativism and the Know-Nothings
1917–1918   Suppression of dissent during World War I
1920s   "Red Scare"; the Ku Klux Klan; the Sacco-Vanzetti case
1940s   Internment of Japanese Americans during World War II
1950s   Second "Red Scare" (McCarthyism)

CONSTITUTIONAL AND LEGAL ISSUES

Major constitutional and legal issues divided Americans in the 1920s. Many of them reflected the struggle between modern and traditional values. They also showed how international affairs affected domestic policies.

The Red Scare

As you read in Unit 3, the government took drastic steps during World War I to suppress dissent. Stern measures continued through 1919 and into 1920 in a crusade against internal enemies known as the **Red Scare**. Some Communists were affected, although they made up only one-half of 1 percent of the population. However, the crackdown targeted many other Americans viewed as "un-American," among them socialists, anarchists, labor leaders, and foreigners.

The crusade was led by U.S. Attorney General **A. Mitchell Palmer**. It was sparked by several events that took place after the war ended. There were race riots in over 25 cities. A series of strikes climaxed with a walkout by Boston police. Several unexplained bombings added to the hysteria. All these events were seen as part of a Communist conspiracy.

The Attorney General ordered the first so-called **Palmer raids** late in 1919. In 33 cities, police (without warrants) raided the headquarters of Communist and other dissident organizations. Eventually they arrested 4,000 people, holding them without charges and denying them legal counsel. Some 560 aliens were deported. Palmer's extreme actions and statements soon turned the public against him. But the Red Scare had lingering effects, discouraging many Americans from speaking their minds freely in open debate.

SACCO AND VANZETTI   Closely linked to the Red Scare was the fate of **Nicola Sacco** and **Bartolomeo Vanzetti**. These two Italian immigrants, admitted anarchists, were convicted of murder in 1921 in connection with a Massachusetts robbery. Many people questioned the evidence against Sacco and Vanzetti, concluding that the two men were convicted more for their beliefs and their Italian origin than for a crime. In spite of mass demonstrations and appeals, the two men were executed in 1927. In 1977, 50 years later, the Massachusetts governor cleared the two men.

THE KU KLUX KLAN   Anti-foreign attitudes encouraged a revival of the Ku Klux Klan. The first organization, active during the Reconstruction period, had died out in the late 1800s. A reorganized Klan, formed in 1915, grew slowly until 1920. In that year, it added 100,000 members. The KKK of the 1920s was not only anti-black but also anti-Catholic, anti-Semitic, and anti-foreign. The Klan stood for "100 percent Americanism," which meant that the only true Americans were white, Protestant, and American-born.

Restricting Immigration

The nativism expressed in the Red Scare, the Sacco-Vanzetti case, and the new KKK was also evident in new immigration legislation. As you read in Unit 2, the "new immigrants" of the late 1800s and early 1900s were seen by many as "different" and somehow threatening to American values. This bias led to the **Immigration Act of 1924**, with its system of **national quotas**. The law not only limited the total number of immigrants, but also set quotas for each country. These were calculated on the basis of the foreign-born population of the United States in 1890. Since the totals for eastern and southern Europe at that time were still low, the quotas were, too. The 1924 immigration act also excluded all immigration from Asia.

Prohibition

Both the rebirth of the Klan and the movement to restrict immigration reflected the struggle in the 1920s between what some saw as old, rural American values and the new values of a changing urban, industrialized culture. However, the clash between these two sets of values did not divide on the basis of where one lived.

For example, the movement for **Prohibition** was not confined to rural America, though it received much support there. The 18th Amendment, allowing Prohibition, became part of the Constitution in 1919.

Congress passed the **Volstead Act** in 1920 to implement Prohibition, but the law turned out to be unenforceable. The majority of Americans were simply unwilling to accept a total ban on alcohol. In 1933, the 21st Amendment ending Prohibition was ratified.

The Scopes Trial

A trial held in Dayton, Tennessee, in 1925 received nationwide attention because it pitted the scientific ideas of Darwinian evolution against the Protestant fundamentalist view of biblical creationism. John Scopes, a biology teacher, had deliberately violated a state law forbidding anyone to teach the theory of evolution. Scopes was represented by a famous trial lawyer, **Clarence Darrow**. The prosecution relied on the assistance of **William Jennings Bryan**, three-time presidential candidate and a firm believer in fundamentalist Christianity. Although Scopes was convicted, Bryan's confused testimony weakened fundamentalist arguments.

MAKING CONNECTIONS

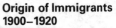

Immigration to the United States 1900–1940

Origin of Immigrants 1900–1920

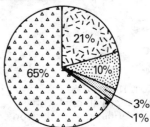

21%

65%

10%

3%

1%

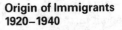

Origin of Immigrants 1920–1940

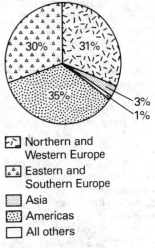

30%

31%

35%

3%

1%

Northern and Western Europe

Eastern and Southern Europe

Asia

Americas

All others

Source: *Historical Statistics of the United States*

Regents Tip Comparing graphs is an important skill.

From what area do you see the biggest percentage change in immigration between the two time periods shown on the graphs?

Regents Questions for Practice _____

Review the Test-Taking Strategies section of this book. Then answer the following questions, drawn from actual Regents examinations. Circle the *number* of the word or expression that best completes the statement or answers the question. Hints on good ways to approach these questions are provided in the margins.

Test Hints   The first five questions all deal with similarities or comparisons. Questions 1 and 2 compare time periods. If you only know about farmers in *one* of the time periods mentioned in question 1, you should still be able to answer the question.

In question 2 the words "most similar" indicate that you must know something about *both* time periods.

Question 3 asks about time periods without giving specific dates—the 1920s and 1970s.

Question 4 compares two presidencies. You should be able to answer the question based on knowledge of just one of these presidencies.

Question 5 asks you to find a *similarity* in *reactions to* a law of the 1850s and one of the 1920s.

1. Which was a major problem faced by United States farmers in both the 1890s and 1920s?
   1 lagging technology
   2 lack of tariff protection
   3 overproduction of basic staples
   4 inflationary currency

2. In which respect were the decades of the 1920s and the 1960s in the United States most similar?
   1 organized militancy by ethnic minorities
   2 public concern with pollution of the environment
   3 widespread government activity dealing with social issues
   4 significant changes in manners and morals

3. Which statement describes United States reaction after both World War I and the Vietnam conflict?
   1 The United States turned to a policy of global intervention.
   2 Many Americans turned inward and tried to ignore events in other parts of the world.
   3 The United States paid large indemnities to its wartime enemies.
   4 Congress quickly voted funds to expand the military.

4. Which is most commonly associated with the presidencies of Ulysses S. Grant and Warren G. Harding?
   1 depression in business
   2 corruption of public officials
   3 humanitarian reforms
   4 territorial expansion

5. In the United States, the widespread disregard of the fugitive slave laws and of Prohibition laws most clearly indicated that
   1 strongly held values are difficult to regulate
   2 the federal government is generally unable to enforce its own laws
   3 little respect is given to the legal system
   4 the judicial system is too lenient in its treatment of offenders

6. In the "return to normalcy" following World War I in the United   **MAKING CONNECTIONS**
States, a policy of the government was to
1 return the railroads to private ownership
2 prosecute monopolies
3 encourage the growth of labor unions
4 enact a low tariff policy

7. During the decade 1920–1930, Congress and the President
approved important laws providing for
1 conservation of natural resources
2 increases in tariff rates
3 regulation of the sale of stocks and bonds
4 guaranteed prices for farm products

8. The desire of the United States in the 1920s to isolate itself from
direct involvement in European conflicts is best illustrated by its
1 participation in disarmament conferences
2 efforts to solve the reparations problem
3 rejection of the principle of international organization
4 lowering of tariff barriers

9. The greatest contribution of the United
States to world peace during the period
between World War I and World War II was
1 support of the League of Nations
2 support of the disarmament movement
3 membership in the World Court
4 adoption of free trade

10. Which is the most valid generalization to be
drawn from the study of Prohibition in the
United States?
1 Social attitudes can make laws difficult
to enforce.
2 Increased taxes affect consumer
spending.
3 Morality can be legislated successfully.
4 People will sacrifice willingly for the
common good.

11. The enactment of Prohibition in the United
States during the 1920s and the laws against
the polygamy practice by the early
Mormons both involved attempts to legislate
1 public morality
2 political responsibility
3 civil rights
4 cultural assimilation

12. One indication of the changing role of the
family as a social institution is the fact that
today
1 families are less mobile than they were
in the early 1900s
2 the family operated as an important unit
in keeping the society economically
stable
3 other institutions share responsibility for
many functions that traditionally were
assumed by the family
4 the family usually acts as a closely knit
social unit and a powerful political
force

13. The income of which group declined
throughout the 1920s?
1 automobile workers   3 stockholders
2 communication workers 4 farmers

14. Since the 1920s, which has been the most
persistent problem confronting United
States farmers?
1 deteriorating roads and waterways
2 decreasing government price supports
3 rising production costs and decreasing
income
4 proliferating pests and diseases

The Great Depression

The end of the prosperity of the 1920s was marked by the **Great Stock Market Crash** of fall 1929. Remember that this stock market had grown on speculation by people who bought on margin and in fact owned only a small portion of their stocks. Many could not meet margin calls or demands to put up the money to cover their loans. The result was panic selling. On October 29 ("Black Tuesday") alone, stock prices fell $14 billion. They dropped lower and lower in the weeks that followed.

Some Economic Changes Between 1928 and 1932
(Figures in millions unless otherwise noted.)

	1928	1929	1930	1931	1932
A. United States exports (merchandise)	$5,030	$5,157	$3,781	$2,378	$1,576
B. Spending for new housing	$4,195	$3,040	$1,570	$1,320	$485
C. Farm spending for lime and fertilizer	$318	$300	$297	$202	$118
D. Federal spending	$2,933	$3,127	$3,320	$3,578	$4,659
E. Cash receipts from farming	$10,991	$11,312	$9,055	$6,331	$4,748
F. Lumber production (billions of board ft.)	36.8	38.7	29.4	20	13.5
G. Unemployment (in thousands)	2,080	1,550	4,340	8,020	12,060
H. Average weekly earnings of production workers in manufacturing (actual dollars)	$24.97	$25.03	$23.25	$20.87	$17.05

The crash triggered the start of the **Great Depression**. It broke the public's feelings of optimism and confidence in the nation and its future that had been so much a part of the lifestyle of the 1920s. It exposed the fact that under the confidence and optimism that had led to speculation and mass consumption, the national economy was weak. If the economy had been stronger, it is doubtful that the nation would have slid from a mild **recession** deeper and deeper into the worst **depression** in its history.

CAUSES OF THE GREAT DEPRESSION

The Great Depression was caused by a variety of factors.

Weaknesses in the Overall Economy

Weaknesses in the economy had existed before 1929 and were expanding.

- Farming had been depressed throughout the 1920s with a worldwide drop in prices.
- There was unemployment in the railroad, coal, and textile industries well before 1929.
- Speculation in real estate and the building boom that was part of it had eroded while automobile sales had slowed.
- As early as the summer of 1929, the economy showed signs of underconsumption as inventories of goods grew due to slower customer demand.

Unequal Distribution of Income

One of the factors contributing to underconsumption and the overall weakness of the economy was unequal distribution of wealth.

- In the 1920s, some 40 percent of all families had an income under $1,500, which put them below the poverty line. At the same time, America's 24,000 richest families had a total income three times as large as the total income of the six million poorest families. In short, while 1 percent of the population owned 59 percent of the nation's wealth, 87 percent of the population owned only 10 percent.
- As a result, the economy was very dependent on the spending of a very small portion of the population. These wealthy people spent their money on luxury goods and on investments. This type of spending was very much affected by the stock market crash.
- The wealthy, not the great mass of the population, had benefited from increased output per worker in the face of stable salaries. Production costs had dropped and profits had risen with increased output, but the workers could not buy what they produced. As a result, demand dropped. As the economy weakened, this nonpurchasing group grew in size and became less and less able to buy even the necessities of life.

Weak Corporate Structure

The crash set off the collapse of the nation's business structure.

- The business consolidations of the 1920s resulted in a few large companies in each industry. Holding companies controlled the stock of

MAKING CONNECTIONS

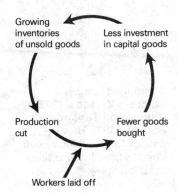

Causes of Great Depression

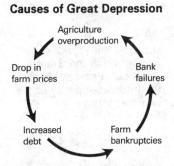

Vocabulary:
UNDERCONSUMPTION or OVERPRODUCTION means that people buy fewer goods than are produced, *i.e.*, supply is greater than demand.

MAKING CONNECTIONS

many different corporations. They depended on the earnings of the various companies they held.

- This was a very fragile system because when one company collapsed it affected, in a domino fashion, the rest of the holding company.

Weak Banking Structure

The weakness of the nation's banking structure was shown by the failures of over 7,000 banks in the 1920s.

Weak International Economy

The international economy depended heavily on that of the United States.

Continuing Issues
Compare Wilson's 1913 Underwood Tariff to Hoover's 1930 Hawley-Smoot Tariff, which raised rates to their highest level in U.S. history.

- Foreign nations owed the United States money that they could repay only by the United States buying foreign goods and making foreign investments and loans. But high American tariffs kept foreign goods out of this nation and led to high foreign tariffs. Meanwhile, Americans invested at home in businesses or in the stock market rather than abroad.

- When the economy weakened, foreign nations bought even less from this country and defaulted on loans. At the same time, the United States made fewer foreign investments and had less money to lend. The international nature of the banking system can be seen by the fact that banks in both Europe and the United States failed as a result of defaults on loans.

U.S. and the World   The way in which the Great Depression spread shows the interdependence of the world economy.

Government Policies

Actions by the federal government contributed to the depression.

- Stock market speculation was unregulated by the government.
- Tax policies that favored the wealthy resulted in even more uneven distribution of income.
- The consolidation of corporations was not challenged under antitrust laws.
- The Federal Reserve Board allowed the low discount (interest to member banks) rate that led to stock speculation and raised rates in 1931, just when spending would have helped the economy.

Enduring Issues

Property/Economic Policy

HOOVER'S RESPONSE TO THE GREAT DEPRESSION, 1929–1933

Background   Hoover campaigned on the slogan, "A chicken in every pot and a car in every garage."

Herbert Hoover was the President who first had to deal with the increasingly deeper depression in the United States. Hoover had taken office in 1929, after having served as Coolidge's Secretary of Commerce. An engineer by training, Hoover was a good businessperson, self-made millionaire, and humanitarian. During and after World War I, he had an international reputation as the leader of the relief effort to aid starving people and to help Europe recover economically.

Hoover's Actions to Halt the Depression

In order to improve economic conditions, Hoover took the following actions:

- Tried to restore confidence in the American economy with such statements as, "Prosperity is just around the corner."

- Altered his view that government should not become directly involved in the economy. He promoted programs that aided businesses on the grounds that as businesses recovered the economic benefits would "trickle down" to the people.

- Organized the Reconstruction Finance Corporation (1932) to lend money to railroads, mortgage and insurance companies, and banks on the verge of bankruptcy.

- Set a precedent for Franklin Roosevelt's New Deal with his use of federal works projects in order to create jobs and stimulate the economy.

- Worked for voluntary agreements from businesses not to lower wages or prices. But as companies increasingly faced collapse, they often could not honor these promises.

- Halted payment of war debts by European nations.

MAKING CONNECTIONS
Election of 1928

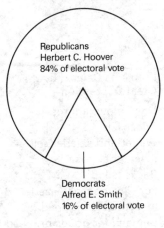

Republicans
Herbert C. Hoover
84% of electoral vote

Democrats
Alfred E. Smith
16% of electoral vote

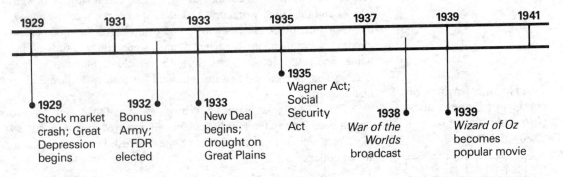

| 1929 | 1931 | 1933 | 1935 | 1937 | 1939 | 1941 |

1929
Stock market crash; Great Depression begins

1932
Bonus Army; FDR elected

1933
New Deal begins; drought on Great Plains

1935
Wagner Act; Social Security Act

1938
War of the Worlds broadcast

1939
Wizard of Oz becomes popular movie

Failure of Hoover's Program

Despite these efforts, Hoover's refusal to provide direct relief damaged his image as the nation's leader. Also damaging was his insistence, in the face of worsening conditions, that the economy was improving.

In the summer of 1932, thousands of unemployed World War I veterans and their families set up camps in Washington, D.C., to demand early payment of the bonus due to them for their war service. When the bill was defeated by Congress, most of the Bonus Expeditionary Force, or **Bonus Army**, refused to leave town. Hoover insisted that the veterans were influenced by Communists and other agitators. He called out the United States Army under Chief of Staff Douglas MacArthur to break up the Bonus Army's camps and disperse the veterans. The pictures showing tanks and tear gas being used against veterans undermined what little popularity Hoover had left.

Regents Tip The following slogans are associated with the Presidents of the 1920s. What does each phrase tell you about that President's political philosophy?

Harding: "Return to normalcy"

Coolidge: "The business of America is business."

Hoover: "Rugged individualism"

Problems Caused by the Great Depression

Unemployment rose
Prices fell
Wages and salaries fell
Inventories rose
Banks failed
Foreclosures increased
Investments dropped
Demand for goods dropped
Supplies increased
Exports declined
Construction dropped
Production fell

The Human Impact of the Great Depression: Unemployment, 1920–1932

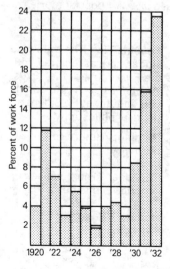

Herbert Hoover took many steps to use the power of the federal government to stop the growing depression. In the end, his efforts were still too little. Historians still debate whether he should be praised for the efforts he did make or condemned for not going far enough.

Hoover's ability to act was limited by his beliefs. He had great faith in the American economic system, insisting that the forces of the market would eventually set the economy right again. He stood for the Puritan work ethic—the idea that one will be rewarded for hard work. He also believed in voluntary rather than governmental action to solve problems of society. He believed in self-help and therefore opposed direct relief, or the "dole," on the grounds that it would destroy people's "rugged individualism."

THE HUMAN IMPACT OF THE GREAT DEPRESSION

The human toll of the collapse of the American economy with 12 million people, or 25 percent of the labor force, unemployed by 1932 was seen in soup lines and bread lines. Even these relief efforts by organizations like the Red Cross had to be limited as the voluntary contributions that supported them slowed down. As banks failed, people lost their savings; as companies failed, they lost their jobs as well. Blacks and unskilled workers were the first to experience unemployment. In 1931 black unemployment was estimated as 30 to 60 percent greater than white unemployment. Women were criticized for working while men could not find jobs. In truth, female occupations such as nursing and clerical work were less hard hit than male positions in manufacturing.

Family life was disrupted. Women at home looked for ways to stretch what money the family had. Families moved in with relatives. Marriages were postponed. The birth rate dropped. Fewer were able to attend college.

Life in the Cities

As more Americans lost their homes, "**Hoovervilles**" grew in the cities. These were sites of shacks lacking heating or water, often made of crates, in which the homeless lived. These homeless slept under old newspapers called "Hoover blankets." Others slept in city parks. People selling apples and shoelaces on the street became a common sight. Malnutrition increased as did death from starvation. There were more cases of diseases such as tuberculosis and typhoid as well as an increase in the suicide rate. Parents starved themselves to give what food they had to their children.

Life in the Country

With more people unable to even buy food, farmers found that their already depressed income dropped by one-half. Farm foreclosure sales grew in number. The farmers' desperate situation only grew worse in the 1930s with a drought in the Great Plains. Parts of Texas, Oklahoma, Kansas, Colorado, and New Mexico suffered from year after year of drought, which resulted in the loss of the topsoil through dust storms. The **Dust Bowl**'s effect created a group of migrant farmers called "Okies" who moved to California in search of work. Their sufferings were made famous in John Steinbeck's novel, *The Grapes of Wrath*.

The Culture of the Great Depression

The Great Depression dominated every aspect of life in the 1930s. Therefore, it is understandable that the conditions it created are mirrored in the popular culture of that decade. In the 1930s people sought inexpensive and escapist leisure activities. Spectator sports remained popular, but fewer people could afford to attend. Instead, they played miniature golf or softball, pinball machines, the new board game *Monopoly*, or they read comic books. *Dick Tracy* was one of the popular comic strips of the decade. About one-third of the nation's movie theaters closed during the depression, but each week between 60 and 90 million people turned out to see films like *King Kong*, *Gone With the Wind*, *The Wizard of Oz*, the latest cowboy adventure, serials, musicals, or Walt Disney cartoons. It cost nothing to listen to the radio, which offered the comedy of George Burns and Gracie Allen or Jack Benny, as well as soap operas and serials.

The literature, photography, and paintings of the 1930s all reflected the concerns of the times. The photographs of Walker Evans and Margaret Bourke-White revealed the suffering of the people. Bourke-White's work appeared in the new *Life* magazine, which for decades depicted American life in pictures until television took over that role. Paintings were often of ordinary people. Some novels such as those of John Dos Passos or John Steinbeck protested life of the 1930s. Other works, such as those of William Faulkner, were less political. Music of the 1930s continued to be dominated by jazz and jazz greats such as Louis Armstrong and Duke Ellington. It was also the age of swing (big) bands such as those of Glenn Miller and Benny Goodman. The musical became a popular form of theater with music by greats such as George Gershwin, Irving Berlin, Cole Porter, and Jerome Kern.

FRANKLIN DELANO ROOSEVELT AND THE NEW DEAL

"I pledge you, I pledge myself, to a new deal for the American people."

The election of 1932 brought to office Franklin Delano Roosevelt, the 32nd President (1933–1945). He was educated at Harvard University and the School of Law at Columbia University. He served as a Democrat in the New York State Legislature, as Assistant

MAKING CONNECTIONS

Regents Tip   Be prepared to compare different time periods when taking a Regents examination. How were the cultures of the 1920s and 1930s similar, and how were they different?

Election of 1932

Democrats
Franklin D. Roosevelt
89% of electoral vote

Republicans
Herbert C. Hoover
11% of electoral vote

MAKING CONNECTIONS

Regents Tip Note that cartoons can express different attitudes on the same subject.

Which cartoonist supports FDR and which disagrees with him?

What opinion of the President does each cartoon express?

A   Old Reliable

Source: Berryman, Graff Collection Apr 12, 1938

B   "Yes, You Remember Me"

Source: Batchelor, 1936 Library of Congress

Background In his 1933 inaugural address, Franklin D. Roosevelt announced, "The only thing we have to fear is fear itself."

Secretary of the Navy under Wilson, and as Governor of New York before being elected President.

Roosevelt as a Political Leader

Franklin Roosevelt was a leader. He inspired support and confidence in people. He is ranked by historians as one of our greatest Presidents.

Roosevelt was a master politician. He was intelligent, energetic, self-confident, charming, and optimistic. He had been tested by a victory over infantile paralysis that left him crippled but tougher, more patient, and more compassionate.

He was also a master communicator. He held press conferences and used the radio for "fireside chats" with the American public. He involved the public emotionally in his explanations of what he was doing to solve the nation's economic problems. He was able to convince people that he had confidence in himself and in our nation as well as genuine concern for the people.

As is true of all strong leaders, Franklin Roosevelt was a controversial President. While many respected and even loved him, others saw him as taking on almost dictatorial powers for himself and for the government. His attempt to make major changes in the Supreme Court is one example of controversy in his administration.

Another is his decision to break the so-called unwritten Constitution and run for a third term in 1940. Roosevelt ran for and was elected to a fourth term in 1944. He died in office in 1945. In 1951 the 22nd Amendment was added to the Constitution, limiting a President to two terms in office. Some saw it as a reaction against Franklin Roosevelt.

Preparing to Lead the Nation

In the months between his election and his inauguration, Roosevelt surrounded himself with a group of formal and informal advisers. The formal advisers, or Cabinet members, included Postmaster James Farley, Secretary of State Cordell Hull, and the first woman to hold a Cabinet post, Frances Perkins, as Secretary of Labor. The informal advisers, who became known as the "Brain Trust," were a group of intellectuals and lawyers, several of whom were Columbia University professors. They favored reform and strongly influenced Roosevelt's New Deal administration. The most well-known "Brain Trust" member was social worker Harry Hopkins.

Another major influence on Franklin Roosevelt and his New Deal was his wife, Eleanor Roosevelt. She was a humanitarian, active on behalf of women and minorities, especially African Americans. She helped to mold New Deal policy through active intervention with her husband on behalf of social reform, through her syndicated newspaper column, and through her travels and speeches around the nation. Through her travels, she served as his eyes and ears. After Franklin

Roosevelt's death in 1945, Eleanor Roosevelt became a leader in the issue of human rights, playing a key role in the creation of the United Nations Declaration on Human Rights (1948).

MAKING CONNECTIONS

FDR's New York State Model for Dealing with the Depression

Franklin Roosevelt's terms as Governor of New York helped him to gain experience dealing with the depression in that state and offered insights into his political philosophy. New York's handling of the depression is often called the "Little New Deal." Under FDR, New York was the first state to provide public money for relief for those who were unemployed through the Temporary Emergency Relief Administration (1931). Roosevelt also created jobs through publicly financed reforestation and land reclamation projects. An old-age pension law was passed that became a model for social security. Leading figures in Roosevelt's New Deal gained experience working with FDR in New York.

New York's cities also responded to the crisis. Rochester created jobs for the unemployed. New York City mayor, Fiorello LaGuardia (1934–1945), the "Little Flower," introduced health insurance programs for city workers and worked to create jobs through major subway, bridge, and housing construction projects, often financed by the federal government.

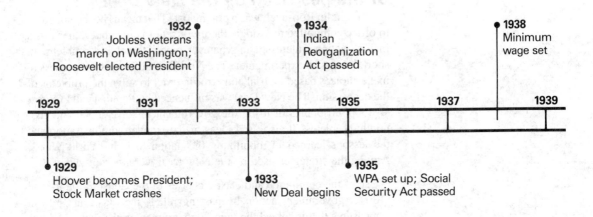

1932 Jobless veterans march on Washington; Roosevelt elected President

1934 Indian Reorganization Act passed

1938 Minimum wage set

1929   1931   1933   1935   1937   1939

1929 Hoover becomes President; Stock Market crashes

1933 New Deal begins

1935 WPA set up; Social Security Act passed

THE NEW DEAL IN ACTION

The New Deal programs had the following goals:

RELIEF for those people who were suffering.
RECOVERY for the economy so that it could grow again.
REFORM measures in order to insure against future depressions.

Stages of the New Deal

1. 1933–early 1935: New Deal legislation dealt with relief and recovery. Much of this legislation was passed in the "First Hundred Days" after FDR took office in March 1933. The 1934 Congressional elections increased the size of the Democratic majority in each house, which helped the New Deal legislative effort.

2. 1935 and early 1936: Often called the "Second Hundred Days" or the "Second New Deal," this period's legislation focused more on social reform.

3. 1936 election: This year is considered the high point of the New Deal.

4. 1937–1938: A setback, or recession, led to a new collapse in the weak economy that had just been starting to improve. The recession was due in part to New Deal cutbacks in spending after the 1936 election.

5. 1938: By 1938 the New Deal had ended due to increased opposition in Congress and preoccupation with the danger of world war. Unemployment did not improve significantly until World War II created jobs in the production of war goods.

Strategies Used by the New Deal

Franklin Roosevelt was a pragmatist. That means he did not come to office committed to a single theory or set of beliefs but rather was a man of action, interested in whatever works to solve a problem. In short, he was an experimenter. The New Deal shows his willingness to make choices based on trial and error in order to solve the problems of the depression. The New Deal was influenced by Populist and Progressive's philosophies of using the government to solve social and economic problems. It also used ideas of the Hoover administration and the lessons learned in mobilizing the nation to fight World War I. Among the strategies used by the New Deal were the following:

• Use of the commerce and elastic clauses of the Constitution to take direct government action by passing relief, recovery, and reform measures that involved the federal government in the nation's economy to a greater degree than at any time in the past.

• Taking fiscal action to stimulate the economy and lower unemployment by lowering taxes and increasing government spending.

• Assuming responsibility for the general welfare by protecting people against risks that they could not handle on their own.

• Increasing the regulatory role of the federal government over banks, businesses, and the stock exchange.

- After the 1936 recession, **deficit spending** was adopted as an economic means of reviving the economy. As stated by the economist John Maynard Keynes, only by spending huge amounts of money would production levels grow and purchasing power increase, thereby bringing a nation out of a depression.

MAKING CONNECTIONS

Regents Tip In what year was the budget deficit the largest?

Federal Income and Spending, 1928–1940

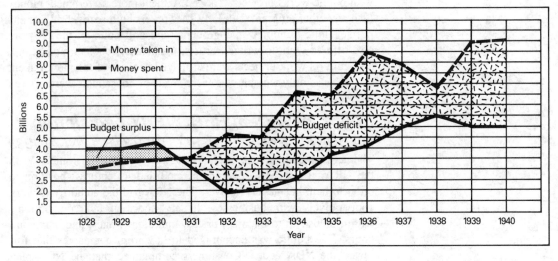

Major New Deal Relief Legislation

EMERGENCY BANKING ACT 1933 Roosevelt's first act as President was to close the nation's banks by declaring a bank "holiday" in order to stop the collapse of the national banking system. The time was used to assure the public through a fireside chat that it could have confidence in the reopened banks. The law provided for examination of banks to insure that only sound banks were operating.

FEDERAL EMERGENCY RELIEF ACT (FERA) 1933 Between 1933 and 1935, one-half million dollars was provided for distribution by states and cities for direct relief and work projects for the hungry, homeless unemployed.

PUBLIC WORKS ADMINISTRATION (PWA) 1933 Operating from 1933–1939, the PWA had two objectives. First, it provided jobs through construction projects that included bridges, low-cost housing, hospitals, schools, and aircraft carriers. Secondly, its aim was to get government money into the economy. It was hoped that this **"pump-priming"** would create jobs, revive production, and lead to more consumer spending.

Enduring Issues

National Power

Background Many agencies were created to carry out New Deal laws. Identified by their various initials—FERA, PWA—they were sometimes called the "Alphabet Agencies."

CIVILIAN CONSERVATION CORPS (CCC) 1933

Between 1933 and 1941, the CCC provided work conserving natural resources for 2.5 million young men ages 18–25. Only 8,000 young women joined the CCC.

WORKS PROGRESS ADMINISTRATION (WPA) 1935

In the years from 1935 to 1943, the WPA provided temporary jobs for 25 percent of adult Americans. It was created to replace direct relief with public works projects. The WPA spent more government money than any other program. While WPA workers built roads, bridges, airports, public buildings, playgrounds, and golf courses, the program also offered work to writers, artists, musicians, scholars, and actors. The cultural work projects were criticized because of the money spent and because only women who were heads of households were offered WPA jobs.

Major New Deal RECOVERY Legislation

NATIONAL INDUSTRIAL RECOVERY ACT (NRA) 1933

The act created the NRA or National Recovery Administration. With the NRA, the federal government modified its antitrust position in order to help businesses recover. The NRA had the authority to work cooperatively with businesses. It set "codes of fair competition" within industries to maintain prices, minimum wages, and maximum hours. The public was encouraged to buy from companies that followed the NRA codes. Consumers complained that the NRA plan raised prices. Companies opposed the provisions giving unions the right to organize. Small companies felt at a disadvantage to larger companies. Even before it was declared unconstitutional in 1935, the NRA was unpopular.

HOME OWNERS LOAN CORPORATION (HOLC) 1933

This agency was created to help home owners save their houses from foreclosure by providing funds to pay off mortgages and financing new long-term mortgages at lower fixed interest rates.

FEDERAL HOUSING ADMINISTRATION (FHA) 1934

The FHA was created by the National Housing Act to insure bank mortgages. These mortgages were often for 20–30 years and at down payments of only 10 percent.

Enduring Issues

Property/Economic Policy

FIRST AGRICULTURAL ADJUSTMENT ACT (AAA) 1933

The AAA aim was to control agricultural overproduction so that farmers would be able to sell their crops at the "parity prices" of the years 1909–1914, a time when farm prices were high. To guarantee parity, the government paid farmers for reducing the number of acres they planted. The plan was financed through a processing tax on companies that made the wheat, corn, cotton, hogs, milk, and tobacco into consumer products. Large farmers, rather than small farmers and tenant farmers benefited from the AAA. The public was outraged at the destruction of crops and animals in order to keep production down. In

1936 the law was declared unconstitutional. However, the principle of farm price supports had been established. The AAA was replaced with a law that encouraged using soil conservation methods.

SECOND AGRICULTURAL ADJUSTMENT ACT (AAA) 1937

The second AAA was passed in response to the fall in farm prices in 1937. The government paid farmers to store portions of over-produced crops until the price reached "parity."

In spite of New Deal efforts, America's farmers did not regain prosperity until World War II brought increased demand for food.

TENNESSEE VALLEY AUTHORITY (TVA) 1933

The TVA was a government project that provided jobs, cheap electricity, and flood control through dam construction in a poor rural area. The TVA was made possible due to the efforts of Senator George Norris, a Republican and a Nebraska Progressive. It was praised as a bold, planned experiment of government intervention to meet regional inter-dependent needs and attacked as "creeping socialism" with the government in the business of doing business.

Major New Deal REFORM Legislation

GLASS-STEAGALL BANKING ACT 1933

The 1933 Banking Act created the Federal Deposit Insurance Corporation (FDIC) that guaranteed individual deposits up to $5,000. The law also increased the powers of the Federal Reserve Board so that it had more control over speculation on credit.

MAKING CONNECTIONS

Unemployment, 1929–1940 (in millions)

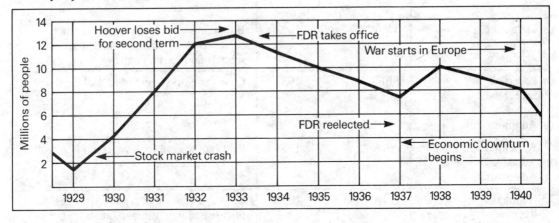

SECURITIES EXCHANGE ACT 1934

This act created the Securities and Exchange Commission (SEC), which had the authority to regulate stock exchanges and investment advisers. SEC powers included the right to bring action against those found practicing fraud. The SEC could require financial information about stocks and bonds before they were sold.

MAKING CONNECTIONS

SOCIAL SECURITY ACT 1935   The 1935 Social Security Act was a combination of public assistance and insurance. (1) It provided for old-age insurance to be paid by a tax on both the employer and employee while the employee is working. (2) It provided for unemployment insurance paid by employers. (3) There was also assistance to the elderly, ill, and handicapped and to dependent children. Today aid to dependent children is the largest government welfare program.

NATIONAL LABOR RELATIONS ACT (WAGNER ACT) 1935   The Wagner Act, named for its author, New York Senator Robert Wagner, guaranteed labor the right to organize, or to form unions, and to **collective bargaining**. It created the National Labor Relations Board (NLRB) to ensure that elections to select unions were conducted fairly. The NLRB could also halt practices such as **blacklisting**, made illegal by this law.

FAIR LABOR STANDARDS ACT 1938   This law set a **minimum wage** (originally 25 cents per hour) and maximum workweek (originally 44 hours) for workers in industries involved in interstate commerce. It is only one of many examples of New Deal legislation passed using the power given to Congress to regulate interstate commerce.

New Deal Programs

Program	Initials	Begun	Purpose
Civilian Conservation Corps	CCC	1933	Provided jobs to young men to plant trees, build bridges and parks, and set up flood control projects
Tennessee Valley Authority	TVA	1933	Built dams to provide cheap electric power to seven southern states; set up schools and health centers
Federal Emergency Relief Administration	FERA	1933	Gave relief to unemployed and needy
Agricultural Adjustment Administration	AAA	1933	Paid farmers not to grow certain crops
National Recovery Administration	NRA	1933	Enforced codes that regulated wages, prices, and working conditions
Public Works Administration	PWA	1933	Built ports, schools, and aircraft carriers
Federal Deposit Insurance Corporation	FDIC	1933	Insured savings accounts in banks approved by government

Rural Electrification Project	REA	1935	Loaned money to extend electricity to rural farmers
Works Progress Administration	WPA	1935	Employed men and women to build hospitals, schools, parks, and airports; employed artists, writers, and musicians
Social Security Act	SSA	1935	Set up a system of Act pensions for elderly, unemployed, and handicapped

THE GROWTH OF ORGANIZED LABOR IN THE 1930s

MAKING CONNECTIONS

Franklin Roosevelt was interested in helping workers primarily through social legislation such as social security. He also wanted to work cooperatively with business, as seen in the NRA legislation. When the NRA was ruled unconstitutional and with it the part that ensured labor the right to form unions, Roosevelt turned to the NLRA as a means of aiding labor. By 1935 he had turned away from business and saw organized labor unions as a force in society that would balance the power of big business.

This pro-labor attitude of the New Deal resulted in an increase in union membership between 1933 and 1935, of more than 1.5 million members. After the Wagner Act became law, membership grew another 3 million so that by 1938 it had reached 7 million organized workers. These gains took place during a split within organized labor over how to unionize workers.

The **American Federation of Labor (AFL)**, whose craft unions of skilled workers had dominated the movement since 1886, was challenged for control by a new union organized by industry. These new unions organized all workers—skilled and unskilled—in a given industry such as textiles, coal, steel, and automobiles, much like the old Knights of Labor. Unlike the Knights of Labor, the industrial unions concentrated on "bread and butter" issues of wages, hours, and working conditions. Led by John L. Lewis of the United Mine Workers, the new industrial unions formed the Committee for Industrial Organization (CIO) within the AFL. In 1937 the CIO became a separate union, the **Congress of Industrial Organization (CIO)**. Not until 1955 did the two organizations merge. In addition to the way it organized workers, the CIO differed from the AFL because its members included women, blacks, and immigrants from southern and eastern Europe. These groups made up a large percentage of the unskilled work force who comprised the CIO unions.

Key Social Studies Concepts

Diversity
Describe how the AFL and the CIO were different.

THE NEW DEAL AND MINORITIES AND WOMEN

NATIVE AMERICANS   As you read in Unit 2, the policies of the United States government toward Native Americans have undergone a series of changes. You reviewed the means by which Native Americans lost their lands and were forcibly removed to reservations. You have also reviewed the fact the United States government dealt with Native Americans through treaties, as it would deal with sovereign, independent nations.

In 1924, Native Americans were granted citizenship by Congress. This change of status did not alter the situation in which Native Americans found themselves in the 1920s. They were suffering under a government policy of forced assimilation enacted in 1887 by the Dawes Act, which aimed at breaking up the tribal structure of Native American life and forcing them to become landowning farmers.

Under Franklin Delano Roosevelt and the New Deal, government policy changed to one of tribal restoration (1934–1953). The Reorganization Act, or Wheeler-Howard Act of 1934, was passed due to the energies of Roosevelt's commissioner of Indian affairs, John Collier. The bill's aim was restore Indian tribal self-government as well as Indian languages, customs, and religious freedom. Another New Deal program provided for education for Indian children under the Bureau of Indian Affairs. In 1946 the Indian Claims Commission was established to handle claims for money for Indian lands lost by illegal means.

AFRICAN AMERICANS   African Americans were not a well-organized interest group in the 1930s and therefore benefited less from the New Deal than did other groups. Franklin Roosevelt was not a strong advocate of civil rights, although within the New Deal Eleanor Roosevelt and Harry Hopkins gave strong support to African Americans. Within the New Deal administrations as many as 50 African Americans were appointed to various agencies. The most active influence among them was Mary McLeod Bethune who served in the National Youth Administration. While blacks protested discrimination within New Deal agencies, about 40 percent of the nation's African Americans are estimated to have received help through one of the New Deal agencies.

MEXICAN AMERICANS   Many Mexican Americans worked in agriculture and were particularly hard hit by the depression. While the New Deal provided relief for these workers, its policy was to stop immigration and return to Mexico any unemployed non-citizens.

WOMEN   Like African Americans, women were not an organized group during the 1930s. You have reviewed the bias during the depression against working women who, it was claimed, took jobs away from male heads of families. This ignored the fact that single women and female heads of families made up a large portion of the female work force. While women made no progress in the field of work, the New Deal did help women in government. Eleanor Roosevelt, Perkins, and Bethune were only a few of the women visibly active in the New Deal administration. More women also ran for and won political office.

REACTIONS TO THE NEW DEAL

From the beginning of the New Deal with his first fireside chat to "my friends," Franklin Roosevelt had won the support of large numbers of Americans. Popular belief in him translated into votes. Roosevelt put together a New Deal program that attempted to offer something to all interest groups—business, labor, farmers, the unemployed, the old, the young, the worker, the intellectual. Therefore, it is understandable that Roosevelt was able to build what has come to be known as the "New Deal coalition," or voting bloc that included votes from the "Solid Democratic South," the "new immigrant" workers, the big cities, blacks who had previously voted Republican, organized labor, the elderly, and even business people and farmers who usually voted Republican.

However, criticism of the New Deal came from both the right and the left—from those who it felt that it was too radical or went too far and from those who felt its programs were too conservative or did not go far enough. In his first two terms, Roosevelt's strongest opposition was from big business. In 1934 a group of conservative Democratic and Republican businessowners and politicians formed the **American Liberty League**. It attacked Roosevelt because he was exercising too much power as President. It attacked the New Deal because programs were being financed through budget deficits or deficit spending. It expressed fear that the American free enterprise system was being destroyed. Radical groups offered alternatives to the New Deal but failed to gain any major public support. On the left, these included the **Communist Party of the United States of America**. At its peak in 1938, it had only 55,000 members and its candidate for the presidency in 1936 won only 80,000 votes. On the right a pro-Nazi German-American Bund became active as did the "Black Shirts" who were fascists supporting the views of Benito Mussolini, the Italian dictator.

The Socialist Party in America drew support, although some members began to vote for Roosevelt. It was led by Eugene Debs and Norman Thomas. Unlike the Communist Party, the Socialists believed in the use of democratic means to make changes in the American economic structure.

As frustration grew in the face of the prolonged depression, a group of individuals entered the political scene, each criticizing the New Deal and offering his own often simplistic solutions to the economic crisis. These men are called "**homegrown demagogues**" because their philosophies did not come from a foreign nation and

MAKING CONNECTIONS

List an example of a New Deal program that might have caused members of each of the following groups to vote for FDR.

Farmers:

Organized Labor:

The Unemployed:

Enduring Issues

Civil Liberties

MAKING CONNECTIONS

because they appealed to the common people's emotions and prejudice. These demagogues included:

- **Dr. Francis E. Townsend** created a financially impossible plan to provide government pensions for the elderly.
- **Father Charles E. Coughlin** was a Catholic priest who blamed business owners, especially Jewish ones, for the economic crisis.
- **Senator Huey Long** proposed that income and inheritance taxes on the wealthy be used to give each American a $2,500 income, a car, and a college education. Long was assassinated in 1935.

Supreme Court Reacts to New Deal

Another source of criticism of the New Deal came from within the federal government—from the Supreme Court. In a series of decisions, the Court ruled unconstitutional several key New Deal laws.

- The NRA was declared unconstitutional in *Schecter Poultry Corporation* v. *United States* (1935). The Court ruled that the law illegally gave Congress power to regulate intrastate commerce and violated separation of powers by giving the executive branch legislative powers.
- In *United States* v. *Butler* (1936), the Supreme Court ruled the AAA unconstitutional on the grounds that agriculture was a local, not an interstate, matter under the provisions of the 10th Amendment.

Enduring Issues

The Judiciary

Background The *Schechter* case is often called the "sick chicken" case because the company was charged with, among other things, selling uninspected, unhealthy chickens. Schecter claimed that it could not be regulated by the NRA because it sold chickens only in New York State.

FDR Reacts to Supreme Court

The "Court-Packing" Proposal Franklin Roosevelt asked Congress to approve a law which would permit the President to increase the number of judges from nine to fifteen if the judges refused to retire at the age of 70. This "court-packing" plan was aimed at making the Supreme Court approve the New Deal laws. It never became law because Americans defended the separation of powers.

An Assessment of the New Deal

For New Deal	Against
1. Was willing to use power of the government to help the less fortunate	1. Created too large a government and too large a bureaucracy
2. Acted on the constitutional goal of "providing for general welfare"	2. Established a welfare state
3. Saved the free enterprise economic system and kept the profit motive	3. Brought the nation close to socialism

4. Acted in the reform tradition of Populists and Progressives	4. Acted in a revolutionary, radical manner
5. Used powers of presidency and government within the guidelines of the commerce clause to help the people and nation	5. Too much power was assumed by President and the rest of government
6. Acted boldly to solve problems of the Great Depression	6. Did not solve unemployment, agricultural problems, or revive the economy
7. Willing to reform tax structure, and enter into deficit spending to help the nation	7. Criticized both for not spending enough money and for not balancing budget
8. Gave new groups of people a voice and active role in government and the political process	8. Responded only to organized interest groups

Regents Questions for Practice ____

Review the Test-Taking Strategies section of this book. Then answer the following questions, drawn from actual Regents examinations. Circle the *number* of the word or expression that best completes the statement or answers the question. Write your answers to essay questions on a separate piece of paper. Hints on good ways to approach these questions are provided in the margins.

Base your answers to questions 1 through 3 on the cartoon below and on your knowledge of social studies.

Franklin Delano Roosevelt

MAKING CONNECTIONS

Test Hints   Questions 1, 2, and 3 are based on the same cartoon. Before answering them, practice what you have learned about answering cartoon-based questions.

A. Look at the cartoon and read the three questions about it.
B. Read all of the words in the cartoon, including those on the signs.
C. Who is the person leading all the others? How do you know? What does the way the cartoonist has drawn him tell you about that person?
D. What animal is shown? What does that animal represent? What is the animal doing?
E. Who are the other people in the cartoon? Do they represent more than one group?
F. Answer the three questions.

1. Which conclusion may best be drawn from this cartoon?
   1 President Roosevelt's program was hurriedly put together and consisted almost entirely of stop-gap, temporary legislation.
   2 The great mass of the people in the United States were indifferent to President Roosevelt's program.
   3 President Roosevelt was being pushed into taking quick action by the Republican Party.
   4 President Roosevelt quickly carried his program into legislative action with forcefulness, optimism, and enthusiasm.

2. The emergency legislation indicated in the cartoon most probably refers to the
   1 declaration of war against Japan in 1941
   2 reorganization of the Supreme Court
   3 measures for dealing with the depression
   4 neutrality laws before World War II

3. The cartoon pictures the role of the President as one in which he
   1 provides leadership for his party, the public, and the Congress
   2 takes his direction from congressional leaders
   3 plays an essentially passive part in the legislative process
   4 affects legislation through the use of his veto power

4. Which conditions are most characteristic of a depression?
   1 high production and high demand
   2 few jobs and little demand
   3 much money in circulation and high stock prices
   4 supply meeting demand and high employment

5. In the United States, one of the basic causes of the Great Depression that began in 1929 was the
   1 lack of available credit
   2 abundance of purchasing power of farmers
   3 low protective tariffs of the 1920s
   4 overexpansion of industrial production

6. One important cause of the Great Depression in the United States was that by the end of the 1920s
   1 the government controlled almost every aspect of the economy
   2 tariffs were so low that foreign products had forced many United States companies out of business
   3 investors were too cautious and put their money only into government bonds
   4 factories and farms were able to produce far more than buyers could afford to purchase

7. The development and operation of the Tennessee Valley Authority by the United States Government is an example of
   1 Federal intervention to meet regional needs
   2 experimentation with nuclear technology
   3 government's attempt to earn maximum profits in business
   4 a return to laissez-faire economics

8. New Deal legislation brought about protection of investors by
   1 nationalizing all banks in the United States
   2 preventing the practice of buying on margin
   3 regulating the issuance of new stocks
   4 determining dividend rates

9. Labor unions in the United States increased their power during the administration of Franklin D. Roosevelt mainly because
   1 there were so many unemployed workers
   2 unions gained major rights under Federal law
   3 more people went to work for the Federal Government
   4 union leaders were elected to high government offices

10. Which action is often viewed as the most serious attempt to undermine the independence of the judiciary?
    1 appointment of conservative Supreme Court Justices by President Ronald Reagan
    2 President Franklin D. Roosevelt's plan to reorganize the Supreme Court
    3 appointment of Supreme Court Justices to unlimited terms of office
    4 periodic increases in the salaries of Supreme Court Justices

11. Andrew Jackson, Theodore Roosevelt, and Franklin D. Roosevelt were similar in that all
    1 had difficulty in carrying through most of their legislative programs
    2 were elected by a small popular vote
    3 were able to exercise great influence because of personal popularity
    4 felt that the President should be purely an executive officer

12. The New Deal changed United States political thinking because it advanced the principle that
    1 corporations should have the right to operate without government interference
    2 government officials should inform the public of major political decisions
    3 the President should have a leadership role in determining foreign policy
    4 the Federal Government should become more involved in the social and economic life of the people

13. An important criticism of the New Deal was that it
    1 greatly increased the national debt
    2 weakened the power of the Chief Executive
    3 did not deal with important issues
    4 promoted the idea of laissez faire

14. During President Franklin D. Roosevelt's first two terms, the strongest opposition to his New Deal policies came from
    1 big business
    2 labor union members
    3 the poor
    4 western farmers

15. In describing the New Deal era, most historians agree that the Federal Government
    1 increased its control over the economy of the United States
    2 preserved states' rights as supreme over federal powers
    3 restricted the activities of labor unions
    4 prevented the establishment of social welfare programs by the states

Essay Questions

Following are essay questions about the Unit that you have been reviewing. Before answering each, apply the lessons you have learned in the Test-Taking Strategies section by blocking each essay. The first block has been organized for you to help you get started with the pre-writing that is so necessary in preparing a good Regents essay answer.

1. Since the 1790s, the United States has changed from a nation of farmers to a highly industrialized nation. This development has created changes in the United States. Some of the areas in which change has occurred include:

> Population distribution
> The role of women
> Immigration
> Standard of living
> The environment
> Agriculture

a Select *three* of the areas listed above. For *each* one chosen, show how industrialization brought about change in that area of United States society. [4, 4, 4]

b For *one* of the changes identified in your answer to *a*, discuss the extent to which this change has had a positive or negative effect on United States society. [3]

Area of Change	A How industrialization brought about change	B Positive or negative effect
immigration	created factory jobs for unskilled workers which encouraged immigration [4]	positive: encouraged growth of business and industry and added to nation's cultural diversity [3]
	  [4]	
	  [4]	

2. Throughout United States history, there have been many instances where political, economic, or social difficulties led to demands for reform. In response to these demands, movements or programs such as those listed below developed.

Movements/Programs

Agrarian Protest/1870–1900

Progressivism/1900–1920

New Deal/1933–1945

Great Society/mid-1960s

New Federalism/1980s

Select *two* movements or programs from the list above and for *each* one chosen:

- Describe a specific problem that led to the movement or program
- Describe a specific reform advocated by the movement or program to deal with this problem
- Discuss the extent to which this reform was successful in solving the problem   [15]

3. Creativity in the United States has been influenced by a number of factors.

Factors

Education

Immigration

Patriotism

Philanthropy

Political or social dissent

Select *three* of the factors from the list above. For *each* one selected, describe a specific example of how that factor has influenced artistic or scientific creativity in the United States.[5, 5, 5]

4. The economy of the United States has been affected by many actions in history. Several such actions are listed below.

Economic Actions

- Implementation of Alexander Hamilton's financial program—1790s
- Invention of the cotton gin—1790s
- Building of the Erie Canal—1820s
- Passage of the Sherman Antitrust Act—1890
- Establishment of New Deal programs by Franklin Roosevelt—1930s
- Deregulation of some United States industries—1970s

Choose *three* of the economic actions listed above and for *each* one chosen:

- Explain the purpose of the action
- Discuss an impact of the action on the United States economy   [5, 5, 5]

UNIT

5

The United States in an Age of Global Crisis

Section 1 Peace in Peril, 1933–1950
Section 2 Peace with Problems, 1945–1960

This unit covers the time period from 1933 to 1960. It is especially concerned with United States foreign policy and how it affected life in the United States during those years.

As you review this unit remember the basic social studies concepts of this course. In this unit the concepts to focus on are power, human rights, and interdependence. Remember also to look for the Enduring Issues highlighted in the margin. Among the issues that are most important in this unit are the following: Presidential Power in Wartime and Foreign Policy; Civil Liberties: Balance Between Government and the Individual; The Rights of Ethnic and Racial Groups Under the Constitution.

You will need to know the answers to the following questions about this unit to pass the Regents examination.

Section 1: How did World War II force the United States to make an increasingly heavy commitment to global involvement?
Section 2: What efforts were made after World War II to achieve continuing peace?

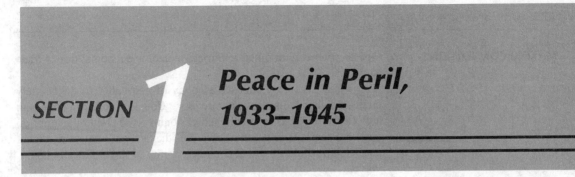

SECTION 1

Peace in Peril, 1933–1945

In Unit 3 you reviewed American reluctance to enter World War I. Fighting had begun in Europe in 1914, but the United States did not enter the actual fighting until 1917. Between April 1917, when the United States formally declared war, and Germany's surrender in November 1918, 48,000 American soldiers were killed in battle, 2,900 were declared missing in action, and 56,000 soldiers died of disease. Although these losses were far less than those of the European nations, after World War I Americans took a close look at the reasons for our entry into the war and at the conduct of the nation's foreign policy.

MAKING CONNECTIONS

Key Ideas It is important to remember that the causes of World War II can be traced to events earlier in the twentieth century.

ISOLATIONIST SENTIMENT AFTER WORLD WAR I

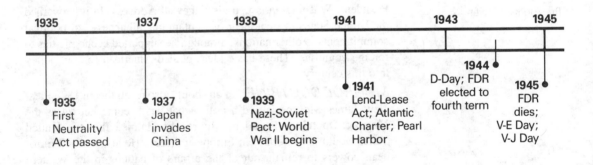

1935	1937	1939	1941	1943	1945

1935
First Neutrality Act passed

1937
Japan invades China

1939
Nazi-Soviet Pact; World War II begins

1941
Lend-Lease Act; Atlantic Charter; Pearl Harbor

1944
D-Day; FDR elected to fourth term

1945
FDR dies; V-E Day; V-J Day

The issue of American involvement in world affairs had been important to the United States before World War I, and it became important once again when the war ended. American disillusionment after World War I contributed to a desire for neutrality and to a revival of isolationism in United States foreign policy.

Isolation and Neutrality

Isolationism and neutrality are similar foreign policies, but an important difference exists between them. **Isolationism** is a national foreign policy of remaining apart from political or economic entanglements with other countries. Countries that practice this type of policy are referred to as isolationist. Strict isolationists do not support *any*

The U.S. and the World
As you learned in Global Studies, Switzerland is famous for following a policy of neutrality. Japan for centuries followed a policy of isolationism.

type of contact with other countries, including economic ties or trade activities.

When a country chooses a policy of **neutrality**, it deliberately takes no side in a dispute or controversy. Countries following this path are often referred to as nonaligned or noninvolved. Neutral nations do not limit their trading activities with other nations, unless a trading partnership would limit that country's ability to stay politically noninvolved.

Historical Roots of Isolationism and Neutrality

The roots of isolationist and neutralist sentiments in the United States can be traced to the late eighteenth and early nineteenth centuries.

PRECEDENTS SET BY GEORGE WASHINGTON
You should remember from your review of Unit I that George Washington set the important precedent of an American foreign policy of neutrality—but not isolationism—in his years as President. He knew that the young nation needed to trade to prosper. He also believed, however, that foreign alliances might force it into war.

Enduring Issues

Presidential Power

In 1793 Washington issued his **Proclamation of Neutrality**, making it clear that the United States would not respond to requests for aid during the French Revolution. In 1796, in his concluding days as President, Washington issued his **Farewell Address**. In it he warned the United States to steer clear of "entangling alliances," or political commitments to other nations, although he supported economic ties to foreign countries. These basic ideas guided American foreign policy into this century.

MONROE DOCTRINE
You should also recall that in 1823 President James Monroe issued a policy that has become known as the **Monroe Doctrine**. President Monroe proclaimed that the United States would not interfere in European affairs. He also warned European powers to remain out of the affairs of nations in the Western Hemisphere. This doctrine formed the backbone of American foreign policy for many years.

Isolationism in the 1930s

In 1934, when the United States was trying to recover from the worst economic depression in its history, Senator Gerald Nye led an investigation into the reasons the United States entered World War I. The committee concluded that the United States had gone to war at the encouragement of financiers and armament makers, eager for profits. As a result of this investigation, many Americans supported a return to isolationism. They believed that the country would be secure without worrying about the actions of the rest of the world.

The United States' refusal to join the League of Nations was reinforced by the Senate's move in 1935 to forbid the United States to join the World Court. In 1935 Congress also passed the first of a series of **Neutrality Acts**, intended to prevent Americans from making loans to nations at war. Any sales of goods to such nations were to be strictly on a "cash and carry" basis. In 1937 President Roosevelt made his famous **quarantine speech**, in which he likened the spreading world lawlessness to a disease. He stated that the United States would attempt to quarantine the "patients" in order to protect the rest of the community of nations.

MAKING CONNECTIONS

EVENTS LEADING TO WORLD WAR II

Historians point out that the causes of World War II were rooted in events earlier in the twentieth century. The rise of totalitarian governments in Germany and Italy in the 1930s set the stage for World War II.

The Rise of Totalitarian Governments

To understand the meaning of the word **totalitarian**, think of its root, *total*. You will recall that in totalitarian governments the government has complete, or total, control over the lives of its citizens. After the Russian Revolution in 1917, the government established there was called totalitarian because Russian citizens lost the ability to control many aspects of their lives. Totalitarian governments rely on terror and the use of secret police to conduct the daily business of government. Basically, totalitarian governments are the opposite of all that the United States considers its tradition of political freedom and liberty. Hitler's Nazi government under the Third Reich and Mussolini's Fascist control in Italy are examples of totalitarian regimes in the 1930s.

Key Social Studies Concepts:
Power

Major World Events, 1919–1941

The chart on the next page presents a summary of the activities of major nations in the years between World War I and World War II. This period is seen as a time when peace failed and aggressors achieved their goals, even though their success did not last long. As you review the chart, look for relationships between events in order to understand how certain events caused others that occurred later.

Major World Events, 1919–1941

- **1918** Germany surrenders. World War I is concluded.
- **1919** Germany signs the Treaty of Versailles. The United States refuses to approve the Treaty of Versailles.
- **1921** Great Britain, France, and Japan attend the Washington Naval Conference on limiting arms. The conference produces the Four Power and Nine Power treaties.
- **1922** Benito Mussolini becomes Italy's Fascist dictator. The USSR is officially formed, following the Communist victory in the Russian Revolution.
- **1923** Adolf Hitler writes *Mein Kampf* in prison.
- **1924** In the USSR, Lenin dies. Stalin continues his rise to power.
- **1928** The Kellogg-Briand Pact outlawing war is signed by 62 nations. The pact contains no method of enforcement.
- **1929** The most serious economic depression in history begins, continuing into the 1930s.
- **1930** Japan occupies Manchuria.
- **1932** Japan seizes Shanghai. The United States issues the Stimson Doctrine, condemning Japanese aggression against Manchuria.
- **1933** Hitler assumes power in Germany. Japan withdraws from the League of Nations. President Roosevelt announces the Good Neighbor Policy in Latin America. The USSR is formally recognized by the United States. Nazi Germany begins operation of the first concentration camp at Dachau, near Munich.
- **1935** Italy invades Ethiopia. The United States passes the first Neutrality Act.
- **1936** Hitler rearms the Rhineland. The German/Italian Axis is formed. The Spanish Civil War begins (ending in 1939). The United States passes the second Neutrality Act. The United States votes for nonintervention at the Pan-American Conference.
- **1937** Japan invades China. Japan sinks an American gunboat in China. The United States passes the third Neutrality Act, including a "cash and carry" plan.
- **1938** Germany annexes Austria (the Anschluss). Hitler demands the Sudetenland of Czechoslovakia. Great Britain, France, and Germany sign the Munich Pact, giving in to Hitler's demands.
- **1939** A German/Soviet nonaggression pact is signed. Japanese and American relations are deadlocked. The United States Senate refuses to grant aid to Great Britain or France. Hitler invades Poland, marking the beginning of World War II.
- **1940** Germany occupies Norway, Denmark, the Netherlands, Belgium, Luxembourg, and France. Germany attacks Great Britain. Japan joins the Axis powers. President Roosevelt arranges to supply destroyers to Great Britain. Congress passes the Selective Service Act, the first peacetime draft in United States history.
- **1941** Germany invades the USSR. The United States passes the Lend-Lease Act, granting aid to countries whose defense was seen as critical to the defense of the United States. President Roosevelt and Prime Minister Churchill agree to the Atlantic Charter. Japan attacks the United States at Pearl Harbor. The United States enter World War II.

Some events in the preceding chart are so significant that they require further discussion.

1938 MUNICH AGREEMENT   With this agreement **Adolf Hitler** convinced Prime Minister **Neville Chamberlain** of Great Britain and French Premier **Edouard Daladier** that if the Sudetenland of Czechoslovakia were separated from the rest of that country, Germany would make no further territorial demands there. Germany was thereby permitted by these two countries to seize the Sudetenland. When Chamberlain returned to Britain with this agreement, he told the world that he had achieved "peace in our time." Six months later, however, Hitler seized the rest of Czechoslovakia.

Great Britain and France had resorted to the policy of **appeasement**, which means to agree to the demands of a potential enemy in order to keep the peace. Hitler demonstrated by his action that he could not be permanently appeased, and the world learned a costly lesson.

JAPAN'S ATTACK ON PEARL HARBOR   Until the United States was attacked by Japan at **Pearl Harbor**, Hawaii, on December 7, 1941, the country had not taken a direct military part in the war. President Roosevelt had continued to promise Americans that the United States would not fight in a war in which the country was not directly involved.

Roosevelt called the Sunday morning attack on the naval base at Pearl Harbor a day that would "live in infamy," a day that Americans would never forget. This surprise attack shattered the American belief that the Atlantic and Pacific oceans would safely isolate the United States from fighting in Europe and Asia. Although the Japanese did not intend to fuel American attitudes of nationalism and patriotism, that was the effect the bombing of Pearl Harbor had on the outraged nation. Suddenly the war was no longer oceans away. By the very next day, Congress had agreed to President Roosevelt's request to declare war on Japan.

WORLD WAR II IN REVIEW

World War II began in 1939 with Germany's invasion of Poland. The war lasted for six years. The United States fought for only four years of the war after the Japanese attacked Pearl Harbor. The European Front ceased-fire in May 1945. It was not until August 14, 1945 that the Japanese surrendered, thus marking the end of World War II.

Major Powers

The war pitted fifty nations united together as the **Allies** against nine **Axis Powers**. The major powers among the Allies were Great Britain, the USSR, and the United States. Germany, Italy, and Japan were the major Axis nations. Leaders of the major powers are listed on the next page.

MAKING CONNECTIONS

The U.S. and the World
The civil war in Spain provided a testing ground where Fascist Germany and Italy tried out new weapons and tactics that they would later use in World War II.

Continuing Issues   The results of appeasement in 1938 have influenced American Presidents to take strong stands against aggression. President Bush's response to Iraq's invasion of Kuwait in 1990 is one example.

Regents Tip   Remember that maps can provide information about time and movement.
From what nation did the Allies begin advances in 1942 and 1944?

World War II in Europe and North America

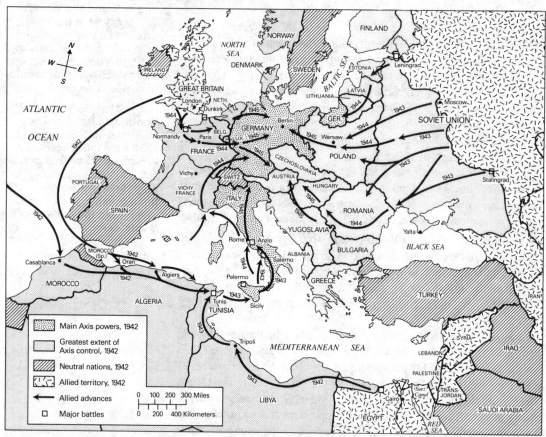

World War II in Europe and North America

Leaders During World War II

Allies	
• Great Britain	Winston Churchill, Prime Minister
• USSR	Josef Stalin, Communist dictator
• United States	Franklin D. Roosevelt, President until his death in April 1945 Harry S Truman, President following Roosevelt's death Dwight D. Eisenhower, Supreme Commander of Allied troops in Europe Douglas MacArthur, Commander of the Allied troops in the Pacific
• France	Charles de Gaulle, leader of the Free French during the Nazi occupation
Axis Powers	
• Germany	Adolf Hitler, leader of the National Socialist Workers Party (Nazis), known as ''Der Fuhrer''
• Italy	Benito Mussolini, Fascist dictator known as ''Il Duce''
• Japan	Emperor Hirohito Hideki Tojo, General and Prime Minister

Major Events

Major military engagements and turning points in World War II are presented in the chart below.

Major Events of World War II

- 1939   Germany invades Poland with a rapid attack by armored vehicles supported by airplanes that is called **blitzkrieg,** or "lightning war."
- 1940   Denmark, Norway, Belgium, the Netherlands, and much of northern France fall to Nazi invasion. Battle of Britain—months of terrifying air raids by Germany against Britain known as the **blitz.**
- 1941   Germany invades the Soviet Union. The siege of Leningrad begins and lasts well over two years. Japan attacks Pearl Harbor, Hawaii. The United States enters the war.
- 1941–1942   Japan seizes the Philippines, Burma, Singapore, the Dutch East Indies, and French Indochina. Japan continues to press southward toward Australia.
- 1942   Battle of Midway in the Pacific. The United States regains naval superiority in the Pacific.
- 1942–1943   Battle of Stalingrad. German troops are forced to surrender after thousands have been killed. This battle marks a turning point in the East and allowed Russian soldiers to begin to move west.
- 1943   In North Africa, Allied troops defeat Axis armies for control of the Mediterranean Sea and the Suez Canal.
- June 6, 1944   Allied invasions of Normandy, France, across the English Channel. This was the largest such invasion in history, involving over 120,000 soldiers.
- 1944–1945   Bitter fighting in the Pacific (for example at Leyte, Iwo Jima, and Okinawa) costs thousands of American lives.
- December 1944   Battle of the Bulge. A surprisingly strong response by German troops slows the movement of Allied forces eastward to Germany.
- April 12, 1945   Franklin Roosevelt dies unexpectedly from a cerebral hemorrhage.
- April 1945   Allied troops from the East and West meet at the Elbe River in Germany. Hitler commits suicide.
- May 8, 1945   The end of war in Europe, celebrated as V-E Day (Victory in Europe).
- August 6, 1945   The United States drops an atomic bomb on the Japanese city of Hiroshima.
- August 9, 1945   The United States drops an atomic bomb on the Japanese city of Nagasaki.
- August 15, 1945   Hirohito announces Japan's defeat to the Japanese people. The day is known as V-J Day (Victory in Japan).
- September 2, 1945   Japan formally surrenders.

World War II in the Pacific

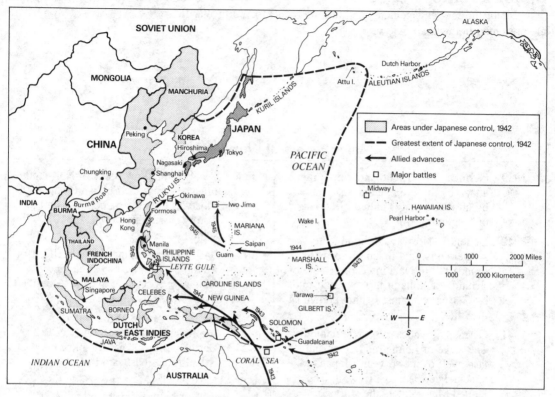

Casualties During World War II

World War II was the most costly war in history. See the chart below for the number of casualties suffered by the major powers.

Casualties in World War II

	Military Dead	Military Wounded	Civilian Dead
Britain	398,000	475,000	65,000
France	211,000	400,000	108,000
Soviet Union	7,500,000	14,102,000	15,000,000
United States	292,000	671,000	*
Germany	2,850,000	7,250,000	5,000,000
Italy	77,500	120,000	100,000
Japan	1,576,000	500,000	300,000

All figures are estimates
*Very small number of civilian dead

Wartime Diplomacy

During the war, leaders of the Allied nations met in a series of conferences to discuss wartime strategies and plans for the postwar world. Key meetings are described below.

ATLANTIC CHARTER MEETING, 1941   Roosevelt and Churchill meet on battle ships in the North Atlantic to agree on certain principles for building a lasting peace and establishing free governments in the world, which they set out in a document called the **Atlantic Charter**.

CASABLANCA, 1942   Roosevelt meets with Churchill to plan "victory on all fronts." The term **unconditional surrender** is used to describe the anticipated victory.

CAIRO, 1943   Roosevelt, Churchill, and Chiang Kai-shek of China plan the Normandy invasion.

TEHERAN CONFERENCE, 1943   Roosevelt and Churchill meet with Stalin to discuss war strategy and plans for the postwar world.

YALTA, 1945   Roosevelt, Churchill, and Stalin discuss the division of postwar Germany and plan for the trials of war criminals. The USSR promises to enter the war against Japan.

POTSDAM, 1945   Allied leaders (Truman now replacing Roosevelt) warn Japan to surrender to prevent utter destruction.

The Atomic Bomb

In an effort to bring the war to a speedy conclusion and to prevent further destruction and loss of life, Allied leaders decided to embark on an atomic research project.

THE MANHATTAN PROJECT   In the spring of 1943, a group of scientists from the United States, Canada, Britain, and other European countries began work on the top-secret atomic research program known as the **Manhattan Project**. The research was done primarily at Los Alamos, New Mexico, under the direction of Dr. Robert Oppenheimer. By July 1945, the first atomic bomb was tested in New Mexico. The success of this project left the United States in the position of determining the ultimate use of the new weapon.

THE BOMBINGS OF HIROSHIMA AND NAGASAKI
Within days after the first atomic test, Allied leaders warned Japan to surrender or face "prompt and utter destruction." Since no surrender occurred, atomic bombs were dropped on the Japanese cities of Hiroshima and Nagasaki. The world had entered the Atomic Age. President Truman, who had been President for only four months since the death of Roosevelt, explained that the new weapon was just that—a weapon to be used as needed in the fighting of the war. For a time after World War II, the United States held a monopoly on atomic weapons.

MAKING CONNECTIONS

Key Ideas Modern methods of transport made possible the meetings of Allied leaders during the war. These gatherings were the first of a series of summit meetings of world leaders that continue to this day.

Key Social Studies Concepts:

Technology, Power

JAPAN SURRENDERS   Japan surrendered within days after the bombings of Hiroshima and Nagasaki. Following Japan's surrender, the United States occupied Japan under the leadership of General Douglas MacArthur. A new constitutional monarchy went into effect introducing democratic reforms to Japan. However, Emperor Hirohito retained his throne.

THE HOLOCAUST

Key Social Studies Concepts:

Human Rights, Empathy

When Adolf Hitler rose to power in Germany, he did so by finding a **scapegoat**, someone to blame for Germany's problems after World War I. By appealing to **anti-Semitism**, feelings of hatred against Jewish people, Hitler encouraged the Germans to turn viciously on all Jewish citizens.

The "Final Solution"

Early in his rise to power, Hitler had seized Jewish property, homes, and businesses and barred Jews from many jobs. At the Wannsee Conference of 1941, the Nazis set as a primary goal the total extermination, or **genocide**, of all Jews under their domination. This effort was to be kept secret from the German people and from the rest of the world. Hitler's plan to eliminate the Jews was known to the Nazis as the **Final Solution**.

The Horror of Concentration Camps

In the 1930s the Nazis started to build **concentration camps** to isolate Jews and other groups from society and provide slave labor for industry. As Hitler's conquest of Europe continued, the camps became factories of death. Over six million Jews died in the camps as did another four million people—dissenters, Gypsies, homosexuals, the mentally and physically handicapped, Protestant ministers, and Catholic priests. Today, concentration camp names such as Auschwitz, Treblinka, and Dachau stand as memorials to the incredible human suffering and death of this time, a period now called the **Holocaust**.

The United States and other nations failed to take strong action to rescue Jews from Nazi Germany before World War II. After war broke out, the Allies still failed to speak out forcefully against the treatment of Jews or to make direct attempts to stop the genocide. Only toward the end of the war did creation of a War Refugee Board begin to provide aid for Holocaust survivors.

Key Social Studies Concepts:

Justice

The Nuremberg Trials

A final chapter to the Holocaust occurred in Nuremberg, Germany, in 1945 and 1946. At that time an international military court tried thousands of Nazis for atrocities committed during World War II. By finding former Nazis guilty of "crimes against humanity," a precedent was established that soldiers, officers, and national leaders could be held responsible for such actions. Escaped Nazis who have been found since the end of the war have also been brought to trial for war-related crimes.

AMERICAN PATRIOTISM DURING WORLD WAR II

MAKING CONNECTIONS

With its entry into World War II, the United States faced new challenges. The country had avoided direct involvement in war for as long as possible. In early 1941, however, the United States had begun selling arms and defense materials to Britain, assuming a role as the "**arsenal of democracy**." After December 1941, the United States moved to full-scale wartime production and mobilization of the armed forces. Americans rallied behind the war effort.

With the exception of the attack on Pearl Harbor and battles on several Pacific islands, World War II was not fought on American soil. Nonetheless, Americans were constantly preparing for attack. America's coastal areas and large cities held blackout drills. Americans were encouraged to support the war effort by rationing food, gasoline, and other necessities and luxuries. Government campaigns encouraged Americans to have "meatless Tuesdays," and many Americans planted "victory gardens" of their own to increase the food supply. Hollywood entertainers made special presentations to encourage citizens to buy war bonds to help the government finance the war.

The lives of all Americans were affected by World War II. American women, African-Americans, and Japanese Americans experienced particularly significant changes.

Enduring Issues

National Power

The Role of American Women

World War II brought dramatic changes to the lives of American women.

IN THE MILITARY   By the end of the war over 200,000 women had joined the military services. Women performed a variety of military duties. They operated radios, repaired planes and vehicles, and were assigned along with men to clerical duties.

IN THE CIVILIAN WORK FORCE   As millions of men joined the military, new employment opportunities outside the home opened up to women. Women who had been working before the war eagerly applied for better-paying jobs, and women who had not been working also entered the work force. Many women took jobs that had once been open to men only. Over five million women eventually worked in factories devoted to wartime production, although their pay never came close to equaling men's pay of the time. One song, "Rosie the Riveter," became popular during the war years because it captured the sense of duty and patriotism felt by millions of women.

Background   Women in the armed forces during World War II were confined to noncombatant jobs, those that did not directly involve fighting.

RESULTING CHANGES   Important changes in employment and lifestyle resulted from the expanded role of women in the work force. Before the war, young single women made up the majority of employed women in the United States. During the war, large numbers of married women and mothers who had never worked outside the home before took jobs. This trend continued after the war. Although many women willingly returned to their homes and the roles of wife and mother at the end of the war, thousands more found the challenge of employment outside the home and the extra paycheck a way to improve their standard of living.

The increased employment of women during World War II marked the beginning of changes in the employment and lifestyle of American women that would mark the remaining years of the century. For example, the increased number of women in the work force gave rise to a need for child care. This became an issue during the war years and remains an important one today.

African Americans

Key Ideas Prejudice toward racial and ethnic groups tends to emerge at times of national crisis and can lead to such groups being deprived of their rights.

The setbacks and gains of African Americans during the war years provided the seeds of the civil rights movement of the 1950s and 1960s.

IN THE MILITARY   Nearly one million black men and women served in the military during World War II. At that time the armed services practiced segregation. Only as black soldiers distinguished themselves on battlefields did they begin to receive recognition for their sacrifices.

AT HOME   Discrimination and racism that had been common in the South spread rapidly to the North in the early twentieth century as northern whites confronted blacks in competition for jobs and housing. Race riots that broke out as whites protested the movement of southern blacks to northern cities added to the frustration of black Americans. Membership in civil rights organizations grew rapidly as blacks struggled against discrimination.

African Americans experienced gains during the war years. Politically, blacks recognized that their migration north had made them a significant voting bloc in urban areas. Economically, new jobs in war industries brought many black Americans the chance to earn more than they ever had before. The black press urged that the struggle for freedom be fought on two fronts—overseas and at home as well.

Japanese Americans

Enduring Issues

- Ethnic and Racial Groups;
- Civil Liberties

Thousands of Japanese Americans faced hardship and economic losses after the attack on Pearl Harbor.

IMMIGRATION TO AMERICA   Immigrants from Japan began arriving in the United States shortly after the Civil War. These immigrants had settled mainly on the west coast of the United States. By

1941, thousands of Americans of Japanese descent, called **Nisei**, had been born in the United States and were American citizens. Thousands of them had never been to Japan, and many had no desire to go there.

MOVEMENT TO INTERNMENT CAMPS   Because of Japan's attack on the United States, many Americans feared that Japanese Americans presented a threat to national security. Anti-Japanese sentiment grew, and in 1942 President Roosevelt issued **Executive Order 9066**, establishing military zones for the imprisonment of Japanese Americans. Over 100,000 innocent people were removed from their homes and businesses and forced to move to **internment camps**, hastily constructed military-style barracks ringed with barbed wire and guarded by troops. This discrimination was focused entirely on Japanese Americans; no such action was taken against citizens or residents of German or Italian descent.

KOREMATSU V. UNITED STATES   In the 1944 landmark case **Korematsu** v. **United States**, the Supreme Court upheld the forced evacuation as a reasonable wartime emergency measure. However, no acts of Japanese-American sabotage or treason were ever identified, and thousands of Nisei fought honorably in the war. Almost fifty years after the internments, the United States government admitted that the wartime relocation program had been unjust. In 1988, Congress voted to pay $20,000 to each of the approximately 60,000 surviving Americans who had been interned. The first payments were made in 1990, and the Government also issued a formal apology.

MAKING CONNECTIONS

Regents Questions for Practice

Review the **Test-Taking Strategies** section of this book. Then answer the following questions, drawn from actual Regents examinations. Circle the *number* of the word or expression that best completes the statement or answers the question. Write your answers to essay questions on a separate piece of paper. Hints on good ways to approach these questions are provided in the margins.

1. A major reason why a working system of international law has been difficult to achieve is that
   1 the many different languages in the world make communication difficult
   2 nations are unwilling to give up some of their sovereignty
   3 no precedent for international law exists
   4 many nations still lack even an internal system of law

Test Hint   Eliminate obvious wrong answers first. For example, there are many translators available; eliminate answer 1.

MAKING CONNECTIONS

Test Hint Be alert to the time frame of questions. Remember that the term "domino theory" came from a later period than the 1930s.

2. A major reason for the United States neutrality in the 1930s was the nation's
1 belief in the domino theory
2 disillusionment resulting from World War I
3 strong approval of political conditions in Europe
4 military and naval superiority

3. At the outbreak of both World War I and World War II in Europe, public opinion in the United States generally favored
1 remaining neutral
2 entering the war on the side of the Allies
3 invading Europe in order to acquire territory
4 settling the conflict through an international peace organization

Test Hint Note that questions 4 and 5 are two different ways of testing the concept of balance of power.

4. Nations have often followed balance of power politics on the assumption that
1 nations will form alliances only when other means of collective security have failed
2 nations will not go to war with enemies of equal or superior strength
3 the existence of a weak nation between two powerful enemy nations will prevent war
4 peaceful and open negotiations will solve international conflicts

5. "Nations strive to prevent any one country from becoming all-powerful and domineering."
Which concept is referred to by this statement?
1 militarism   3 national sovereignty
2 imperialism   4 balance of power

6. During the period between World Wars I and II, which general foreign policy was followed by the United States?
1 overseas expansion   3 militarism
2 internationalism   4 isolationism

Test Hint To help you keep track of the time period, write the decades involved out in the margin. Remember the correct answer must apply to both decades.

7. Which statement best describes the international situation in the decades just prior to both World War I and World War II?
1 The United States was reluctant to become actively involved in European political affairs.
2 Great Britain and France gave in to the demands of aggressive nations.
3 Formal world peace organizations were effective in settling international crises.
4 Germany annexed neighboring territories in order to improve the economic status of their peoples.

8. Evidence that the United States generally followed a policy of isolationism during the period 1919–1939 is that the United States
1 condemned Fascist aggression
2 rejected the policy of appeasement
3 refused to join the League of Nations
4 participated in disarmament conferences

9. Isolationism as a foreign policy is more difficult to achieve in the 20th century than in prior times mainly because
1 the increase in the world's population has forced people to live more closely together
2 there are more sovereign nations today than in the past
3 modern technology had made nations more interdependent
4 public opinion on issues is more easily disregarded

10. Which is a secondary source of information about the period between World Wars I and II?
1 a passage in a social studies textbook about the Munich Pact of 1938
2 the Treaty of Versailles
3 Adolf Hitler's autobiography *Mein Kampf*
4 one of President Franklin Roosevelt's Fireside Chats

11. "We Americans live in a world we can no longer dominate, but from which we cannot isolate ourselves."
The author of this quotation is saying that the United States should
1 become less dependent on foreign nations
2 realize that it is no longer a world power
3 recognize important changes in international relations
4 increase its economic and military strength

12. The appeasement policy followed by Western European leaders in the late 1930s was based primarily on the belief that war could be avoided by
1 satisfying Hitler's desire for territorial expansion
2 encouraging Communist expansion into Nazi Germany
3 limiting the development of Germany's armed forces
4 appealing to the League of Nations for international cooperation

13. During the early 1940s, the United States aided the Soviet Union mainly in order to
1 strengthen Soviet resistance to Nazi Germany
2 persuade Josef Stalin not to become an ally of Japan
3 encourage anti-Communist uprisings among the Russian people
4 increase Soviet agricultural production

14. The most accurate description of United States foreign policy toward Japan between 1900 and 1941 is that the United States
1 supported Japan's territorial ambitions
2 attempted to restrict Japan's growth and power
3 encouraged Japan to develop a strong industrial base
4 lacked interest in Japanese policies

15. Which statement is accurate concerning the forced relocation of Japanese Americans during World War II?
1 President Franklin D. Roosevelt authorized the action as a military necessity.
2 Few of those relocated were actually United States citizens.
3 Widespread Japanese American disloyalty and sabotage preceded the forced relocation.
4 The Japanese American experience was similar to what happened to German Americans at this time.

Peace with Problems, 1945–1960

Every country forms its foreign policy based on its self-interest. You will recall that after World War I the United States Senate refused to support President Wilson's plan for the League of Nations. Because of strong isolationist sentiment, the United States never joined the League. Eventually, however, the nation abandoned its isolationist policy to fight in World War II.

It is important to recall that the United States emerged from World War II as the world's greatest military power. The nation had suffered relatively little physical destruction compared to the rest of the world. Also, though only for a short time, the United States held a monopoly on the ability to use nuclear power. After World War II, the United States was aware of its strength as a nation and its responsibility to preserve world peace.

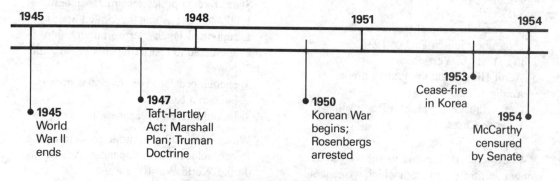

| 1945 | 1948 | 1951 | 1954 |

1945
World War II ends

1947
Taft-Hartley Act; Marshall Plan; Truman Doctrine

1950
Korean War begins; Rosenbergs arrested

1953
Cease-fire in Korea

1954
McCarthy censured by Senate

INTERNATIONAL PEACE EFFORTS: THE UNITED NATIONS

Key Ideas Increased interdependence among nations in the modern world is one factor that has led this nation to participate in organizations like the UN.

American foreign policy changed dramatically as a result of World War II. Even before the conclusion of the war, the United States began planning for an **international peacekeeping organization**. Plans were made at the Yalta Conference for a **United Nations Conference** to be held in San Francisco in April 1945. The Soviet Union, under the leadership of Josef Stalin, agreed to participate in planning the new organization that would be known as the United Nations. The United States Senate approved the United Nations Charter by a vote of 82 to 2.

The United Nations

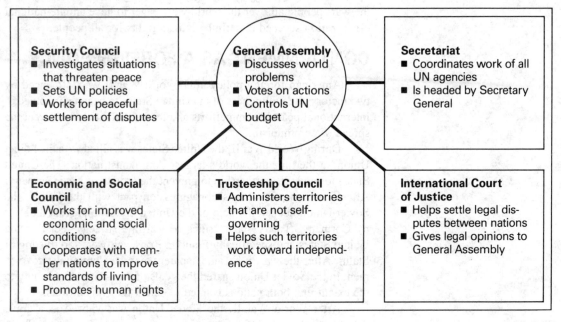

Security Council
- Investigates situations that threaten peace
- Sets UN policies
- Works for peaceful settlement of disputes

General Assembly
- Discusses world problems
- Votes on actions
- Controls UN budget

Secretariat
- Coordinates work of all UN agencies
- Is headed by Secretary General

Economic and Social Council
- Works for improved economic and social conditions
- Cooperates with member nations to improve standards of living
- Promotes human rights

Trusteeship Council
- Administers territories that are not self-governing
- Helps such territories work toward independence

International Court of Justice
- Helps settle legal disputes between nations
- Gives legal opinions to General Assembly

Organization of the United Nations

The structure of the United Nations includes a **General Assembly** of all its members and a **Security Council** of fifteen members. The Security Council consists of five permanent members (the United States, Great Britain, the Soviet Union, China, and France) and ten rotating member nations.

In the years since the founding of the United Nations, the General Assembly has served as a forum for world leaders to speak on a variety of concerns. Although the UN has become militarily involved in a number of world crises, most of its members would agree that its greatest accomplishments have been in fighting hunger and disease and in education. United Nations headquarters are in New York City.

UNIVERSAL DECLARATION OF HUMAN RIGHTS   President Truman appointed Eleanor Roosevelt, the former first lady, as a United Nations delegate in 1946, the only woman on the American delegation. Eleanor Roosevelt was quoted later as saying that she was very concerned that she represent all women to the best of her ability. Eleanor Roosevelt's committee authored the **Universal Declaration of Human Rights**, a proclamation that is still part of the guiding philos-

MAKING CONNECTIONS

Regents Tip An organizational chart shows the different parts of an overseeing body like the UN.
Which part of the UN is most similar to the World Court that the United States refused to join in 1935 (mentioned in Section 1 of this Unit)?

ophy of the UN today. Remember that in the years immediately after the war, people all over the world were eager to have an international organization succeed at defining human rights for all people.

CONTAINMENT AS A FOREIGN POLICY

American foreign policy after World War II was influenced by two factors: the willingness of the United States to become involved in international peacekeeping efforts and its determination to prevent the spread of communism.

During World War II, the United States was allied with the Soviet Union, at the time the world's largest Communist nation. The United States formed this partnership to prevent the growth of Nazi Germany. After Germany violated its nonaggression pact with the USSR, the Soviet Union needed the help of the United States to prevent a defeat by Germany. Today some critics of wartime strategy feel that the United States and specifically Franklin Roosevelt were too trusting of Stalin. After the war, it became apparent that the Communist government in the Soviet Union shared the goals of the United States only to the extent that both nations wanted to defeat the Axis powers.

After World War II, the Soviet Union was viewed as a grave threat to the security of the non-Communist world. The United States had emerged from World War II as the most powerful nation in the world. It took on the task of offsetting Communist expansion. The United States developed a foreign policy of **containment**. Its goal was to confine communism to the area in which it already existed—the Soviet Union and the Eastern European nations. American presidential power increased during this time period as the United States sought to carry out this policy.

Following are key foreign policy developments related to the containment of communism immediately after World War II.

Churchill's "Iron Curtain" Speech

In defeating Nazi Germany, the Soviets had moved troops into the nations of Eastern Europe. After the war the Soviet Union actively supported Communist governments in those nations.

In 1946 British Prime Minister Winston Churchill, speaking at Westminster College in Fulton, Missouri, sounded an "alarm" to the free world. In this famous speech, Churchill warned that "from Stettin in the Baltic to Trieste in the Adriatic, an Iron Curtain has descended across the Continent." Churchill's phrase **iron curtain** drew a clear picture of the postwar world. There had come to be recognizable division between the free world and the Communist world. Russian actions soon reinforced Churchill's words.

The Truman Doctrine

Before World War II, Britain had been a powerful force in the Mediterranean. Following the tremendous losses and expense of

Step on it, Doc!

Roy Justus, *The Minneapolis Star*, 1947.

World War II, however, Britain was no longer able to maintain its military presence there. As a result, the Soviets, who had long been striving for access to the Mediterranean Sea by way of the Turkish straits, sought to increase their influence in the area.

Attempts by Communist rebels to topple the government of Greece moved the United States to try to contain the spread of communism to the Mediterranean region. On March 12, 1947, President Truman asked Congress for $400 million in aid to Turkey and Greece. He called on the United States to support free people in resisting control by armed minorities or outside pressures. Truman believed that the United States' failure to act at this time would endanger both the nation and the free world.

Congress approved Truman's request. By 1950, more than $660 million had been spent in aid to Turkey and Greece. This policy of economic and military aid became known as the **Truman Doctrine**. It represents a major step in the evolution of American foreign policy.

The Marshall Plan

After World War II, Europe was a scene of ruin and destruction. Thousands of people in almost every country were homeless, many without families or jobs. Major cities and industrial centers had been destroyed. Survivors of the war struggled to find food, shelter, and clothing. Dissatisfaction with such conditions grew rapidly. In many war-torn countries, the Communist party claimed to offer solutions to such problems.

To prevent the spread of Communist influence in Europe, General **George C. Marshall**, Secretary of State under President Truman (the first military man to hold such a position), announced a new program. In a speech delivered on June 5, 1947, Marshall announced that the United States was against ''hunger, poverty, desperation and

Enduring Issues

Presidential Power

Germany Divided

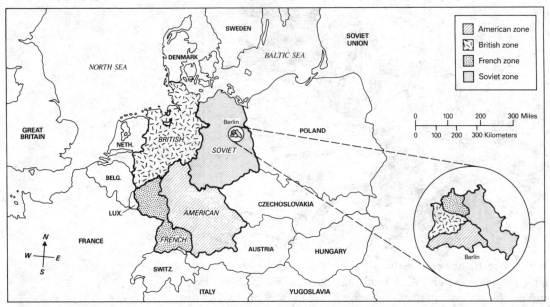

MAKING CONNECTIONS

Continuing Issues In November of 1990, an arms-reduction treaty was signed in Paris which formally marked the end of the Cold War. The failed overthrow of Gorbachev in 1991 and the collapse of the Soviet Union in 1992 made it certain that whatever role the Communist Party plays, communism in the new Commonwealth of Independent States is ended. What effect do these events have on attitudes toward democracy and communism today compared to attitudes in the late 1940s and early 1950s?

chaos.'' Between 1948 and 1952, about $12 billion in economic aid was allocated by the Republican-dominated Congress for the rebuilding of Europe under the so-called **Marshall Plan**. More than half the total went to Britain, France, and West Germany.

This aid enabled the businesses and industries of Western Europe to begin consumer production and to prosper. Both Western Europe and the United States felt that with stabilized and improving economies, Communist expansion would be halted.

The Beginning of the Cold War: Germany 1948–1949

At the conclusion of World War II, Germany was divided into four zones of occupation controlled by Great Britain, France, the Soviet Union, and the United States. Berlin, the capital of Germany, was located in the Russian-controlled sector. It too was divided into four sections, each run by one of the four Allies. Lack of agreement on German unification marked the beginning of the **Cold War**, a period of tension between the United States and the Soviet Union from the end of World War II to 1990.

THE BERLIN BLOCKADE The United States, France, and Great Britain cooperated in governing the western sectors of Germany. Unable to reach agreement with the Soviet Union over the unification of Germany, the three Western powers unified their zones in June 1948 and established the German Federal Republic, which came to be known as West Germany. The Soviets opposed the establishment of a separate government in Germany run by the Western powers. On June 24, 1948, the Soviets began a **blockade** of all land traffic to the western zone of Berlin. Remember that access to West Berlin was through the Soviet-controlled sector of Germany. By their action the Soviets hoped to force the other Allies out of Berlin.

THE BERLIN AIRLIFT   The United States, Great Britain, and France would not back down from the Soviets and began an airlift of food, clothing, coal, medicine, and other necessities to West Berlin.

Almost a year later, on May 12, 1949, the Soviets recognized their defeat in the area and ended the blockade. Shortly afterward the Soviets announced the formation of the German Democratic Republic, commonly known as East Germany. In 1955 West Germany was given full sovereignty. The West had learned once again that although World War II was over, its struggle against aggressor nations was not.

Point Four Program

The United States recognized that the Soviet Union's expansionist aims threatened not only Europe but developing nations of the world

MAKING CONNECTIONS

MAKING CONNECTIONS

Regents Tip   Sometimes maps do not give complete information about a subject.
Name one NATO nation that is not shown on this map.

The Cold War in Europe

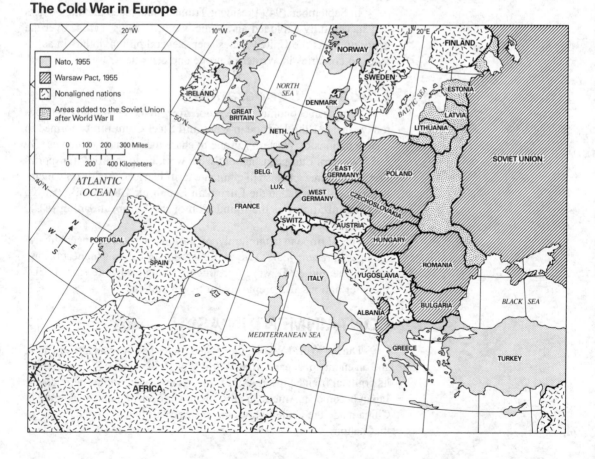

Nato, 1955

Warsaw Pact, 1955

Nonaligned nations

Areas added to the Soviet Union after World War II

as well. For this reason, in 1949 President Truman proposed and Congress approved nearly $400 million for technical development programs in Latin America, Asia, and Africa. The goal of this **Point Four Program** was to modernize and strengthen the economies of developing nations and thereby discourage the growth of communism.

The North Atlantic Treaty Organization

The United States and other Western European nations decided that another effective method of containing the Soviets would be to form alliances. In April 1949 the United States approved the North Atlantic Treaty. Under it the United States joined with eleven other western nations in a **collective security agreement**. Such an agreement binds participating nations to act together for their common defense. Members pledged that an attack on any one of them would be considered an attack on all of them. Defense arrangements were coordinated through the **North Atlantic Treaty Organization** (NATO).

The Soviets later formed an opposing alliance. The USSR and seven Eastern European nations joined together under the **Warsaw Pact**.

In September 1949 President Truman announced that the Soviets had successfully exploded an atomic bomb. For this reason, over the next few years the United States spent several billion dollars in assistance to countries in Western Europe and elsewhere.

European Cooperation

European economic cooperation grew in the 1950s and continues today. In 1951 the **European Coal and Steel Community** formed to enable nations of Western Europe to share their natural resources. By 1957 Western Europeans nations were working to improve transportation in their area and also to eliminate tariff barriers. At this time member nations were called the **European Economic Community** (EEC). This organization was the foundation of the **European Union (EU)** that exists today.

The European community of nations has experienced many changes in recent years. Two of the European Union's highest priorities in the mid-1990s were introducing a single currency for all EU member nations and preparing for new members.

CONTAINMENT IN ASIA

During World War II, the United States had been an ally of China and an enemy of Japan. After World War II, the United States reversed its political friendships in Asia. With its new constitutional democracy, Japan became an American ally. Meanwhile a Communist takeover in China made the United States increasingly suspicious of and hostile to that nation.

Communist Victory in China

Since the 1930s China had been divided by civil war. **Mao Zedong**, leader of the Communist forces in China, sought to defeat the nationalist regime of **Chiang Kai-shek**. In 1949, the Communist forces defeated the nationalists, and the nationalists fled to the island of Taiwan. The United States was alarmed by this development. Since the United States had overseen the initial rebuilding of postwar Japan and had helped put a new constitutional democracy in place, this nation was not willing to allow Japan to fall to the Communist influence of its giant neighbor to the west. Support for Japan was now seen as a way of offsetting Communist China's influence in Asia.

The Korean War

At the end of World War II, the nation of Korea, which had been occupied by the Japanese during the war, was divided along the **38th parallel**, or line of latitude. The northern zone was under the influence of the Soviet Union, and the southern zone was controlled by the United States. By 1948 the southern zone had elected an anti-Communist government headed by Syngman Rhee and was now called the Republic of Korea. In the northern zone, now named the Democratic People's Republic of Korea, a Communist government ruled.

FIGHTING BEGINS   By 1950 most American and Soviet forces had withdrawn from Korea. However, after North Korea invaded South Korea on June 25, 1950, President Truman committed American troops to major involvement in the Korean conflict.

MacARTHUR IN COMMAND   **General Douglas MacArthur**, a World War II hero, was sent to command the United States troops in Korea. The United States, along with small numbers of soldiers from other UN member nations, were soon involved in battles as fierce as those of World War II. A particularly devastating loss came at the Yalu River, when Chinese forces entered the conflict and pushed UN troops south. By the middle of 1951, the war had reached a stalemate, with neither side able to advance successfully.

Disagreement over the objectives and military strategies of the Korean War caused a major conflict between President Truman and General MacArthur. Although Truman was a civilian, the Constitution makes the President the commander-in-chief of the armed forces. When General MacArthur disagreed with Truman publicly about the conduct of the war, the President recalled him to the United States and dismissed him from command.

HOSTILITIES END   Although peace talks began in June 1951, no resolution was reached before the American presidential election of 1952. During that campaign the Republican candidate, World War II hero **Dwight D. Eisenhower**, promised that if he were elected President he would go to Korea to aid in the peace negotiations.

MAKING CONNECTIONS

Key Ideas   The Constitution gives Congress the power to declare war. Congress never did so during the Korean conflict. Sending U.S. troops into battle without such a declaration caused controversy at the time and again during the Vietnam War.

MAKING CONNECTIONS   **The Korean War**

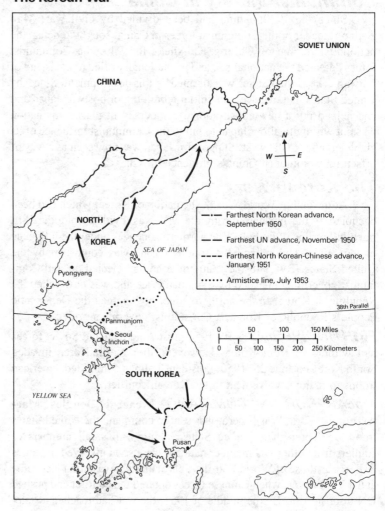

Regents Tip You can use information from maps to understand why events took place.
Why do you think Communist China decided to enter the Korean War in November 1950?

Although Eisenhower won the election and did keep his campaign promise, a cease-fire was not officially signed until July 27, 1953.

The war in Korea lasted for more than three years and cost over $15 billion. Over 54,000 Americans died in the conflict. More than 1 million Koreans and Chinese were also killed.

NEW DIRECTIONS   The policy of containment took a different course with American involvement in the Korean conflict. Early efforts at containment had revolved primarily around economic aid programs. The United States now showed its willingness to undertake military action to contain communism if it was necessary. American experiences in Korea were a warning of future global confrontations between democratic and Communist opponents.

THE POSTWAR UNITED STATES

World War II and the tensions of the cold war that followed it had long-lasting effects on American society. The United States had been spared the destruction other nations had felt during the war. Its factories, geared up for wartime production, had helped the nation recover from the depression of the 1930s. Now the challenge was to convert from a wartime to a peacetime society.

Demobilization

Demobilization means the movement from a military to a civilian status. This meant reducing the nation's armed forces from 12 million members to 3 million. However it also meant seeing that factories that had made planes and tanks could now begin producing consumer goods. It also meant ensuring that the nation would not slip back into depression.

Key Social Studies Concepts:
Change, Choice

Under President Truman's administration, legislation was passed to deal with different issues raised by demobilization.

SERVICEMEN'S READJUSTMENT ACT   Also known as the **GI Bill of Rights**, this act authorized billions of dollars to pay for such veteran's benefits as college education, medical treatment, unemployment insurance, and home and business loans.

EMPLOYMENT ACT OF 1946   This act made full employment a national goal and set up a **Council of Economic Advisors** to guide the President on economic matters.

AN END TO PRICE CONTROLS   Wartime legislation had put controls on the prices of most goods. In 1946 the government moved to end most such controls. However, the end of controls coupled with a tax cut caused a rapid increase in inflation. For example, food prices soared 25 percent in just two years.

THE TAFT-HARTLEY ACT   Workers' wages could not keep up with inflation after the war. Major strikes hit the nation as unions pushed for higher wages. Antiunion feelings grew and led Congress to pass the **Taft-Hartley Act** over Truman's veto. The act

- provided an 80-day "cooling-off" period through which the President could delay a strike that threatened national welfare,
- barred the **closed shop**, under which workers had to belong to a union before being hired,
- allowed states to pass "**right-to-work laws**" which said workers could take jobs and not have to join a union,
- banned union contributions to political campaigns,
- required union leaders to swear they were not Communists.

National Security Concerns

Truman also moved to help the nation meet postwar international concerns. The **National Security Act** of 1947 changed the administration of the armed forces and created a new, Cabinet-level Department of Defense. The act also created the **Central Intelligence Agency** to oversee intelligence gathering activities.

As Commander-in-Chief, Truman also issued an executive order banning discrimination in the armed forces.

The "Baby Boom"

In addition to problems caused by converting to a peacetime economy, the nation also had to cope with the largest population explosion in its history. Refugees doubled the immigrant population in the years after the war. Meanwhile, the economic hardships of the depression that had encouraged smaller families were gone. Families grew larger again. By 1950 the rate of the nation's population growth was 14.5 percent. Between 1950 and 1960, it reached 18.5 percent. This "**baby boom**" brought with it the expansion of many public services, especially schools. You will learn more about the long-term effects of the "baby boom" in the next unit.

The Election of 1948

Inflation, strikes, Truman's actions on civil rights, and cold war challenges abroad left many voters dissatisfied with Truman. Polls predicted that the Republican candidate, Governor Thomas Dewey of New York, would defeat Truman easily in the 1948 presidential election. Yet Truman pulled off the greatest upset in American political history by winning reelection. He then attempted to build on this victory by proposing a program called the **Fair Deal** that aimed to extend reforms started under FDR's New Deal.

IMPACT OF THE COLD WAR AT HOME

During World War II, feelings of nationalism and patriotism ran high in the United States. After the war, as the nation defended democratic freedoms worldwide, it discovered that sometimes those freedoms were in danger at home. As Communists took over the government of China and the Soviet Union tested its first atomic bomb, fears of a Communist takeover in the United States led some Americans to take actions that violated the civil rights of others.

In the years after World War II, what has been called the **politics of subversion** became a new issue. "To subvert" means "to corrupt, undermine, or destroy." Many Americans charged that this was what Communists were trying to do in the United States. Other Americans responded that the actions of anti-Communists were more subversive of American values and more dangerous to the nation.

Key Ideas Tensions between feelings of patriotic loyalty and the right to dissent often increase during times of national crisis.

Looking for Communists

MAKING CONNECTIONS

Anti-Communist activity in the United States began well before World War II.

HUAC   In 1938 the **House Un-American Activities Committee** (HUAC) was formed as a temporary investigative unit to look into Communist activity in the United States. HUAC operated for more than 20 years. Its probe of the movie industry in the 1940s and 1950s was especially famous. This probe led to the **blacklisting**, or cutting off from employment, of many actors, writers, and directors.

J. Edgar Hoover, director of the Federal Bureau of Investigation, often aided investigations like HUAC's. He held his position and conducted anti-Communist activities that often violated the civil rights of Americans until the 1970s.

THE SMITH ACT   In 1940 Congress passed the **Smith Act**. This made it illegal for anyone to advocate "overthrowing . . . any government in the United States by force" or to "affiliate" with groups that called for such action.

In the landmark case of *Dennis* v. *United States*, 1951, the Supreme Court upheld the Smith Act. Eugene Dennis, General Secretary of the Communist Party in the United States, and ten others were convicted of teaching and advocating the violent overthrow of the government.

Two court decisions in 1957 weakened the intent of the Smith Act. In *Watkins* v. *United States*, the court ruled the HUAC could not punish witnesses who refused to cooperate at will. In *Yates* v. *United States*, the court ruled that the Smith Act applied only to those who teach or advocate direct "action" to overthrow government, not to those who merely advocate it in principle.

THE LOYALTY PROGRAM   President Truman added to anti-Communist feelings. In 1947 he ordered a **Loyalty Review Board** to conduct security checks of thousands of government employees. Those whose loyalty was considered doubtful were dismissed.

THE HISS CASE   Fears of Communists in government increased due to the Hiss case. **Alger Hiss** had been a strong backer of the New Deal in the 1930s. During the war, he had been an advisor to Roosevelt and had accompanied him to the Yalta Conference.

In 1948, however, **Whittaker Chambers**, a former Communist Party member, charged that Hiss had been a Communist spy in the 1930s. Hiss denied the charges, but a Congressional committee continued to probe them.

One committee member, **Richard Nixon**, a young Republican from California, believed Hiss to be guilty. His pursuit of the case and Hiss' eventual conviction on perjury charges made Nixon a national

Continuing Issues   In the landmark case of *Schenck* v. *United States*, the Supreme Court ruled that the government could place limits on free speech during wartime. Was the United States at war when the Smith Act was passed?

Enduring Issues

- Civil Liberties
- Criminal Penalties

MAKING CONNECTIONS

figure. The conviction also added weight to Republican charges that Roosevelt and Truman had not been alert enough to the dangers of communism.

McCarthyism

Against this political background, Senator Joseph McCarthy of Wisconsin began his own hunt for subversives. In 1950 McCarthy charged he had a list of State Department employees known to be Communists yet still working for the government. Over the next four years McCarthy went on to charge that many other people and government agencies had been corrupted by communism.

McCarthy made bold accusations without any evidence. This tactic became known as **McCarthyism**. He ruined the reputations of many people he carelessly accused of being Communists. Two related events during this period helped win public support for McCarthy's actions.

THE ROSENBERG CASE

In 1950 a German-born British citizen, **Klaus Fuchs**, was convicted of atomic espionage. Fuchs had worked on the American atom bomb program. Soon after, three Americans, **Ethel** and **Julius Rosenberg** and **Martin Sobell**, were charged with giving atomic secrets to the Soviets. In 1951 they were convicted and the Rosenbergs sentenced to death and Sobell to prison. The Rosenbergs were executed in 1953.

CONGRESSIONAL LEGISLATION

In the same year the Rosenbergs were arrested, Congress passed the **McCarran Internal Security Act**. The law aimed at limiting the actions of anyone the government considered a threat to United States security. The **McCarran-Walter Immigration Act** of 1952 restricted the immigration of persons from Communist countries and of anyone who could be considered a subversive.

Continuing Issues
Remember that the United States had gone through "Red Scare" in the 1920s. How were conditions then similar to conditions during the "Red Scare" after World War II?

McCARTHY'S CENSURE

In 1954 McCarthy charged that there were Communists in the Army. He held televised investigations into these charges. For the first time, millions of Americans saw McCarthy's bullying tactics for themselves. His public support quickly faded, and in December 1954 the Senate **censured**, or denounced, him for "conduct unbecoming a member."

The fall of McCarthy ended the "Red Scare" of the 1950s. But anti-Communist attitudes endured as the cold war dragged on for decades. Meanwhile, changes on the domestic front, especially in the area of civil rights, were having a lasting impact on American society. These will be key subjects for discussion in the next unit.

Regents Questions for Practice _____

Review the Test-Taking Strategies section of this book. Then answer the following questions, drawn from actual Regents examinations. Circle the *number* of the word or expression that best completes the statement or answers the question. Write your answers to essay questions on a separate piece of paper. Hints on good ways to approach these questions are provided in the margins.

MAKING CONNECTIONS

1. Which action by the United States government best demonstrated President Harry Truman's post–World War II containment policy?
   1 reaching an agreement with the Soviet Union to restrict military conflicts in Asia
   2 increasing scientific research in the field of armaments
   3 refusing to officially recognize most Communist countries
   4 establishing economic and military programs to stop communism

Test Hint Remember that you must be able to link Presidents with their policies.

2. United States economic aid to Western Europe after World War II was intended primarily to
   1 create a tariff free Common Market
   2 provide the United States with badly needed raw materials
   3 bring about political unity in Europe under United States leadership
   4 rebuild the economies of European nations

3. The purpose of the Marshall Plan was to provide Europe with
   1 defensive military weapons   3 cultural exchange programs
   2 economic aid   4 political alliances

4. The formation of the North Atlantic Treaty Organization (NATO) in 1949 is a significant event in United States diplomatic history because it
   1 committed the United States to a peacetime military alliance
   2 strengthened United States influence in oil-producing nations
   3 eased tensions with the Soviet Union and its satellites
   4 created new patterns of international trade

Test Hint Note the time period. Remember that the United States and the Soviet Union had just begun to face off in the cold war.

5. In its dependence upon members to enforce human rights declarations, the United Nations most closely resembles the
   1 Soviet Union under Josef Stalin
   2 United States under the federal Constitution
   3 United States under the Articles of Confederation
   4 Japanese government before World War II

6. ''The parties agree that an armed attack against one or more of them in Europe or North America shall be considered an attack against them all. . . .'' This quotation is most closely associated with which concept?

1 collective security   3 ultimatum
2 intervention   4 appeasement

7. Since World War II, collective security has been developed to
1 limit the development of nuclear weapons
2 prohibit the formation of local alliances
3 prevent the outbreak of war between the major powers
4 protect a nation from being weakened by internal subversion

8. An international policy whereby nations agree to take joint measures against an aggressor nation is called
1 unilateral action
2 an offensive alliance
3 benevolent neutrality
4 collective security

9. Which has been a primary difficulty of international organizations in dealing with world problems?
1 ineffective leadership
2 lack of Third World membership
3 lack of participation by the Communist bloc nations
4 emphasis on national self-interest by member nations

10. Since World War II, relations between the Soviet Union and the United States have been marked by
1 conflicts where the superpowers supported opposing sides, but did not confront each other directly
2 refusal to negotiate on any issues
3 slow but steady decreases in military forces and armaments
4 reliance on international peace organizations to solve disputes

11. After the end of World War II. the United States Government policy toward the Soviet Union was influenced primarily by the
1 existence of Soviet control in Eastern European countries
2 close alliance between the United States and China
3 abundance of Soviet aid during the war
4 cooperation between Soviet and American scientists on nuclear projects

12. After World War II, Untied States foreign policy in Western Europe was based primarily on the belief that
1 Western Europe required assistance to preserve its an ancient cultures
2 the threat of communism to Western European nations must be counteracted
3 Western Europe possessed abundant agricultural resources needed by the United States
4 the attitude of militarism found in most Western European nations threatened world peace

13. Which has been a major goal of United States foreign policy in Europe since 1945?
1 development of nuclear weapons for World War II Allies of the United States
2 liberation of nations under the control of the Soviet Union
3 military support for nationalist movements within individual European nations
4 promotion of international cooperation through political and economic agreements

14. During the Cold War era of the 1950s United States foreign policy was characterized by
1 a policy of nonalignment
2 an increase in the number of trade agreements with Communist nations
3 a willingness to compromise with Communist nations
4 a willingness to protect allies against Communist aggression

15. The term "cold war" referring to the period following World War II, primarily signifies the
1 struggle to overcome disease and poverty throughout the world
2 efforts to rebuild the economies of war-damaged countries in Europe
3 attempts by Third World nations to develop their military strength
4 political, economic, and military rivalry between the United States and the Soviet Union

16. "We Americans live in a world we can no longer dominate, but from which we cannot isolate ourselves." The author of this quotation is saying that the United States should
1 become less dependent on foreign nations

2 realize that it is no longer a world power
3 recognize important changes in international relations
4 increase its economic and military strength

17. Following the end of World War II United States foreign policy changed significantly in that the United States
1 assumed a more isolationist stance
2 began to rely on appeasement to reduce world tensions
3 perceived the containment of Communist expansion as a major goal
4 concentrated most heavily on events within the Western Hemisphere

18. One important result of the Red Scare of the 1920s and the McCarthy Era of the 1950s was the realization that
1 large numbers of Soviet agents had infiltrated high levels of the Federal Government
2 fears of subversion can lead to the erosion of constitutional liberties
3 communism gains influence in times of economic prosperity
4 loyalty oaths by government employees prevent espionage

Essay Questions

Following are essay questions about the Unit that you have been reviewing. Before answering each, apply the lessons you learned in the Test-Taking Strategies section by blocking each essay. The first block has been organized for you to help you get started with the pre-writing that is so necessary in preparing a good Regents essay answer.

1. At various times, the United States has followed one or more of the foreign policies listed below.

Foreign Policies
Imperialism
Isolationism
Containment

Nonrecognition
Formation of military alliances
Reliance upon international organizations

Choose three of the policies listed above. For each one chosen,
discuss a specific application of that policy by the United States.
Include in your discussion one reason the United States applied
that policy and one result of that policy.   [5, 5, 5]

Policy	Specific Application	Reason for Policy	Result of Policy
containment	Marshall Plan 1947	U.S. wanted to strengthen West European economies against Communist postwar expansion.	Communists were not able to gain control of any Western European nation. [5]
			[5]
			[5]

2. The foreign policy of a nation changes as conditions change. At
various times since the Civil War, the United States followed the
policies listed below.

Foreign Policies
Collective Security
Detente
Imperialism
Isolationism
Nuclear deterrence
Support of dictatorships

Select three of the foreign policies listed. For each one chosen, describe conditions that led the United States to adopt the policy at a particular time since the Civil War, and explain how the policy was implemented.   [5, 5, 5]

3. Some of the major goals of United States foreign policy are listed below

Goals

To foster foreign trade and United States economic interests
To provide for the military security of the United States
To promote the spread of the democratic ideals and values of the United States

a Select two of the goals listed and for each one chosen:
   • Describe an action taken by the United States government at any time before the end of World War II (1945) to achieve the goal
   • Describe an action taken by the United States Government since the end of World War II (1945) to achieve the goal   [12]
b Discuss one way in which life in the United States has been significantly influenced by one of the actions described in answer a.   [3]

4. The United States has initiated various foreign policy programs to deal with changing situations.
a Choose two of the programs or proposals listed below. For each one chosen, describe the program or proposal and the historical circumstances that led to its formulation.   [6, 6]

Washington's Farewell Address
Monroe Doctrine
Open Door Policy
Good Neighbor Policy
Marshall Plan
Membership in the North Atlantic
Treaty Organization
Membership in the United Nations

b For one of the programs or proposals described in answer to a, discuss to what extent the United States honored a principle of that program or proposal.   [3]

UNIT 6

The World in Uncertain Times, 1950–the Present

In Unit 5 you reviewed how the United States became involved in World War II and emerged from that conflict as the strongest nation in the world. You also saw how the nation set out on a foreign policy that deepened its involvement in many parts of the world.

In Unit 6 you will see how the foreign policies begun after World War II continued to shape America's responses to events abroad for decades. The policy of containment, begun under President Truman, finally led the nation into its longest war, one that caused deep splits within American society.

You will also see how life changed at home for Americans from the 1950s to the present. An expanding civil rights movement, a major constitutional crisis, new technologies, and a changing economic picture are some of the highlights of these years.

Almost all the Enduring Constitutional Issues are discussed in this unit. Key social studies concepts to focus on include change, diversity, justice, empathy, technology, and power.

You will need to know the answers to the following questions in order to pass the Regents examination:

Section 1: How did the foreign policy concerns of the United States become more global in scope?

Section 2: What were the goals and achievements of the black civil rights movement?

Section 3: What effects did the war in Vietnam have on American society?

Section 4: How did United States relations with the Soviet Union change under Presidents Reagan and Bush?

Section 5: What are some of the major challenges that the nation will face in the years to come?

Containment Abroad and Agreement at Home

Unit 5 discussed how United States foreign policy took shape in the years immediately after World War II. This section shows how the foreign policy that took shape then influenced events in the 1950s.

THE COLD WAR CONTINUES

The United States had emerged from World War II as the strongest nation in the world. It controlled the atomic bomb, and its economy had emerged undamaged by the destruction of war. The Soviet Union, however, quickly became America's chief rival. By 1949 it too had the atomic bomb. It had also taken control of most of the nations of Eastern Europe and was seeking to extend its influence elsewhere.

President Truman began the policy of containment after the war in an attempt to limit the spread of communism. As the United States and the Soviet Union—the two world "superpowers"—attempted to maintain a **balance of power**, a cold war developed.

Eisenhower's Foreign Policy

As President, **Dwight D. Eisenhower** continued Truman's basic policy of containment. However, he and his Secretary of State **John Foster Dulles** introduced some new ideas.

MASSIVE RETALIATION   Eisenhower worried that defense spending would bankrupt the nation. Yet he feared that the Soviets might see cutbacks in military spending as a sign of weakness.

Eisenhower and Dulles instead came up with a "new look" in national defense. The United States would rely more heavily on air power and nuclear weapons than on ground troops. Dulles announced a policy of **massive retaliation**. This meant the United States would consider the use of nuclear weapons to halt aggression if it believed the nation's interests were threatened.

Dulles further stated that the nation must be ready to go "to the brink of war" in order to preserve world peace. This policy of **brinkmanship** greatly increased world tensions during the 1950s.

THE ARMS RACE   The United States and the Soviet Union began an **arms race**, stockpiling nuclear and nonnuclear weapons. The

Enduring Issues

Presidential Power

Key Social Studies Concepts:

Power

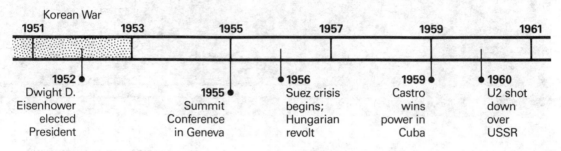

Korean War

| 1951 | 1953 | 1955 | 1957 | 1959 | 1961 |

1952 •
Dwight D.
Eisenhower
elected
President

1955 •
Summit
Conference
in Geneva

• **1956**
Suez crisis
begins;
Hungarian
revolt

1959 •
Castro
wins
power in
Cuba

• **1960**
U2 shot
down
over
USSR

MAKING CONNECTIONS

Regents Tip Maps can
illustrate aspects of
government policies.
On this map, note that most
of the trouble spots are
along the borders of the
Communist bloc nations.
This might serve to support
the idea that the United
States was continuing to
follow what foreign policy
in the 1950s?

United States exploded a hydrogen bomb in 1952, and the Soviets
tested one a year later.

Both nations rushed to develop missiles capable of carrying
nuclear weapons. The balance of power became more and more a
"balance of terror."

In 1957 the Soviets used a missile to launch a satellite, *Sputnik I*,
into orbit around the earth. The arms race then became a space race as
the United States rushed to launch its own satellites, some for military
purposes.

Foreign Policy in Asia

Asia became a major area of concern for United States foreign
policy. The Communist victory in China in 1949 raised fears of further
Communist expansion. The war in Korea, even though it ended in what
was basically a draw in 1953, added to these fears.

Trouble Spots of the Cold War, 1950s

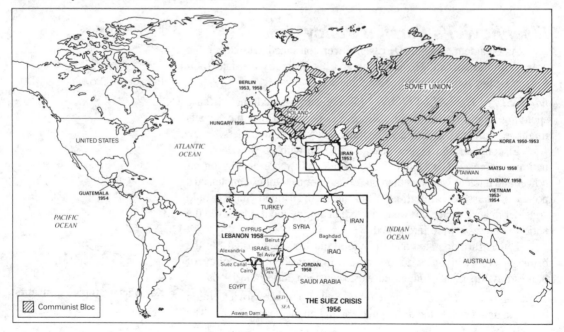

THE DOMINO THEORY   The fall of China and later the fall of the nations of Southeast Asia increased American worries of Communist expansion. Eisenhower stated that the United States must resist further aggression in the region. He explained this policy in what came to be known as the "**domino theory.**" The nations of Asia, he said, were like a row of dominoes standing on end. If one fell to communism, the rest were sure to follow.

SEATO   One way to resist aggression, Dulles claimed, was through alliances. To mirror the formation of NATO in Europe, Dulles in 1954 pushed for the creation of the **Southeast Asia Treaty Organization** (SEATO). Its original members—Pakistan, Thailand, the Philippines, Australia, New Zealand, Great Britain, and the United States—pledged to meet any "common danger" from Communist aggression.

Foreign Policy in the Middle East

The Middle East was the scene of several outbreaks of trouble during the Eisenhower administration.

IRAN   The United States sometimes attempted to advance its foreign policy by covert, or undercover, means. In 1954 the prime minister of Iran tried to nationalize that country's foreign-owned oil industry. The United States, through the Central Intelligence Agency, secretly arranged the overthrow of the prime minister's government and the restoration of the Shah to the throne of Iran. This action helped secure America's supply of oil at the time but would cause problems for the nation in years to come.

EGYPT   **Gamel Abdel Nasser**, president of Egypt, had counted on economic support from the Soviet Union and the United States to build a huge dam at Aswan on the Nile River. Nasser's friendliness to the Soviet Union led the United States to withdraw its support. Nasser then nationalized the Suez Canal, which was run by a British and French company. He planned to use revenues from the canal to pay for the dam.

Great Britain and France, joined by Israel, sent troops to seize the canal. Fearing that fighting would spread through the region, both the United States and the Soviet Union supported a United Nations resolution condemning the attack. Britain, France, and Israel withdrew, and the canal remained under Egyptian control.

THE EISENHOWER DOCTRINE   Troubles in the Middle East led Congress to adopt what became known as the **Eisenhower Doctrine** in 1957. The nation pledged to help any Middle Eastern nation resist Communist aggression.

LEBANON   In 1958 the Eisenhower Doctrine was tested when the governments of Lebanon and Jordan asked for help. The United States sent marines to Lebanon, and Great Britain sent troops to Jordan to help restore political calm in those nations.

MAKING CONNECTIONS

Foreign Policy in Latin America

Troubles also flared up closer to home during Eisenhower's time in office. Three instances were especially notable.

GUATEMALA   The CIA staged a successful covert operation in Guatemala in 1954. It arranged a revolt that toppled a government considered to be too friendly to Communists.

NIXON'S TOUR   In 1958 Vice President Richard Nixon went on a goodwill tour of Latin America. In Peru and Venezuela, however, angry mobs surrounded his limousine, throwing rocks and eggs at it. This event revealed the strong anti-American feelings that had built up in Latin America in response to this nation's repeated interventions in the region.

CUBA   In 1956 **Fidel Castro** began a revolt against the government of Cuban dictator Fulgencio Batista. When the revolt ended with Castro's victory in 1959, the United States quickly recognized the new government.

Castro, however, soon adopted policies that angered the Eisenhower administration. He limited civil liberties and imprisoned political opponents. He also nationalized key industries and turned to the Soviet Union for aid.

Large numbers of Cubans fled Castro's rule, with many settling in southern Florida. Some worked actively to end Castro's rule. Meanwhile, they became one more immigrant group that contributed to the richness of the American multicultural experience.

Continuing Issues
Remember that events begun in Cuba during the Eisenhower administration had effects on President Kennedy's foreign policy decisions in the 1960s.

Changing Relations with the Soviet Union

Tensions between the United States and the Soviet Union rose and fell during Eisenhower's time in office.

NEW SOVIET LEADERSHIP   Joseph Stalin, leader of the Soviet Union since the 1920s, died in 1953. In time, **Nikita Khrushchev** took over as the head of the Soviet government. This change marked a temporary easing of cold war tensions as the Soviets began to focus more on improving conditions within their nation.

"PEACEFUL COEXISTENCE"   Relations between the superpowers gradually improved. Leaders of the United States, the Soviet Union, Great Britain, and France held the first **summit meeting** since World War II in Geneva, Switzerland, in 1955. The superpower leaders began talks on disarmament that in time led to a suspension of nuclear testing.

POLAND AND HUNGARY   In 1956 riots by Polish workers won concessions from the Communist government of that satellite nation. Inspired by this, students and workers in Hungary began demonstrations that fall that ended with the Soviet Union sending tanks and troops to bring that nation back firmly under Communist control. The crushing of the Hungarian revolt cooled relations between Americans and Soviets.

Regents Tip   Practice your summarizing skills by explaining how United States foreign policy differed in the 1930s (before World War II) and the 1950s (after World War II).

CAMP DAVID Relations had improved again by 1959. Khrushchev visited the United States for two weeks. He and Eisenhower held lengthy talks at **Camp David**, the presidential retreat near Washington. The spirit of goodwill that grew at these talks encouraged the leaders to announce another summit meeting in Paris in 1960.

THE U-2 INCIDENT The Paris summit proved a disaster. Shortly before it opened, the Soviet military shot down an American U-2 aircraft deep in Soviet territory. The pilot admitted that he had been spying on Soviet military bases.

Eisenhower said that he had approved the U-2 flights and promised to suspend them. Khrushchev denounced the United States and demanded an apology. Eisenhower refused and the summit collapsed before it really started.

In summary, Eisenhower's foreign policy had been primarily one of a continuation of the Truman policy of containment. Many of the events of the 1950s can be compared to kettles ready to boil over in the 1960s. In later years the Eisenhower administration was criticized by some as not being aware enough of the struggles of the Third World nations and of their desires to end colonial rule.

AN IMPROVING ECONOMY AT HOME

When Dwight Eisenhower became President in 1953, he was the first Republican President since 1933—the year Herbert Hoover left office and one of the worst years of the Great Depression. Since that time, Democrats Franklin D. Roosevelt and Harry S Truman had called for New Deal and New Society policies that had vastly increased both the federal government's spending and its role in society. Would Eisenhower act to end such programs?

Eisenhower's Economic Policies

Eisenhower made it clear that he had a deep dislike for strong centralized government. In addition, he generally believed policies that were good for big business were good for the nation as a whole.

EISENHOWER'S DOMESTIC POLICIES Eisenhower attempted to cut back on the federal government's size and power. He reduced spending for defense and foreign aid.

Eisenhower did recognize that many social programs begun under the New Deal were very popular. He extended some of these and, in some cases, started new programs. The Social Security program was expanded to include 10 million more people, and a new Cabinet post, the Department of Health, Education, and Welfare, was created.

THE FARM PROBLEM Conditions on the nation's farms pulled Eisenhower between his desire to cut government spending and his wish to extend some social programs. Farm production had been increasing while prices for agricultural products had been declining.

MAKING CONNECTIONS

Background Camp David was named for President Eisenhower's young grandson, who later married Richard Nixon's daughter Julie. What other important meeting was held at Camp David?

Major Ideas The changing world balance of power made efforts to restore normal domestic life after World War II and Korea more complicated.

Enduring Issues

Federalism

MAKING CONNECTIONS

Major Ideas Recovery of the American economy was also aided by the fact that the nation's industries had not been destroyed by fighting during World War II.

Regents Tip Regents questions may test your ability to make connections between what you have learned in different parts of the course.
How is the number of Representatives a state has in the House of Representatives determined?
How might population shifts such as the one described here affect New York State's representation in the House?

Farmers had been receiving payments from the federal government to make up for changes in market conditions. Eisenhower's Secretary of Agriculture wanted to be able to cut such payments. Farmers protested, and in 1956 Congress approved a new program that paid farmers for *not* planting crops. Both types of payments are **subsidies**, or direct payments by a government to private individuals.

"Eisenhower Prosperity" and Consumer Spending

Despite the problems noted above, the American people generally prospered during the 1950s. There were several reasons for this.

- During World War II, Americans had worked hard and generally earned good wages. Due to rationing and shortages, however, they could usually only spend their money on basic necessities.

- By war's end, Americans had accumulated huge amounts of **capital**, wealth in the form of money or property. They were ready to spend this capital on consumer goods.

- By the 1950s, wartime price controls were over and factories had time to convert from the production of military supplies to production of consumer goods.

- Americans were now eager and able to buy new cars, washing machines, refrigerators, and a host of new and improved goods. This spending helped the nation's booming economy.

NEW HOMES As you read in Unit 5, the postwar years saw the start of a "baby boom." The growth in family size, the accumulation of capital, and the availability of government loans to veterans brought a rapid increase in home building.

SUBURBS Much new home building was done in areas surrounding major cities (urban areas). These areas are called **suburbs**. The suburbs offered limited jobs and services for their residents, most of whom worked in the cities. For this reason, suburbs are sometimes called "bedroom communities."

The suburbs grew rapidly. In Levittown, New York, some 17,000 "tract" houses were built in four years. By the 1960s, almost a third of all Americans lived in suburbs.

The growth of suburbs contributed to the decline of many cities. As people moved out of cities to suburbs, fewer taxpayers remained to help pay for essential services. At the same time, a greater concentration of poorer people in the cities increased the demand for many social services.

AUTOMOBILES Cars made the growth of suburbs possible, and suburbs increased the demand for cars. Since public transportation systems grew more slowly than suburbs, people in suburbs relied increasingly on their cars. As the demand for automobiles increased, many areas of the nation's economy benefited. Factories turned out the steel, glass, and rubber that went into new cars. Refineries also produced oil and gas that powered them.

The federal government stepped into the transportation picture with passage of the Highway Act of 1956. This provided funding for what became a 41,000-mile network of interstate highways.

A NATION ON THE MOVE Americans moved from central cities to suburbs. They also moved to new areas of the country. Many people moved from the industrialized but decaying cities of the Northeast and Midwest and from the farms of the Midwest to the **Sunbelt**. This was the name given to the states of the South and West, including Florida, Texas, Arizona, and California, that experienced a faster than average population growth beginning in the postwar years.

The sun and warm climate of these states attracted both retirees and businesses that wished to relocate. As this region grew, it attracted more industry and prompted both population and job loss in what came to be called the "Rust Belt." This region included the states of the Northeast (including New York and Massachusetts) and Midwest (including Ohio and Michigan).

TELEVISION National broadcasting began in 1946. Television became the leading form of popular entertainment, and its growth, both as a source of amusement and a tool for learning, has continued to the present day.

A RENEWED STRUGGLE FOR CIVIL RIGHTS

Since the period of Reconstruction after the Civil War, black Americans faced discrimination, especially in Southern states. "Jim Crow" laws limited the freedoms of African Americans. For generations, descendants of former slave owners maintained economic, social, and political control over descendants of former slaves.

Beginnings of Change

Until well into this century, much of the South was **segregated**, or separated by race. Although such segregation was less apparent in the North, blacks were still by and large forced to live in poorer neighborhoods and work at lower-paying jobs than whites. Although African Americans fought for change, until the 1950s their gains were limited.

Not until 1947, for example, were African Americans permitted to play on major league baseball teams in this country. In that year,

MAKING CONNECTIONS

Homes with Television Sets

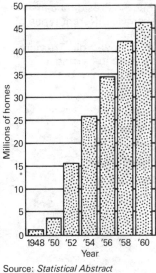

Source: *Statistical Abstract of the United States*

Enduring Issues

Ethnic and Racial Groups

Regents Tip Read the labels on the axes of graphs carefully. In what year did homes with television sets increase the most? How many homes had television sets that year?

MAKING CONNECTIONS

Regents Tip Remember that the President can exercise different types of power.
What power did Truman exercise in barring segregation in the armed forces?

Enduring Issues

The Judiciary

Regents Tip This case is the most frequently tested of all the Supreme Court's landmark decisions. Make sure you understand its significance.

Background Thurgood Marshall, who argued the case for the Brown family, was later appointed to the Supreme Court by President Lyndon Johnson. He was the first black to hold such a position.

Jackie Robinson joined the Brooklyn Dodgers. This was one sign that public attitudes on segregation were beginning to change.

TRUMAN'S POLICIES ON CIVIL RIGHTS President Truman appointed a presidential commission on civil rights in 1946. Based on its report, Truman called for establishment of a Fair Employment Practices Commission. Congress, however, failed to act on the idea.

Using his powers as commander in chief, Truman issued an executive order banning segregation in the armed forces. He also strengthened the Justice Department's civil rights division, which aided blacks who challenged segregation in the courts.

Civil Rights and the Courts

THE WARREN COURT In 1953 a vacancy occurred on the Supreme Court. President Eisenhower then appointed **Earl Warren**, former governor of California, as Chief Justice.

Warren came from a political rather than a purely legal background. He presided over the Supreme Court until 1969. During that period the Court reached a number of decisions that deeply affected many areas of American life. The liberal nature of many decisions later prompted Eisenhower to remark that Warren's appointment was one of his biggest mistakes. Among the most far-reaching of the Warren Court's decisions were those dealing with civil rights for blacks.

BROWN V. BOARD OF EDUCATION Only a year after he became Chief Justice, Warren presided over the court as it reached a landmark decision in *Brown* v. *Board of Education*. Linda Brown, a young African American student in Topeka requested the right to attend a local all-white school in her neighborhood rather than attend an all-black school that was further away.

The landmark *Plessy* v. *Ferguson* decision of 1896 had held that separate but equal public facilities for white and blacks were legal. Schools were such public facilities, and Brown was refused admittance to the all-white school.

The National Association for the Advancement of Colored People (NAACP) joined the case and appealed it all the way to the Supreme Court. There, reversing *Plessy* v. *Ferguson*, the unanimous Court ruled that in the field of public education "the doctrine of separate but equal has no place."

LITTLE ROCK The Brown case opened the door for desegregation, but integration did not follow immediately. Many Americans were shocked by the decision. In the South, whites began campaigns of "massive resistance" to public school desegregation.

Although the Supreme Court had ordered that school integration go forward "with all deliberate speed," many school systems openly defied the ruling. In 1957 the governor of Arkansas ordered the state's National Guard to prevent the integration of Little Rock high schools.

President Eisenhower was reluctant to step in, but mob violence in Little Rock forced him to act. He placed the Arkansas National Guard under federal control and now used it to enforce integration. After the school year ended, the governor ordered the high schools closed for the following year to prevent integration. This happened in other Southern states, as deep-seated racism and bigotry came to the surface.

Black Activism

In addition to schools, movie theaters, lunch counters, drinking fountains, restrooms, buses, and trains throughout the South were segregated. Rather than wait for court rulings to end segregation, in the 1950s African Americans began to take direct action toward that goal.

THE MONTGOMERY BUS BOYCOTT In 1955 **Rosa Parks**, a black seamstress in Montgomery, Alabama, refused to give up her seat to a white man and move to the back of the bus as required by law. She was arrested for violating the law, and her action was the inspiration for one of the most significant events of the civil rights movement of the 1950s.

Black citizens quickly organized a boycott of the city's buses. **Martin Luther King, Jr.**, a young Baptist minister, emerged as a leader of the protest. King had studied the nonviolent methods of Mohandas Gandhi and Henry David Thoreau. His dynamic speaking style drew the attention and support of large numbers of blacks and some whites.

The boycott went on for 381 days. In the end, the Supreme Court ruled that segregation of public buses was illegal. Parks later commented that she had not planned or anticipated the results of her action that day, but that it was an action that had to happen. Her stand against injustice lead the way for others.

Civil Rights Legislation

The Congress also made some moves to ensure civil rights for black Americans. In August 1957, it passed the first civil rights act since Reconstruction. The bill created a permanent Commission for Civil Rights and increased federal efforts to ensure blacks the right to vote. Another bill in 1960 further strengthened voting rights.

These bills had only limited effectiveness, but they did mark the beginning of change. Martin Luther King, Jr., once remarked that it was impossible to legislate what was in a person's heart, but that laws can "restrain the heartless."

MAKING CONNECTIONS

Major Ideas The responses of Southern authorities and individuals to nonviolent efforts by blacks to achieve integration encouraged a spirit of empathy among Americans from other regions who followed these events in newspapers and on television.

Enduring Issues

Equality

Regents Tip Review the section by listing two ways in which blacks were denied full rights of citizenship in this period.

1.

2.

What amendment should have prevented this from happening?

Regents Questions for Practice _____

Review the Test-Taking Strategies section of this book. Then answer the following questions, drawn from actual Regents examinations. Circle the *number* of the word or expression that best completes the statement or answers the question. Hints on good ways to approach these questions are provided in the margins.

Test Hint   To answer this question, think about other U.S. goals in postwar Europe. Was the spread of communism more likely in rich or poor countries?

1. United States economic aid to Western Europe after World War II was intended primarily to
   1 create a tariff-free Common Market
   2 provide the United States with badly needed raw materials
   3 bring about political unity in Europe under United States leadership
   4 rebuild the economies of European nations

2. "Nations strive to prevent any one country from becoming all powerful and domineering."
   Which concept is referred to by this statement?
   1 militarism   3 national sovereignty
   2 imperialism   4 balance of power

Test Hint   Remember to associate Castro and Communist goals.

3. Since Fidel Castro assumed control in 1959, many nations have considered Cuba a threat because the Castro regime
   1 overthrew a democratic Cuban government when taking control
   2 has seriously hindered trade among countries of the Western Hemisphere
   3 has supported revolutions in various parts of the world
   4 has refused to sell sugar or tobacco to industrialized nations

Test Hint   Underline and think about the word "original" here.

4. Which reason was usually given by the United States government to explain its original involvement in Indochina?
   1 Vietnam's long tradition of democracy
   2 the evidence of an immediate danger to the United States from a Communist-controlled Vietnam
   3 the desire of the United States to prevent the spread of Communist influence in Southeast Asia
   4 United States investments in the development of Vietnam

Test Hint   You can answer this question using common sense. Think about technological changes in the 20th century.

5. In the United States during the 20th century, which contributed most to the development of the suburbs?
   1 improvements in transportation systems
   2 a decrease in the average per capita income
   3 an increase in the number of women employed in industry
   4 a strong desire by the middle class to develop original ideas and styles

6. In the United States, which has been a result of the movement of the population from urban to suburban areas?
   1 a decrease in the value of property in most rural areas
   2 an increase in the importance of the city as a commercial center
   3 an intensification of financial problems in many cities
   4 an increase in the educational cost per pupil in suburban areas

MAKING CONNECTIONS

Test Hint You need to know this vocabulary: urban, suburban, and rural.

7. Which is the most valid conclusion that may be drawn from a study of the population shift in the United States from the inner city to the suburbs?
   1 The middle class is moving to the suburbs because of the loss of federal aid to the cities.
   2 Metropolitan governments are being created which are able to solve financial problems through regional planning.
   3 The city leaders are better able to deal with urban problems because growth in suburban areas widens the tax base.
   4 The urban situation is becoming more critical because of the reduction of the tax base.

8. The relationship between the automobile and the development of suburbs is most similar to the relationship between
   1 television and increased uniformity of United States culture
   2 skyscrapers and the decline of commuter railroads
   3 political parties and the growth of big business
   4 nuclear power plants and rising oil prices

9. One method the United States Federal Government has used to stimulate consumer spending has been to
   1 increase taxes on imports
   2 raise yields on government bonds
   3 reduce personal income taxes
   4 cut unemployment benefits

Base your answer to questions 10–12 on the chart to the right and on your knowledge of social studies.

United States Population Changes

	1910	1960	Percent Change
Urban Population (percent of total)	45.5%	69.3%	+52.3%
Rural Population (percent of total)	54.5%	30.7%	−43.7%
Farm Employment (percent of total employed)	14.7%	3.9%	−75.5%
Per Capita Gross National Product (GNP)	$608	$1,396	+129.6%

10. Which statement concerning population changes is best supported by the data in the chart?
1 Urbanization has accompanied economic growth.
2 There is little connection between population changes and prosperity levels.
3 Urban workers earn more money than rural workers.
4 The decrease in farm employment resulted in increased urban unemployment.

11. Which situation would most likely account for the changes in population shown in the chart?
1 Greater educational opportunities were available in the cities.
2 Greater economic opportunities were available in the cities.
3 The crime rate was lower in rural areas.
4 Housing became scarce in rural areas.

12. Which factor would best explain the change in farm employment?
1 Immigration was restricted after 1910.
2 The amount of available farmland decreased.
3 Mechanization reduced the need for farm workers.
4 Imports provided a higher percentage of food needs.

13. The post-World War II baby boom in the United States indicated that population growth has been directly related to the
1 general movement of the population
2 movement of population to rural areas
3 change of political leadership
4 general economic and social conditions

14. In the case of *Brown* v. *Board of Education*, 1954, the United States Supreme Court decided that
1 separate educational facilities are inherently unequal and unconstitutional
2 busing of children to overcome segregation is constitutional
3 the use of civil disobedience to achieve legal rights is constitutional
4 closing public schools to avoid integration is unconstitutional

Base your answers to questions 15 and 16 on the quotation below from a United States Supreme Court decision and on your knowledge of social studies.

"We conclude that in the field of public education the doctrine of 'separate but equal' has no place. Separate educational facilities are inherently unequal. Therefore, we hold that the plaintiffs . . . are, by reason of the segregation complained of, deprived of the equal protection of the laws guaranteed by the 14th amendment."

15. This Supreme Court decision is based on the idea that segregation in education is likely to
1 deny individuals the opportunity to make upward social and economic progress
2 create unnecessary administrative problems in the nation's schools
3 place excessive burdens on school transportation systems
4 result in unfair tax increases to support dual school systems

16. This Supreme Court ruling can most accurately be said to have marked the beginning of the end of
1 racial violence
2 public education
3 legal racial discrimination
4 the civil rights movement

Decade of Change

In 1960 Democrat **John F. Kennedy** defeated Republican Richard M. Nixon to gain the presidency. After Kennedy's assassination in November 1963, Vice President **Lyndon B. Johnson** took over as President, later winning election in 1964. These two Democratic Presidents led the nation through one of its most stormy periods, the 1960s. These years introduced major changes into American society. Many of the most important changes had to do with civil rights.

MAKING CONNECTIONS

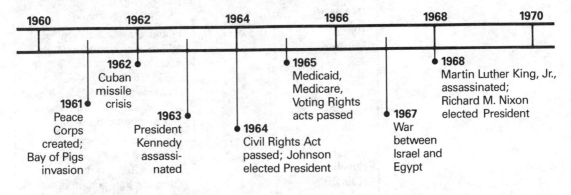

| 1960 | 1962 | 1964 | 1966 | 1968 | 1970 |

1962 Cuban missile crisis

1961 Peace Corps created; Bay of Pigs invasion

1963 President Kennedy assassinated

1964 Civil Rights Act passed; Johnson elected President

1965 Medicaid, Medicare, Voting Rights acts passed

1967 War between Israel and Egypt

1968 Martin Luther King, Jr., assassinated; Richard M. Nixon elected President

THE STRUGGLE FOR CIVIL RIGHTS CONTINUES

During the 1960s the struggle of African Americans to win equality before the law grew more intense. In their fight, blacks were seeking to overcome a heritage of racism that had become a part of American thought and tradition for more than 300 years.

The first Africans destined for slavery had arrived in Virginia in 1619, the same year that representative government, in the form of the House of Burgesses, became a part of colonial life. By the end of the Civil War, blacks had endured more than two centuries of slavery and discrimination. Almost a full century of discrimination lay ahead after Reconstruction.

By the 1960s, however, African Americans were working together for the common goal of justice and equality in a way that white America had never seen. The successes they gained would deeply affect many parts of American society.

Enduring Issues

∞

Ethnic and Racial Groups

Election of 1960

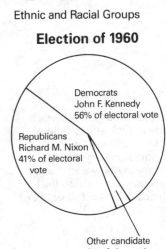

Democrats John F. Kennedy 56% of electoral vote

Republicans Richard M. Nixon 41% of electoral vote

Other candidate 3% of electoral vote

African Americans Organize

The pressure for change came mostly from blacks themselves. They formed a number of different groups that used different approaches in the attempt to better conditions for all African Americans.

Organization	Date of Founding	Background
National Association for the Advancement of Colored People (NAACP)	1909	Organized by black and white progressives; W. E. B. Du Bois an early leader; favored court challenges to segregation; appealed primarily to the professional and college-educated.
Black Muslims	1931	Founded as a black separatist religious group; became the voice of black nationalism in the 1960s; Muhammed Ali converted in 1965; Malcolm X, a leading spokesperson, was assassinated in 1965.
Congress on Racial Equality (CORE)	1942	Became best known for the "freedom rides" of the 1960s, efforts to desegregate interstate transportation.
Southern Christian Leadership Conference (SCLC)	1957	Founded by Martin Luther King, Jr., to encourage nonviolent passive resistance; organized black Christian churches.
Student Nonviolent Coordinating Committee (SNCC)	1960	In early days, used nonviolent civil disobedience in sit-ins and boycotts; later supported the idea of "black power" put forward by Stokely Carmichael.

Major Idea   Stereotyped ideas that whites held of blacks often slowed understanding and empathy between those groups and slowed the black drive for full rights of citizenship.

In the early 1960s, many groups working for black rights followed the nonviolent methods of Dr. Martin Luther King, Jr. Many of their actions involved **civil disobedience**. This means the deliberate breaking of a law to show a belief that the law is unjust. For example, they also attempted to use segregated facilities at interstate train stations and bus depots. Usually they were arrested for such acts; often they were beaten.

JAMES MEREDITH   The push to integrate education begun in the 1950s continued. In 1962 **James Meredith**, a black Air Force veteran, made headlines when he tried to enroll at the all-white University of Mississippi. The governor of the state personally tried to stop Meredith from enrolling. Riots broke out and federal marshals and the National Guard were called up. Although he had to overcome continued harassment, Meredith did finally enter and eventually graduate from the university.

GREENSBORO   Civil rights demonstrators used the concept of civil disobedience to protest such discrimination as segregated lunch counters and buses. Sit-ins at lunch counters—the 1960s version of fast-food restaurants—began at Greensboro, North Carolina, in 1960. There a group of blacks sat at a "whites only" lunch counter and refused to leave until served. As such protests became popular, sympathetic whites often joined with blacks in sit-ins.

BIRMINGHAM   In 1963 Dr. Martin Luther King, Jr., and the SCLC began a campaign to bring integration to Birmingham, Alabama, which white city officials proudly hailed as the most segregated city in the South. King planned to use marches, demonstrations, and other nonviolent methods of civil disobedience to focus public attention on Birmingham. Police used dogs and firehoses to break up the marchers and arrested over 2,000 people.

One of those jailed was King, who then wrote his famous "**Letter from a Birmingham Jail**" in which he defended his methods of nonviolent civil disobedience and restated the need for direct action to end the moral wrong of segregation.

After weeks of protest, support for the black cause grew nationwide. The Kennedy administration worked to resolve the crisis and helped arrange a settlement that satisfied many of the blacks' demands.

MEDGAR EVERS   White reaction to African American protests sometimes turned deadly. **Medgar Evers**, field secretary of the Mississippi NAACP, had been trying to win a similar settlement to Birmingham's for Jackson, Mississippi. In June 1963, Evers was murdered by a sniper outside his home.

UNIVERSITY OF ALABAMA   In that same month, Governor George Wallace of Alabama vowed to personally stop two black students from registering at the state university. Pressure from President Kennedy and the later arrival of the National Guard forced Wallace to back down. The two students enrolled peacefully.

THE MARCH ON WASHINGTON   The continuing agitation over civil rights moved President Kennedy to address the issue head on. In June 1963 Kennedy delivered a televised speech to the nation on the need to guarantee the civil rights of blacks. This marked the first

MAKING CONNECTIONS

Key Social Studies Concepts:
Citizenship; Empathy

U.S. and the World
Remember that Mohandas Gandhi's nonviolent struggle against British rule in India greatly influenced King's ideas on civil disobedience.

MAKING CONNECTIONS

Enduring Issues

Equality

Enduring Issues

Change and Flexibility

Major Ideas Improvement in rights and opportunities for blacks and other groups who have suffered discrimination requires action on the national, state, and local levels.

speech by a President specifically on this issue. Eight days later, he sent the most comprehensive civil rights bill in the nation's history to Congress.

Black groups organized a huge **March on Washington, D.C.,** in August 1963 to show support for the bill. At the march, Dr. Martin Luther King, Jr., delivered his famous ''I have a dream'' speech to a crowd of more than 200,000. In it, he eloquently expressed his hopes for a unified black and white America.

Not all Americans shared King's dream. Just a few weeks after the March on Washington, white terrorists bombed a black church in Birmingham, killing four little girls.

JOHNSON AND THE CIVIL RIGHTS ACT   With the assassination of John F. Kennedy in November 1963, it seemed that the civil rights bill might no longer be a top government priority. Yet the new President, Lyndon Johnson, had been deeply involved with civil rights legislation when he had served in Congress. He recognized the urgency of pushing forward with the bill.

Within days of taking office, Johnson appealed to Congress for passage of the legislation. He also worked tirelessly behind the scenes for the bill, and in July 1964 Johnson signed the **Civil Rights Act of 1964**, the most sweeping civil rights law in American history. The bill called for

• protection of voting rights for all Americans

• opening of public facilities (restaurants, hotels, stores, restrooms) to people of all races

• a commission to protect equal job opportunities for all Americans

Passage of the Civil Rights Act came just months after ratification of the 24th Amendment to the Constitution, which abolished the **poll tax** in federal elections. A poll tax was a fee that had to be paid before a person could vote. Abolishing the tax would mean opening elections to the poorest Americans, many of whom were Southern blacks.

THE VOTING RIGHTS ACT OF 1965   Black Americans welcomed the new legislation. They recognized, however, that having legislation on record did not necessarily mean that laws would be obeyed. Many Southern states resisted the new legislation. Demonstrations and protest marches continued, and arrests and deaths mounted.

Southern resistance to civil rights laws angered Johnson. He proposed new legislation, which was passed as the **Voting Rights Act of 1965**. This bill

• put an end to **literacy tests**, tests of a person's ability to read and write that had often been misused to bar black voters

• authorized federal examiners to register voters in areas suspected of denying blacks the right to vote

- directed the Attorney General of the United States to take legal action against states that continued to use poll taxes in state elections

MAKING CONNECTIONS

CHANGES IN THE CIVIL RIGHTS MOVEMENT   The summer of 1964 had been know as "Freedom Summer" for its many demonstrations, protests, voter registration drives, and the March on Washington. Freedom Summer and the passage of the Voting Rights Act a year later marked highpoints of the civil rights movement.

Change came as black frustration over continuing economic and social inequality erupted in riots in major cities across the United States. Hundreds of people died and millions of dollars worth of property was lost in these clashes.

Many white Americans claimed that blacks wanted too much, too fast. Blacks responded that new legislation had not improved conditions enough. Many African Americans demanded "**Black Power**," stressing that blacks should take total control of the political and economic aspects of their lives. Some advocated the use of violence. More moderate leaders continued to call for nonviolent methods of protest. These splits weakened the effectiveness of the civil rights movement.

DEATH OF DR. MARTIN LUTHER KING, JR.   Dr. Martin Luther King, Jr., had been awarded the Nobel Peace Prize in 1964 "for the furtherance of brotherhood among men." He remained a leading speaker for black rights even as splits developed in the civil rights movement. He also remained firmly on the side of nonviolence.

As a supporter of the underprivileged and the needy, King went to Memphis, Tennessee, in April 1968 to back a sanitation workers' strike. There he was shot and killed by a white assassin. The death of the leading spokesperson for nonviolence set off new rounds of rioting in American cities.

Just two months after King's death, Robert F. Kennedy, brother of the late President and now a presidential candidate himself, was assassinated. The shock of these deaths and the increasing urban violence made the goals of King and the Kennedys seem far off to many Americans.

THE WOMEN'S RIGHTS MOVEMENT

Enduring Issues

The Rights of Women

Like African Americans, women had been denied equal rights in the United States for hundreds of years. Like blacks, women played no part in the Constitutional Convention that shaped the nation's system of government. Like blacks, they had long been denied the right to vote. Like blacks, they had won some concessions over time but were still denied full equality in society. The successes of the black civil rights movement in the 1960s highlighted the need for organized action by women to achieve similar goals.

Women Working Outside the Home

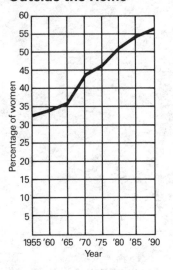

Source: *Statistical Abstract of the United States*

Past Successes, New Goals

The women's rights movement was not just a product of the 1960s. The struggle for equality had been a long one. Some of the key events in the struggle are listed below.

1848   The Seneca Falls Convention marked the beginning of the organized women's rights movement in this nation.

1868   Passage of the 14th Amendment granted the vote to black males but not to women. Susan B. Anthony arranged to have a women's suffrage amendment introduced in Congress. It was defeated there, but Anthony and others continued the fight.

1920   Ratification of the 19th Amendment gave women the right to vote.

1940s   Thousands of women took jobs in war-related industries.

By the 1960s, women had exercised the right to vote for 40 years. Yet women still had not achieved equal status with men economically and socially. Women's groups renewed demands for a variety of goals including more job opportunities, equality of pay with men, and an end to discrimination based on sex.

Presidents Kennedy and Johnson appointed no women to major posts in their administrations. Yet in those years fundamental changes did occur. For example, more and more women entered fields that men had traditionally dominated such as law, medicine, engineering, and the sciences. Below is a list of some important events concerning women's rights in the 1960s and early 1970s.

- In 1963 Betty Friedan wrote *The Feminine Mystique*, a book arguing that society had forced American women out of the job market and back into the home after World War II. She said that not all women were content with the role of homemaker and that more job opportunities should be open to women.

- Title VII of the Civil Rights Act of 1964 barred job discrimination on the basis of sex as well as race.

- The **National Organization for Women** (NOW) was formed in 1966 to push for legislation guaranteeing equality for women.

- Congress approved an **Equal Rights Amendment** (ERA) in 1972 and sent it to the states for ratification. The amendment stated that "equality of rights under the law shall not be denied or abridged by the United States or any state on account of sex."

- The Equal Employment Opportunity Act of 1972 required employers to pay equal wages for equal work.

- Title IX of the Educational Amendments Act of 1972 gave female college athletes the right to the same financial support as male athletes.

- In the landmark case of *Roe* v. *Wade* (1073), the Supreme Court decided that a woman's right to an abortion is constitutionally protected. Laws making abortion a crime were overturned because they violated a woman's right to privacy; the Supreme Court held that the states could only limit abortion after the first six months of pregnancy. Challenges to the decision in *Roe* v. *Wade* have continued, and the possibility remains that the Supreme Court may reverse the decision in another case.

AFFIRMATIVE ACTION   Some of the laws guaranteeing equal opportunities for women and blacks and other minority groups called for **affirmative action**. This meant taking positive steps to eliminate the effects of past discrimination in hiring. In practice it often meant giving preference to members of such groups when hiring workers or accepting applicants to schools. These affirmative action programs were begun during the Johnson administration of the 1960s.

WOMEN'S RIGHTS VOCABULARY   "Feminism" and "sexism" became two key vocabulary words for understanding the women's rights movement. "Feminism" refers to the belief that women should have the same economic, social, and political rights as men. The women's rights movement is sometimes called the feminist movement.

"Sexism" refers to belief or practices that discriminate against a person on the basis of sex. The women's movement directed its efforts at removing sexist terminology, practices, and literature from American business and education.

Setbacks for the Movement

Not all Americans—nor all women—agreed with the goals of the women's rights movement. Some argued that women already had equal rights. Others claimed that those goals undermined "traditional" values. Such opposition led to a number of setbacks for the movement.

- In 1971 President Nixon vetoed a bill that would have provided for a national system of day care for working mothers on the grounds that the family rather than the government should be responsible for the care of children.

- Critics charged that affirmative action programs were a kind of "reverse discrimination" in which white males lost chances at jobs to less qualified women and members of minority groups. A number of affirmative action programs have been challenged in court, with mixed results.

For example, in 1979 the Supreme Court ruled in the landmark case of *Regents of the University of California* v. *Bakke* that the school used explicit racial quotas when deciding on applicants to medical school. This meant that Allan Bakke was rejected in favor of

MAKING CONNECTIONS

Continuing Issues   Most of the Supreme Court justices who supported the decision in *Roe* v. *Wade* have retired. Conservative Presidents have since appointed new justices to the Court. Those Americans who opposed the original decision hope that this new group of justices will overturn the *Roe* v. *Wade* ruling.

Continuing Issues   The fact that courts have upheld some affirmative action programs while rejecting others indicates that more court cases on this topic can be expected in the future.

MAKING CONNECTIONS

Background   It is
important to remember that
the ERA was only
proposed, never *ratified.*
Only 35 states voted for the
ERA; it takes the approval
of 38 states for a proposed
amendment to become part
of the Constitution.

Enduring Issues

Ethnic and Racial Groups

Key Social Studies Concepts:

Justice

less qualified applicants. The Court ruled that Bakke had been
denied equal protection under the 14th Amendment. It nevertheless
found that other affirmative action programs may be constitutional.

- The proposed ERA generated tremendous controversy. Opponents
claimed that the women's rights movement had led to rising divorce
rates, increasing numbers of abortions, and the growing acceptance
and recognition of homosexuality—all threats to traditional values,
said critics. Ratification of the ERA, they argued, would cause still
more problems for American society. By the 1982 deadline, the
ERA was three states short of ratification and thus was defeated.

OTHER GROUPS STRUGGLE FOR THEIR RIGHTS

Other groups besides women and blacks demanded equal rights.
Among them were Hispanic Americans, Native Americans, and disabled Americans.

Hispanic Americans

Three fifths of the Spanish-speaking people in the United States
are Hispanic Americans from Mexico. Although they have moved to
many parts of the country, most still live in the Southwest, in states that
were once part of Mexico. These people are often known as "Chicanos."

Large numbers of Chicanos were farm workers, often migrants.
They faced problems of discrimination, poor pay, and often hazardous
working conditions. In 1962 a Chicano named **Cesar Chavez** emerged
as a labor leader, starting a union for migrant farm workers. The following year that union merged with another as the United Farm Workers Organizing Committee and later became affiliated with the AFL-
CIO. Chavez's work was especially helpful to lettuce and grape pick-
ers in their struggle for higher wages.

Chavez, like Dr. Martin Luther King, Jr., believed in nonviolent
methods. He was a devout Roman Catholic, and this also helped his
organizing efforts. Chavez continued to serve as spokesperson for
farm workers until his death in 1993. He helped raise the self-esteem
of the nation's growing Hispanic population by making their contributions to the American economy and culture more visible.

Native Americans

During World War II, many Native Americans, like many African Americans, fought in foreign lands to maintain or restore democracy. These experiences made both groups more aware of how the
rights they were fighting for were often denied them at home.

As you remember from Unit 4, Indians had been admitted to full
citizenship in 1924 under the Snyder Act. Roosevelt's Indian "New

Deal'' of the 1930s had changed earlier government policies and aimed to rebuild tribes and promote tribal cultures. Conditions for Indians improved, and their population began to increase.

Nevertheless, conditions remained poor for Indians when they were compared to the overall population. The per capita income of Native Americans was well below the poverty level. Rates of alcoholism and suicide were the highest of any ethnic group in the United States. Unemployment rates among Indians were far higher than the national average, and the high-school dropout rate was near 50 percent.

NATIVE AMERICANS ORGANIZE   In the early 1950s, Congress had enacted legislation to lessen government control over reservations, but this led to the loss of property by many Indians and forced some onto welfare. During the Johnson administration, the government tried to improve conditions by starting new programs to improve housing and to provide medical facilities, educational institutions, and vocational training.

Many Indians felt these programs were not enough. They demanded greater responsibility in making decisions that affected their lives. Like the Hispanic Americans, the Indians took some direction from the black civil rights movement. They began to call for "Red Power" and formed the **American Indian Movement** (AIM) to further their goals.

In 1969 a group of militant Indians seized Alcatraz Island in San Francisco Bay with the demand that it be turned into an Indian cultural center. In 1972 members of AIM occupied the Bureau of Indian Affairs in Washington, D.C., demanding rights and property they said were guaranteed Indians under earlier treaties. In 1973 AIM members occupied the reservation village of Wounded Knee, South Dakota, site of the last battle in the Indian wars of the 1800s. The takeover lasted two months, as militants demanded changes in policies toward Indians.

Although these actions did not always achieve Indians' goals, they did draw attention to the Indians' problems. Throughout the 1970s, court decisions tried to remedy earlier treaty violations. By 1989 Native Americans had been awarded over $80 million as compensation for lost land.

In addition, government policies changed again. The Indian Self-Determination and Education Assistance Act of 1975 gave Indians more say in the running of reservations and in education programs there. Also the post of Assistant Secretary of the Interior for Indian Affairs was created in 1975 to advance Indian interests.

NEW YORK STATE AND NATIVE AMERICANS   New York State has been the scene of major cases involving Indian rights and lands in recent years. For example, the Supreme Court in 1985 ruled in *County of Oneida* v. *Oneida Indian Nation of New York State* that Indians had a right to sue to enforce their aboriginal land rights.

MAKING CONNECTIONS

Regents Tip   Try to connect recent events with your previous learning.

List three examples of failure by the federal government or white Americans to show empathy with Native Americans.

1.

2.

3.

Continuing Issues   How have Indians contributed to the cultural diversity of the United States?

In that case the Court further said that the state's purchase of 872 acres from the Oneida Indians in 1795 was illegal because it was neither witnessed by federal agents nor approved by Congress. Both these steps were required under the federal Indian Trade and Non-Intercourse Act of 1793. Such court decisions have encouraged other Native American groups both in New York State and across the nation to sue for return of lost lands.

More recent controversies have arisen in northern New York regarding the St. Regis Mohawk Reservation, or Akwesasne Mohawk Reservation as it is also known. Violence erupted on the 28,000 acre reservation, which stretches into southern Canada, in the spring of 1990. At issue was gambling on the reservation. The incident involved questions of which Native American group controlled reservation policy as well as the role New York State has in dealing with the reservation.

Disabled Americans

Americans with disabilities have endured a long struggle to gain their full rights in American society. Ignorance and superstition have often resulted in prejudiced attitudes and actions directed against handicapped Americans.

In the nation's early years, care of the handicapped was usually left to their families. This often resulted in the neglect or abuse of the disabled. During the early 1800s, however, reformers began to put forward the idea that society as a whole should work to aid the handicapped. For example, **Dorothea Dix** led a one-person campaign to expose conditions for the mentally ill. Over thirty state institutions for the mentally ill were started as a result of her efforts.

Major Ideas It is important to remember that almost 36 million Americans (one out of every six) have some form of physical, mental, or emotional disability.

In 1865 President Lincoln signed a bill establishing **Gallaudet College** in Washington, D.C., for the hearing impaired. Today that institution is internationally recognized for its work. The school drew national attention in the late 1980s when its students successfully demonstrated to win appointment of a hearing-impaired person as president of the college.

In New York State, the National Technical Institute for the Deaf at the Rochester Institute of Technology is another school for the hearing impaired whose programs have won wide recognition. The school provides deaf students with college training in technical and scientific fields.

In 1832 the **Perkins Institute for the Blind** opened in Boston and quickly became a model for schools for the blind elsewhere. Although such schools still exist and serve important functions, many blind students today attend regular schools under a practice called **mainstreaming**. The idea behind mainstreaming is to bring handicapped students out of the isolation of special schools and into the "mainstream" of student life.

NEW PROGRAMS FOR THE HANDICAPPED   The federal government has been especially active in setting out new programs and policies for the handicapped.

MAKING CONNECTIONS

Key Social Studies Concepts:
Change; Justice

- President Kennedy established a Presidential Commission on Mental Retardation to study and highlight the problems of the mentally handicapped individuals in American society. This helped focus national attention on both the needs and the abilities of handicapped Americans.

- President Kennedy also backed the establishment of the Special Olympics to provide both a showcase and encouragement for athletes with handicapping conditions.

- The Rehabilitation Act of 1973 barred discrimination against handicapped persons in programs, activities, and facilities that were supported by federal funds.

- The Education for All Handicapped Children Act of 1975 required states to provide suitable education for children with physical or mental handicaps.

- Different pieces of legislation in the 1970s set up requirements that public buildings and transportation be made handicapped accessible.

- In 1990 President Bush signed a Bill of Rights for Handicapped Americans. The legislation prohibited discrimination on the basis of disability in employment, public services, and public accommodations. It required new buses and trains to be accessible to people with disabilities and required telecommunication companies to operate systems that would permit hearing- and speech-impaired people to use telephone services.

     In addition to new laws, newspapers, magazines, radio, and television as well as court cases directed public attention to the problems of handicapped Americans. School programs, especially in health classes, educated non-handicapped students in the problems facing handicapped students.

THE NEW FRONTIER AND THE GREAT SOCIETY

Continuing Issues   As you read, underline those New Frontier and Great Society programs still in effect.

     Not all legislation on domestic issues during the 1960s concerned civil rights. Kennedy's programs, known as the **New Frontier**, and Johnson's, known as the **Great Society**, continued and expanded upon traditions begun during Franklin Roosevelt's New Deal of the 1930s.

Kennedy

- **The space program**. Following the successful launch of a Soviet cosmonaut in 1961, the first man in space, President Kennedy committed the nation to a space program that had the goal of landing a person on the moon by the end of the 1960s. In July 1969, six years after Kennedy's death, that goal was met when astronaut Neil Armstrong stepped onto the moon's surface. The effort had cost some $24 billion.

- **The Peace Corps**. This program sent thousands of American volunteers, at first mostly young college graduates, to developing nations where they worked at training local peoples in technical, educational, and health programs. The Peace Corps program was intended to offset the growth of communism in such nations. The program is still in existence.

Johnson

- **The VISTA program**. Volunteers in Service to America (VISTA) was meant as a domestic Peace Corps, aiding poor citizens in rural and impoverished areas.

Enduring Issues

- National Power;
- Federalism

- **The Office of Economic Opportunity**. Set up in 1964, this was the directing agency in President Johnson's "War on Poverty." Its branches included **Project Head Start**, to provide education for preschoolers from poor families, **Project Upward Bound** to aid high-school students from low-income families attend college, and the **Job Corps**, to provide vocational training for high-school dropouts.

- **The Elementary and Secondary Education Act**. This 1965 measure provided over $1 billion in federal aid to education, with the largest share going to school districts with large numbers of students from poor families. Sections of the bill required that schools accepting the money be integrated.

- **Medicare**. Amendments to the Social Security Act provided health insurance and some types of health care to those over 65. A Medicaid program provided states with funds to help the needy who were not covered by Medicare.

- **Department of Housing and Urban Development**. This Cabinet post was meant to oversee federal efforts to improve housing and aid economic development of cities. Its first head, Robert C. Weaver, was the first black to hold a Cabinet post.

Enduring Issues

Presidential Power

FOREIGN POLICY IN THE 1960s

United States foreign policy under both Kennedy and Johnson continued cold war policies begun under President Truman. The United States remained committed to stopping the spread of communism. In the next section, you will review how that commitment led the nation into its longest war, the war in Vietnam. In this section, you will see how cold war concerns affected other aspects of United States policy in the 1960s, especially in Latin America.

A History of Involvement

As you remember, the United States has been deeply involved in the affairs of Latin America since early in its history. Latin American nations often resented such intervention, and United States policies have left a legacy of anger and hostility.

Some of the key events in United States-Latin American relations are listed below. For a fuller discussion of these events, see Unit 3, Section 2.

The Monroe Doctrine	In 1823 President Monroe warned the nations of Europe not to interfere with the nations of the Western Hemisphere, thus assuming the role of protector of the Western Hemisphere. However, this policy earned the United States a negative image in much of Latin America.
Spanish-American War (1898)	Victory in a war with Spain brought the United States an overseas empire. It also increased the nation's role in Latin America by giving it possession of Puerto Rico and much control over the government of Cuba.
Panama Canal (1901–1914)	The United States gained control over land where it wanted to build a canal by interfering in the internal affairs of Colombia. As a result, the United States made many enemies in Latin America.
Roosevelt Corollary (1904)	Under this addition to the Monroe Doctrine, President Theodore Roosevelt claimed the United States had the right to intervene in the affairs of Latin American nations guilty of "chronic wrongdoing."
"Dollar Diplomacy" (early 1900s)	This term described President Taft's plan of increasing U.S. influence in Latin America through economic investment backed by military force.
"Good Neighbor" Policy (1933)	This was President Franklin Roosevelt's effort to improve relations with Latin America by stressing increased cooperation.

MAKING CONNECTIONS

Major Ideas The 1920s marked a time when the United States began to shift its policy in Latin America toward one of regional cooperation. However, these efforts have not been completely successful.

MAKING CONNECTIONS

Kennedy and Latin America

Some of President Kennedy's most significant foreign policy decisions involved Latin America.

The Caribbean and Central America

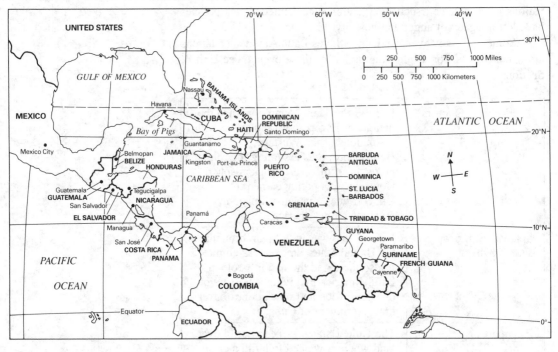

Regents Tip Maps can help you understand reasons behind actions taken by a government.

How far is Cuba from the United States?

Major Ideas The United States saw Castro's communism as a threat to its political dominance in Latin America.

THE ALLIANCE FOR PROGRESS Kennedy hoped to improve relations with Latin America and stop the spread of communism there through the **Alliance for Progress**. This nation pledged $20 billion to help economic development in the region. However, funds often went to aid repressive governments simply because they were anti-Communist.

THE BAY OF PIGS In Section 1 of this Unit, you read how Fidel Castro established a Communist regime in Cuba. When President Kennedy took office he approved a CIA plan to overthrow Castro. The plan called for Cuban exiles—supplied with U.S. arms, material, and training—to invade Cuba, setting off a popular uprising against Castro. The invasion took place on April 17, 1961, at a location called the Bay of Pigs, about 90 miles from Havana. No uprising followed, and Castro's troops quickly crushed the invading forces to the embarrassment of Kennedy and the United States government.

THE CUBAN MISSILE CRISIS Fearing another U.S. invasion attempt, Castro agreed to a Soviet plan to base nuclear missiles aimed at the United States in Cuba. Kennedy learned of the plan while the bases were under construction. On October 22, 1962, he announced a naval blockade of Cuba and demanded that the Soviets withdraw the missiles. The world seemed on the brink of nuclear war, but the Soviets backed down and pulled out their missiles.

Kennedy had clearly demonstrated that the United States would not tolerate a Soviet presence in the Western Hemisphere just 90 miles from its shores. By doing so, Kennedy also helped the nation recover some of the prestige it had lost in the failed Bay of Pigs invasion.

MAKING CONNECTIONS

Kennedy and Berlin

Study the timeline below. It can help you understand how the events you have just read about in Latin America influenced and were influenced by events in Europe.

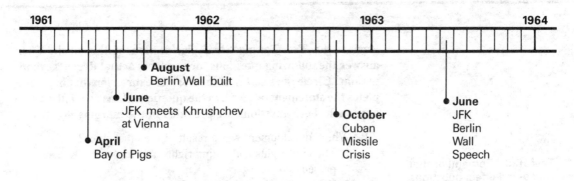

Since World War II, the division of Germany into a Communist East and a democratic West had added to cold war tensions. President Kennedy and Soviet Premier Nikita Khrushchev met in Austria in June 1961 to discuss the issue. Khrushchev thought that the Bay of Pigs disaster revealed American weakness, and he tried to threaten Kennedy into removing NATO troops from Europe. Instead, Kennedy increased U.S. military and financial commitment to West Germany.

Response to the American moves came in August 1961 when the East German government built a wall between East and West Berlin. The wall was meant to stop the flood of East Germans escaping to freedom in the West. The wall quickly became a symbol of tyranny as many East Germans lost their lives trying to escape over it. In June 1963 Kennedy visited West Berlin, renewing the American commitment to defend that city and Western Europe. In a famous speech, he said that he and all people who wanted freedom were citizens of Berlin.

The Berlin Wall stood as a symbol of the division between the Free World and the Communist World until 1989. In that year the

Background Remember that Berlin was the scene of the blockade and airlift reviewed in Unit 5. Also remember that West Berlin at this time was within Communist-controlled East Germany.

MAKING CONNECTIONS

political changes sweeping through Eastern Europe led East Germany to tear down the wall to great celebration on both its sides. By October 1990 the rapid political changes in the region had led to the reunification of the two Germanys as a single nation for the first time since the end of World War II.

IMPACT OF KENNEDY'S DEATH Kennedy's energetic voice for world democracy and his multilingual wife, Jacqueline, helped to make friends for the United States in many areas of the world. His tragic and unexpected assassination in November 1963 caused an outpouring of grief from around the world as dozens of foreign heads of state came hurriedly to Washington, D.C., for Kennedy's funeral.

Regents Questions for Practice ____

Review the Test-Taking Strategies section of this book. Then answer the following questions, drawn from actual Regents examinations. Circle the *number* of the word or expression that best completes the statement or answers the question. Hints on good ways to approach these questions are provided in the margins.

1. Which development was a result of the other three?
   1 The civil rights and voting rights acts of the 1960s were passed.
   2 Blacks were barred from voting in several states.
   3 State laws supported racial segregation.
   4 Several civil rights movements were formed.

Test Hint Remember that cause-and-effect questions are ways of asking what happened *after* some event.

2. Which action would be most in accord with the ideals of Dr. Martin Luther King, Jr.?
   1 underpaid workers sabotage the machinery at their factory
   2 a minority worker assaults a bigot
   3 an 18-year-old pacifist accepts a jail term rather than register for military service
   4 radical leaders advocate black separatism if their group's demands are not met

Test Hint Note the vocabulary you will need to know for Regents questions. Remember to review the Vocabulary and Glossary sections at the back of this book.

3. The movements led by Mohandas Gandhi of India and Martin Luther King, Jr., of the United States were similar because both
   1 supported attempts to overthrow the established government
   2 advocated civil disobedience to bring about social change
   3 appealed solely to the upper classes for financial support
   4 resulted in their leaders gaining national political office

Test Hint Remember that you may be asked to make connections to what you have learned in your Global Studies course.

4. Civil disobedience would involve
1 unknowingly breaking a law
2 deliberately breaking a law considered unjust
3 insisting upon serving as one's own lawyer
4 lobbying for changes in the legal code

Base your answers to questions 5 and 6 on the graph below and on your knowledge of social studies.

Median Income in Current Dollars

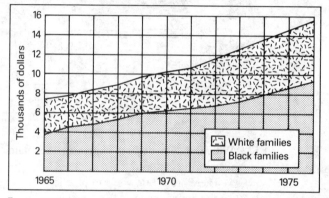

MAKING CONNECTIONS

Test Hint Remember to underline or write key points on charts or graphs. If necessary, do the math directly on the test page to get an answer.

5. In 1975 the median income of black families was approximately
1 $14,000   3 $9,000
2 $10,000   4 $6,000

6. Which is a valid statement based on the data in the graph?
1 The gap between the median income of black families and the median income of white families increased during the period.
2 There was improvement in black employment rates between 1965 and 1975.
3 The median income of black families will reach the level of white families by 1990.
4 In 1970 half of the black families in the United States had incomes over $7,000.

7. In the United States, de facto segregation has existed primarily as a result of
1 court ordered busing   3 housing patterns
2 voting restrictions   4 immigration quotas

8. Which demand of black civil rights leaders in the 1970s is most different from the demands of the earlier civil rights movements of the 1950s?
1 greater involvement in making decisions basic to everyday life
2 integration of public facilities
3 increased voting rights in the Southern states
4 increased opportunities in the field of education

9. Which statement best explains why a woman needs a college degree in order to earn more than a man with an eighth-grade education?
   1 There are more jobs for men which require little education.
   2 Men are more productive employees.
   3 There is unequal access to many types of jobs.
   4 Men have to support families, while women's income generally only supplements the family income.

"Founding Fathers! How come no Founding Mothers?" Drawing by D. Fradon, © 1972 The New Yorker Magazine, Inc.

10. Which is a valid generalization that can be drawn from the cartoon?
    1 Women have not had a role in United States history.
    2 Women have become more appreciative of American art.
    3 Women have developed a consciousness with regard to their role in American society.
    4 Women artists are demanding greater respect for their contributions to the field.

11. In the United States, economic opportunities for women expanded during the last quarter of the 19th century primarily because of the growth of
    1 opportunities to buy farms in the West
    2 industry and technology
    3 big-city political machines
    4 organized labor

Base your answer to question 12 on the cartoon below and on your knowledge of social studies.

12. Which statement best expresses the main idea of the cartoon?
    1 There are subtle ways to practice discrimination.
    2 Affirmative action programs have practically eliminated sex discrimination in business.
    3 It is legal and just to give men and women different job titles for the same work.
    4 Discriminatory attitudes are more commonly found among lower paid employees than among executive level employees.

13. In the United States, changes in occupational titles from busboy to dining room attendant and stewardess to flight attendant illustrate an attempt to deal with the problem of
    1 racism   3 sexism
    2 ethnocentrism   4 age basis

14. Which situation best illustrates the idea of affirmative action?
1 An organization actively recruits qualified women and members of minority groups for an on-the-job training program.
2 A corporation hires people on first-come, first-served basis.
3 A university's sole criterion for admission is performance on an entrance examination.
4 A graduate school accepts all students who apply.

15. Women's liberation groups would be most likely to oppose which action?
1 the changes in women's dress styles in the 1970s
2 the passage of laws to protect women from long hours of employment and strenuous jobs
3 the establishment of day-care centers
4 the widespread distribution of information concerning birth control methods and devices

16. A valid generalization concerning the women's movement in the United States during the 20th century is that the women's movement
1 has made the public more aware of sexism
2 stresses that women are superior to men
3 represents the views of very few women
4 has eliminated discrimination

17. The programs of the Progressive Movement (1900–1920), the New Deal (1930–1941), and the Great Society (1965–1968) were similar in that they
1 emphasized the expansion of civil rights for blacks and other minority groups
2 were passed by Congress despite strong opposition by the President and party leaders
3 took effect during periods of extended economic depression
4 resulted in the greater involvement of the Federal Government in the daily lives of Americans

18. In which respect were the decades of the 1920s and the 1960s in the United States most similar?
1 organized militancy by ethnic minorities
2 public concern with pollution of the environment
3 widespread government activity dealing with social issues
4 significant changes in manners and morals

3 *Limits of Power*

MAKING CONNECTIONS

As you recall from Section 1, United States fears of Communist expansion led the nation to become increasingly involved in Southeast Asia. In this section, you will learn how this involvement led to the longest war in United States history. The following chart helps you to review some of the key historical events in the build up to the Vietnam War.

Unrest in Asia, 1945–1960

Date	Event
September 1945	World War II ends in Asia; Ho Chi Minh, a member of the Communist Party since 1920, proclaims the Democratic Republic of Vietnam.
1946–1949	France, which had controlled Vietnam since the 19th century, appoints a "puppet leader" named Bao Dai, who is ineffective against the power of Ho Chi Minh.
1949	Mao Zedong declares the (Communist) People's Republic of China and recognizes the Vietnamese government of Ho Chi Minh.
1950–1953	United States fights the Korean War and provides the French with financial aid in their struggle to hang onto Vietnam.
1953–1954	President Eisenhower debates how far the United States should go in backing the French.
1954	The forces of Ho Chi Minh defeat the French at Dienbienphu; Geneva Accords divide Vietnam at the 17th parallel; North and South Vietnam agree to hold elections in 1956 to reunite the country; the United States joins with seven Asian and European nations in the Southeast Asia Treaty Organization (SEATO), an anti-Communist pact which extends protection to Vietnam.
1955	United States under Eisenhower increases aid to South Vietnam.
1956	South Vietnamese President Ngo Dinh Diem, fearing the popularity of Ho Chi Minh, refuses to hold elections scheduled under the Geneva Accords.
1960	Ho Chi Minh recognizes the Vietcong, Communist guerrillas in South Vietnam, as the National Liberation Front (NLF) of Vietnam; President Kennedy sends Vice President Johnson to study the crisis in Vietnam.

KENNEDY AND VIETNAM

Kennedy shared Eisenhower's belief in the domino theory. He, therefore, continued to support the Diem regime. By 1963 the total number of United States "advisers" in South Vietnam totaled about 17,000. That year, 489 Americans died in the fighting in Vietnam.

Debate Over Involvement

United States advisers urged Diem to adopt reforms to broaden his support. Diem, however, brutally suppressed all opponents and ruled as a dictator. On November 2, 1963, the South Vietnamese military overthrew Diem, with the knowledge and approval of the United States. Around the same time, the White House announced that it intended to withdraw all United States military personnel from Vietnam by 1965. Whether Kennedy would have kept this promise will never be known. As you recall, the President was assassinated on November 22, 1963.

JOHNSON AND ESCALATION

It is important to remember that under the Constitution only the United States Congress can declare war. However, by 1964, three Presidents—Eisenhower, Kennedy, and Johnson—had sent United States aid and troops into Vietnam. Each did so by acting as the commander in chief of the nation's military forces.

The Tonkin Gulf Resolution

On August 4, 1964, President Johnson **escalated** the war dramatically. He announced on television that United States destroyers had been the victim of an unprovoked attack by North Vietnamese gunboats. (It later appeared that the ships might have been protecting South Vietnamese boats headed into North Vietnamese waters.) The next day Johnson asked Congress for the authority to order air strikes against North Vietnam. With only two dissenting votes, Congress passed the **Gulf of Tonkin Resolution**. The resolution empowered "the President, as Commander in chief, to take all necessary measures to repel any armed attack against the forces of the United States and to prevent further aggression." Johnson used the resolution to justify expansion of the war. By April 1965, United States planes regularly bombed North Vietnam.

A GUERRILLA WAR   At first, United States military leaders expected that the nation's superior technology would guarantee victory. However, they soon found themselves bogged down in a guerrilla war fought in the jungles of Southeast Asia. The enemy did not wear uniforms, and no clear battlefront emerged. Thousands of Vietnamese casualties occurred each month as the United States dropped more

MAKING CONNECTIONS

Enduring Issues

Presidential Power

Regents Tip Reading maps can help make relations between nations clearer.

What nation is to the north of North Vietnam?

What kind of government does that nation have?

Vietnam

Key Social Studies Concepts:

Technology

Why might technology be of limited use in fighting a guerilla war?

bombs on Vietnam, an area about twice the size of New York, than it had used on Nazi Germany during the heaviest months of fighting during World War II.

REASONS FOR WAR   The massive commitment in Vietnam raised questions in the minds of many Americans: Why did the United States get involved in Vietnam? And why did the United States stay there?

The administration offered several answers to these questions. These included

- to prevent the fall of Vietnam to communism
- to stop the rise of aggressor governments
- to protect the nation's position as a superpower and defender of democracy

However, as the war dragged on, a number of Americans began to question United States motives in Southeast Asia.

Resistance to the War

By late 1965, an antiwar movement had taken shape in the United States.

HAWKS AND DOVES   Congress no longer stood solidly behind the President. Those who argued in favor of victory at any cost were known as "hawks." Those who favored immediate withdrawal were known as "doves."

STUDENT PROTESTS   College campuses became the centers of political activity against the war. Students organized a new form of protest called **teach-ins**, or meetings in which speakers, usually promoting unconditional American withdrawal from Vietnam, held study sessions and rallies. The strongest antiwar group in the 1960s was Students for a Democratic Society (SDS), founded in 1960. SDS was anti-establishment, or anti-big business and government. It led demonstrations, sit-ins, draft-card burnings, and protests against universities with "pro-establishment" regulations.

By 1969 the organization had collapsed into a number of splinter groups. However, SDS's legacy of protest against authority remained a strong force into the 1970s.

PROTEST MARCHES   People of all ages joined in protest marches against the war. The first huge march took place in Washington, D.C., in 1965. In 1967 some 300,000 Americans marched in New York City. That same year, another 100,000 tried to shut down the Pentagon.

DRAFT RESISTERS   By 1968 about 10,000 draft resisters, people unwilling to serve in the military after being drafted, had fled the country for Canada. The nation's youth became increasingly divided as some chose to fight for the United States in Vietnam and others sought deferments to go to college. A large number of minorities, who could not afford the cost of college, responded to the draft and went to Vietnam. The attitude of American youth became increasingly hostile toward the Johnson administration and all war-related issues.

1968—A Crucial Year at Home and Abroad

In 1968 American society became increasingly divided. The following chart shows major events that year.

MAKING CONNECTIONS

Major Ideas Note that accountability in foreign policy finally rests with the President, who must answer for all foreign policy decisions made while in office.

Month	Event
February	• North Vietnam launches the Tet (New Year's) offensive, using Soviet-made jets and weapons for the first time.
March	• Eugene McCarthy, a peace candidate and leading "dove," wins the Democratic Presidential primary in New Hampshire. • Robert Kennedy announces his candidacy for the Presidency. • President Johnson announces that he will not seek reelection and that he will devote the remainder of his term to trying to end the war.
April	• American forces in Vietnam reach 549,000; combat deaths climb to 22,951. • North Vietnam announces its willingness to enter into peace talks. • An assassin claims the life of Dr. Martin Luther King, Jr.
May	• Preliminary peace talks with the North Vietnamese begin, but serious negotiations do not take place for several years.
June	• An assassin claims the life of Robert Kennedy shortly after his victory in the California Democratic presidential primary.
August	• The Democratic National Convention nominates Hubert Humphrey amid the worst political rioting and demonstrations any convention has ever experienced; Humphrey (Johnson's Vice President) inherits a divided party and seeks election in a divided nation. • The Republican National Convention nominates Richard Nixon, whose only serious challenger is Ronald Reagan. • The American Independence Party nominates Governor George Wallace of Alabama, showing that a third party could attract white-backlash voters who opposed the civil rights movement.
November	• Nixon wins the 1968 election with 43.4% of the popular vote; Humphrey claims 42.7%; Wallace takes 13.4%.

MAKING CONNECTIONS

Major Ideas Only the Civil War had a more divisive impact on American society than the Vietnam War.

THE 1960s—POLITICAL AND SOCIAL UPHEAVAL

Some political analysts who studied the events of 1968 believed the nation had survived one of the biggest tests to its political institutions since the Civil War. The 1960s had been shaped by two movements: the civil rights movement and the antiwar movement. The political turmoil of the decade helped produce great social upheaval, especially among the nation's youth.

Cultural Changes

Some young people became disillusioned with traditional American values. For the first time in United States history, thousands of Americans flaunted the use of illegal drugs, often popularized in rock music.

Many young Americans referred to themselves as "hippies" or "flower children." They claimed to be searching for a freer, simpler way of life. Communal living attracted thousands of youth who adopted lifestyles foreign to older Americans. Some spoke of a "generation gap" between youth and people over 30.

The civil rights movement and the Vietnam War also divided Americans. The assassinations of Robert Kennedy and Dr. Martin Luther King, Jr., heightened emotions.

NIXON AND VIETNAM

President Nixon faced a national crisis. The Vietnam War had turned into the nation's longest and most costly war. In 1968 American support for the war was at an all-time low.

Winding Down the War

Nixon did not bring an end to the war right away. In fact, for a time, he widened American military activities, attacking North Vietnamese supply routes out of Laos and Cambodia.

VIETNAMIZATION Nixon called for **Vietnamization** of the war, or a takeover of the ground fighting by Vietnamese soldiers. Both Kennedy and Johnson had favored this approach, but neither had been able to make it work. While Nixon promoted Vietnamization, he also bombed neighboring Cambodia, which he claimed served as a base for North Vietnamese guerrillas. The bombings triggered a large student protest at Kent State University in Ohio. By the time the National Guard broke up the demonstration, four students lay dead and nine others wounded. More and more Americans were questioning the role of the United States in Vietnam, yet President Nixon increased bombing raids on North Vietnam throughout 1970.

PEACE WITH HONOR   Henry Kissinger, Nixon's chief foreign policy advisor, met in Paris with North Vietnamese officials seeking an end to the war. For several years, negotiations remained deadlocked. Finally, on January 15, 1973, Nixon announced that a "peace with honor" had been reached and that a cease-fire would soon take effect.

The War Powers Act

In November 1973, Congress passed the **War Powers Act** over Nixon's veto. This law helped reverse the precedent set by the Gulf of Tonkin Resolution, which gave the President sweeping powers in Vietnam. The War Powers Act included the following provisions:

- The President had to notify Congress within 48 hours of sending troops into a foreign country. At that time, the President would have to give Congress a full accounting of the decision.

- The President had to bring the troops home within 60 days unless both houses voted for them to stay.

Vietnam and Limits on United States Power

When the United States finally withdrew from Vietnam, the North Vietnamese overran South Vietnam. For two years, the United States poured billions of dollars of aid into South Vietnam. However, on April 29, 1975, the government in Saigon collapsed. Bitterness over the war still persisted. When President Ford, who replaced Nixon (See Section 4), asked for funds to evacuate the South Vietnamese who had helped the United States, Congress refused. In the end, some 100,000 people fled the country.

The United States had tried for 20 years to guarantee freedom to the people of South Vietnam. However, the United States ultimately could not count its efforts as a success. In the conflict, 56,000 Americans died and another 300,000 were wounded. The United States spent over $150 billion on the war effort. Not only did Vietnam fall to communism, but so did its neighbors Cambodia (Kampuchea) and Laos. Throughout the late 1970s and 1980s, the United States sought to understand the Vietnam experience. It was the subject of films, books, and national monuments such as "the wall" in Washington, D.C.

Conclusions Drawn from U.S. Involvement in Vietnam

The following is a list of conclusions drawn from the Vietnam War era.

- The American political system acts in response to a variety of public pressures.

- Modern war technology is not always powerful enough if an opponent is armed with a determined spirit of nationalism.

MAKING CONNECTIONS

- Successful military efforts require a well-prepared and supportive public. (Compare, for example, the differing experiences in Vietnam and World War II.)
- The United States was committed to a foreign policy that supported the global nature of United States involvement in foreign affairs.

Regents Questions for Practice _____

Review the Test-Taking Strategies section of this book. Then answer the following questions, drawn from actual Regents examinations. Circle the *number* of the word or expression that best completes the statement or answers the question. Hints on good ways to approach these questions are provided in the margins.

1. The War Powers Act of 1973 is an example of a
  1 congressional expansion of Presidential power
  2 congressional check of Presidential power
  3 Presidential expansion of congressional power
  4 Presidential check of congressional power

Test Hint Remember that you will need to know specific information about specific events.

2. United States actions in the Vietnam War demonstrated that
  1 the domino theory is an effective military tactic
  2 military policy in a democracy is affected by popular opinion
  3 advanced technology insures victory
  4 limited use of tactical nuclear weapons can be successful

3. Which has occurred in Southeast Asia since the end of the Vietnam War in the early 1970s?
  1 Military dictatorships have been replaced by democratic governments.
  2 Communist economic practices have brought about substantial industrial growth.
  3 A strong middle class has emerged as the dominant economic force.
  4 Conflicts have developed among the Communist factions in the area.

Test Hint Note that this is really a cause-and-effect question. What happened as a result of the war?

4. The use of the draft during the Civil War and the Vietnam War was similar in that in both instances
1 substitutes were often paid to replace the draftees
2 riots and demonstrations of resistance occurred
3 a constitutional amendment was adopted to punish draft evaders
4 draftees could pay a set fee to the government to avoid military service

5. Susan B. Anthony's vote in the 1870s, Plessy's disregard of Jim Crow laws in the 1890s and the burning of draft cards by young men in the 1960s were all examples of
1 antiwar sentiment
2 the struggle for minority rights
3 civil disobedience
4 cultural empathy

6. A nation usually demands the greatest conformity from its citizens during times of
1 war
2 prosperity
3 scientific and artistic creativity
4 industrial expansion

7. Isolationism as a foreign policy is more difficult to achieve in the 20th century than in prior times mainly because
1 the increase in the world's population has forced people to live more closely together
2 there are more sovereign nations today than in the past
3 modern technology has made nations more interdependent
4 public opinion on issues is more easily disregarded

8. Which was the primary effect of the Vietnam conflict on later United States foreign policy decisions?
1 return to a policy of isolationism
2 increased emphasis on the United States military as the world's police force
3 reassessment of commitments to other nations
4 acceptance of the expansion of Chinese influence

MAKING CONNECTIONS

Test Hint Note that you must compare different time periods here.

Test Hint Here you are being asked to compare events from three time periods. Take your time with such questions.

Base your answers to questions 9 and 10 on the statements of the speakers below and your knowledge of social studies.

Speaker A: The United States should trade with any and all countries on a friendly basis but should not take sides in other nations' disputes.

Speaker B: We should not get involved with other nations.

Speaker C: We must bear any burden and pay any price to advance the cause of freedom.

Speaker D: The United States cannot serve as policeman to the entire world. It is not within our ability to do so.

9. Which speaker's statement expresses a viewpoint that led to disputes among the United States, Germany, and Great Britain during the early part of World War I?
(1) A   (2) B   (3) C   (4) D

10. Which speaker expresses a viewpoint that gained new strength immediately after the Vietnam War?
(1) A   (2) B   (3) C   (4) D

11. The Korean and Vietnam conflicts were similar in that both
1 represented United States efforts to contain communism
2 involved unilateral military action on the part of the United States
3 brought the United States into direct military conflict with China
4 were military defeats for the United States

The Trend Toward Conservatism

Turmoil rocked the United States during the 1960s. The nation's experiences in Vietnam had changed the way Americans thought about United States policies at home and abroad. As the 1970s unfolded, a new attitude of conservatism replaced the liberalism of the decade before. Americans wanted to end the long, drawn out Vietnam War and quiet the violent upheavals at home. President Nixon captured the mood of the nation when he announced that the theme of his presidency would be to bring Americans together again.

MAKING CONNECTIONS

FROM COLD WAR TO DÉTENTE

As you read in the last section, Nixon's main foreign policy objective was ending the Vietnam War. However, he had other foreign policy interests too.

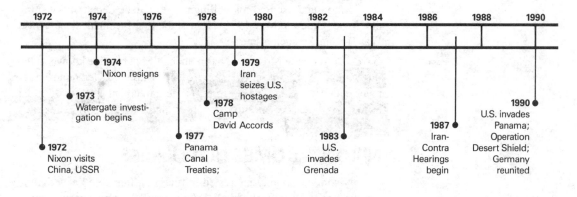

Nixon Doctrine

In 1969 Nixon announced what became known as the **Nixon Doctrine**. This doctrine stated that the United States would no longer provide direct military protection in Asia. Nixon warned Asian nations that they must assume greater responsibility for their own development and national defense. Even though the Vietnam War was not yet concluded, Nixon promised Americans that there would be no more Koreas or Vietnams for the United States.

A New Policy Toward China

Nixon also adopted a new foreign policy toward China.

PRESIDENTIAL VISIT   In 1971 Nixon stunned Americans by announcing that he had accepted an invitation to visit the People's Republic of China. As you recall, the United States had not had diplomatic relations with the People's Republic since right after the 1949 Communist Revolution. On February 21, 1972, Nixon arrived in China. Secretary of State Henry Kissinger accompanied the President on his "peace mission."

OPENING THE DOOR   After more than 20 years of hostility, Nixon and Chinese leaders Mao Zedong and Premier Zhou Enlai agreed to "open the door" to normal diplomatic relations. Nixon's visit cleared the way for economic and cultural exchanges. United States manufacturers, for example, now had a new market for their products. By following a separate policy toward the People's Republic, Nixon underscored the splits that had occurred in communism.

A New Policy Toward the Soviet Union

Nixon balanced his openness with China by looking for ways to ease tensions with the Soviet Union, China's Communist rival.

DÉTENTE   Nixon and Kissinger shaped a policy called **détente**. The goal of détente was to bring about a warming, or thaw, in the cold war. Truman, as you recall, aimed at containment, or boxing in the Communists. Under détente, however, Nixon's objective was to prevent open conflict.

Nixon underscored his willingness to pursue détente by visiting the Soviet Union in May 1972. He was the first President since World War II to make such a journey.

SALT   While in Moscow, Nixon opened what became known as the Strategic Arms Limitations Talks (SALT). These talks led to an agreement called the **SALT Agreement**. The agreement set limits on the number of defensive missile sites and strategic offensive missiles each nation would keep.

NIXON'S DOMESTIC POLICIES

Nixon was mainly interested in foreign affairs. He knew that he faced a Congress controlled by a Democratic majority. Because of the system of checks and balances, Nixon realized that it would be almost impossible to push Republican policies through Congress. Therefore, he limited his domestic policy goals.

New Federalism

Like Eisenhower, Nixon wanted to reduce the role of the federal government and turn over more activities to the states. Nixon called this policy the **New Federalism**. He criticized Johnson's Great Society as too costly and tried to reduce involvement of the federal government in social welfare programs. To achieve this goal, Nixon instituted **revenue sharing**, a policy in which the federal government gave part of its income or, revenue, to the states to spend on social welfare as they saw fit.

Curbing Inflation

The Vietnam War had helped trigger inflation, which was one of Nixon's biggest domestic problems. During the 1968 election, Nixon had promised to end inflation and balance the budget. By the time he took office, prices were rising faster than they had in 20 years. Unemployment was rising too. At the same time, the nation's Gross National Product (GNP) was declining. To bring the economy under control, Nixon implemented a 90-day wage-price freeze in August 1971. He was the first President to impose mandatory wage-price controls in peacetime.

Nixon, Civil Rights, and the Supreme Court

Under separation of powers and checks and balances, the Supreme Court can exercise a great deal of power over domestic policy. As a result, each President hopes to influence the decisions of the Court through the appointment of justices. However, the appointees do not always rule as a President might expect. For example, you may recall that President Eisenhower regretted his appointment of Earl Warren to the Supreme Court. This was because Warren made many liberal decisions that opposed Eisenhower's conservative political views.

NIXON APPOINTEES In 1969 Warren retired, and Nixon appointed **Warren Burger** as Chief Justice. During his administration, Nixon also had the opportunity to appoint three other justices. Not all of these appointees were approved by the Senate on the first nomination.

Nixon's appointees were all **strict constructionists**, or people who hold that Congress and the President have only those powers specifically given to them by the Constitution. The "Nixon Court," however, did not overturn many of the liberal rulings of the 1960s as Nixon had expected.

To get a better understanding of the nature of Supreme Court decisions during the 1960s and 1970s, study the following table.

MAKING CONNECTIONS

Major Ideas Government regulations are designed to protect public health and safety, but putting them into practice costs money and may reduce profits of private businesses.

Enduring Issues

The Judiciary

Number of Black Supreme Court Judges Appointed by Presidents from FDR to Bush

Court	Number of Judges	Appointing President
Supreme Court	1	Johnson
	1	Bush

MAKING CONNECTIONS

Enduring Issues

Criminal Penalties

Number of Women Judges Appointed to the Supreme Court

Court	Number of Judges	Appointing President
Supreme Court	1	Reagan
	1	Clinton

Landmark Supreme Court Decisions, 1962–1973

Case	Date	President/ Chief Justice	Issue/ Decision
Engle v. *Vitale*	1962	Kennedy/Warren	Freedom of religion: States cannot write prayers for students to recite; students cannot be forced to pray in public.
Gideon v. *Wainwright*	1963	Kennedy/Warren	Due process: Courts must provide a lawyer for the accused.
Escobedo v. *Illinois*	1964	Johnson/Warren	Due process: The accused has the right to a lawyer at the time of questioning.
Miranda v. *Arizona*	1966	Johnson/Warren	Due process: Accused persons must be told of their rights at time of arrest.
Tinker v. *Des Moines*	1969	Nixon/Burger	Freedom of speech: Students and teachers have the right to use symbols under freedom of speech; "the schoolhouse gate" does not limit that freedom.
New York Times v. *United States*	1971	Nixon/Burger	Freedom of the press: Publication of stolen Defense Department documents (the Pentagon Papers) was permitted because it did not endanger national security.
Roe v. *Wade*	1973	Nixon/Burger	Privacy: A woman's right to an abortion was protected within certain limits.

OTHER DOMESTIC EVENTS UNDER NIXON

The United States enjoyed triumphs in outer space. The civil rights movement that had begun in the 1960s also continued into the 1970s, resulting in gains for many groups.

The Space Program

In 1969 the United States scored another first in the space race. That year American astronaut **Neil Armstrong** became the first person to walk on the moon. The triumph of seeing Armstrong plant a United States flag on the moon's surface marked a bright spot in an otherwise troubled decade.

The 26th Amendment

In 1971 Congress proposed the 26th Amendment to the Constitution. This amendment extended the vote to people ages 18 and older. By lowering the voting age from 21 to 18, Congress added almost 12 million new voters to the American electorate.

Women's Rights Movement

In the 1970s, more and more women enrolled in schools of law, medicine, engineering, and business, fields that had been traditionally reserved for men. However, full-time working women in 1971 were paid only 59 percent as much as men. They also did not hold positions equal to their talents. As you read in Section 2, the Equal Rights Amendment failed to win ratification.

Consumer Rights Movement

A strong consumer rights movement also developed in the early 1970s to address abuses by major American industries. The movement was led by **Ralph Nader**, a young Washington lawyer who organized a protest in the 1960s against the automotive industry. Nader attracted a number of young volunteers, known as "Nader's Raiders," to his cause. They championed environmental and consumer protection. Nader continues to be a consumer advocate.

THE WATERGATE AFFAIR

In 1972 the Republicans nominated Nixon for reelection. The Democrats selected George McGovern. During the campaign, McGovern charged that Nixon and the Republicans had engaged in a number of covert, or secret, activities. However, Nixon claimed credit for bringing down inflation and scoring foreign policy triumphs abroad. He swept to victory, carrying the largest popular majority in United States history. Yet less than two years later, Nixon resigned from office. The following chart shows key facts in the opening act of the **Watergate affair**.

MAKING CONNECTIONS

Enduring Issues

Change and Flexibility

Continuing Issues
Remember that the term "muckraker" was used for an individual who exposed dangers to workers and consumers in the early 1900s. Ralph Nader is a modern example of such an individual.

Enduring Issues

The Separation of Powers

MAKING CONNECTIONS

WHAT HAPPENED   An illegal break-in to "bug" the Democratic Party headquarters with electronic surveillance equipment.

WHERE   Watergate Towers, an apartment complex in Washington, D.C.

WHEN   June 17, 1972.

WHO   The Committee to Reelect the President (CREEP), acting with the knowledge of several high-level Nixon advisors.

WHY   To secure information to undermine the Democratic campaign against Nixon.

HOW   Attempted to wiretap phones in the Democratic headquarters.

The Cover-Up

Police captured the "burglars," who carried evidence linking them to the White House. Nixon did not know about the plan until after it happened. However, he then ordered a cover-up, a crime under federal law.

THE INVESTIGATION   Reporters from the *Washington Post* probed into the case, but their reports did not hinder Nixon's reelection. Then in 1973 the Senate set up a committee to look into "illegal, improper, or unethical activities" in the 1972 election. For over a year, the Senate committee came closer and closer to implicating the President.

RESIGNATION OF AGNEW   While the Watergate hearings were under way, the Justice Department charged Vice President Spiro Agnew with income tax evasion. Agnew resigned, and Nixon appointed **Gerald R. Ford**, the minority leader in the House of Representatives, as Vice President.

THE TAPES   In early 1973 the Senate committee learned that the White House had kept tape recordings of key conversations between Nixon and his top aides. Nixon refused to turn over the tapes. During the summer, the committee opened the hearings to television. The televised proceedings had the appeal of a soap opera as millions of Americans watched, fascinated by tales of "dirty tricks."

Continuing Issues
Remember that use of the impeachment process is an example of checks and balances.

NIXON RESIGNATION   The situation ended when the Supreme Court ordered Nixon to hand over the tapes in a case called *United States* v. *Richard Nixon*. Based on evidence in the tapes, the House Judiciary Committee began voting on articles of impeachment against the President. On August 9, 1974, Nixon resigned, becoming the first President ever forced to leave office before the end of his term. On noon of that day, Gerald Ford took the oath of office.

Significance of Watergate

Although Nixon was never charged with any specific crimes, President Ford issued a Presidential pardon to him. Ford hoped to end what he called "our long national nightmare." Dozens of Nixon's advisers, however, were found guilty of crimes and sentenced to prison. The incident showed, as Ford put it, that "the Constitution works." The system of checks and balances had stopped Nixon from placing the Presidency above the law.

THE FORD ADMINISTRATION

Many people called Nixon's administration the "Imperial Presidency" because of his disregard of the Constitution. Ford tried to rebuild the image of the President. However, the Watergate affair had disillusioned many Americans with the office of President.

Ford's Domestic Policies

One of Ford's first acts as President was to appoint a new Vice President. He chose Nelson Rockefeller, the governor of New York and grandson of multimillionaire oil tycoon John D. Rockefeller. Ford was the first President to be appointed in United States history. Neither the President nor Vice President had been elected by the American people.

From the start, Ford faced a number of domestic problems.

- **Nixon's Pardon**: Many Americans questioned Ford's decision to free Nixon when so many of his advisers were jailed.

- **Amnesty Plan**: Ford stirred bitter debate when he offered amnesty to thousands of young men who avoided military service in Vietnam by violating draft laws, fleeing the country, or deserting the military.

- **Inflation**: In 1973 the Organization of Petroleum Oil Exporting Countries (OPEC) placed an oil embargo on the United States for its support of Israel. The price of oil and gasoline more than doubled, setting off a new round of inflation. Temporary rationing of gasoline and federal incentives to research energy alternatives helped ease shortages. Even so, Americans remained highly dependent on foreign oil. Inflation topped 10 percent, and the nation entered into its worst recession since World War II.

Ford's Foreign Policies

Henry Kissinger continued working with the Ford administration. Kissinger helped

- negotiate a cease-fire agreement between Egypt and Israel, thus ending the 1973 Yom Kippur War and OPEC oil embargo.

MAKING CONNECTIONS

Enduring Issues

Change and Flexibility

Enduring Issues

Criminal Penalties

Inflation; Cost of Living in the 70s

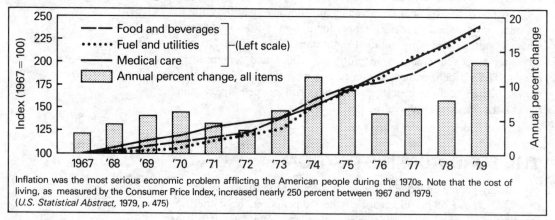

Inflation was the most serious economic problem afflicting the American people during the 1970s. Note that the cost of living, as measured by the Consumer Price Index, increased nearly 250 percent between 1967 and 1979.
(*U.S. Statistical Abstract,* 1979, p. 475)

MAKING CONNECTIONS

Regents Tip Be aware of reasons behind trends shown on graphs.

What factors help explain the trend shown on this graph?

Election of 1976

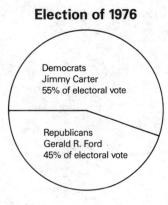

Democrats
Jimmy Carter
55% of electoral vote

Republicans
Gerald R. Ford
45% of electoral vote

• continue the policy of détente with the Soviet Union, including the sale of tons of grain to the Soviets and a hookup of Soviet and American space capsules.

• oversee the end of the Vietnam War, including the withdrawal of the last American personnel from Saigon in 1975.

The Election of 1976

The nation's bicentennial in 1976 gave the Ford presidency a boost. However, it was not enough to help Ford completely shake off his negative association with the Nixon years. He lost a close election to James (Jimmy) Earl Carter, former Democratic governor of Georgia.

THE CARTER ADMINISTRATION

Jimmy Carter won the 1976 election, in part, because of his appeal to the American sense of honesty and integrity. He stated a desire to return to basic American "down home" values. He wanted to prove that an "outsider" could make government more responsive to the people. However, Carter's unfamiliarity with Washington politics proved a disadvantage. His most trusted adviser became First Lady Rosalynn Carter.

Carter's Domestic Policies

Carter's presidency was made more difficult by changes that had taken place within Congress because of Watergate. Newly elected members tended to question every executive act.

"STAGFLATION" Carter ran into the same economic woes as Ford—inflation coupled with rising unemployment. The problems were worsened by many welfare programs that increased the cost of government. With the economy apparently stalled in place, economists

coined a new term, "**stagflation**," to describe the situation. (The term referred to the stagnation of the economy and simultaneous inflation of prices.)

ENERGY PROBLEM   As the world's leading industrial power, the United States was also the world's leading consumer of energy. By the late 1970s, the nation had to import more than 30 percent of its oil. OPEC kept prices high, and American dollars flowed out of the country, worsening the **trade deficit**—the situation in which a nation buys more foreign goods than it exports abroad.

CORPORATE BAILOUTS   Some American corporations were hard hit by stagflation and the decline in purchasing power at home. Foreign imports undersold some American goods, especially automobiles. The Chrysler Corporation and Lockheed Aircraft faced possible bankruptcy. Fearing the effect of massive layoffs on the economy, the federal government authorized huge loans to both corporations to keep them in business.

ENVIRONMENTAL PROBLEMS   President Nixon had taken steps to end harmful industrial pollution by creating the **Environmental Protection Agency** in 1970. Carter supported environmental programs too. **Acid rain**, created by toxic air pollution, threatened forests, lakes, and wildlife in both the United States and Canada. However, inflation and energy shortages prevented Carter from undertaking ambitious programs to protect the environment. Coal polluted the air, but the nation needed coal to offset oil shortages. The nation needed to clean up the air, but emission devices for cars and factories pushed up prices.

NUCLEAR ENERGY   Carter supported **nuclear energy** as an alternative to coal and oil. However, in 1979 an accident occurred at the Three Mile Island nuclear plant near Harrisburg, Pennsylvania. Although the problem was brought under control, the incident highlighted the hazards of the nuclear power industry, which by the late 1970s supplied 12 percent of the nation's energy.

Carter's Foreign Policies

Carter inherited many foreign policy problems from the Ford administration.

HELSINKI AGREEMENT   In 1975 the United States and other nations signed the **Helsinki Agreement** promising to respect basic human rights. Carter took this agreement seriously and believed that the United States should withhold aid from nations that violated human rights.

CAMP DAVID ACCORDS   In 1977 Egyptian President Anwar el-Sadat surprised the world by visiting Israeli Prime Minister Menachem Begin. President Carter seized the opportunity for bringing peace to the Middle East by inviting the two leaders to Camp David,

MAKING CONNECTIONS

U.S. and the World   The oil crisis of the 1970s highlighted increasing global interdependence.

Enduring Issues

Property/Economic Policy

Key Social Studies Concepts:

Technology

Major Ideas   Remember that the Middle East is a geographic region of great strategic value for many nations.

Enduring Issues

Presidential Power

Election of 1980

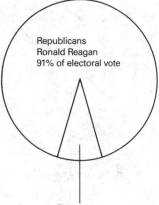

Republicans
Ronald Reagan
91% of electoral vote

Democrats
Jimmy Carter
9% of electoral vote

Major Ideas Remember that debate over the amount of power the federal government should have and how that power should be used goes back to the nation's beginnings.

the President's retreat in Maryland. Here Sadat and Begin hammered out the terms for a peace treaty known as the **Camp David Accords**. The two leaders signed the treaty in 1979. Other Arab nations, however still refused to recognize Israel.

PANAMA CANAL TREATIES In 1977 President Carter signed two treaties promising to turn over control of the Panama Canal to Panama in 1999. The treaties aroused bitter debate, but the Senate narrowly ratified them in 1978.

PROBLEMS WITH DÉTENTE In June 1979, Carter met with Soviet leader Leonid Brezhnev to negotiate the **SALT II Treaty**. However, a Soviet invasion of Afghanistan later that year ended détente under Carter. The President cut off grain shipments to the Soviet Union and boycotted the 1980 summer Olympic games held in Moscow. Carter's tough line spurred debate at home.

HOSTAGE CRISIS The biggest foreign policy crisis for Carter came in Iran. In 1979 a revolution led by Islamic fundamentalists toppled the pro-American Shah, Rezà Pahlavi. The Shah, suffering from terminal cancer, requested treatment in the United States, and Carter agreed. Islamic rebels struck back by seizing the United States embassy in Teheran and taking more than 50 Americans hostage.

The 1980 Election

When Carter announced his intention to run for reelection in 1980, he was haunted by the continuing hostage crisis, persistent energy shortages, and lingering inflation. **Ronald Reagan**, former governor of California and conservative Republican, promised Americans a "new beginning," and a restoration of confidence at home and abroad. Reagan swept to victory, and on the day of his inauguration, Iran released the hostages.

REAGAN AND THE CHALLENGES OF THE 1980s

A former actor, Reagan appealed to Americans with his references to the "good old days" and his patriotic speeches. He used his prepared speeches to promote a conservative approach to government and the economy. He targeted inflation as his top priority. He also emphasized that big government and big-government spending were the cause of inflation. "In the present crisis," said Reagan, "government is not the solution to our problem; government is the problem."

New Federalism

Reagan supported a domestic program backed by both Eisenhower and Nixon. Like his Republican predecessors, he supported New Federalism, a policy that turned over federal control of some social welfare programs to the states.

SUPPLY-SIDE ECONOMICS   Reagan called for cuts in taxes on businesses and individuals, especially those with large incomes, so that they could reinvest in more businesses. These businesses would hire more workers and increase the "supply" of goods and services. Reagan argued that "**supply-side economics**" would end inflation without increasing the national debt. His ideas later became known as **Reaganomics**.

BALANCED BUDGET   Reagan tried to balance the budget by reducing many social welfare programs. He also made sharp cuts in the Environmental Protection Agency. Despite such efforts, however, the national debt climbed throughout Reagan's presidency.

"STAR WARS"   Reagan felt national security rested on defense. So he made every effort to fight off cuts in the military budget. He even asked for increased spending on missiles, ships, bombers, and a program for space weapons that came to be called "Star Wars."

FARM AID   In the 1980s farmers experienced their worst economic problems since the Great Depression. A worldwide recession made it impossible for farmers to sell their surpluses—and to repay their loans. The Reagan administration responded by paying farmers not to plant millions of acres of land to reduce the supply and raise prices. However, this never happened, and the national debt grew.

Foreign Affairs

Reagan adopted a tough stand toward communism, describing the Soviet Union as an "evil empire."

QUESTIONING DÉTENTE   Reagan's attitude hardened toward communism in December 1981 when the Polish government cracked down on Solidarity, an independent labor party. Reagan called for economic sanctions to force the Communist-backed government to end martial law. A renewal of détente did not take place until Reagan's second term.

INTERVENTION IN CENTRAL AMERICA   Reagan believed that unstable economic conditions opened the door to communism. He asked for aid to Latin American groups fighting Communist takeovers and approved limited military intervention in some nations.

- **El Salvador**: Reagan sent arms and military advisors to El Salvador to back anti-Communist forces in a civil war. He also pressured the government to hold democratic elections.

- **Nicaragua**: In 1979 Marxist guerrillas called the **Sandinistas** overthrew anti-Communist dictator Anastasio Somoza. Because the Sandinistas accepted aid from Cuba and the Soviet Union, Reagan

MAKING CONNECTIONS

Regents Tip   Read questions that accompany graphs and other art work carefully.

By how much did the federal budget deficit increase during President Reagan's first term in office?

Federal Budget Deficit 1980–1985

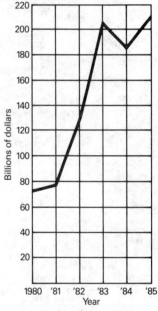

Source: *Statistical Abstract of the United States*

Enduring Issues

Civil Liberties

approved aid to the **Contras**, rebels seeking to oust the Sandinistas. Actions by the CIA to help the Contras angered Congress, and it cut off aid to the Contras until 1987.

* **Grenada**: In October 1983, a rebellion on the Caribbean island nation of Grenada raised fears that it might become a Communist base in the Caribbean. To prevent such a possibility Reagan ordered a surprise United States invasion.

TURMOIL IN THE MIDDLE EAST   Religious conflicts in the Middle East increased tensions in an already unstable region. An international peacekeeping force went into Lebanon to try to end bloody fighting between Christians and Muslims. In September 1983, American marines became the target of terrorists when a bomb-laden truck drove into their barracks, killing 241. In 1984 Reagan admitted the peacekeeping effort had failed and withdrew American troops.

TERRORISM   **Terrorism,** random acts of violence to promote a political cause, raised global concern. In some countries, Islamic fundamentalists engaged in terrorism as part of a **jihad,** or a struggle to protect the Islamic faith. Charges of terrorism were also leveled against the Soviets in September 1983 when they shot down a Korean airliner that strayed into their air space, killing some 269 innocent people.

The Election of 1984

In 1984 Reagan announced a second bid for the presidency. He chose **George Bush** as his running mate. **Walter Mondale** ran for the Democratic nomination against several contenders including **Reverend Jesse Jackson**, a black minister. Mondale won and selected Representative Geraldine Ferraro as his vice presidential running mate.

A TWO-TERM PRESIDENCY

Reagan was the first President since Eisenhower to serve two full terms in office.

Domestic Policies

Reagan, nicknamed the "Great Communicator" by some journalists, used his charm and persuasive talents to convince Americans to back a plan aimed at creating a balanced budget by the early 1990s.

Reagan and his supporters promised to make deep cuts in federal programs. Only a few select programs, such as Social Security and defense were to be spared. Reagan also called for simplification of tax laws and tax cuts for about 60 percent of Americans. Some people charged that the cuts favored the rich. However, the Tax Reform Act passed in 1986 freed some six million low-income earners from paying any income taxes at all.

TRADE IMBALANCE Despite drastic actions by the federal government, the national debt climbed. This was due, in part, to a huge **trade imbalance**, a situation in which a nation imports more goods than it exports. At the start of Reagan's second term, the trade deficit topped $100 billion.

Foreign Affairs

Reagan redirected his foreign policy to meet changes taking place in the Soviet Union. However, an issue that arose out of United States dealings in the Middle East and Latin America took up much of his attention.

THE IRAN-CONTRA AFFAIR In 1986 the United States public learned that several top presidential aides had sold arms to Iran in exchange for Iranian help in freeing American hostages held in Lebanon. The money from the sale of arms was then channeled to Nicaragua to support the Contras.

Reagan had vowed never to bargain with terrorists or kidnappers. Also, Congress had banned aid to the Contras. A Congressional committee cleared the President of any wrongdoing and concluded that the actions had been illegally undertaken at the direction of Colonel Oliver North and members of the CIA.

REOPENING OF DÉTENTE In 1985 **Mikhail Gorbachev** became the new charismatic leader of the Soviet Union. Gorbachev criticized Reagan's policy of ''Star Wars'' and called for a renewal of détente.

Gorbachev helped further relations by announcing his new policies of **glasnost** and **perestroika**. Glasnost called for greater ''openness,'' including increased political freedom in the Soviet Union and Eastern Europe. Perestroika allowed a measure of free enterprise to improve economic conditions within the Soviet Union.

ARMS REDUCTIONS In 1987 the United States and Soviet Union reached an agreement to reduce short-range and medium-range missiles.

TROUBLES ELSEWHERE Troubles over other foreign policy issues were not so easily resolved. These included:

- **Continuing Terrorism**: Terrorists continued to claim American lives. In 1985, for example, Palestinian terrorists killed an American passenger aboard the Italian cruise ship, the *Achille Lauro*. In 1988 a bomb destroyed a Pan Am jet over Scotland.

MAKING CONNECTIONS

Continuing Issues List other incidents of terrorism that have affected the United States in earlier times.

Enduring Issues

- Political System
- Choice

Election of 1984

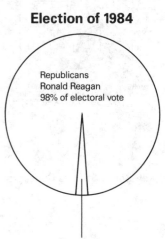

Republicans
Ronald Reagan
98% of electoral vote

Democrats
Walter Mondale
2% of electoral vote

MAKING CONNECTIONS

Major Ideas Domestic economic conditions have an effect on American citizens' attitudes toward foreign trade.

Regents Tip Cartoonists may use figures in one setting to comment on events in another setting.

What is this cartoonist's attitude toward the Iran-Contra affair?

"I TAKE THE IRAN-CONTRA DEFENSE—I WOULDN'T HAVE HAD TO BREAK ANY LAWS IF YOUR STUPID LAWS HAD FIT IN WITH WHAT I WANTED TO DO"

From Herblock at Large (*Pantheon Books, 1987*)

Key Social Studies Concepts:

Change

- **Battling the Drug Trade**: First Lady Nancy Reagan launched an antidrug campaign with the slogan, "Just say NO!"
- **Ending Apartheid**: Many Americans demanded **divestiture**, a policy that called for the end of American investments in South Africa to protest **apartheid** there. In 1986 Congress overrode Reagan's veto and imposed strict economic sanctions against South Africa until it ended apartheid.

The 1988 Election

George Bush won the Republican nomination for President. Bush surprised the nation by choosing a little-known Indiana Senator, Dan Quayle, as his running mate. Within the Democratic party, a primary battle shaped up between Jesse Jackson and Michael Dukakis, son of a Greek immigrant and governor of Massachusetts. Dukakis eventually won the nomination and selected Texas Senator Lloyd Bentsen as his running mate. In November, voters chose Bush as the next President.

THE BUSH ADMINISTRATION

The biggest issues of the Bush years were the budget, events abroad, and the economy.

Domestic Events

Bush inherited several of Reagan's problems from the late 1980s.

ECONOMIC TROUBLES During the campaign, Bush had promised voters no new taxes. However, as the budget deficit mounted, Bush was forced to break this promise in 1990. By 1992 a continuing economic recession caused increased layoffs and rising unemployment.

SAVINGS AND LOANS SCANDAL In 1990 misuse of funds by savings and loan institutions surfaced. At the end of 1990, it was estimated that it would cost American taxpayers billions of dollars to bail out the savings and loan industry.

SUPREME COURT APPOINTMENTS President Bush appointed two new justices to the Supreme Court—David Souter in 1990 and Clarence Thomas in 1991. Thomas was confirmed by the Senate after controversial hearings in which he was charged with sexual harrassment by Anita Hill, a former employee.

URBAN VIOLENCE After five white Los Angeles police officers were found innocent in the beating of African-American motorist Rodney King in 1992, that city erupted in riots.

Events Abroad

END OF THE COLD WAR   In November 1989, the world watched in amazement as Germans tore down the Berlin Wall—a symbolic reminder of the division between the Communist and non-Communist worlds. Throughout the winter of 1989, Communist governments in Eastern Europe crumbled. In 1990 Gorbachev received the Nobel Peace Prize for relaxing control over former Soviet satellites. In November of that year, East and West Germany were formally reunited. A failed coup by hard-line Communist leaders in 1991 led to the dissolution of the Soviet Union and the 1992 formation of a democratic Commonwealth of Independent States.

INVASION OF PANAMA   As President, Bush continued Reagan's war on drugs. He ordered United States troops into Panama to capture General Manuel Noriega, the dictator of Panama, and return him to the United States to face drug charges. In 1992 Noriega was sentenced to serve 40 years in federal prison.

WAR IN THE GULF   In August 1990 Iraqi leader Saddam Hussein invaded the oil-rich nation of Kuwait. Bush responded to the aggression by sending United States troops into Saudi Arabia, with the agreement of Saudi leaders. The United Nations condemned Iraq's actions and approved economic sanctions against Iraq. The UN also authorized a joint military buildup in Saudi Arabia, called Operation Desert Shield.

Operation Desert Shield became Operation Desert Storm in January 1991 when the United States with a troop force of over 400,000 (the largest American military commitment since Vietnam) and Allied troops from a number of other nations began a total air assault on Iraq. By the end of February Bush ordered a cease-fire and Iraq accepted all U.N. demands to end the War. More than three hundred Allied lives were lost but the Iraqi death toll was estimated at 100,000.

The 1992 Election

George Bush was nominated to run for a second term as President by the Republican Party as was Vice President Dan Quayle. The Democrats selected Arkansas Governor Bill Clinton as their Presidential nominee with Al Gore for Vice President. An Independent challenger, Texas billionaire Ross Perot also entered the race. The major issues revolved around the state of the American economy.

Clinton carried 32 states with a total of 370 electoral votes. Although Perot did not earn any electoral votes, he received over 19 million popular votes. Women, blacks and Hispanics were elected to Congress in record high numbers in 1992.

MAKING CONNECTIONS

Key Social Studies Concepts:

Choice

Election of 1992

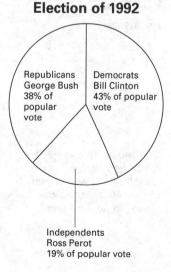

Republicans
George Bush
38% of
popular
vote

Democrats
Bill Clinton
43% of popular
vote

Independents
Ross Perot
19% of popular vote

MAKING CONNECTIONS

THE CLINTON ADMINISTRATION

Clinton entered office with an ambitious domestic program. Two important areas of concern to Clinton were health-care reform and improving economic growth. However, events in other nations also demanded much of Clinton's attention.

Domestic Issues

HEALTH-CARE REFORM In 1993 Clinton presented to Congress a health-care reform plan that would ensure health insurance for all Americans. Critics of the plan complained that it would cost too much and prove too complex to implement effectively. In 1994 Congress rejected Clinton's plan.

SUPREME COURT APPOINTEES With the nomination of Ruth Bader Ginsburg to the Supreme court in 1993, Clinton became the first Democratic President in 26 years to name a Supreme Court justice. In 1994, due to another retirement, Clinton had the opportunity to appoint a second justice, Stephen Breyer.

THE 1994 CONGRESSIONAL ELECTIONS In 1994, running with a platform called the "Contract with America," the Republican Party took majority control of both houses of Congress for the first time in 40 years. Led by new Speaker of the House Newt Gingrich, the House soon passed bills dealing with topics from the Contract, such as welfare reform and a constitutional amendment to balance the budget. Most of the bills, however, failed to pass the Senate or were vetoed by President Clinton.

THE 1996 ELECTIONS At the end of 1995, disagreement between Republicans and Clinton over the federal budget led to a shutdown of the federal government. The public largely blamed Republicans for the shutdown, and Clinton used that sentiment to help jump-start his 1996 presidential campaign. During the campaign, Clinton usurped several Republican issues. He signed welfare reform into law and supported a balanced budget. He also focused public attention on how the economy had improved during his first term. With these tactics, Clinton easily won reelection over his major challengers, Republican Bob Dole and the candidate of the new Reform Party, Ross Perot. The Republican Party maintained its majority in both houses of Congress.

Enduring Issues

Presidential Power

Continuing Issues
According to the Constitution, which branch of government has the power to declare war?

Foreign Affairs

HAITI In 1991, the Haitian military had overthrown President Jean-Bertrand Aristide, Haiti's first freely elected leader. Desperate Haitian refugees then fled by the thousands, most seeking asylum in the United States. In 1994, Haiti's military rulers—under threat of U.S. invasion—agreed to give up power. United States forces landed in Haiti to oversee the transition to democratic rule.

SOUTH AFRICA   In 1994 the United States welcomed the news of the first free elections in South African history. Nelson Mandela, the internationally recognized spokesman for the anti-apartheid movement, was elected president.

THE MIDDLE EAST   In 1993 the Palestine Liberation Organization (PLO) recognized Israel's right to exist, and Israel recognized the PLO as the representative of the Palestinian people. The following year Israel and Jordan signed a peace treaty. Major obstacles to peace remained, however. Arab opponents of the peace process launched terrorist attacks against Israel, and in 1995 a Jewish extremist assassinated Israel's prime minister, Yitzhak Rabin. By mid-1998, peace talks remained at an impasse.

THE FORMER YUGOSLAVIA   Beginning in 1991, when republics of the former Yugoslavia began declaring independence, thousands died in bitter ethnic fighting. In 1995 the United States hosted a meeting of the warring sides in Dayton, Ohio, where they signed an agreement calling for an end to the war. Foreign troops, including many from the United States, went to Bosnia to enforce the peace plan. Yet tensions in the area remained extremely high.

NATO EXPANSION   At a summit in Madrid, Spain, in July 1997, the North Atlantic Treaty Organization (NATO) planned to offer membership to some Central and Eastern European nations. Russia initially opposed this expansion of NATO, but negotiations between President Clinton and Russian president Boris Yeltsin resolved this issue, allowing the post–Cold War expansion to go forward.

ASIA   In mid-1998 India set off five nuclear tests, drawing worldwide condemnation and causing Pakistan to retaliate by launching nuclear tests of its own. The United States placed economic sanctions on both countries and took a more watchful stance to guard against an arms race in South Asia. In Southeast Asia, a nationwide protest led by students brought about the resignation of President Suharto of Indonesia, who had ruled the country since 1967. Suharto turned over his office to his vice president, B. J. Habibe.

Regents Questions for Practice _____

Review the Test-Taking Strategies section of this book. Then answer the following questions.

1. The balance-of-terror theory in relations between the super powers is based primarily on the belief that
   1 providing nuclear weapons to as many allies as possible assures military superiority
   2 war can provide a powerful stimulus for social change
   3 nuclear superiority guarantees an adequate defense
   4 the fear of nuclear war helps preserve peace

Test Hint Again, note the importance of knowing key vocabulary terms.

2. "Despite all changes in the world, one key reality has remained unchanged: United States participation is still the indispensable condition for any stable and harmonious world order."
In this statement President Nixon was advocating the policy of
1 isolationism
2 militarism
3 internationalism
4 imperialism

MAKING CONNECTIONS

Test Hint This question gives you an effect and asks you to name the cause.

3. Since the early 1970s, the United States and the People's Republic of China have moved toward establishing better relations mainly because
1 China had democratized its government and meets United States standards for protecting human rights
2 both countries wish to counteract the rising industrial strength of Japan
3 the United States needs China as a supplier of vital raw materials
4 both countries are seeking to balance the power of the Soviet Union

4. Since World War II, a major goal of United States foreign policy in the Middle East has been to bring about
1 a peaceful settlement of Arab-Israeli issues
2 an end to United States cooperation with Arab nations
3 ownership of oil resources by western nations
4 permanent United Nations control of disputed territories

5. During the 1970s a major reason that the United States was willing to negotiate increased Panamanian control of the Panama Canal was that the United States
1 was planning to build a new canal
2 had lost interest in Latin American affairs
3 had insufficient military strength to defend the Canal
4 regarded the Canal has having reduced strategic importance

Test Hint Questions 5 and 6 both deal with Panama. One asks about recent events there. The other requires you to have knowledge of earlier U.S. actions in the region.

6. The Panama Canal Treaty (1978) represented a partial reversal of an earlier United States foreign policy in that it
1 ended United States isolation by the formation of an alliance with Panama
2 returned to Panamanian control an area that the United States had controlled for decades
3 recognized and accepted a new Communist government in Panama
4 accepted the principle of European involvement in the management of the Panama Canal

7. Détente, as applied to United States foreign policy in the 1970s, is based on the belief that
   1 where peaceful coexistence fails a display of force frequently leads to suitable compromise
   2 formal alliances should be avoided, since they often cause small conflicts between two countries to broaden into international wars
   3 ideological differences need not prevent peaceful economic and cultural contacts among countries
   4 internal problems of foreign countries are best solved by a joint agreement of major powers not to intervene

Test Hint This question is another way of asking you to supply a definition of a particular term.

8. The United States foreign policy of détente with the Soviet Union has been mainly concerned with
   1 promoting democratic ideals
   2 easing tensions
   3 promoting the arms race
   4 lowering tariffs

9. Which best accounts for the fact that in the United States in 1947, blue-collar workers outnumbered white-collar workers, whereas by 1975 white-collar workers outnumbered blue-collar workers?
   1 White-collar workers received higher wages than blue-collar workers.
   2 The increase in the number of college graduates led to an increase in the need for white-collar workers.
   3 Many jobs have been reclassified from blue-collar to white-collar status.
   4 Technological advances have increased the need for white-collar workers.

10. Which action involves the President of the United States in the criminal justice system?
    1 reviewing the decisions of the Secretary of Defense
    2 granting pardons and reprieves
    3 presiding at an impeachment trial of the Vice President
    4 determining the legality of Cabinet decisions

11. As United States involvement in world affairs has increased the power of the Presidency has also increased because
    1 congressional leaders have been unwilling to divert their attention from domestic issues
    2 according to custom and tradition, Congress does not discuss foreign policy issues
    3 the Senate has consistently failed to check the President's power by refusing to ratify treaties
    4 the Constitution gives primary responsibility for foreign relations to the President

12. In recent years which measure has most often been proposed to reduce the influence of special interest groups on candidates running for political office?
    1 increasing the length of political campaigns
    2 increasing public funding of political campaigns
    3 decreasing the number of elected offices
    4 decreasing voter registration drives

13. In 1972 and 1984, Republican candidates for President won overwhelming electoral victories while, at the same time, Democrats gained majorities in the United States House of Representatives. This fact illustrates that
   1 winning presidential candidates have ''coattail effects''
   2 many Democrats do not vote in presidential elections
   3 Republicans outnumber Democrats nationally
   4 many voters split their ballots

14. A strong United States dollar in the world market would be most likely to aggravate which domestic economic issue?
   1 the trade deficit
   2 cost of military defense
   3 funding for education
   4 Social Security benefits

15. To offset competition from foreign imports, a country's labor unions would most likely favor
   1 laws to protect domestic industries
   2 lower tariffs on foreign imports
   3 government control of all industries
   4 a reduction in domestic production of goods

16. The United States sells manufactured products to Third World nations and purchases raw materials from these nations. This fact illustrates
   1 economic protectionism
   2 global interdependence
   3 pooling of resources
   4 finance capitalism

17. The use of United States military forces in the Dominican Republic (1965), Vietnam (1960s and 1970s), and Grenada (1984) was legally justified by the
   1 power of Congress to declare war
   2 precedents established in the Nuremberg War Crimes Trial
   3 provisions of the Monroe Doctrine
   4 President's power as Commander in Chief

Base your answers to questions 18 and 19 on the cartoon below and on your knowledge of social studies.

"THE RUSSIANS ARE GAINING! THE RUSSIANS ARE GAINING!"

"THE AMERICANS ARE GAINING! THE AMERICANS ARE GAINING!"

18. Which best summarizes the main idea of the cartoon?
   1 ''Soviet and American Détente''
   2 ''Containment of Communism''
   3 ''The Search for Democracy''
   4 ''A Reason for the Arms Race''

19. Which point of view does the cartoon best support?
   1 The United States should place greater restrictions on trade with the Soviet Union
   2 Soviet and American leaders are failing to modernize their armed forces.
   3 Competition to achieve military superiority should be ended.
   4 Ideological differences between the Soviet Union and the United States make arms limitation talks useless.

20. Which is a valid generalization about United States relationships with Latin America in the last 100 years?
1 The success of democracy in Latin America is due largely to United States intervention.
2 Latin American resentment of the United States is due to Communist influences.
3 The United States has gradually realized that events in Latin America have little bearing on United States security.
4 Economic interests have generally influenced United States policy toward Latin America.

21. Which is characteristic of both democracy and capitalism?
1 guarantees of a high standard of living
2 equality among people
3 very limited competition
4 considerable individual choice

22. The cartoon implies that the United States is
1 attempting to take a balanced view of the situation in South Africa
2 allowing economic concerns to affect its view of a moral problem
3 being threatened with the loss of an ally if it opposes South Africa's government
4 willing to get involved in an internal political dispute of another country

23. The major South African issue referred to in the cartoon is the
1 problem of apartheid
2 question of reciprocal trade agreements
3 difficulty of doing business in a country that has civil unrest
4 problem of minority rights in a democracy

Base your answers to questions 22 and 23 on the cartoon below and on your knowledge of social studies.

Toward a Postindustrial Society: Living in a Global Age

The United States began as a nation of farmers. Today it is one of the leading economic and political powers in the world. Because of the advanced technology of the postindustrial age, the world has become what some call a "global village." Because of increased interdependence, major events in one part of the world have an impact upon the rest of the world.

Key Social Studies Concepts:

Change

RAPID PACE OF CHANGE

In both Global Studies and United States History you learned about the causes and effects of the Industrial Revolution, one of the most far-reaching developments in human history. Although the Industrial Revolution began in the late 1700s, some historians argue that it has not yet ended.

Toward a Service Economy

Every generation since the Civil War has experienced the effects of the Industrial Revolution. However, the pace of technological change has picked up dramatically since World War II. Today the United States is moving into a postindustrial age. That is, the American economy no longer rests on the development of new factories and heavy industries such as the production of steel or coal. Instead, because of technological changes, service-related industries now occupy a larger sector of the economy.

Technology—What Is It?

Continuing Issues Why are the concepts of change and technology so important to an understanding of American culture in the 1990s?

Technology is the application of scientific knowledge to commerce and industry. To appreciate the effect of technological change, think of the following situations out of the past.

- George Washington, the nation's first President, never called a member of Congress on the telephone, never rode in a limousine, and never saw his photograph in a newspaper.

- Abraham Lincoln, President during the Civil War, never called generals on the telephone and never listened to battle reports on the radio.

- Franklin Roosevelt, President during World War II, never had a speech transmitted by satellite to Europe and never watched a program on television.

- John F. Kennedy, President in the early 1960s, never wrote a speech on a computer and never ate a snack heated up in a microwave.

- All recent Presidents have supported the American space program, but none has yet traveled into space. It is difficult even to imagine the changes that await future Presidents.

The Post-World War II Era

Since the end of World War II, a number of forces have had a great impact upon the economy and upon the lifestyles of Americans. These forces include the following:

SCARCE ENERGY SOURCES   Scarce oil supplies have led scientists to research alternative energy sources, such as solar power. Nuclear power is being used in some parts of the world. However, the hazards associated with **nuclear energy**, such as the storage of **nuclear waste**, of spent radioactive fuel, have created controversy. The accident at a nuclear power plant at Chernobyl, Russia, in 1986 has increased debate even more.

USE OF NEW MATERIALS   Inventions since World War II have replaced wood and steel in many jobs with synthetics such as plastic. In some cases, these new materials are lighter and more durable than traditional materials.

SPREAD OF COMPUTERS   The widespread use of computers in American homes and businesses in the 1980s has revolutionized record keeping and the storage of information. Advocates of computers praise their ability to process and store large volumes of information. Critics charge that computers have increased the chances for the invasion of privacy as people access private records without permission.

DEVELOPMENT OF MULTINATIONAL CORPORATIONS   Since the 1800s, American business organization has changed from individual proprietors (single owners) and partnerships to corporations. In the post-World War II period, many corporations have become multinationals—businesses with bases of operation in many nations.

INCREASED JOB OPPORTUNITIES   The greatest areas of occupational growth in the 1990s and early 2000s promise to be in the service fields. The most significant declines will occur in agricultural employment. Technological advancements have made it possible for fewer farmers to produce more food, reducing the need for agricultural labor.

RISE OF NEW LIFESTYLES   American attitudes toward family size and divorce have also changed since the 1950s. The average

MAKING CONNECTIONS

U.S. and the World   The accident at Chernobyl illustrates global interconnectedness, as radioactive waste from the accident was spread by the winds to other nations. What nation do some Canadians blame for much of the acid rain that falls in Canada?

Key Social Studies Concepts:

Technology

MAKING CONNECTIONS

family size has declined. After years of expansion, many school districts throughout the nation, including New York, experienced declining school enrollments in the 1980s. The divorce rate has also remained constant since the late 1980s, creating the largest number of single-parent households in the nation's history.

LONGER LIFE SPANS   Improvements in health care, resulting from advanced technological procedures, such as laser surgery and organ transplants, have increased average **life spans**. This in turn has increased the number of older Americans, who in recent years have organized to protect their rights and improve their lives.

EXPANSION OF PUBLIC EDUCATION   Access to free public education has always been a method for Americans to improve their standard of living. As individuals complete higher levels of education, they have the chance to secure better-paying jobs and more desirable housing. Thus education helps further social mobility.

As the 1900s draw to a close, American schools are struggling with public expectations about the role of educators in solving social problems. Also, schools must find ways to keep up with the latest technology while teaching students basic skills.

DEALING WITH THE AIDS CRISIS   Throughout the 1980s, medical researchers gathered more information about a fatal disease known as **Acquired Immune Deficiency Syndrome** (AIDS). Even so, AIDS spread through some sectors of the American population at an alarming rate. Without a known cure, scientists and public officials tried to increase public awareness and prevention of the disease. Many critics of government policy have condemned the federal government for not acting faster and with more money to find a cure for AIDS.

HELPING THE HOMELESS   Not everyone enjoyed the prosperity of the post-World War II years. President Johnson's Great Society programs in the 1960s tried to reduce poverty in America. However, cuts in social programs under the Reagan administration in the 1980s caused a rise in the number of Americans living below the poverty line. A problem unknown in the United States since the depression of the 1930s has arisen—the problem of homelessness. Thousands of people of all ages in the 1980s had no place to live. Local communities and private charitable organizations tried to provide relief. But as the 1990s unfold, the issue of homelessness remains a troubling social issue.

Key Social Studies Concepts:

Empathy

THE UNITED STATES AND CONTEMPORARY WORLD PROBLEMS

Just as the United States is attempting to deal with economic and social changes at home, it is also reviewing its position within the global community. The United States can no longer effectively isolate itself from problems abroad. Some international issues that concern Americans today include the following:

Population Growth

Although the United States and most other developed nations have experienced a decline in their birth rates, the developing nations of the world have an overpopulation problem. Millions of the world's people suffer from starvation, and millions more live only a marginal existence. Foreign aid has become of vital economic importance to regions such as Sub-Saharan Africa. The role of foreign aid has affected the conduct of foreign relations, raising questions about the obligations of both giving and receiving nations.

Environmental Concerns

Because of increased **interdependence**, an environmental problem in one nation frequently raises global concern. An example includes destruction of tropical rain forests by Brazil.

ENVIRONMENTAL ACTIVISTS Disasters such as the Exxon oil spill off the coast of Alaska have helped increase public awareness of the ecological threats to the planet's life forms. A number of groups have gained international attention for their efforts to curb the negative effects of industry. Greenpeace is one such group. Animal rights' activists have also gained publicity for their efforts to stop people from killing animals for their furs or for using animals for laboratory research.

Recycling efforts have been organized on the local level, including New York, to reuse paper, glass, and aluminum. Community organizers have become more vocal in rejecting plans to convert vacant lands into dump sites. Communities are studying the effects of industrial pollution on the ground water that people drink.

In response to public pressure, the federal government has enacted laws requiring automobile manufacturers to put antipollution devices on their cars. The federal government also faces the problem of finding acceptable ways to store the spent fuel from nuclear power plants and weapons firms. Since the first Earth Day celebration in 1970, the American people, along with the rest of the world, have begun to realize their obligation to protect the environment for future generations.

Emerging Power Relationships

The following pairs of terms illustrate economic categories into which nations were grouped in the years after World War II.

developed   [or]   developing
West   [or]   East
haves   [or]   have-nots
North   [or]   South

MAKING CONNECTIONS

Regents Tip   Try to understand a cartoonist's attitude toward his subject.

What does this cartoonist think is a major cause of pollution?

Do you think the cartoonist is optimistic that the problem of pollution can be ended? Explain your answer.

"Where there's smoke, there's money."

Drawing by Joe Mirachi. © 1985 The New Yorker Magazine, Inc.

MAKING CONNECTIONS

In the late 1900s, the nations that had traditionally fallen in the left column are being joined by nations once described as "developing." For example, some Eastern European nations now may be described as developed. However, the gap between the rich and poor nations is widening. Parts of Africa, Asia, and Latin America (have-not nations in the southern hemisphere) are still without many of the basic services in the developed nations of North America and Western Europe (have nations in the northern hemisphere). Basic economic differences can be expected to cause problems in the decades ahead as developing nations struggle to raise their standards of living while resisting dependence upon the developed nations.

During much of the 20th century, the United States devoted huge sums of foreign aid to reducing the gap between the developed and developing nations (haves and have-nots). However, the growing federal budget deficit may cause Americans to reassess their commitment to foreign aid in the future.

Regents Questions for Practice ___

Review the **Test-Taking Strategies** section of this book. Then answer the following questions, drawn from actual Regents examinations. Circle the *number* of the word or expression that best completes the statement or answers the question. Write your answers to essay questions on a separate piece of paper. Hints on good ways to approach these questions are provided in the margins.

1. Which has been an effect of technological advances in most developing nations?

Note Technology is one of the key concepts.

1 Class distinctions have disappeared.
2 Subsistence agriculture has been emphasized.
3 Traditional family ties have been strengthened.
4 Urbanization has been stimulated.

2. Maintaining stability in a pluralistic society is difficult because

Regents Tip Plural means more than one.

1 individuals are often forced to encounter the views of others which may challenge their own ideas
2 there is usually no defined order of governmental authority
3 new members in the society are often unwilling to obey established laws of the society
4 the wide variety of citizens' abilities hinders the management of labor resources

3. Which will most likely be a major effect of the declining birth rate in the United States?

1 an increased effort on the part of advertisers to capture the youth market

2 a surge in the building of public schools

3 an increase in the political power of retired people

4 a strengthening in the power of college students as a special interest group

MAKING CONNECTIONS

4. Which will be the most likely outcome of the increasing life expectancy in the United States?

1 decreased need for health care facilities

2 decreased political power of senior citizens' organizations

3 increased demands for mandatory retirement at age 65

4 increased concern for economic security for the elderly

5. Which best explains why divorce rates in the United States are higher today than at the beginning of the century?

1 Marriage is no longer considered an important element in society.

2 Divorce statistics at the beginning of the century were not accurate.

3 Divorce rates generally increase during periods of economic stability.

4 Social and legal restrictions concerning divorce have been reduced.

6. Upward social mobility would be most likely to occur in a society that has

1 undergone widespread economic expansion

2 produced a relatively low per capita income

3 provided few educational opportunities

4 maintained a traditional economy

Vocabulary You must know the meaning of social mobility to answer this question.

7. Which is a valid generalization about world population growth?

1 Population growth rates are unequal, with the less developed nations gaining population most rapidly.

2 Industrialized nations are increasing in population more rapidly than are the less developed nations.

3 Death rates are increasing more rapidly than birth rates in most nations.

4 Population growth rates are about the same in most nations.

Regents Tip Note that this is a global question, not only about the United States.

8. In the United States the idea of the need for a compulsory and free public education system was primarily built on the premise that

1 an effective democracy depends on educated people

2 people in a democratic society need to be informed about the arts and sciences

3 the nation will advance in the sciences if the people are educated

4 education for all people is guaranteed by the federal Constitution

MAKING CONNECTIONS

Test Hint   Read all parts of essay questions carefully before beginning to block them.

Essay Questions

At various times, the United States has followed one or more of the foreign policies listed below.

Foreign Policies
Imperialism
Isolationism
Containment
Nonrecognition
Formation of military alliances
Reliance upon international organizations

1. Choose *three* of the policies listed above. For each one chosen, discuss a specific application of that policy by the United States. Include in your discussion one reason the United States applied that policy and one result of the application of that policy.

[5, 5, 5]

Three Policies	Specific Application	Reason for Policy	Result of Application
containment	American involvement in war in Vietnam	U.S. feared that all of Asia would become Communist (domino theory).	U.S. fought losing fight in Vietnam; divisions at home; Vietnam is now communist. [5]
			[5]
			[5]

2. Many aspects of United States society have been greatly affected by technological changes. Choose three of the aspects of United States society listed below. Explain how each one chosen has been affected by a specific technological development. (Use a different development for each aspect.)

Aspects of United States Society
Urbanization
Agriculture
Cultural homogeneity
Rights of the individual
Politics
Environment

[5, 5, 5]

3. The growing interdependence of nations has made the United States increasingly affected by global problems such as those listed below.

Global Problems
Environmental pollution
International drug trafficking
International terrorism
Human rights violations
Rapid population growth
Economic needs of emerging nations

Assume that you are an adviser to a United States presidential candidate. Select three of the problems from the list above and for each one chosen:

• Describe the global nature of the problem and explain how the problem affects the United States.

• Recommend and justify a position that the candidate should take concerning the problem.

[5, 5, 5]

4. Listed below are issues confronting United States society:

Issues
Students with AIDS attending public schools
Media censorship
Environmental protection
The homeless
Prayer in public schools

MAKING CONNECTIONS

Test Hint Underline words in essay questions that tell you what to do.

Test Hint Be sure to study directions in the bulleted lists.

MAKING CONNECTIONS

Test Hint Be sure to do all the required parts of each essay question.

Select *three* of the issues listed and for each one chosen:

• Discuss a controversy related to the issue.

• Identify one specific argument on each side of the controversy.

• Discuss one specific action through which the government has attempted to deal with the issue.

[5, 5, 5]

5. Presidential decisions have had an important effect on the United States and the world. Listed below are headlines representing important presidential decisions.

Headlines
"McKinley Asks for War with Spain"
"Wilson Proposes the Fourteen Points"
"Truman Orders Dropping of Bomb on Hiroshima"
"Kennedy Orders Blockade of Cuba"
"Johnson Increases Military Forces in Vietnam"
"Carter Signs Camp David Accords with Sadat and Begin"

Select *three* of the decisions above. For each one selected, describe the circumstances which led to the decision and discuss two major results of that decision.

[5, 5, 5]

6. Many factors have influenced United States social and economic life. Select *three* of the factors from the list below. For each *one* selected, discuss two ways in which that factor has affected United States social and/or economic life.

Factors
Immigration
Women's movement
Environmental protection
The media
Regional difference
Growth of suburbs

[5, 5, 5]

English Vocabulary for the Regents: What You Need to Know _____

Sometimes students have trouble with a question because they do not know the meaning of an English vocabulary term, or non-social studies term. The following English vocabulary terms have appeared on past Regents Examinations in United States History and Government.

abolish to end, or do away with, completely

absolute complete; unmixed; not limited by a constitution

accurate free from errors

acquire to gain by one's own knowledge or efforts

acquisition something someone has acquired or added

adapt to change or adjust [*adapt* to new conditions]

adherence attachment to, support of

adopt to choose and follow; to vote to accept

advocate to speak or write in support of something; a person who supports a cause

affect to influence or produce a change in; to stir emotions; to bring about an effect or result

aggression a forceful, hostile, or warlike act; **aggressive** inclined toward militant or direct action

agrarian of agriculture or farmers

allocate to set apart for a specific purpose

allocation that which is set apart or allocated

alter to change

analysis examination of the parts making up a whole

appease to pacify or quiet; to satisfy or relieve

assert to declare, or defend

assimilate to absorb or make alike [*assimilate* into a culture]

assume to suppose or take for granted; to take upon oneself [to *assume* responsibility]

assumption anything that someone takes for granted; a supposition

assure to convince or promise

authority the power to enforce or impose obedience; a person or source considered expert in a field; a government agency that administers a project; **authorize** to delegate power

balance to weigh off the importance of ideas, values, and so to achieve a state of equality or stability

basic fundamental; essential

basis foundation; fundamental principle or theory

caprice a sudden, impulsive change in the way one thinks or acts

cease to bring or come to an end

characterize to describe features, traits, or qualities of an item, idea, or person

characteristic a distinguishing trait, feature or quality

chronic lasting a long time or recurring often

cite to mention by way of example or proof

classify   to arrange or group according to some system or principle

coalition   a combination; union

commit   to turn over for safekeeping; to make known an opinion or point of view; **commitment**   a pledge or promise to turn over or do something

compel   to force or bring together by force

compete   to enter into rivalry; **competition**   a contest or match; rivalry in business

compromise   a mutual agreement; midway point between two positions; to settle a dispute by making concessions on both sides

compulsory   obligatory; required

concept   an idea or generalized notion

concern   a matter of interest or importance; **concerned**   to be worried or interested

conclusion   judgment, decision, or opinion based upon a clear line of reasoning

confine   to limit or restrict

conflict   fight, struggle, or disagreement

conform   to adapt or make similar

confront   to bring face to face or oppose; **confrontation**   act of opposition

consequence   outcome or result

consistent   in agreement; holding to the same principles; **consistently**   in a similar manner

conspiracy   secret plan or act for an unlawful or harmful purpose

contain   to hold or check [to *contain* expansion]

controversial   subject to dispute; **controversy** debate or subject open to argument

crucial   of great importance

curb   to check or restrain

curtail   to cut short

decade   ten-year period

decline   to descend or lessen in force

demand   to ask for as a right; a strong request

denounce   to accuse publicly

deny   to refuse to accept or grant

derive   to trace from a source or a line of reasoning

destiny   fate; the seemingly inevitable or necessary happening of events

discontent   dissatisfaction; desire to change a situation

disillusion   disappoint; to take away ideals; **disillusionment**   the state of feeling stripped of former ideals

dissent   to differ in belief or opinion; disagree

diversify   to give variety to, to vary, to divide up among different companies, to expand a line of production; **diversity**   variety

divert   to turn aside; deflect

domestic   having to do with one's own house or country; native products or industries

dominant   ruling or prevailing power; **dominate**   to exercise power over others; **domination**   rule or control over others

dwindle   diminish; shrink

effective   able to produce a desired result

efficient   working well or producing a desired result with the least effort possible

eliminate   to reject or omit; **elimination**   the act of excluding

elite   group or part of a group selected or regarded as the finest, best, most powerful, etc.

embroil   to confuse; mix up; to draw into a conflict

emerge to become visible or to rise up

enact to pass or decree [to *enact* a law]

enforce to compel or impose by force

ensure to make certain

equalize to make uniform or equal

era an event or period in time

essential fundamental or absolutely necessary

establish to set up, enact, or make happen

ethical of or conforming to moral standards

evidence data that tends to prove something

excess action or conduct going beyond the reasonable; **excessive** characterized by excess

exclude to bar, keep out, or refuse to consider

exclusive given or belonging to no other; not shared or divided; sole

exercise to use or perform [to *exercise* power]

exert to put into action, to put forth

existence a state of fact, living, or being [to call into *existence*, or being]

expand to spread or make greater in size; **expansion** an increasing of size [the *expansion* of territory]

exploit to make unethical use of for one's advantage or profit

expose to reveal, disclose, to allow to be seen

extent the range or limits of something [the *extent* of power]; **extend** to stretch out or give to [to *extend* power to]; **extension** a giving or expanding of something [*extension* of the vote to women]

factor circumstances, people, or conditions that help bring about a result

flourish to grow; succeed; thrive

foster to help grow or develop

frivolous of little value; unimportant

fulfill to carry out or complete established requirements

function duty or stated purpose; to perform in the expected manner

fundamental basis, principle, or most important part

generalization a general idea or statement based on available information; **generally** usually; widely accepted

generate to produce or bring about; **generated from** came from or was produced by

goal an object or aim that one aims to achieve

guarantee a pledge, assurance, or safeguard that something will happen

hinder to prevent or keep back

hostility antagonism or act of ill will

ideal principle, model, or image thought to be perfect

ideological of the study of ideas, their nature and source

illustrate to make clear or explain by examples

impact the power of an event or idea to bring about change

implement to provide the means for putting something into effect; **implementation** putting a plan into action

imply to hint at or suggest

impose to place a burden or responsibility on someone or something [to *impose* a tax]

indicate to point out or show

individual   single or separate; **individualism** following self-interest or expressing individual character

ineffective   not capable of producing the desired result

inequities   instances of unfairness or lack of justice

infiltrate   to attack or seize control from within

influence   the power to affect the actions of others or to produce a change; **influential** having a powerful effect

initiate   to start or bring into practice; **initiative**   the act of beginning or taking the first step

institute   to set up; establish; initiate

intensify   to strengthen or increase; **intensity** the degree of strength, energy, or force

interest   feeling of concern or importance by a person or group [took an *interest* in]

interfere   to meddle or hinder; **interference** act of blocking or meddling

interpret   to explain the meaning of something; **interpretation**   explanation or expression of a person's understanding of something

intervene   to come in between; **intervention** the act of coming in between two parties or events [*intervention* between warring nations]

involve   to include or become entangled in; **involvement**   the act of becoming included

isolate   to set apart from others

justify   to show reason or cause for an action

lenient   merciful or mild; not harsh

limit   to impose boundaries or restrictions

major   greater in importance or strength

mandatory   required

mobility   movement from one place to another

moral   good or right conduct

motivate   to provide with a cause; to incite or inspire

motley   having many or clashing elements; heterogeneous

mutual   shared, in common; to have similar interests

negative   lacking a positive or affirmative quality

negotiate   to bargain or discuss with the purpose of reaching an agreement

noninvolvement   the act of not taking part in something

obligate   to bind by a promise or contract

opponent   adversary; **opposition**   act of resisting; the person or group contrary to a course of action

originate   to start or bring into being

outstripped   excelled; surpassed

overwhelm   to make helpless; overcome; overpower

perceive   to observe or recognize

periodic   occurring at regular intervals; occurring from time to time

persuade   to cause to do something by urging or reasoning

philosophy   search for wisdom or knowledge; general principles or laws underlying a system of thought

pluralistic   a multitude of characteristics or traits; a nation or society made up of distinctive ethnic or racial groups

pluralism   existence within a nation of groups distinctive in ethnic, religious, cultural patterns

policy   principle or plan of action

populace   the common people

portray   to depict or describe

positive   tending toward progress or agreeable action; definite proposition or statement

precede   to come before in time, order, or rank [Washington *preceded* Jefferson]

precedent   an act, decision, or law that may be used to justify later actions

precedence   the act or right of coming first because of preceding in time, or, rank, status

predominate   dominating influence over others; superior

preferential   of, having, giving, or receiving one's first choice

preoccupy   to absorb totally

preserve   to keep from harm or damage

prevent   to stop or keep something from happening by taking prior action

primary   first in time; fundamental or basic; **primarily**   mainly

principle   prime source; fundamental truth, doctrine, or belief

priority   preceding in time, order, importance

procedure   particular method or course of action

process   a continuous action involving many steps or operations

prohibit   to forbid, bar, or hinder; **prohibition** order or law banning some action

promote   to further or advance; to move forward; to support a position

proportion   relationship between parts; a part or share of the whole

propose   to set forth or to suggest a plan of action

prosperity   good fortune or state of material well being

provide   to furnish or to supply [to *provide* evidence]

provision   act of supplying or preparing; a clause in a legal document; an anticipatory action

pursue   to follow or go according to a plan of action

react   to respond

reaffirm   to declare firmly again

receptive   able or ready to receive new ideas, etc.

recur, recurrence   to happen again, to repeat, to appear at intervals

reduce   to lessen; **reduction**   anything made smaller; the amount by which something is lessened

reflect   to give back; to contemplate or think about

reflective   thoughtful

regulate   to control or govern; **regulatory** governing

reject   to discard or refuse to agree

reliance   trust, dependence, or confidence

replenish   to make full or complete again, as by furnishing a new supply

represent   to present accurately; to stand in place of; to act or speak for another; **representative**   one who acts for another

repressive   keeping down or holding back; restraining

resent   to feel bitterness; **resentment**   a sense of being wrongfully harmed

resistant   offering opposition

resolve   to reach a decision; **resolution** decision or solution to a problem; a formal statement or opinion

restraint   loss or limitation of liberty; confinement

restrict   to limit; **restriction**   limitation of something that confines

result   consequence or end product

resumption   the act of beginning again or going on after interruption

sabotage   deliberate obstruction or damage to any cause, movement, activity, effort, etc.

sanction   act of confirming or ratifying a course of action; approval

scope   the range or extent of an activity, concept, etc.

secure   free of danger or trouble; to make safe

self-sufficient   independent; to get along without help

significant   important or having meaning

stimulate   to arouse or increase [*stimulate* trade]

strategy   plan of action to best achieve a stated goal

subjugation   to bring under control

submit   to yield

substantiate   to show to be true or real by giving evidence

summarize   to state briefly

support   to carry or bear; to show that something is true; to lend help or backing [to *support* a law]

suppress   to put down by force; to subdue

supremacy   the quality or state of being the highest in rank, power, or authority

tactic   method to achieve an end

tradition   beliefs, customs, or practices handed down from generation to generation

tranquility   calm or peace

transaction   a business deal or agreement

trend   general course or direction of events

ultimate   farthest, utmost, or maximum

unanimous   united in opinion

unbiased   without prejudice; objective; impartial

uniform   always the same; without differences

universal   applies to every case or individual without exception

uphold   to give support or encouragement

valid   sound or free from error

vital   necessary or essential; of crucial importance

widespread   spread over a large area

withdraw   to recall or remove from use; to pull out of a situation

wretched   unhappy or miserable

yearn   to be filled with desire

Important People in United States History

The following list includes the key people other than Presidents who have been mentioned in the Regents Examinations. They represent the pluralism that is America.

Numerals indicate how often the person has been mentioned on Regents Examinations.

MC in a multiple choice question
E   in an essay question
Q   quoted

Ansel Adams E1	• Photographer whose natural landscapes of the western United States are also a statement about the importance of the preservation of the wilderness.
Jane Addams E2, MC2	• Social reformer and humanitarian during the Progressive Era. • Founder of settlement house in Chicago. • Awarded Nobel Peace Prize.
Susan B. Anthony E3	• Reformer. Leader in Women's Rights Movement from 1851 until her death in 1906. • Most active for women's suffrage, but also worked for women's property rights and rights of married women.
Neil Armstrong E1	• Astronaut. First person to set foot on the moon as part of the first manned lunar landing, made by Apollo 11, July 20, 1969.
Matthew Brady E1	• Photographer of Civil War and Ante Bellum period, providing the chief visual information about the period. • Helped determine role of photography as an influence in American culture and politics.
Dee Brown E1	• Author of *Bury My Heart At Wounded Knee,* an account of how the Native American way of life, rooted the land, was destroyed.
William Jennings Bryan E1	• Unsuccessful Democratic presidential candidate in 1896 and 1900. • Populist who supported farmers and free. silver. Orator, religious fundamentalist (Scopes Trial) and anti-imperialist.
Warren Burger MC1	• Chief Justice of the United States (1969-87)
John C. Calhoun E1	• United States Senator from South Carolina (1832-43 and 1845-50). • Vice President (1825-29 and 1829-32). • Leader of southern States' Rights position, favoring nullification and the extension of slavery into the territories.
Stokely Carmichael MC1	• Civil Rights leader in 1960s. • President of SNCC (Student Nonviolent Coordinating Committee) in 1966. • Advocate of Black Power, disagreeing with Martin Luther King, Jr.

Andrew Carnegie E1	• Industrialist and Philanthropist. • Immigrant who built Carnegie Steel Company (later part of U.S. Steel).
Rachel Carson E4 MC1	• Helped start modern environmental reform movement in 1962 with book, *Silent Spring* which pointed out effects of chemical pesticides.
Winston Churchill MC3 Q1	• Prime Minister of Great Britain during World War II.
James Fenimore Cooper E1	• Nineteenth-century novelist and naval historian from New York. • Best known for his series, *The Leatherstocking Tales*, set on the frontier.
Aaron Copland E1	• Twentieth-century composer and writer about American music. • Incorporated American folk music and jazz into his music.
Dorothea Dix E1	• Nineteenth-century social reformer who revolutionized mental health reform.
Frederick Douglass E1	• Escaped slave, abolitionist, orator, writer. • Founded *North Star,* an abolitionist paper. • Supported black suffrage and civil rights.
Theodore Dreiser E1	• Author and major literary naturalist of early twentieth century. • Wrote *Sister Carrie* and *An American Tragedy*
W.E.B. DuBois E1 MC5 Q2	• African American civil rights leader, historian, writer, sociologist • Founder of Niagara Movement and a founder of NAACP (National Association for the Advancement of Colored People) • Disagreed with Booker T. Washington and Marcus Garvey
Bob Dylan E1 Q1	• Folk singer and songwriter whose social protest music was popular in the 1960s.
Duke Ellington E1	• Twentieth-century songwriter, band leader, jazz composer, pianist. • His tours helped to publicize American music around the world.
Henry Ford E1	• Industrialist who headed Ford Motor Co. • His design and production methods made it possible for the average person to own an automobile.
Betty Friedan E5	• Author and leader in Women's Rights Movement which began in 1960s, influenced by her book, *The Feminine Mystique*, questioning the theory that women could find personal fulfillment only in home and family. • A founder of NOW (National Organization For Women).
Marcus Garvey E1	• African American nationalist leader. • Advocated black pride and self-help as means of empowering blacks. • Leader of Back-to-Africa movement.
Samuel Gompers E3	• Organizer and President of American Federation of Labor, a craft union for skilled workers. • Stressed ''bread and butter'' issues such as wages and hours.

Alexander Hamilton E1 MC5	• New Yorker at Constitutional Convention who worked for a strong central government. • Wrote fifty-one of *The Federalist Papers* in support of ratification of the Constitution. • Nationalist, who as first Secretary of the Treasury promoted the economic development of the nation.
William Randolph Hearst MC1	• Newspaper publisher who pioneered "Yellow Journalism." • Helped create public pressure for Spanish American War.
Langston Hughes E1	• Poet, playwright, novelist. • A leader of Harlem Renaissance of 1920s and 1930s.
Helen Hunt Jackson E2	• Author of *A Century of Dishonor* (1881) which documented unjust treatment of Native Americans by federal government and influenced a reform movement.
Scott Joplin E1	• Composer and Ragtime pianist of late nineteenth and early twentieth centuries.
Chief Joseph E1	• Chief of Nez Perce Tribe. • Symbol of Native American resistance.
Jack Kerouac E1	• Novelist associated with Beat movement of 1950's and 1960's counterculture.
Martin Luther King, Jr. E3 MC5 Q2	• Civil Rights leader who founded Southern Christian Leadership Conference in 1957. • Believed in civil disobedience and nonviolent demonstrations. • Led Montgomery, Alabama bus boycott. • Led March from Selma to Montgomery for voting rights. • Gave "I Have Dream" Speech in Washington, D.C. • Won Nobel Peace prize. • Assassinated in 1968.
Sinclair Lewis E1	• Twentieth-century author known for novels, such as *Main Street* in which he attacked middle class values.
Harper Lee E1	• Author of Pulitzer prize winning novel, *To Kill a Mockingbird,* about race relations in Alabama in the 1930s.
Charles Lindbergh E1	• Aviator, environmentalist. • In 1927 made first solo and first nonstop flight from New York to Paris.
General Douglas MacArthur MC3	• Led U.S. troops in the Pacific in World War II. • Commander of U.S. occupation forces in Japan after World War II. • Relieved of command by Truman after publicly disagreeing with him as to how to conduct KOREAN WAR.
Malcolm X E1 MC1	• Leader in Black Power movement. • Assassinated in 1965.

John Marshall E1 MC10	• Chief Justice of the United States (1801-1835). • Established prestige of the Supreme Court and strengthened power of federal government. • In Marbury confirmed right of Court to declare federal laws unconstitutional.
Arthur Miller E1	• Twentieth-century playwright whose play *The Crucible*, written at the time of the Senator Joseph McCarthy Red Scare, deals with the hysteria and fear of the 1692 Salem witch trials.
Grandma Moses E1	• Twentieth-century artist who began painting in her seventies. • Her simple scenes of farm life are examples of art known as primitivism
Ralph Nader E5 MC1	• Leader in consumer protection movement starting in the 1960s with his book, *Unsafe At Any Speed* which detailed safety hazards in automobiles.
Thomas Nast MC2	• Post–Civil War political cartoonist known for cartoons on the corruption of the Tweed Ring.
Rosa Parks E1	• Her refusal, in 1955, to give up her seat to a white person led to the Montgomery, Alabama bus boycott, and helped to launch the Civil Rights Movement.
Elvis Presley E1	• One of first stars of Rock 'n' Roll whose style influenced American music. • Rock 'n' Roll combines elements of blues, gospel music, country and western.
Frederick Remington E1	• Sculptor, painter, writer on the American west and frontier.
Jacob Riis MC3	• Danish immigrant and journalist-photographer of the Progressive Era. • His book, *How the Other Half Lives* (1890) documented life in New York's tenements. • Led reform movement to improve housing.
Jackie Robinson E1	• Professional baseball player. • In 1947, he became first African American to play in major league baseball, joining the Brooklyn Dodgers.
John D. Rockefeller E1	• Industrialist and philanthropist of late nineteenth and early twentieth centuries. • Founder of Standard Oil Company.
Norman Rockwell E1	• Twentieth-century illustrator of life in rural and small town America. • His paintings appeared often on cover of *The Saturday Evening Post*.
Eleanor Roosevelt E3	• Led effort to focus attention on world problem of human rights. • Played key role in creation of United Nations Declaration on Human Rights (1948) • Chaired Kennedy's Presidential Commission on the Status of Women. • Early and long time activist for rights for Black Americans and women from within the New Deal as First Lady and as political activist in her own right.
Jonas Salk E1	• Scientist who developed the first vaccine to immunize people against poliomyelitis.

Margaret Sanger E3	• Pioneering birth control advocate. Organized first American birth control conference in 1921 and that same year organized a birth control lobbying group which, in 1942, became Planned Parenthood.
Upton Sinclair E2 MC3	• Muckraking journalist of Progressive Era. • His novel, *The Jungle* is about exploitation of the poor and factory conditions which resulted in contaminated meat influenced passage of the 1906 Meat Inspection Act.
Elizabeth Cady Stanton E2	• Leading crusader for women's rights; also for abolition and temperance. • Began women's rights movement with Seneca Falls (N.Y.) convention in 1848. • Wrote Declaration of Sentiments (1848).
John Steinbeck E2 MC1	• Author whose novels often deal with problems of the working class during the 1930s. • *The Grapes of Wrath* tells of farmers forced to leave Oklahoma in Dust Bowl years and relocate to California where they must work as migrant laborers.
Harriet Beecher Stowe	• Author of *Uncle Tom's Cabin,* a novel which helped to solidify feelings against slavery. Its popularity also led to increased respect for women who choose to be active in public affairs.
Ida Tarbell E2	• Muckraking journalist of Progressive era whose *History of Standard Oil Company* exposed Rockefeller's unfair and often ruthless business practices.
Henry David Thoreau E1 MC1 Q1	• Naturalist, poet, antislavery reformer. • Practiced and wrote on civil disobedience. • Authored *Walden: Or Life in the Woods.*
Harriet Tubman E2	• Abolitionist, spy, scout and escaped slave who returned to the South again and again to lead hundreds to freedom. • Scout, spy, nurse during the Civil War.
Lillian Wald MC1	• Social reformer of Progressive era. • Founded Henry Street Settlement House in New York.
Andy Warhol E1	• Artist and most well-known figure in the Pop art movement. Best known for 1962 "Campbell's Soup Can."
Earl Warren MC4	• Chief Justice of the Supreme Court (1953-1969). • Landmark cases such as *Brown, Miranda Gideon* and the reapportionment cases marked his tenure.
Booker T. Washington E1 MC6 Q2	• Educator and founder in 1881 of Tuskegee Institute. • Author of *Up from Slavery.* • Progressive era leader of African Americans.

The Fifteen Basic Concepts

In New York State fifteen major concepts have been identified for
emphasis in the 7–12 social studies program. The following chart is
arranged to show how some topics and events that you have studied in
United States History and Government relate to each concept. As you
review, try to think of other examples of concept usage.

ONE: CHANGE

Unit One
Supreme Court may reverse its decisions
Custom and usage in the United States
    Constitution

Unit Three
Role of the muckrakers
Civil service reform
Growth of public education
Temperance movement
Progressivism
Women's rights movement
Imperialism

Unit Five
FDR and Latin America
U.S. and World War II
Urban to suburban

Unit Six
Civil rights for minorities
Great Society programs
AIDS epidemic
Growing percentage of elderly in the population
Population shifts to Sunbelt

TWO: CHOICE

Unit One
Civil War

Unit Two
Reconstruction

Unit Five
Entry into World War II
Marshall Plan and Truman Doctrine

THREE: CITIZENSHIP

Unit One
Rights of British colonists
Process of electoral college

Unit Two
Due process of law and the 14th Amendment
Rights of Native Americans

Units Three through Six
All Supreme Court cases

FOUR: CULTURE

Unit One
Contributions of Greece, Rome, and England to
    colonial ideas of government

Unit Two
Native Americans and conflicts with westward
    expansion
Life on the frontier
Immigrant experiences

Unit Three
Prohibition

FIVE: DIVERSITY

Unit Two
Immigration
Social mobility

Unit Four
Immigration

Unit Six
Cultural pluralism

SIX: EMPATHY

Unit One
Abolitionist movement

Unit Two
Slavery and the Civil War
Understanding Native Americans

Unit Five
The Holocaust and result of Nuremburg Trials

Unit Six
AIDS crisis

SEVEN: ENVIRONMENT

Unit Three
Theodore Roosevelt and conservation

Unit Six
Threats to the environment
Rachel Carson and others
Impact of technology on problems of pollution

EIGHT: HUMAN RIGHTS

Unit One
Abolitionist movement and Frederick Douglass

Unit Two
13th, 14th, 15th Amendments

Native Americans

Unit Three
Anti-immigration acts
Muckrakers

Unit Six
Affirmative action programs
Martin Luther King, Jr.
Death penalty controversy
International terrorism

NINE: IDENTITY

Unit Two
Immigrant contributions

Unit Four
Harlem Renaissance

Unit Six
Martin Luther King, Jr., and nonviolence

TEN: INTERDEPENDENCE

Unit One
Need for colonial union against Great Britain

Unit Two
Sectionalism

Unit Five
International organizations—the UN and NATO

ELEVEN: JUSTICE

Unit One
The Great Compromise
Marbury v. *Madison* and judicial review

Unit Three
Political machines
Role of third parties
Women's rights movement

What You Need To Know:
Landmark Supreme Court Cases _____

This chart presents seventeen of the landmark Supreme Court cases which influenced the development of our Constitution.

Year	Name of Case	Enduring Issue	Why Case Is Important
1803	*Marbury* v. *Madison*	• Separation of powers • The Judiciary	• Established right of judicial review, strengthening the judiciary in relation to other branches of government
1819	*McCulloch* v. *Maryland*	• Federalism • National power	• Supported use of the "elastic clause" to expand federal power
1824	*Gibbons* v. *Ogden*	• Federalism • Property Rights/Economic Policy	• Established basis of Congressional regulation of all types of interstate commerce • Declared supremacy of national to state law when the two conflicted
1857	*Dred Scott* v. *Sanford*	• The Judiciary • Equality • Ethnic and racial groups • Change and flexibility	• Declared that slaves were property and could be taken anywhere • Stated blacks were not citizens • Declared the Missouri Compromise unconstitutional; this decision was overturned by the 13th and 14th Amendments
1866	*Ex parte Milligan*	• Presidential power • Civil liberties	• Ruled that the President could not suspend the right to due process and suspend the writ of habeas corpus as long as civilian courts are still functioning in an area
1896	*Plessy* v. *Ferguson*	• The Judiciary • Equality • Ethnic and racial groups • Change and flexibility	• Permitted legal segregation by ruling that "separate but equal" facilities did not violate the Constitution's equal protection clause
1919	*Schenck* v. *United States*	• Civil liberties	• Established limits on the free speech, holding that this right is not absolute • Set the "clear and present danger" standard for when free speech can be restricted

1935	*Schechter Poultry Corporation* v. *United States*	• Separation of powers • Property rights • National power	• Placed limits on the ability of Congress to delegate legislative powers to the President • Narrowly defined interstate commerce • Declared the New Deal's NRA unconstitutional
1944	*Korematsu* v. *United States*	• Civil liberties • Presidential power	• Ruled that the executive order that sent Japanese-Americans to internment camps during World War II was constitutional because of threat posed to national security
1954	*Brown* v. *Board of Education*	• The Judiciary • Equality • Ethnic and racial groups	• Overturned *Plessy* v. *Ferguson* by ruling that the "separate but equal" doctrine violated the 14th Amendment
1962	*Engel* v. *Vitale*	• The Judiciary • Civil liberties	• Ruled that prayer in schools violated the 1st Amendment establishment clause
1963	*Gideon* v. *Wainwright*	• Criminal penalties • Federalism • Constitutional change	• Ruled that the 14th Amendment due process clause guaranteed a 6th Amendment right to a lawyer to all defendants in a criminal case, thus extending 14th Amendment protection to defendants in the states
1964	*Reynolds* v. *Sims*	• Avenues of representation • The Judiciary	• Established the doctrine of "one man, one vote," setting equal population as the only basis for drawing up electoral districts of state legislatures
1966	*Miranda* v. *Arizona*	• Criminal penalties • The Judiciary	• Ruled that police must inform suspects when arrested of their right to remain silent, their right to have a lawyer when questioned, and that what they say may be used against them
1971	*New York Times* v. *United States*	• Civil Liberties • Presidential power	• Stated arguments that prior restraint violated principle of a free press • Ruled national security not threatened by publication of Pentagon Papers
1973	*Roe* v. *Wade*	• Rights of women • Civil liberties • The Judiciary	• Gave women the right to abortion • Supported this decision based on a constitutional right to privacy
1978	*Regents of the University of California* v. *Bakke*	• The Judiciary • Equality • Ethnic and racial groups • Rights of women	• Ruled university's quota system under its affirmative action plan was unconstitutional • Held that affirmative action programs could be legal

Presidents of the United States _____

Below is a list of all the Presidents of the United States, their years in office, and their political parties. Additional information that you need to know appears next to those Presidents who have figured in Regents Examination questions.

The following codes indicate how often information on these individuals has appeared in Regents Examinations. The letters MC stand for multiple-choice questions and E for essay questions. The notation MC3 means the person has been cited in three multiple-choice questions. An E2 would mean information about the person was asked in two essay questions. A ‹Q› or an ‹E› means that the only time a person was named was in a quotation or an essay.

Blank Spaces indicate that Regents questions have not yet been asked about those Presidents. Write important facts that you think might be tested about those Presidents in the blanks.

George Washington 1789–1797 E3	• President of Constitutional Convention • Commanded Continental army during American Revolution • Set precedents such as the Cabinet that were followed by other Presidents • Strengthened new government through support of Hamilton's financial policies and use of force against the Whiskey Rebellion • Kept peace through Proclamation of Neutrality and Jay Treaty • Set basis of U.S. foreign policy in his Farewell Address
John Adams 1797–1801 Federalist	• Helped draft Declaration of Independence • First Vice President of the United States • President during time of wars in Europe • Alien and Sedition Acts contributed to his unpopularity and the fall of his party
Thomas Jefferson 1801–1809 Democratic-Republican MC2; Q1	• Major author of Declaration of Independence • Opposed Federalists, instead favoring limited, decentralized government • Opposed Hamilton's financial plan and the Alien and Sedition Acts • Approved the Louisiana Purchase from France which doubled the size of the nation
James Madison 1809–1817 Democratic-Republican E1; Q1	• Called Father of the Constitution, an author of the Virginia Plan; his journals provide a record of events at the Constitutional Convention (1787) • Wrote 29 of the *Federalist Papers* • Proposed the Bill of Rights to Congress • Lost popularity over lack of leadership in War of 1812

James Monroe 1817–1825 Democratic-Republican E1	• Established U.S. foreign policy in this hemisphere with the Monroe Doctrine • Settled boundaries with Canada (1818) • Acquired Florida (1819)
John Quincy Adams 1825–1829 National-Republican	
Andrew Jackson 1829–1837 Democratic	
Martin Van Buren 1837–1841 Democratic	
William Henry Harrison 1841 Whig	
John Tyler 1841–1845 Whig	
James K. Polk 1845–1849 Democratic	
Zachary Taylor 1849–1850 Whig	

Millard Fillmore 1850–1853 Whig	
Franklin Pierce 1853–1857 Democratic	
James Buchanan 1857–1861 Democratic	
Abraham Lincoln 1861–1865 Republican E3; MC3	• Used war powers of the presidency during Civil War to achieve his goal of preserving the nation • Assassinated before he could act on his plans for Reconstruction
Andrew Johnson 1865–1869 Unionist-Republican E1; MC2	• Impeached by House after bitter disagreements with Congress over Reconstruction, he escaped conviction in the Senate by one vote
Ulysses S. Grant 1869–1877 Republican ⟨E⟩	• War hero who served as supreme commander of the Union (Northern) army during Civil War • Scandals including the Credit Moblier and the Whiskey Ring marred his presidency
Rutherford B. Hayes 1877–1881 Republican	• Compromise led to his election and prevented a constitutional crisis after a dispute over electoral votes • As a result of the compromise, the last federal troops were removed from the South, marking the end of Reconstruction
James A. Garfield 1881 Republican	

Chester A. Arthur 1881–1885 Republican	
Grover Cleveland 1885–1889 and 1893–1897 Democratic	
Benjamin Harrison 1889–1893 Republican	
William McKinley 1897–1901 Republican E1	• President during turn-of-century expansionism marked by the Spanish-American War • A high tariff and the Gold Standard Act passed during his administration
Theodore Roosevelt 1901–1909 Republican E3; MC8	• Progressive Era President whose program was called the Square Deal • Known as a trustbuster, conservationist, reformer, and nationalist • Used the power of the presidency to regulate economic affairs of nation and to expand its role in Asia and the Caribbean • Issued the Roosevelt Corollary to the Monroe Doctrine
William H. Taft 1909–1913 Republican	• His policy of "Dollar Diplomacy" gave diplomatic and military support to U.S. business investment in Latin America • Continued Progressive policies of business regulation, but his tariff and conservation policies, which were conservative, split the party.
Woodrow Wilson 1913–1921 Democratic E1; MC4	• Progressive Era President whose program was known as New Nationalism • Reform regulation included Clayton Antitrust Act, Federal Trade Commission Act, and Underwood Tariff Act, which lowered rates • Led the nation in World War I • Supported the Treaty of Versailles and League of Nations which failed to pass Senate.

Warren G. Harding 1921–1923 Republican E2	• Led nation into the "roaring rwenties" on a call for "normalcy" • Administration known for scandals, fraud, and bribery including the Teapot Dome scandal. • Opened Washington Conference on Naval Disarmament in 1921, although he opposed internationalism
Calvin Coolidge 1923–1929 Republican	• Conservative, laissez-faire attitudes toward business • Presided over "Coolidge Prosperity"
Herbert Hoover 1929–1933 Republican Q1	• Used government resources against the Great Depression without success • Supported loans through Reconstruction Finance Corporation • Opposed direct relief • Used federal troops against World War I veteran "Bonus Marchers"
Franklin D. Rosevelt 1933–1945 Democratic E6; MC18	• His New Deal policies to fight the Great Depression and his leadership in World War II increased the power of the federal government • Tried to expand number of Supreme Court justices when the Court opposed his programs • His social welfare legislation included the Social Security Act • His programs were criticized as both inadequate and too extreme • Urged cooperation in Western Hemisphere under the "Good Neighbor" Policy • Supported Japanese American internment during World War II
Harry S Truman 1945–1953 Democratic E2; MC2; Q1	• Made decision to drop two atomic bombs on Japan in 1945 to end World War II • The Truman Doctrine began the policy of containment of communism • The Marshall Plan supported economic recovery in Europe • His Fair Deal programs continued the philosophy of the New Deal
Dwight D. Eisenhower 1953–1961 Republican	
John F. Kennedy 1961–1963 Democratic E1; Q1	• His New Frontier program centered on containment, the Peace Corps, and the Alliance for Progress in foreign policy and civil rights at home • Blockaded Cuba during the Cuban Missile Crisis
Lyndon B. Johnson 1963–1969 Democratic E1; MC2	• His Great Society programs promoted the War on Poverty and brought strong new civil rights laws • Used the Gulf of Tonkin Resolution to expand the Vietnam War • Divisions over his war policy led to his failure to seek reelection

Richard M. Nixon 1969–1974 Republican E2; MC2	• His "Vietnamization" policy and increased bombings were followed by a 1973 cease-fire in Vietnam • Relaxed relations with the USSR and the People's Republic of China • Resigned as President because of Watergate affair
Gerald R. Ford 1974–1977 Republican	
Jimmy Carter 1971–1981 Democratic E1	• Domestic problems included inflation and oil shortages • His foreign policy supported human rights and Panama Canal treaties and opposed the Soviet invasion of Afghanistan • Camp David Accords which led to peace between Egypt and Israel were his greatest success
Ronald Reagan 1981–1989 Republican E2; MC7	• New Federalism took a conservative viewpoint on social issues such as abortion and prayer in school • "Supply-side" economic policy or "Reaganomics" was based on the belief that government can destroy individual initiative • During his presidency the U.S. ran up huge trade and budget deficits • Agreed to arms control with USSR after summit meetings in 1985, 1986, and 1987 • His foreign policy aimed at keeping communism out of Latin America • The Iran-Contra scandal hurt his popularity and foreign policy
George Bush 1989–1993 Republican E	• Vice-President under Reagan, he inherited high deficits, savings and loan scandal, and legacy of Iran-Contra affair • His administration saw the end of the Cold War and the end of Communist governments in Eastern Europe and the Soviet Union • Ordered troops into Panama against Noriega • Led the United States and an international force against Iraq in 1990–91 when Iraq invaded Kuwait • His administration saw the disintegration of the Soviet Union and subsequent formation of the Commonwealth of Independent States
William (Bill) Clinton 1993– Democrat	• First Democrat elected to two presidential terms since Franklin Roosevelt • Domestic policies centered on health care reform and on other economic issues such as reduction of the national deficit • Secured approval of NAFTA (North American Free Trade Agreement) • Agreed to economic aid for Russian president Boris Yeltsin, ordered U.S. troops to Haiti to oversee transition to democracy, ordered U.S. troops to Bosnia to enforce peace agreement • His administration was troubled by a series of investigations into potential scandals, including an investigation of a real estate investment known as Whitewater

Regents Examinations _____

This section contains additional Regents exams for you to take for practice. These are actual Regents Examinations in United States History and Government that have been given in New York State.

Circle your answers to Part I in all of these exams and write your answers to essay questions on separate sheets of paper. Be sure to use the blocking technique described in the Test-Taking Strategies section of this book as you prepare to answer essay questions.

Part I (55 credits)

Answer all 48 questions in this part.

Directions (1–48): For each statement or question, write on the separate answer sheet the *number* of the word or expression that, of those given, best completes the statement or answers the question.

1 Which idea had a major influence on the authors of the Articles of Confederation?

① A strong central government threatens the rights of the people and the states.

2 All of the people must be granted the right to vote.

3 Three branches of government are needed to protect liberty.

4 The central government must have the power to levy taxes and to control trade.

Base your answers to questions 2 and 3 on the discussion below and on your knowledge of social studies.

Speaker A: States must be represented in the national government solely on the basis of population. It is indeed the only fair situation.

Speaker B: The national legislature must be based on equal representation of the states to protect the interests of the small states.

Speaker C: States must accept the supremacy of the national government on all issues; otherwise, the system will fail.

Speaker D: The national Congress should consist of two houses: one in which representation is based on population, and one in which states are equally represented.

2 Which document was being written when this discussion most likely occurred?

1 Declaration of Independence

② United States Constitution

3 Covenant of the League of Nations

4 Charter of the United Nations

3 Which speaker's idea about representation was actually included in the document that was written?

(1) A   (3) C

(2) B   ④ D

4 Which United States governmental principle includes the concepts of reserved powers, delegated powers, and concurrent powers?

1 the amending process

2 judicial review

③ federalism

4 the unwritten constitution

5 The majority of cases heard by the United States Supreme Court come to the Court because of its constitutional power to

1 exercise jurisdiction in legal situations involving foreign governments

2 advise Congress on the legality of bills

3 mediate disagreements between states

④ act on decisions appealed from lower courts

6 The major reason the Bill of Rights was added to the United States Constitution was to

1 limit the power of state governments

② protect individual liberties against abuse by the Federal Government

3 provide for equal treatment of all people

4 separate powers between the three branches of government

7 ". . . I desire you would Remember the Ladies, and be more generous and favorable to them than your ancestors. Do not put such unlimited power into the hands of the Husbands. . . . If particular care and attention is not paid to the Ladies, we . . . will not hold ourselves bound by any Laws in which we have no voice, or Representation."

—Abigail Adams, 1776

This statement was an early expression of women's support for

1 abolition   3 suffrage rights

2 affirmative action   4 divorce rights

8 Once an amendment has been added to the United States Constitution, which process must be used to change that amendment?

1 ratifying a new amendment
2 convincing the states to ignore the amendment
3 having Congress pass a law repealing the amendment
4 having the President issue an executive order canceling the amendment

9 Which governmental practice established under the unwritten constitution was later included in the written Constitution by an amendment?

1 appointing members of the Cabinet
2 exercising judicial review
3 holding political party conventions
4 limiting the President's time in office to two terms

10 Which statement best explains why critics have called for a change in the electoral college system?

1 A person who did not receive the largest percentage of popular votes can be elected President.
2 The system is a threat to the two-party system.
3 Electors often vote for candidates not listed on the ballot.
4 States with small populations have greater influence on Presidential elections than more populated states do.

11 "Compromise Enables Maine and Missouri To Enter Union" (1820)
"California Admitted to Union as Free State" (1850)
"Kansas-Nebraska Act Sets Up Popular Sovereignty" (1854)

Which issue is reflected in these headlines?

1 enactment of protective tariffs
2 extension of slavery
3 voting rights for minorities
4 universal public education

12 The main goal of the Seneca Falls Convention (1848) was to

1 obtain equal rights for women
2 make the public aware of environmental problems
3 correct the abuses of big business
4 organize the first labor union in the United States

13 A major reason the Radical Republicans opposed President Abraham Lincoln's Reconstruction plan was that his plan

1 demanded payments from the South that would have damaged its economy
2 postponed the readmission of Southern States into the Union for many years
3 granted too many rights to formerly enslaved persons
4 offered amnesty to nearly all Confederates who would swear allegiance to the United States

14 How were many African Americans in the South affected after Reconstruction ended in 1877?

1 A constitutional amendment guaranteed their social advancement.
2 The Freedmen's Bureau helped them become farmowners.
3 Jim Crow laws placed major restrictions on their rights.
4 Southern factories offered them job training and employment opportunities.

15 In which pair of events did the first event most directly influence the second?

1 discovery of gold in California → Louisiana Purchase
2 building of the transcontinental railroad → disappearance of the frontier
3 settling of the Oregon Territory → passage of the Homestead Act
4 assimilation of Native American Indians into American society → passage of the Dawes Act

16 "I am tired of fighting. . . . Hear me, my chiefs. I am tired. My heart is sick and sad. From where the sun now stands, I shall fight no more forever!"
— Chief Joseph, 1877

In this statement, Chief Joseph of the Nez Percé expressed his reluctant acceptance of a government policy of

1 placing Native American Indian tribes on reservations
2 requiring Native American Indians to settle west of the Mississippi River
3 granting immediate citizenship to Native American Indians
4 forcing Native American Indians to assimilate into American culture

[OVER]

17 Although the Populist Party failed to elect its candidates to the Presidency, some of the Party's aims were later achieved by the

1 adoption of the gold standard
2 elimination of racial segregation laws in the South
3 creation of a graduated income tax and the direct election of Senators
4 establishment of higher protective tariffs on manufactured goods

Base your answers to questions 18 and 19 on the chart below and on your knowledge of social studies.

UNITED STATES CROP PRICES, 1878–1897

Years	Wheat (per bushel)	Corn (per bushel)	Cotton (per pound)
1878–1881	$1.00	$.43	$.09
1882–1885	$.80	$.39	$.09
1886–1889	$.74	$.35	$.08
1890–1893	$.70	$.41	$.07
1894–1897	$.63	$.29	$.05

Source: *History of the United States*, Houghton Mifflin, 1991

18 Which factor was a major cause of the farm problem indicated by the data in the chart?

1 major droughts in the Midwest
2 low farm prices set by government regulations
3 widespread crop failures during the late 1800's
4 overproduction of these farm crops

19 To help solve the problem indicated by the data in the chart, American farmers wanted the Federal Government to

1 reduce regulation of the railroads
2 increase the money supply
3 provide funds to increase crop yields
4 raise tariffs on foreign manufactured goods

20 The principle that the United States has the right to act as the "policeman of the Western Hemisphere" and intervene in the internal affairs of Latin American nations was established by the

1 Good Neighbor policy
2 Open Door policy
3 Roosevelt Corollary to the Monroe Doctrine
4 Marshall Plan

21 Which argument was used to support United States acquisition of overseas possessions in the late 1800's?

1 The United States needed to obtain raw materials and new markets.
2 The spread of Marxist ideas had to be stopped because they threatened world peace.
3 The United States should be the first world power to build a colonial empire.
4 The doctrine of Manifest Destiny had become obsolete.

22 A belief shared by Presidents Theodore Roosevelt, William Taft, and Woodrow Wilson is that the Federal Government should

1 allow the free-enterprise system to work without regulation
2 use its power to regulate unfair business practices
3 provide jobs for unemployed workers
4 support unions in labor-management disputes

23 The actions of Jane Addams, Ida Tarbell, and Booker T. Washington illustrate that reform in the United States has

1 utilized a variety of methods to achieve many goals
2 depended on support from religious groups
3 relied on programs initiated by the Federal Government
4 promoted women's suffrage as its main goal

24 Which factors were the major causes of the Red Scare and the Palmer Raids, which followed World War I?

1 success of the Communist Party in congressional and Presidential elections
2 race riots in Los Angeles and the revival of the Ku Klux Klan
3 failure of the United States to join the League of Nations and the unpaid German war debts
4 the Bolshevik Revolution of 1917 in Russia and workers' strikes in the United States

Base your answers to questions 25 through 27 on the statements below and on your knowledge of social studies.

Speaker A: To preserve our American culture, people whose national origins do not match the origins of our nation's founders must be refused admission.

Speaker B: . . . let us admit only the best educated from every racial and ethnic group . . .

Speaker C: . . . there is an appalling danger to the American wage earner from the flood of low, unskilled, ignorant, foreign workers who have poured into the country . . .

Speaker D: Give me your tired, your poor, your huddled masses yearning to breathe free . . .

25 In the early 20th century, most labor unions supported the view of Speaker
- (1) *A*
- (2) *B*
- (3) *C*
- (4) *D*

26 People who support unrestricted immigration would agree most with Speaker
- (1) *A*
- (2) *B*
- (3) *C*
- (4) *D*

27 United States immigration legislation of the 1920's most closely reflected the views of Speakers
- (1) *A* and *C*
- (2) *A* and *D*
- (3) *B* and *C*
- (4) *C* and *D*

28 Based on a study of the trial of Sacco and Vanzetti (1920's) and the internment of Japanese Americans (1940's), which conclusion is most accurate?
1 The Bill of Rights is not intended to apply to naturalized citizens.
2 Racial and ethnic hostilities are effectively checked by adherence to due process of law.
3 Internment of suspected criminals is necessary during wartime.
4 Nativism and racism sometimes override the ideals of constitutional democracy.

29 After World War I, which factor was the major cause of the migration of many African Americans to the North?
1 the start of the Harlem Renaissance
2 increased job opportunities in Northern cities
3 laws passed in Northern States to end racial discrimination
4 Federal Government job-training programs

30 A major criticism of President Franklin D. Roosevelt's programs to combat the Great Depression was that these programs
1 reduced the power of the Federal Government
2 ignored the plight of homeowners with mortgages
3 provided too much protection for big business
4 made people dependent on the Federal Government

Base your answer to question 31 on the cartoon below and on your knowledge of social studies.

31 The cartoon indicates the foreign policy position of the United States in response to the
1 start of the League of Nations
2 collapse of the global economy
3 beginning of World War II
4 spread of communism to Eastern Europe

[OVER]

Base your answer to question 32 on the cartoon below and on your knowledge of social studies.

32 What is the main idea of the cartoon?

 1 President Franklin D. Roosevelt used a system of trial and error to improve the economy.
 2 President Franklin D. Roosevelt consistently adopted the Depression remedies proposed by Congress.
 3 Congress and the President were unable to cope with the Depression.
 4 The President and Congress constantly fought over Depression-Era programs.

33 The Truman Doctrine and the Eisenhower Doctrine were United States foreign policies concerning

 1 the international balance of payments
 2 the containment of communism
 3 worldwide environmental pollution
 4 nuclear disarmament

34 A governmental action that was consistent with the Cold War mentality was the

 1 establishment of loyalty reviews of government employees
 2 reduction in military defense spending
 3 elimination of the Central Intelligence Agency
 4 adoption of the GI Bill of Rights

35 After World War II, the United States was better able than its allies to adjust its economy from wartime to peacetime because the United States

 1 possessed nuclear weapons
 2 raised tariffs on imports
 3 had collected its war debts from the Allies
 4 had suffered no widespread wartime destruction

36 When President Dwight D. Eisenhower sent Federal troops to Little Rock, Arkansas, during the 1957 school integration crisis, he was exercising his constitutional power as

 1 Chief Legislator   3 Chief Diplomat
 2 Commander in Chief   4 Head of State

37 The chief objective of President Lyndon Johnson's Great Society programs was to

 1 increase foreign aid to developing nations
 2 correct environmental pollution
 3 help the disadvantaged in the United States
 4 unite democratic nations and contain communism

38 The decisions of the United States Supreme Court in *Miranda* v. *Arizona*, *Gideon* v. *Wainwright*, and *Escobedo* v. *Illinois* all advanced the

 1 voting rights of minorities
 2 guarantees of free speech and press
 3 principle of separation of church and state
 4 rights of accused persons

39 The primary purpose of the War Powers Act (1973) is to

 1 limit Presidential power to send troops into combat
 2 allow for a quicker response to a military attack
 3 assure adequate defense of the Western Hemisphere
 4 stop the use of troops for nonmilitary purposes

40 The main reason that the United States sent troops to Bosnia in 1995 was to try to

 1 bring a peaceful end to a civil war
 2 contain the spread of communism
 3 take over the area as a protectorate
 4 resettle refugees in North America

41 During the 1990's, which issue has led to the greatest tension between the United States and Japan?

1 immigration quotas
2 use of natural resources
3 trade policies
4 military preparedness

42 What is the main criticism of affirmative action in recent years?

1 The program has been extremely costly to the Federal Government.
2 Hiring quotas for minorities may have denied opportunities to other qualified persons.
3 Very few minority persons have been hired.
4 Most state governments have been unwilling to enforce the program.

43 A study of the women's movement in the United States would show that

1 the National Government granted rights to women long before state governments did
2 the gains made by women usually took considerable periods of time
3 women received voting rights before African-American males did
4 wartime employment slowed progress toward gender equality

44 *How the Other Half Lives*, Jacob Riis (1890)
The Jungle, Upton Sinclair (1906)
The Grapes of Wrath, John Steinbeck (1939)
Unsafe at Any Speed, Ralph Nader (1965)

What has been the impact of these authors and their books on American society?

1 Most Americans have developed a preference for escapist and romantic literature.
2 Most American authors have adopted a conservative viewpoint.
3 American business has corrected poor conditions quickly.
4 These works have had significant influence on social, political, and economic reforms.

45 The response of President George Washington to warring European nations in the 1790's was most similar to the response of President

1 Woodrow Wilson to the start of World War I
2 Harry Truman to the invasion of South Korea
3 Lyndon Johnson to communist expansion in Southeast Asia
4 George Bush to the invasion of Kuwait

46 The concept of collective security is best exemplified by the role of the United States in

1 forming the North Atlantic Treaty Organization (NATO)
2 negotiating the Camp David accords
3 granting China most-favored-nation status
4 becoming a member of the North American Free Trade Agreement (NAFTA)

47 "*Resolved*. . . , that the Congress approves and supports the determination of the President, as Commander in Chief, to take all necessary measures to repel any armed attack against the forces of the United States . . ."
— Gulf of Tonkin Resolution

This congressional resolution provided justification for

1 William Howard Taft's Dollar Diplomacy
2 Woodrow Wilson's Fourteen Points
3 Lyndon Johnson's involvement in Vietnam
4 Ronald Reagan's invasion of Grenada

48 "I suppose that history will remember my term of office as the years when the 'cold war' began to overshadow our lives. I have hardly had a day in office that has not been dominated by this all-embracing struggle. . . and always in the background there has been the atomic bomb."

This quotation best reflects the Presidential administration of

1 Franklin D. Roosevelt   3 Richard Nixon
2 Harry Truman   4 George Bush

[OVER]

Answers to the following questions are to be written on paper provided by the school.

Students Please Note:

In developing your answers to Parts II and III, be sure to

(1) include specific factual information and evidence whenever possible
(2) keep to the questions asked; do not go off on tangents
(3) avoid overgeneralizations or sweeping statements without sufficient proof; do not overstate your case
(4) keep these general definitions in mind:

    (a) <u>discuss</u> means "to make observations about something using facts, reasoning, and argument; to present in some detail"
    (b) <u>describe</u> means "to illustrate something in words or tell about it"
    (c) <u>show</u> means "to point out; to set forth clearly a position or idea by stating it and giving data which support it"
    (d) <u>explain</u> means "to make plain or understandable; to give reasons for or causes of; to show the logical development or relationships of"

Part II

ANSWER ONE QUESTION FROM THIS PART.   [15]

1 United States Supreme Court cases deal with controversial issues. Some of these issues are listed below.

> *Issues*
> Rights of the accused
> Free speech
> Separation of church and state *engle vs. vital*
> Powers of government
> Civil rights *Dred scot case*
> Education *Brown vs. board of ed*
> Right to privacy

Choose *three* of the issues listed and for *each* one chosen:

- Identify a Supreme Court case that dealt with the issue [Use a different case for each issue chosen. The exact name of the case does *not* have to be given.]
- Discuss the controversy involved in the case
- State the Court's decision *and* describe an impact of the decision on American society [5,5,5]

2 The United States Government includes a system of checks and balances. Some features of the system of checks and balances are listed below.

> *Features*
> Judicial review
> Presidential veto
> Treaty ratification
> Impeachment
> Investigative powers of Congress

Choose *three* of the features listed and for *each* one chosen:

- Explain how the feature operates to limit the power of a specific branch of the United States Government
- Describe a specific historical situation in which the feature was used
- Discuss the extent to which the power of a specific branch of the United States Government was limited in this situation [5,5,5]

Part III

ANSWER TWO QUESTIONS FROM THIS PART. [30]

3 United States Presidents have taken actions to achieve their foreign policy goals.
Several Presidents and foreign policy goals they attempted to achieve are listed below.

Presidents — Foreign Policy Goals

George Washington — neutrality
James Monroe — isolation
Theodore Roosevelt — imperialism
Franklin D. Roosevelt — international involvement
John F. Kennedy — containment
Richard M. Nixon — détente
Bill Clinton — post–Cold War stability

Choose *three* of the Presidents listed and the foreign policy goal with which each is
paired. For *each* one chosen:

• Show how a specific action taken by that President was designed to achieve his foreign
policy goal
• Discuss the extent to which the President's action was successful in achieving his goal
[5,5,5]

4 Titles are often used to describe various time periods in United States history.

Titles (Time Periods)

Critical Period (1781–1789)
Reconstruction (1865–1877)
Gilded Age (1880–1900)
Progressive Era (1900–1920)
Roaring Twenties (1920–1929)
New Deal Era (1933–1940)

a Choose *two* of the titles and time periods listed. For *each* one chosen, explain how
the title describes the time period. Include specific social, political, and/or economic
information to support your explanation. [5,5]

b Choose *one* of the decades listed below. Suggest a title for the decade and explain
how this title reflects American society during that decade. Support your explanation
with specific information. [5]

Decades

1950's
1960's
1970's
1980's

[OVER]

5 Many individuals have tried to bring about change in American society.

Individuals

Harriet Beecher Stowe
Susan B. Anthony
Samuel Gompers
William Jennings Bryan
Margaret Sanger
Rachel Carson
Malcolm X

Choose *three* of the individuals listed and for *each* one chosen:

• Describe a condition in American society that the individual tried to change
• Discuss a method this individual used to try to bring about change
• Discuss the extent to which the individual was successful in bringing about change
[5,5,5]

6 At the end of the 20th century, many problems challenge American society.

Problems That Challenge American Society

– AIDS
– Juvenile crime
Social Security reform
Social welfare reform
Deficits and the national debt
–Environmental quality
Health care reform

Choose *three* of the problems listed and for *each* one chosen:

• Identify and discuss a major cause or origin of the problem
• Identify and discuss a specific policy or action designed to deal with or solve the problem
• State *one* argument made by opponents of the policy or action [5,5,5]

7 Many factors contributed to the economic growth of the United States from 1860 to 1920.

Factors

Agricultural developments
Business practices
Transportation
Labor supply
Natural resources
Communications

a Choose *three* factors from the list and for *each* one chosen, discuss how *each* factor contributed to the economic growth of the United States from 1860 to 1920. [4,4,4]

b Show how a specific law or policy of the United States Government contributed to economic growth from 1860 to 1920. [You may *not* repeat information used in part *a*.] [3]

Part I (55 credits)

Answer all 48 questions in this part.

Directions (1–48): For each statement or question, write on the separate answer sheet the *number* of the word or expression that, of those given, best completes the statement or answers the question.

The Virginia House of Burgesses and the Mayflower Compact had a similar effect in that both

1 reinforced the English Parliament's control over the colonies
2 gave settlers the power to establish colonies
3 contributed to the development of representative democracy
4 granted absolute authority to the colonial governors

2 A major purpose of the Declaration of Independence was to

1 guarantee individual rights to citizens
2 state colonial grievances against British rule
3 establish a plan for a national government
4 strengthen the power of the central government

3 A major problem of the government under the Articles of Confederation was that the

1 courts of the national government had nearly unlimited power
2 President could make major decisions without the approval of Congress
3 national government could levy and collect unlimited taxes
4 Congress depended on the states for men and money to support an army

4 "Congress shall have power . . . to make all laws which shall be necessary and proper for carrying into execution the foregoing powers. . . ."

This section of the United States Constitution is used to

1 justify a loose interpretation of the Constitution
2 protect States rights
3 start the amendment process
4 limit the authority given to Congress

Base your answer to question 5 on the table below and on your knowledge of social studies.

POPULATION DATA — 1790

STATE	TOTAL POPULATION	NUMBER OF ENSLAVED PERSONS
Massachusetts	378,787	0
New Jersey	184,139	7,557
New York	340,120	10,088
Virginia	747,610	425,353

Source: Historical Statistics of the United States

5 In terms of representation in the United States Congress, which state benefited most from the three-fifths compromise reached at the Constitutional Convention of 1787?

1 Massachusetts   3 New York
2 New Jersey   4 Virginia

6 What is the primary constitutional principle exemplified by the United States Senate's rejection of a treaty?

1 federalism   3 States rights
2 checks and balances   4 executive privilege

7 Which statement regarding the United States Supreme Court is valid?

1 The power of the Supreme Court has lessened over the last 100 years.
2 Supreme Court rulings usually reflect the attitudes of the times in which they are made.
3 Presidential programs have consistently received favorable rulings from the Supreme Court.
4 All bills must be approved by the Supreme Court before they become laws.

8 Which official of the Federal Government is elected directly by the people?

1 a Cabinet member
2 the President
3 a Member of the House of Representatives
4 a Justice of the Supreme Court

9 The United States Constitution requires that from time to time, the President must

1 inform Congress and the nation about the state of the Union
2 campaign for members of his political party
3 appoint new commissioners of Federal agencies
4 propose bills to Congress for its consideration

10 Which quotation taken from the United States Constitution provides for limiting the power of government?

1 "All persons born or naturalized in the United States . . . are citizens of the United States. . . ."
2 "This Constitution . . . shall be the supreme law of the land; . . ."
3 "The President shall be commander in chief of the army and navy. . . ."
4 "Congress shall make no law respecting an establishment of religion, . . . or abridging the freedom of speech, or of the press. . . ."

11 A decision of the United States Supreme Court can be overturned by

1 an amendment to the Constitution
2 the appointment of a new Chief Justice
3 a national referendum
4 a Presidential veto

12 In the 1780's, the publication of *The Federalist* papers was intended to

1 justify the American Revolution to the colonists
2 provide a plan of operation for the delegates to the Constitutional Convention
3 encourage ratification of the United States Constitution
4 express support for the election of George Washington to the Presidency

13 In deciding to purchase the Louisiana Territory, President Thomas Jefferson had to overcome the problem of

1 obtaining the support of Western settlers
2 passing the constitutional amendment necessary to authorize the purchase
3 avoiding a possible war with England over the purchase
4 contradicting his belief in a strict interpretation of the Constitution

14 The United States Supreme Court decision in *Dred Scott* v. *Sanford* (1857) was important because it

1 strengthened the determination of abolitionists to achieve their goals
2 caused the immediate outbreak of the Civil War
3 ended the importation of slaves into the United States
4 increased the power of Congress to exclude slavery from the territories

15 As the United States became industrialized, an important effect of mechanization and the division of labor was that

1 smaller industries had difficulty maintaining their competitiveness
2 the price of most manufactured goods increased
3 the demand to improve transportation systems decreased
4 pools and trusts became less efficient forms of business organization

16 When the Interstate Commerce Act was passed in 1887, it marked the first time that

1 Congress officially affirmed its laissez-faire economic policy
2 the Federal Government imposed a tariff
3 a third political party was able to influence government policy
4 a Federal regulatory agency was established

17 In the late 1800's, most strikes by unions were unsuccessful mainly because

1 unions were generally considered to be unconstitutional
② government usually supported business instead of workers
3 strikes had never been used before in labor disputes
4 strikers failed to use militant tactics

Base your answers to questions 18 and 19 on this excerpt from a speech and on your knowledge of social studies.

You come to us and tell us that the great cities are in favor of the gold standard; we reply that the great cities rest upon our broad and fertile prairies.
. . . we will answer their demand for a gold standard by saying to them: You shall not press down upon the brow of labor this crown of thorns, you shall not crucify mankind upon a cross of gold.

— Speech at Democratic Convention of 1896
William Jennings Bryan

18 This excerpt reflects William Jennings Bryan's support for

① the free coinage of silver
2 the graduated income tax
3 government regulation of mining practices
4 government ownership of railroads

19 Which group most strongly supported the ideas presented in this speech?

1 industrialists   ③ farmers
2 bankers   4 merchants

20 During the period from 1880 to 1920, the majority of immigrants to the United States settled in urban areas in the North mainly because

1 the Populist Party was successful in preventing immigrants from buying farmland
② rapid industrialization had created many job opportunities
3 labor unions gave financial help to immigrants willing to work in the factories
4 most immigrants had lived in cities in their native countries

21 A basic goal of early-1900's muckrakers such as Lincoln Steffens, Upton Sinclair, and Ida Tarbell was to

1 encourage workers in most industries to join unions
2 bring about equal opportunities for African Americans
3 keep the United States from participating in wars
④ expose corruption in government and business

22 Populism and Progressivism were similar because supporters of both movements

① called for the government to address political and economic problems
2 favored an imperialistic foreign policy
3 appealed to business leaders who wanted to increase profits at any cost
4 encouraged increased immigration

23 The "clear and present danger" test that resulted from the Supreme Court decision in *Schenck* v. *United States* placed limits on the

① free speech protections granted by the first amendment
2 powers of Congress under the elastic clause
3 rights of the accused in criminal cases
4 powers of the President during wartime

24 The conviction of John Scopes in 1925 for teaching about evolution supported the ideas of those Americans who

1 believed in religious freedom and the separation of church and state
2 hoped to lessen the differences between rural and urban lifestyles
③ wanted to promote traditional fundamentalist values
4 favored the changes resulting from the new technology of the 1920's

25 "It is our true policy to steer clear of permanent alliances with any portion of the foreign world . . ."

— George Washington, Farewell Address

In the 1920's and 1930's, some Americans used this statement to justify a policy of

① isolationism   3 mercantilism
2 collective security   4 imperialism

Base your answer to question 26 on the cartoon below and on your knowledge of social studies.

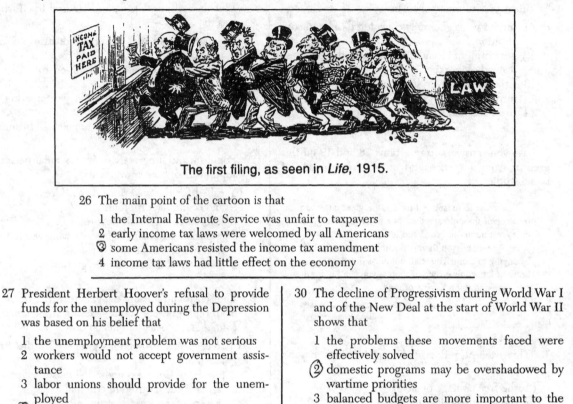

The first filing, as seen in *Life*, 1915.

26 The main point of the cartoon is that

   1 the Internal Revenue Service was unfair to taxpayers
   2 early income tax laws were welcomed by all Americans
   ③ some Americans resisted the income tax amendment
   4 income tax laws had little effect on the economy

---

27 President Herbert Hoover's refusal to provide funds for the unemployed during the Depression was based on his belief that

   1 the unemployment problem was not serious
   2 workers would not accept government assistance
   3 labor unions should provide for the unemployed
   ④ Federal relief programs would destroy individual initiative

28 A major purpose for the creation of the Federal Deposit Insurance Corporation (FDIC) during the 1930's was to

   1 limit government borrowing
   2 break up banking monopolies
   ③ strengthen consumer confidence in the banking system
   4 implement monetary policies to fight the Depression

29 The main purpose of the lend-lease program enacted by the United States during World War II was to

   1 sell weapons to both Allied and Axis nations
   2 rehabilitate countries devastated by war and occupation
   3 encourage the extension of democratic reforms in Germany
   ④ assist countries fighting the Axis Powers

30 The decline of Progressivism during World War I and of the New Deal at the start of World War II shows that

   1 the problems these movements faced were effectively solved
   ② domestic programs may be overshadowed by wartime priorities
   3 balanced budgets are more important to the public than social reforms
   4 Presidents Woodrow Wilson and Franklin D. Roosevelt lacked the leadership to continue these movements

31 Which heading would be the most appropriate for the list below?

> I. _____
> A. Truman Doctrine
> B. Marshall Plan
> C. North Atlantic Treaty Organization (NATO)

   ① Containment Efforts
   2 Tax-Reform Plans
   3 Trade Agreements
   4 Immigration Policies

[OVER]

32 When President Dwight D. Eisenhower said "If you knock down the first of a row of dominoes, all the others will fall in quick order," he was expressing a view that led to

1 decreased foreign aid to Western Europe
2 less restrictive immigration policies toward Africa and Latin America
3 stronger support for United States involvement in Southeast Asia
4 the end of colonialism in Africa

33 Senator Joseph McCarthy built his power on the issue of the

1 need to weaken the role of Congress
2 extent of Communist influence in the Federal Government
3 decline of academic achievement among American students
4 importance of improving race relations

34 Since World War II, what has been a major goal of United States relations with the Middle East?

1 a peaceful resolution to Arab-Israeli conflicts
2 an end to European influence over Arab nations
3 establishment of United Nations control over the Middle East
4 equal access for all nations to the oil reserves in the Middle East

35 The foreign policy actions of Presidents James Monroe, Theodore Roosevelt, and Ronald Reagan were similar in that they all

1 enforced a strict policy of neutrality
2 involved the United States in armed conflict in Europe
3 added to the American colonial empire
4 acted to support United States interests in Latin America

36 Which is a primary source of information about the nature of slavery in the United States?

1 a television program showing life on a Southern plantation
2 a copy of the Supreme Court's ruling in *Brown v. Board of Education*
3 the autobiography of Frederick Douglass
4 a history of slavery written by a 20th-century historian

37 "The civil rights movement would have been vastly different without the shield and spear of the first amendment."

Based on this quotation, which is a valid conclusion?

1 The civil rights movement used the right to assemble peaceably to its advantage.
2 Armed violence was responsible for the gains made by the civil rights movement.
3 Congress ignored the Constitution in its efforts to speed civil rights gains.
4 The executive branch lacked the power to enforce equal rights legislation.

Base your answers to questions 38 and 39 on the section of the law quoted below and on your knowledge of social studies.

> Sec.2 . . . All freedmen, free negroes and mulattoes . . . over the age of eighteen years found . . . with no lawful employment or business . . . and all white persons . . . usually associating with freedmen, free negroes or mulattoes on terms of equality, . . . shall be deemed vagrants, and on conviction thereof shall be fined . . . and imprisoned at the discretion of the court. . . .
>
> — Mississippi Black Code

38 This law was most likely passed during the

1 pre–Revolutionary War period
2 Reconstruction Era
3 Great Depression
4 civil rights movement of the 1960's

39 The principal purpose of this type of law was to

1 maintain racial separation and support white supremacy
2 expand economic opportunities for freedmen
3 encourage formerly enslaved persons to seek skilled jobs
4 establish universal suffrage

40 During the 20th century, agriculture in the United States has experienced a *decrease* in the

1 average size of farms
2 total output of farm products
3 productivity of farmworkers
4 number of farmworkers

Base your answer to question 41 on the cartoon below and on your knowledge of social studies.

IF DAVY CROCKETT RAN FOR OFFICE IN TENNESSEE TODAY HE'D NEED TO:

GET AN
IMITATION
COONSKIN CAP

START WEARING TIES
AND NIX THE BUCKSKINS

SHAVE FOR
TELEVISION

DENY ANY KNOWLEDGE
OF KILLING A BEAR
WHEN HE WAS ONLY 3

RUN ON THE
"GUN IN EVERY
HAND" TICKET

THROW IN THE TOWEL
BECAUSE HE'S NOT A
RICH GUY

BUY SOME
JOGGING SHOES

41 According to the cartoon, candidates for political office in the United States today must

1 be careful not to offend a variety of special-interest groups
2 have firm, knowledgeable opinions on every subject
3 win an election at the state level before running for Federal office
4 solicit the support of women and minorities

---

42 Eugene V. Debs, Samuel Gompers, and John L. Lewis all strongly supported the efforts of

1 the Federal Government to favor business in disputes between labor and management
2 the Populist Party to make government more democratic
3 organized labor to improve conditions for workers
4 business leaders to avoid Federal regulation of their activities

43 Which action would the Federal Reserve Board most likely take to stimulate economic growth?

1 imposing higher income taxes on middle class Americans
2 lowering interest rates on loans to member banks
3 raising the reserve requirement to discourage borrowing
4 initiating antitrust lawsuits to break up monopolies

44 "They have such refined and delicate palates
That they can discover no one worthy of their ballots
And then when someone terrible gets elected
They say 'There, that's just what I expected.'"
— Ogden Nash

In this poem, the poet is expressing an opinion about

1 the operation of the electoral college system
2 the women's suffrage movement
3 term limits for elected officials
4 voter apathy

45 Most recently, one goal of women in the United States Armed Forces has been to gain the right to

1 serve in combat positions
2 become officers
3 travel overseas during wartime
4 receive the same pay as men of comparable rank

Base your answer to question 46 on the cartoon below and on your knowledge of social studies.

"...AND THIS IS OUR WORKING MODEL...."

46 This cartoon suggests that President Ronald Reagan was

1 failing to modernize government operations
2 creating an economic policy that was unlikely to work successfully
3 interfering in economic matters best left to Congress
4 increasing defense spending unnecessarily

47 "I was born upon the prairie — where there were no enclosures and where everything drew a free breath. I want to die there and not within walls . . . So why do you ask us to leave?"

This statement was most likely made by

1 an enslaved person in the South in the pre–Civil War period
2 a Native American Indian during the second half of the 19th century
3 a worker in an industrial sweatshop of the late 19th century
4 a migrant worker in the West during the 1930's

48 Programs designed to increase the representation of minorities and women in the workforce have come under attack during recent years mainly because

1 minorities and women have not been able to point to serious examples of discrimination in employment
2 most laws guaranteeing equal opportunity have been found unconstitutional
3 affirmative action has sometimes been considered reverse discrimination
4 the economy has been too weak to absorb more workers

Answers to the following questions are to be written on paper provided by the school.

Students Please Note:

In developing your answers to Parts II and III, be sure to

  (1) include specific factual information and evidence whenever possible

  (2) keep to the questions asked; do not go off on tangents

  (3) avoid overgeneralizations or sweeping statements without sufficient proof; do not overstate your case

  (4) keep these general definitions in mind:

    (a) <u>discuss</u> means "to make observations about something using facts, reasoning, and argument; to present in some detail"

    (b) <u>describe</u> means "to illustrate something in words or tell about it"

    (c) <u>show</u> means "to point out; to set forth clearly a position or idea by stating it and giving data which support it"

    (d) <u>explain</u> means "to make plain or understandable; to give reasons for or causes of; to show the logical development or relationships of"

Part II

ANSWER ONE QUESTION FROM THIS PART.

1 Throughout United States history, each branch of the Federal Government has made controversial decisions. Some of these decisions are listed below.

Supreme Court Decisions
Plessy v. *Ferguson* (1896)
Miranda v. *Arizona* (1966)
Roe v. *Wade* (1973)

Congressional Decisions
To impeach Andrew Johnson (1868)
To refuse to ratify the Treaty of Versailles (1919)
To pass the Gulf of Tonkin Resolution (1964)

Presidential Decisions
Franklin D. Roosevelt — to pack the United States Supreme Court (1937)
Dwight D. Eisenhower — to send troops to Little Rock, Arkansas (1957)
Gerald Ford — to pardon former President Richard Nixon (1974)

Choose *one* decision from *each* branch of government listed and for *each* one chosen:
- Describe the historical circumstances that led to the decision
- Explain *one* view held by supporters **and** *one* view held by opponents of the decision
  [5,5,5]

2 In United States history, many changes have been made in the Government of the United States.

Governmental Changes

Ratification of the United States Constitution
Expansion of voting rights
Adoption of a civil service system
Direct election of Senators
Limit on Presidential war powers
Limit on campaign financing
Two-term limit on the Presidency

Choose *three* of the changes listed and for *each* one chosen:
- Describe the historical circumstances that led to the adoption of the change in government
- Discuss the extent to which the change has had an impact on the United States Government   [5,5,5]

Part III

ANSWER TWO QUESTIONS FROM THIS PART.   [30]

3 During the 1990's, the United States economy has experienced challenges in many areas.

Areas

Foreign trade
Deficit spending
Health care
Employment
Environment
Education

Choose *three* of the areas listed and for *each* one chosen:
- Identify a specific challenge facing the United States economy in the 1990's
- Discuss a cause of that challenge
- Describe a specific proposal or action of government to try to meet that challenge   [5,5,5]

4 The United States has made many foreign policy decisions concerning other nations. Some of these nations are listed below.

Nations

Bosnia
China
Cuba
Iraq
Korea
Panama
Philippines

Choose *three* of the nations listed and for *each* one chosen:

• State a United States foreign policy decision concerning that nation
• Discuss a specific historical circumstance that led the United States to make that decision
• Explain how this decision affected the relationship between the United States and that nation   [5,5,5]

5 In United States history, decisions made by Presidents have had significant impacts on American society.

Presidential Decisions

George Washington — to support Alexander Hamilton's financial plan
Abraham Lincoln — to preserve the Union
Theodore Roosevelt — to enforce the Sherman Antitrust Act
Franklin D. Roosevelt — to propose the New Deal
Harry S. Truman — to drop atomic bombs on Japan
Lyndon B. Johnson — to declare the "War on Poverty"

Choose *three* of the Presidential decisions listed and for *each* one chosen:

• Describe a problem faced by the President that led him to make the decision
• Discuss an impact of the decision on American society   [5,5,5]

GO RIGHT ON TO THE NEXT PAGE. ⟩

6 Many individuals have made statements about people who have been oppressed in United States history.

> The history of mankind is a history of repeated injuries . . . on the part of man toward woman, having in direct object the establishment of an absolute tyranny over her.
>
> **"Declaration of Sentiments and Resolutions," 1848**

> I regard my people as I regard my machinery. So long as they can do my work for what I choose to pay them, I keep them, getting out of them all I can.
>
> **Factory Manager, 1883**

> I am tired of talk that comes to nothing. It makes my heart sick when I remember all the good words and all the broken promises. If the white man wants to live in peace with the Indians, he can live in peace. Treat all men alike. Give them the same laws. Give them all an even chance to live and grow.
>
> **Chief Joseph, 1879**

> [Route] 66 is the path of people in flight, refugees from dust and shrinking land. The people in flight from the terror behind.
>
> **John Steinbeck, *The Grapes of Wrath*, 1939**

> Of one thing I was sure [in 1944]. The wire fence was real. I no longer had the right to walk out of it. It was because I had Japanese ancestors. It was also because some people had little faith in the ideals of democracy.
>
> **Monica Sone, *Nisei Daughter*, 1953**

> Oppressed people cannot remain oppressed forever. The urge for freedom will eventually come. This is what has happened to the American Negro.
>
> **Martin Luther King, Jr., "Letter from Birmingham City Jail," 1963**

Choose *three* of the statements listed and for *each* one chosen:
- Describe the specific historical circumstances that led to the statement
- Discuss a specific effort made by a group or by government to try to deal with the oppression   [5,5,5]

7 The United States Government has followed a variety of policies toward groups of people coming to live in the United States.

Drawing A   **Drawing B**

a The drawings above illustrate different policies toward immigration to the United States.

(1) Explain the governmental policy toward immigration illustrated by each of the drawings.   [3]

(2) Discuss a reason for the change in policy shown by the drawings.   [3]

b Some of the different groups of people who have immigrated to the United States are listed below.

> Western Europeans (1800–1890)
> Eastern Europeans (1890–1930)
> Asians (1860–1930)
> Latin Americans (1965–today)

Choose *three* of the groups listed. For *each* one chosen, describe a governmental policy related to the immigration of that group to the United States during the time period indicated.   [3,3,3]

Part I (55 credits)

Answer all 48 questions in this part.

Directions (1–48): For each statement or question, write on the separate answer sheet the *number* of the word or expression that, of those given, best completes the statement or answers the question.

1 "The only representatives of the people of these colonies are persons chosen therein by themselves; and that no taxes ever have been, or can be constitutionally imposed on them but by their respective legislatures."

— Statement by the Stamp Act Congress, 1765

What is a valid conclusion that can be drawn from this quotation?

1 The colonial legislatures should be appointed by the English King with the consent of Parliament.
2 Only the colonists' elected representatives should have the power to levy taxes.
3 The English King should have the right to tax the colonists.
4 The colonists should be opposed to all taxation.

2 The authors of the Articles of Confederation established a decentralized political system mainly to

1 cancel state debts incurred during the Revolutionary War
2 assist the southern states in their efforts to gain a manufacturing base
3 promote the common goal of national sovereignty
4 prevent the abuses of power that had existed under British rule

3 Senate ratification of treaties negotiated by the President is required by the United States Constitution as a way of

1 maintaining United States prestige in international affairs
2 preventing Federal abuse of State power
3 implementing the principle of checks and balances
4 expanding the authority of the executive branch

4 The United States Constitution requires that a census be taken every ten years to reapportion

1 membership in the House of Representatives
2 the number of delegates to national nominating conventions
3 Federal aid to localities
4 agricultural subsidies

5 In the United States Congress, differences between Senate and House of Representatives versions of a bill are usually resolved by accepting the version that is

1 preferred by a majority of the State legislatures
2 supported by the Supreme Court
3 preferred by the House in which the bill originated
4 agreed to by a joint conference committee of both Houses

6 "The privilege of the writ of habeas corpus shall not be suspended, unless when in cases of rebellion or invasion the public safety may require it."

This provision is evidence that the writers of the United States Constitution

1 wanted the President to have unlimited power during wartime
2 wanted to balance individual liberty with the needs of the nation
3 did not trust the common people to obey the laws
4 expected the American people to oppose most government policies

7 In the United States, activities such as Cabinet meetings and political party conventions are best described as

1 examples of direct democracy
2 responsibilities of the executive branch
3 features of the unwritten constitution
4 requirements of the system of checks and balances

Base your answer to question 8 on the cartoon below and on your knowledge of social studies.

8 The most commonly proposed solution to the problem shown in the cartoon is to

1 establish poll taxes
2 have candidates finance their own campaigns
3 eliminate primaries from the election system
4 use public funds to pay for political campaigns

9 Actions and policies of the Government under President George Washington generally resulted in the

1 establishment of strong political ties with other nations
2 liberation of many enslaved persons
3 failure to create a sound financial program for the country
4 strengthening of the Federal Government

10 "By the 1850's, the Constitution, originally framed as an instrument of national unity, had become a source of sectional discord."

This quotation suggests that

1 vast differences of opinion existed over the issue of States rights
2 the Federal Government had become more interested in foreign affairs than in domestic problems
3 the Constitution had no provisions for governing new territories
4 the Southern States continued to import slaves

11 Early in his Presidency, Abraham Lincoln declared that his primary goal as President was to

1 enforce the Emancipation Proclamation
2 preserve the Union
3 end slavery throughout the entire country
4 encourage sectionalism

12 In their plans for Reconstruction, both President Abraham Lincoln and President Andrew Johnson sought to

1 punish the South for starting the Civil War
2 force the Southern States to pay reparations to the Federal Government
3 allow the Southern States to reenter the nation as quickly as possible
4 establish the Republican Party as the only political party in the South

13 The poll tax, the literacy test, and the actions of the Ku Klux Klan were all attempts to limit the effectiveness of

1 the 14th and 15th amendments
2 the Supreme Court's decision in *Brown* v. *Board of Education*
3 civil rights legislation passed in all states after the Civil War
4 immigration laws such as the Gentleman's Agreement and the Chinese Exclusion Act

14 According to the theory of <u>laissez faire</u>, the economy functions best when the government

1 subsidizes business so that it can compete worldwide
2 regulates businesses for the good of the majority
3 owns major industries
4 does not interfere in business

15 Businesses formed trusts, pools, and holding companies mainly to

1 increase profits by eliminating competition
2 offer a wide range of goods and services to consumers
3 provide employment opportunities for minorities
4 protect the interests of workers

16 The Rockefeller Foundation, Carnegie Hall, and the Morgan Library illustrate various ways that entrepreneurs and their descendants have

1 suppressed the growth of labor unions
2 supported philanthropic activities to benefit society
3 applied scientific discoveries to industry
4 attempted to undermine the United States economic system

17 The major reason the United States placed few restrictions on immigration during the 1800's was that

1 few Europeans wished to give up their economic security
2 little opposition to immigration existed
3 the growing economy needed a steady supply of cheap labor
4 most immigrants spoke English and thus needed little or no education

18 The American Federation of Labor became the first long-lasting, successful labor union in the United States mainly because it

1 refused to participate in strikes against employers
2 concentrated on organizing workers in industries in the South
3 formed its own political party and elected many prolabor public officials
4 fought for the rights of skilled workers

19 In the late 1800's, the goal of the Federal Government's policy toward Native American Indians was to

1 destroy tribal bonds and thus weaken their traditional cultural values
2 grant them full citizenship and due process
3 give their tribal groups authority over their own affairs
4 increase the land holdings of western tribes

20 W.E.B. Du Bois believed that African Americans should attempt to gain equality in the United States by

1 setting up a separate nation within the United States
2 entering vocational training programs in separate schools
3 demanding full and immediate participation in American society
4 taking over the leadership of the two major political parties

21 In the United States during the late 19th century, much of the prejudice expressed toward immigrants was based on the belief that they would

1 cause overcrowding in farm areas
2 refuse to become citizens
3 support the enemies of the United States in wartime
4 fail to assimilate into American society

22 During the late 19th and early 20th centuries, United States policy toward Latin America was most strongly characterized by

1 friendship and trust
2 intervention and paternalism
3 tolerance and humanitarianism
4 indifference and neglect

23 A major purpose of the Federal Reserve System is to

1 deal with the trade deficit through tariffs and quotas
2 control the minimum wage
3 establish the Federal budget
4 regulate interest rates and the money supply

24 A major goal of reformers during the Progressive Era was to

1 end segregation in the South
2 correct the abuses of big business
3 limit immigration from Latin America
4 enact high tariffs to help domestic industry grow

25 "We are to be an instrument in the hands of God to see that liberty is made secure for mankind."

— President Woodrow Wilson

President Wilson tried to carry out the idea expressed in this quotation by

1 protesting the sinking of the *Lusitania*
2 proposing a program of civil rights for minorities in American society
3 urging the Allies to adopt the Fourteen Points
4 taking control of territories conquered in World War I

26 In stating the principle of a "clear and present danger" in *Schenck v. United States*, the Supreme Court established that

1 constitutional rights are not absolute
2 the Constitution guarantees the right to privacy
3 Congress can pass a law to eliminate any part of the Bill of Rights
4 all individual rights are eliminated during wartime

27 In the 1920's, the Immigration Act of 1924 and the Sacco-Vanzetti trial were typical of the

1 rejection of traditional customs and beliefs
2 acceptance of cultural differences
3 increase in nativism and intolerance
4 support of humanitarian causes

28 The economic boom and the financial speculation of the 1920's were caused in part by

1 installment buying and an unregulated stock market
2 the expansion of civil rights to women and minorities
3 the mobilization of the economy for war
4 increased government restrictions on big business

29 The popularity of escapist novels and movies during the Great Depression is evidence that

1 the Great Depression was not really a time of economic distress
2 popular culture is shaped by economic and social conditions
3 American society did not try to solve the problems of the Great Depression
4 the greatest employment opportunities for the average person in the 1930's were in the field of entertainment

30 The power of labor unions increased during the New Deal mainly because

1 a new spirit of cooperation existed between employers and government
2 a shortage of skilled and unskilled laborers developed
3 management changed its attitude toward organized labor
4 Federal legislation guaranteed labor's right to organize and bargain collectively

31 An immediate result of the Supreme Court decisions in *Schechter Poultry Corporation v. United States* (1935) and *United States v. Butler* (1936) was that

1 some aspects of the New Deal were declared unconstitutional
2 State governments took over relief agencies
3 Congress was forced to abandon efforts to improve the economy
4 the constitutional authority of the President was greatly expanded

32 The United States became involved in World War II primarily because

1 Germany refused to pay its debts from World War I
2 European democracies supported United States policies toward Germany and Japan
3 President Franklin D. Roosevelt did not enforce the Neutrality Acts
4 Germany and Japan achieved important military successes in Europe and Asia

Base your answer to question 33 on the cartoon below and on your knowledge of social studies.

I WANT SIX SUBSTITUTES AT ONCE. THOSE FELLOWS DONT KNOW IT, BUT THEY'RE THROUGH BUT I DONT WANT TO TAKE 'EM OFF THE FIELD!

THE INGENIOUS QUARTERBACK!

33 This cartoon portrays President Franklin D. Roosevelt's attempt to
   1 continue life terms for Supreme Court Justices
   2 increase Presidential influence on the Supreme Court
   3 prevent Congress from interfering with the Federal Court system
   4 strengthen the independence of the Supreme Court

34 In the United States during World War II, the role of women changed as they
   1 were drafted and assigned military roles equal to those held by men
   2 continued to work outside the home only in jobs traditionally performed by women
   3 made major contributions to the war effort by taking jobs in factories
   4 achieved positions of leadership in most major industries

35 After World War II, the United States occupied Japan, joined the North Atlantic Treaty Organization (NATO), and helped organize the United Nations. These actions show that the United States was
   1 concerned solely with rebuilding Europe
   2 taking on greater global responsibility
   3 expanding its imperialistic empire
   4 returning to its policy of neutrality

Base your answer to question 36 on the graph below and on your knowledge of social studies.

U.S. Foreign Aid, 1946–1954
(Billions of Dollars)

NONMILITARY	YEAR	MILITARY
$ 4.0	1946	$ 0.7
$ 5.8	1947	
$ 5.0	1948	$ 0.1
$ 5.7	1949	$ 0.4
$ 4.3	1950	$ 0.2
$ 3.3	1951	$ 1.1
$ 2.8	1952	$ 1.8
$ 2.0	1953	$ 4.4
$ 1.7	1954	$ 3.5

36 Which United States program is most likely reflected in the amounts of nonmilitary foreign aid given from 1947 to 1950?

1 Peace Corps
2 Marshall Plan
3 Alliance for Progress
4 Lend Lease

37 Which is a valid conclusion based on United States involvement in the Korean War?

1 The policy of containment was applied in Asia as well as in Europe.
2 United Nations economic sanctions are more effective than military action.
3 The American people will support United States participation in any war, whether declared or undeclared.
4 United States cooperation with a wartime ally ends when the war ends.

38 Which statement about public education in the United States is most accurate?

1 The Federal Government controls but does not fund education.
2 The problems that affect other segments of American society seldom affect education.
3 Education is largely controlled and financed by state governments and local communities.
4 High school enrollments have decreased over the last 100 years.

39 "Those of us who shout the loudest about Americanism in making character assassinations are all too frequently those who, by our own words and acts, ignore some of the basic principles of Americanism."

— Senator Margaret Chase Smith, 1950

This criticism of Senator Joseph McCarthy and his supporters suggests that

1 Senator McCarthy did not do enough to protect the nation from a Communist conspiracy
2 the tactics of Senator McCarthy were necessary to protect the basic principles of democracy
3 free speech must be limited in times of national crisis
4 Senator McCarthy was a greater threat to the nation than Communist sympathizers were

40 The Great Society programs of the 1960's used the power of the Federal Government to bring about

1 an all-volunteer military
2 antipoverty reforms
3 deregulation of business
4 reduced defense spending

41 A major long-term effect of the Vietnam War has been

1 an end to communist governments in Asia
2 a change in United States foreign policy from containment to imperialism
3 a reluctance to commit United States troops for extended military action abroad
4 a continued boycott of trade with Asia

42 The Camp David accords negotiated during President Jimmy Carter's administration were an attempt to

1 decrease United States control of the Panama Canal
2 encourage the use of solar and other nonpolluting energy sources
3 end inflationary oil prices
4 establish peace in the Middle East

[OVER

43 According to the supply-side economics principles promoted by President Ronald Reagan, economic growth would occur when

  ① corporate business taxes were reduced
  2 business was regulated by antitrust legislation
  3 unemployment benefits were increased
  4 investment in capital goods was decreased

44 The rulings of the Supreme Court in *Dred Scott* v. *Sanford* (1857), *Plessy* v. *Ferguson* (1896), and *Korematsu* v. *United States* (1944) all demonstrate that the Supreme Court has

  1 continued to extend voting rights to minorities
  2 protected itself from internal dissent
  ③ sometimes failed to protect the rights of minorities
  4 often imposed restrictions on free speech during wartime

45 Which characteristic of the American frontier continues to be an important part of life in the United States today?

  1 widespread support for the Populist Party
  2 necessity for families to have many children
  3 a predominantly agricultural and mining economy
  ④ significant opportunities for social and economic mobility

46 The main purpose of a progressive income tax is to

  ① base tax rates on a person's ability to pay
  2 increase government spending on welfare programs
  3 tax everyone at the same percentage rate
  4 ensure a balanced budget

Base your answers to questions 47 and 48 on the statements below and on your knowledge of social studies.

Speaker A: We must take action even if we are not sure it will work. To do nothing to stop them would be a repeat of the Munich mistake.

Speaker B: We must recognize the increasing interdependence of nations and join the United Nations.

Speaker C: Stopping the spread of communism can and must take several forms. We must be willing to do whatever is necessary.

Speaker D: Involvement in European affairs would be a mistake. We should not jeopardize our peace and prosperity over issues that Europe's ambitions and rivalries control.

47 Which speaker best describes the basic foreign policy of the United States until the late 1800's?

  (1) *A*   (3) *C*
  (2) *B*   ④ *D*

48 The "Munich mistake" mentioned by speaker *A* refers to a policy of

  1 interdependence   3 balance of power
  ② appeasement   4 collective security

Answers to the following questions are to be written on paper provided by the school.

Students Please Note:

In developing your answers to Parts II and III, be sure to

(1) **include specific factual information and evidence whenever possible**

(2) **keep to the questions asked; do not go off on tangents**

(3) **avoid overgeneralizations or sweeping statements without sufficient proof; do not over-state your case**

(4) **keep these general definitions in mind:**

(a) <u>discuss</u> **means "to make observations about something using facts, reasoning, and argu-ment; to present in some detail"**

(b) <u>describe</u> **means "to illustrate something in words or tell about it"**

(c) <u>show</u> **means "to point out; to set forth clearly a position or idea by stating it and giving data which support it"**

(d) <u>explain</u> **means "to make plain or understandable; to give reasons for or causes of; to show the logical development or relationships of"**

Part II

ANSWER ONE QUESTION FROM THIS PART.   [15]

1   The United States democratic system includes certain features that are intended to pro-tect against the abuse of power by government and public officials.

Protective Features

— Judicial review
— Impeachment process
   Freedom of expression
   Protection against unreasonable searches
   Equal protection under the law
   Rights of the accused

Choose *three* of the features listed and for *each* one chosen:

- Explain how the feature is intended to protect against abuse of governmental power
- Discuss a specific situation in United States history in which the feature was used to protect against an abuse of governmental power [Use a different historical situation for each feature discussed.]
- Discuss the extent to which the feature was successful in protecting against abuse of governmental power in that situation   [5,5,5]

[OVER

2 Different groups have played a role in influencing policies and shaping legislation in the United States.

Influential Groups

Representatives of foreign nations
Lobbyists
Media
Political action committees
Political parties
Unions

Choose *three* of the groups listed and for *each* one chosen:
- Identify a specific group and show how that group attempted to influence a specific governmental policy or to shape legislation
- Discuss the extent to which the attempt was successful   [5,5,5]

Part III

ANSWER TWO QUESTIONS FROM THIS PART.   [30]

3 At different times in the history of the United States, Presidents have taken various foreign policy actions.

Presidential Foreign Policy Actions

George Washington warns against "entangling alliances" in Farewell Address. (1796)
James Monroe announces the Monroe Doctrine. (1823)
Theodore Roosevelt supports the independence of Panama from Colombia. (1903)
Franklin D. Roosevelt asks Congress for a declaration of war. (1941)
John F. Kennedy orders a blockade of Cuba. (1962)
Ronald Reagan begins a major military buildup. (early 1980's)
Bill Clinton sends United States forces to Bosnia. (1995)

Choose *three* of the foreign policy actions listed and for *each* one chosen:
* Describe a circumstance that motivated the Presidential foreign policy action
* Explain a goal of the United States in taking that action
* Discuss an impact of that action   [5,5,5]

4 Since colonial times, various methods of protest have been used to bring about change.

Methods of Protest

Boycott
Civil disobedience
Demonstration/protest march
Petition
Rebellion
Sit-in
Strike

a Choose *three* of the methods listed and for *each* one chosen, describe a specific historical situation in which that method of protest was used to bring about change and explain why that method was used. [Use a different historical situation for each method.]   [4,4,4]
b For *one* of the methods of protest chosen in answer to part *a*, discuss the extent to which that method was successful in bringing about change.   [3]

5 Certain actions have aroused controversy in American society. Some of these controversial actions are listed below.

Controversial Actions

Proposal of the Virginia Plan (one-house federal legislature) at the
  Constitutional Convention (1787)
Election of Abraham Lincoln to the Presidency (1860)
Annexation of the Philippines by the United States (1898)
Proposal of United States membership in the League of Nations by President
  Woodrow Wilson (1919)
Ratification of the Prohibition amendment (1919)
Proposal of New Deal legislation by President Franklin D. Roosevelt (1933)
Decision concerning abortion in *Roe* v. *Wade* by the Supreme Court (1973)

Choose *three* of the controversial actions listed and for *each* one chosen:
- Discuss *one* argument given by supporters and *one* argument given by opponents of the action
- Discuss *one* result of the action [5,5,5]

6 Certain issues concern American society today. Some of these issues are listed below.

Issues of Concern to Americans

  Changing family patterns
  Crime
  Health care reform
  Homelessness
  Immigration
  Technological change

Choose *three* of the issues listed and for *each* one chosen:
- Discuss *two* reasons the issue concerns Americans today
- Describe a specific proposal that has been suggested to deal with the issue [5,5,5]

7 Songs sometimes describe the experiences and problems of various groups. Excerpts from some songs are given below. Choose *three* of the excerpts and for *each* one chosen:

- Identify the group described in the song and describe a problem suggested by the song
- Show how a specific political or economic policy of government attempted to deal with the problem   [5,5,5]

"HARD TIMES" SONGS

Excerpt 1 —

The farmer is the man, the farmer is the man
Lives on credit 'til the fall
With the interest rate so high, it's a wonder he don't die
For the mortgage man's the one who gets it all.

— Anonymous

Excerpt 2 —

O it's all in the past you can say
But it's still going on here today
The Government now wants the Iroquois land
That of the Seneca and the Cheyenne
It's here and it's now you must help us, dear man
Now that the Buffalo's gone.

— Buffy Sainte-Marie

Excerpt 3 —

It is we who dug the ditches, built the cities where they trade
Blasted mines and built the workshops, endless miles of railroad laid
Now we stand outcast and starving 'mid the wonders we have made,
But the union makes us strong. . .

— Ralph Chaplin
(adapted)

Excerpt 4 —

Bumpy wagons moving through the days and nights
They've been travelin' far in search of women's rights
Not much comfort or supporters but within this country's borders
They won't quit 'til they've won all of the fights.

— Eileen Abrams

Excerpt 5 —

Too old to work, too old to work
When you're too old to work and you're too young to die
Who will take care of you, how'll you get by
When you're too old to work and you're too young to die?

— Joe Glazer

[OVER

Part I (55 credits)

Answer all 48 questions in this part.

Directions (1–48): For each statement or question, write on the separate answer sheet the *number* of the word or expression that, of those given, best completes the statement or answers the question.

1 Which fundamental political idea is expressed in the Declaration of Independence?
1 The government should guarantee every citizen economic security.
2 The central government and state governments should have equal power.
3 If the government denies its people certain basic rights, that government can be overthrown.
4 Rulers derive their right to govern from God and are therefore bound to govern in the nation's best interest.

2 The Articles of Confederation are best described as a
1 statement of principles justifying the Revolutionary War
2 plan of union for the original thirteen states
3 set of arguments supporting ratification of the Constitution
4 list of reasons for the secession of the Southern States

3 When the United States Constitution was written, which compromise was reached by the authors to gain the support of the states with small populations?
1 Congress would consist of both a House of Representatives and a Senate.
2 Five enslaved persons would be counted as three free persons for the purpose of taxation.
3 The President would be selected by the direct vote of the people.
4 Exported goods could not be taxed, but imported goods could be taxed.

4 An example of the unwritten constitution is the
1 establishment of a postal system
2 development of political parties
3 direct election of Senators
4 impeachment process

5 "All communities divide themselves into the few and the many. The first are the rich and well born, the other the mass of the people. . . . The people are turbulent and changing. . . . Give therefore to the first class a distinct permanent share in the government. They will check the unsteadiness of the second."

— Alexander Hamilton

The author of this quotation suggests that
1 the will of the majority should guide public policy
2 wealthy people are too preoccupied to rule well
3 the common people cannot be trusted to run a stable government
4 poorer people must work harder to gain access to economic and political power

6 Which action could eliminate the electoral college?
1 a Supreme Court ruling
2 a Presidential order
3 passage of legislation by Congress
4 ratification of a constitutional amendment

7 "President Delivers State of the Union Address to Congress"
"President Mobilizes the National Guard To Quell Riots"
"President's Appointee Will Enforce Federal Guidelines"

These headlines are evidence that the President of the United States
1 has new added duties not specified in the original Constitution
2 exercises nearly unlimited power under the United States governmental system
3 has specific executive, legislative, and military powers
4 must obtain congressional approval of most executive decisions

8 Sectional differences developed in the United States largely because
1 the Federal Government adopted a policy of neutrality
2 economic conditions and interests in each region varied
3 only northerners were represented at the Constitutional Convention
4 early Presidents favored urban areas over rural areas

9 The dispute between President Andrew Johnson and Congress during the Reconstruction Era illustrates the constitutional principle of
1 equality of justice under the law
2 federalism
3 one man, one vote
4 separation of powers

10 Poll taxes and grandfather clauses were devices used to
1 deny African Americans the right to vote
2 extend suffrage to women and 18-year-old citizens
3 raise money for political campaigns
4 prevent immigrants from becoming citizens

11 Which situation brought about the rapid growth of industry between 1865 and 1900?
1 high worker morale resulting from good wages and working conditions
2 availability of investment capital
3 establishment of western reservations for Native American Indians
4 decline in the number of people attending schools

12 From 1865 to 1900, how did the growth of industry affect American society?
1 The United States experienced the disappearance of the traditional "family farm."
2 Population centers shifted from the Northeast to the South.
3 Restrictions on immigration created a more homogeneous culture.
4 The percentage of Americans living in urban areas increased.

13 During the late 1800's, a major reaction to the activities of labor unions in the United States was that
1 the press in most communities supported unions
2 United States Presidents opposed the use of Federal troops to end strikes called by organized labor
3 courts frequently issued injunctions to stop strikes
4 most factory workers quickly joined the unions

14 Many wealthy American industrialists of the late 19th century used the theory of Social Darwinism to
1 support the labor union movement
2 justify monopolistic actions
3 promote legislation establishing a minimum wage
4 encourage charitable organizations to help the poor

15 Prior to 1880, the number of immigrants to the United States was *not* restricted mainly because
1 industry owners wanted cheap labor
2 the nations of Europe discouraged emigration
3 the United States birthrate was increasing
4 Congress lacked the power to limit immigration

16 "America's strength lies in its diversity. Many immigrant groups have joined the mainstream of American life, while maintaining their languages, religions, and traditions. This has made the United States a strong nation."

The author of this statement could best be described as a supporter of
1 nativism
2 ethnocentrism
3 cultural pluralism
4 limited social mobility

17 A main goal of the Granger movement of the 1870's and 1880's was to
1 force the railroads to lower freight rates
2 reduce the rate of inflation
3 strengthen labor unions
4 improve living conditions in urban slums

[OVER]

18 "Up to our own day American history is the history of the colonization of the Great West. The existence of an area of free land, ... and the advance of American settlement westward explain American development."

This quotation of the 1890's suggests that the American frontier

1 should be preserved for free use by all the people
2 has mirrored European values and social patterns
3 will continue indefinitely as a region to be colonized
4 has had a positive effect on the growth of the United States

19 Involvement in the Spanish-American War, acquisition of Hawaii, and introduction of the Open Door policy in China were actions taken by the United States Government to

1 establish military alliances with other nations
2 gain overseas markets and sources of raw materials
3 begin the policy of manifest destiny
4 support isolationist forces in Congress

20 Which foreign policy position was held by both President James Monroe and President Theodore Roosevelt?

1 Trade with other nations should be sharply reduced.
2 The United States should follow a policy of isolationism.
3 A special relationship should exist between the United States and the nations of Latin America.
4 The United States should send troops to aid revolutionary movements in European nations.

21 Laws requiring individuals to pass civil service examinations to obtain government jobs were enacted to

1 eliminate patronage and corruption in government hiring
2 allow the government to compete with private industry for employees
3 support the development of public employee labor unions
4 encourage the growth of local political parties

22 Which event of the early 1900's is evidence that Upton Sinclair's novel *The Jungle* had an important impact on the United States?

1 adoption of reforms in public education
2 passage of legislation limiting immigration
3 adoption of the 18th amendment establishing Prohibition
4 passage of legislation requiring Federal inspection of meat

23 Which conclusion can be drawn from the occurrence of the Red Scare and the decision of the Supreme Court in *Schenck* v. *United States*?

1 Immigrants to the United States are consistently denied equal protection under the law.
2 A person's best protection from persecution rests with the Supreme Court.
3 Civil rights are sometimes compromised by the public's fear of radical political groups.
4 Violent protests in the United States are usually met with a violent response from the government.

24 In the United States, the decade of the 1920's was characterized by

1 a willingness to encourage immigration to the United States
2 increased consumer borrowing and spending
3 the active involvement of the United States in European affairs
4 major reforms in national labor legislation

25 In the 1920's, the depressed situation of United States agriculture was chiefly caused by

1 overregulation by government
2 mechanization and overproduction
3 inefficient production techniques
4 stock-market speculation

26 When the Great Depression began in 1929, the most common economic belief supported by the Republican Party was that

1 an increase in defense spending would stimulate the economy
2 unemployed workers should receive Federal unemployment benefits
3 the government should assume control of industry
4 the economy would recover on its own

Base your answer to question 27 on the cartoon below and on your knowledge of social studies.

THE PRESIDENT PROPOSES:
THE SENATE DISPOSES

U.S. SENATE

TREATY OF VERSAILLES PART I
LEAGUE OF NATIONS
REJECTIONS

27 Which aspect of the United States Government is best illustrated by the cartoon?

1 system of checks and balances
2 veto power of the President
3 congressional committee system
4 civilian control of the military

28 Which statement is accurate about American culture during the Great Depression?

1 The Federal Government provided money to support the arts.
2 Most movies featured realistic themes and unhappy endings.
3 Rock-and-roll music became popular.
4 Interest in professional sports declined.

29 Which New Deal reforms most directly targeted the basic problem of the victims of the Dust Bowl?

1 guaranteeing workers the right to organize and bargain collectively
2 regulating the sale of stocks and bonds
3 providing farmers low-cost loans and parity payments
4 raising individual and corporate income tax rates

30 In the 1930's, the United States attempted to avoid a repetition of the events leading up to United States involvement in World War I by

1 establishing the Good Neighbor policy with Latin American nations
2 forgiving the foreign debts incurred during World War I
3 officially recognizing the existence of the Soviet Union
4 passing a series of neutrality laws

31 How did the personal diplomacy conducted by President Franklin D. Roosevelt during World War II affect the Presidency?

1 Subsequent Presidents have refused to use this unsuccessful method.
2 The President's role in shaping United States foreign policy was strengthened.
3 The President's war powers as Commander in Chief were sharply reduced.
4 Congress increased its power over the executive branch.

Base your answer to question 32 on the graph below and on your knowledge of social studies.

Federal Income and Spending, 1928–1936

32 Which situation best accounts for the differences in Federal income and spending between 1928 and 1936, as shown in the graph?

1 government funding of programs to combat economic problems
2 increase in personal income tax rates
3 military spending for World War II
4 United States trade imbalance with Japan

Base your answer to question 33 on the quotation below and on your knowledge of social studies.

Many foreign peoples, in Europe at least, are . . . frightened by experiences of the past and are less interested in . . . freedom than in security. They are seeking guidance rather than responsibilities. We should be better able than the Russians to give them this. And unless we do, the Russians certainly will.

33 This advice to President Harry Truman helped influence Truman's decision to

1 drop atomic bombs on Hiroshima and Nagasaki
2 end segregation in the Armed Forces
3 deport any person suspected of being a Communist
4 develop the Marshall Plan

34 As World War II was ending, the United States decided to join the United Nations mainly because the United States

1 sought to meet the American public's overwhelming demand for free-trade agreements
2 wanted to continue to play the same role it had in the League of Nations
3 recognized that efforts to achieve world peace required United States involvement
4 wanted to stop the growing influence of newly independent developing nations

35 In the 1950's, Senator Joseph McCarthy was most closely associated with issues related to

1 Communist infiltration and the denial of civil liberties
2 farm problems and taxation
3 military preparedness and foreign aid
4 collective bargaining and the rights of unions

36 During the Korean War, what was the main reason that President Harry Truman dismissed General Douglas MacArthur as commander of the United States troops?

1 The United States had suffered many severe military losses.
2 Congress refused to appropriate any more money to support the war.
3 President Truman believed that General MacArthur's conduct threatened the concept of civilian control over the military.
4 General MacArthur disobeyed President Truman by deciding to stop fighting the war.

37 During the Cold War Era, the easing of tensions between the United States and the Soviet Union resulted in

1 the organization of the Warsaw Pact
2 the invasion of Hungary and Czechoslovakia
3 the Berlin Airlift
4 a treaty banning nuclear tests

38 The Great Society of Lyndon Johnson is most similar to which other Presidential program?

1 Warren Harding's Return to Normalcy
2 Franklin D. Roosevelt's New Deal
3 Ronald Reagan's New Federalism
4 George Bush's Thousand Points of Light

39 The Presidency of Gerald Ford was different from all previous Presidencies because he was the first President who

1 won the office by running on a third-party ticket
2 resigned from the office of the President
3 ran for office as a nonpartisan candidate
4 was not elected to either the Presidency or the Vice-Presidency

40 Which statement is most accurate about the economy of the United States during the 1970's and early 1980's?

1 The increased cost of imported oil hurt economic growth.
2 The Federal budget was balanced.
3 Inflation declined sharply throughout these years.
4 The number of jobs in farming increased while service jobs decreased.

41 The "supply side" economics of President Ronald Reagan and President George Bush favored

1 raising tariffs to increase the number of imports
2 increasing Federal taxes to support social welfare programs
3 providing incentives to stimulate business growth
4 establishing government programs to provide jobs for the unemployed

42 Since 1980, relations between Japan and the United States have been most influenced by the

1 imbalance of trade between the two nations
2 refusal of the United States to accept Japanese technology
3 immigration restrictions imposed by the Gentlemen's Agreement
4 construction of Japanese military bases in the Pacific area

43 The widespread use of computers has led to a national concern over

1 increased pollution of the environment
2 guarding the right to privacy
3 protection of the right to petition
4 a decline in television viewing

44 A study of voting patterns in the United States today indicates that

(1) the United States has a low voter turnout
(2) urban areas have higher voter turnouts than suburban areas do
(3) people who live in poverty tend to have a high voter turnout
(4) 18- to 25-year-old voters are more likely to vote than senior citizens are

45 In the United States in the 1990's, cuts in defense spending have been proposed because

1 Japan has assumed the peacekeeping responsibilities of the United Nations
2 military technology has become less expensive
3 the United States has returned to an isolationist foreign policy
4 communist governments in Eastern Europe and the former Soviet Union have collapsed

[OVER]

Base your answer to question 46 on the cartoon below and on your knowledge of social studies.

the small society by Bill Yates

46 According to the cartoon, a problem of political elections in the United States is that
1 candidates have few serious issues to consider
2 candidates offer simplistic solutions in television campaigning to gain votes
3 most voters demand quick solutions to national problems
4 television reporting of candidates and their campaigns is biased

47 A valid generalization about reform movements throughout United States history is that
1 reform movements have failed to use the media effectively
2 most successful reform movements affect relatively few people
3 many reform movements have led to long-lasting changes in society
4 most reform movements have had little impact on the economy

48 United States annexation of the Philippines (1898) and military involvement in Vietnam (1960's and 1970's) are similar because in each event the United States
1 achieved its long-range foreign policy objectives
2 put the domino theory into action
3 demonstrated the strength and success of its military power
4 provoked domestic debate about its involvement in the internal affairs of other nations

Answers to the following questions are to be written on paper provided by the school.

Students Please Note:

In developing your answers to Parts II and III, be sure to
(1) include specific factual information and evidence whenever possible
(2) keep to the questions asked; do not go off on tangents
(3) avoid overgeneralizations or sweeping statements without sufficient proof; do not overstate your case
(4) keep these general definitions in mind:
  (a) discuss means "to make observations about something using facts, reasoning, and argument; to present in some detail"
  (b) describe means "to illustrate something in words or tell about it"
  (c) show means "to point out; to set forth clearly a position or idea by stating it and giving data which support it"
  (d) explain means "to make plain or understandable; to give reasons for or causes of; to show the logical development or relationships of"

Part II

ANSWER ONE QUESTION FROM THIS PART.   [15]

1 United States Supreme Court cases have often dealt with the constitutional rights of Americans. Some of these rights are listed below.

Constitutional Rights

Equal protection of the law
Rights of the accused
Right to privacy
Freedom of expression
Freedom of religion

Choose *three* of the rights listed and for *each* one chosen:

* Show how a specific Supreme Court case dealt with that right [Use a different case for each right chosen. The exact name of the case does not have to be given.]
* Describe the historical circumstances of the case
* Show how the Court's decision affected American society   [5,5,5]

2 Since the ratification of the United States Constitution, various methods have been used and various proposals have been made to expand democracy in the United States.

 a Choose *two* of the methods listed below. For *each* one chosen, use a specific example to show how that method has been used to expand democracy in the United States. Cite a specific historical circumstance that led to each example you include in your discussion.   [5,5]

Methods

Constitutional amendments
Congressional legislation
State or local governmental actions
Presidential actions

 b Some of the proposals that have been made to expand democracy in the United States are listed below. Choose *one* proposal and describe *one* argument given by supporters of the proposal and *one* argument given by opponents.   [5]

Proposals

Term limits for members of Congress
Elimination of the electoral college
Public financing of election campaigns

Part III

ANSWER TWO QUESTIONS FROM THIS PART. [30]

3 United States Presidents have made statements about United States involvement in foreign affairs. Some of these statements are listed below.

Presidential Statements

"It is our true policy to steer clear of permanent alliances with any portion of the foreign world . . ."

— George Washington, 1796

". . . I ask the Congress to authorize and empower the President to take measures to secure a full and final termination of hostilities between the Government of Spain and the people of Cuba, ..."

— William McKinley, 1898

"Chronic wrongdoing . . . in the Western Hemisphere . . . may force the United States . . . to the exercise of an international police power."

— Theodore Roosevelt, 1904

"A general association of nations must be formed under specific covenants for the purpose of affording mutual guarantees of political independence and territorial integrity to great and small states alike."

— Woodrow Wilson, 1918

"Yesterday, December 7, 1941 — a date which will live in infamy — the United States of America was suddenly and deliberately attacked. . . ."

— Franklin D. Roosevelt, 1941

"Let every nation know, whether it wishes us well or ill, that we shall pay any price, bear any burden, meet any hardship, support any friend, oppose any foe to assure the survival and success of liberty. . . ."

— John F. Kennedy, 1961

". . . clearly there are limits to what outside forces can do to solve the severe internal problems of countries. . . . (But) we cannot withdraw from the world we have done so much to make."

— Bill Clinton, 1993

Choose *three* of the statements listed. For *each* one chosen, discuss an action taken by the United States during that President's administration that demonstrates the viewpoint or policy expressed in the statement. [5,5,5]

4 During various time periods in United States history, groups of people have been excluded from full participation in American society.

Groups

Native American Indians (1790–1890)
Latinos (1900–1970)
Japanese Americans (1900–1945)
Women (1940–1990)
African Americans (1945–1970)
Persons with disabilities (1910–1970)

a Select *three* of the groups listed. For *each* one selected, discuss a specific historical example of how the group was excluded from full participation in American society during the time period indicated. [4,4,4]

b For *one* of the groups you selected in answer to *a*, discuss a specific action taken by the Federal Government or a state government or an organization during or after the time period indicated to help this group achieve full participation in American society. [3]

5 Throughout United States history, the Federal and state governments have passed legislation to regulate the economy for a variety of purposes. Some of these purposes are listed below.

To protect the consumer
To regulate industry
To improve transportation
To promote business competition
To regulate trade
To regulate banking

Choose *three* of the purposes listed and for *each* one chosen:

• Identify a specific governmental action taken to achieve this purpose [Use a different specific action for each purpose.]
• Explain why the governmental action was taken
• Discuss the impact of the action on the United States   [5,5,5]

6 Individuals have made significant contributions to social, economic, and political change in the United States.

Individuals

W.E.B. Du Bois
Henry Ford
Samuel Gompers
Eleanor Roosevelt
Margaret Sanger
Elizabeth Cady Stanton
Harriet Tubman

Choose *three* of the individuals listed and for *each* one chosen:

- Identify a specific social, economic, *or* political change that individual attempted to bring about in the United States
- Discuss efforts made by that individual to bring about that change
- Describe an impact of that individual's efforts on the United States   [5,5,5]

7 A variety of concerns face the United States during the 1990's.

Areas of Concern

Crime
Education
Employment
Health care
Social Security system
Welfare

Choose *three* of the areas of concern listed and for *each* one chosen:

- Discuss a specific problem of the 1990's in that area of concern
- Show how a specific action that has been taken by government or by an organization has attempted to deal with that problem   [5,5,5]

Part I (55 credits)

Answer all 47 questions in this part.

Directions (1–47): For each statement or question, write on the separate answer sheet the *number* of the word or expression that, of those given, best completes the statement or answers the question.

1 In the Colonial Era, developments such as the New England town meetings and the establishment of the Virginia House of Burgesses represented
  1 colonial attempts to build a strong national government
  2 efforts by the British to strengthen their control over the colonies
  3 steps in the growth of representative democracy
  4 early social reform movements

2 According to the Declaration of Independence, the people have the right to alter or abolish a government if that government
  1 is a limited monarchy
  2 violates natural rights
  3 becomes involved in entangling alliances
  4 favors one religion over another

3 During the debates over the ratification of the United States Constitution, Federalists and Anti-Federalists disagreed most strongly over the
  1 division of powers between the national and state governments
  2 provision for admitting new states to the Union
  3 distribution of power between the Senate and the House of Representatives
  4 method of amending the Constitution

4 Which constitutional provision was intended to give the people the most influence over the Federal Government?
  1 President's duty to give Congress information about the state of the Union
  2 electoral college system for choosing the President
  3 direct election of members of the House of Representatives for two-year terms
  4 process for proposing and ratifying amendments to the Constitution

5 One similarity between the United States Constitution and the New York State Constitution is that both
  1 provide methods for dealing with foreign powers
  2 authorize the coinage of money
  3 establish rules for public education
  4 separate the branches of government

6 The 14th amendment provides that no "state [shall] deprive any person of life, liberty, or property, without due process of law; nor deny to any person within its jurisdiction the equal protection of the laws." A direct result of this amendment was that
  1 the process of amending the Constitution became slower and more complex
  2 the guarantees in the Bill of Rights were applied to state actions
  3 every citizen gained an absolute right to freedom of speech and assembly
  4 the power of the Federal Government was sharply reduced

7 When John Marshall was Chief Justice, United States Supreme Court decisions tended to strengthen the power of
  1 the National Government
  2 state and local governments
  3 labor unions
  4 trusts and monopolies

8 An example of the unwritten constitution in the United States is the
  1 sharing of power by the national and state governments
  2 development of the political party system
  3 separation of powers among the three branches of government
  4 guarantees of due process of law

Base your answer to question 9 on this excerpt from a newspaper article and on your knowledge of social studies.

> WASHINGTON, Dec 4 -- Supporters of limits on Congressional terms gathered in the nation's capital today, ...
>
> Limiting the number of years that members of Congress could serve to 12 years -- six terms for House members and two terms for senators -- would force more competition into the system. . . supporters of term limits said this year's elections, with a 96 percent re-election rate in the House, showed how hard it was for even an angry electorate to defeat incumbents.
>
> -- The New York Times,
> December 1990

9 The major reason for increased support for the change discussed in the article is the public's belief that
1 most current members of Congress have taken bribes
2 the President's political party should have a majority in Congress
3 political disputes in Congress would be reduced
4 the democratic process would be strengthened

---

10 Alexander Hamilton's argument that the government has the power to create a National Bank is based on which part of the Constitution?
1 the Preamble
2 the elastic clause
3 guarantees to the States
4 the Bill of Rights

11 The legal basis for the United States purchase of the Louisiana Territory was the
1 power granted to the President to make treaties
2 President's power as Commander in Chief
3 authority of Congress to declare war
4 Senate's duty to approve the appointment of ambassadors

12 The reason for ending the importation of enslaved persons to the United States after 1807 was the
1 success of the American colonial revolution against Britain
2 rapid industrialization of the South
3 replacement of slave labor by immigrant workers from eastern Europe
4 passage of legislation that forbids the practice

13 After the passage of the 13th, 14th, and 15th amendments, African Americans continued to experience political and economic oppression mainly because
1 the amendments were not intended to solve their problems
2 many African Americans distrusted the Federal Government
3 Southern legislatures enacted Jim Crow laws
4 poor communications kept people from learning about their legal rights

Base your answers to questions 14 and 15 on the speakers' statements and on your knowledge of social studies.

Speaker A: "The business of America is business, and we would be wise to remember that."

Speaker B: "Government ownership of business is superior to private enterprise."

Speaker C: "Strict government regulation of business practices is a means to insure the public good."

Speaker D: "Only through personal effort can wealth and success be achieved."

14 Which speaker best expresses the main idea of rugged individualism?
(1) *A*   (3) *C*
(2) *B*   (4) *D*

15 Which speaker would most likely have supported the ideas of the Progressive movement?
(1) *A*   (3) *C*
(2) *B*   (4) *D*

                                     [OVER]

16 Which term best describes United States economic policy during the era of the rise of big business (1865–1900)?
1 laissez-faire capitalism
2 mercantilism
3 Marxism
4 welfare-state capitalism

17 Which statement best describes the status of the labor union movement in the United States in 1900?
1 Most of the labor force was organized into unions.
2 Government and business opposition had destroyed the labor union movement.
3 Unions were still struggling to gain public acceptance.
4 Unions had won the right to strike and bargain collectively.

18 The purpose of the Interstate Commerce Act (1887), the Sherman Antitrust Act (1890), and the Clayton Antitrust Act (1914) was to
1 eliminate unfair business practices
2 reduce imports from foreign nations
3 reduce the power of the unions
4 increase the power of local governments

19 Why did the United States follow a policy of unrestricted immigration for Europeans during most of the 1800's?
1 Business and industry depended on the foreign capital brought by immigrants.
2 The American economy needed many unskilled workers.
3 Most Americans desired a more diversified culture.
4 The United States wanted to help European nations by taking in their surplus population.

20 In the early 20th century, muckrakers were able to influence American society mainly through their
1 frequent acts of civil disobedience
2 activities as government officials
3 publication of articles and books
4 control over factories

21 The initiative, referendum, recall, and direct primary are all intended to
1 make the President more responsive to the wishes of Congress
2 reduce the influence of the media on elections
3 give political parties more control of the electoral process
4 increase participation in government by citizens

22 The main reason the United States developed the Open Door policy was to
1 allow the United States to expand its trade with China
2 demonstrate the positive features of democracy to Chinese leaders
3 aid the Chinese Nationalists in their struggle with the Chinese Communists
4 encourage Chinese workers to come to the United States

23 President Theodore Roosevelt's policies toward Latin America were evidence of his belief in
1 noninvolvement in world affairs
2 intervention when American business interests were threatened
3 the sovereign rights of all nations
4 the need for European interference in the Western Hemisphere

24 The "clear and present danger" ruling in the Supreme Court case *Schenck* v. *United States* (1919) confirmed the idea that
1 prayer in public schools is unconstitutional
2 racism in the United States is illegal
3 interstate commerce can be regulated by state governments
4 constitutional rights are not absolute

25 A major reason for the isolationist trend in the United States following World War I was
1 a desire to continue the reforms of the Progressives
2 the public's desire to end most trade with other nations
3 the failure of the United States to gain new territory
4 a disillusionment over the failure to achieve United States goals in the postwar world

26 Which events best support the image of the 1920's as a decade of nativist sentiment?
  1 the passage of the National Origins Act and the rise of the Ku Klux Klan
  2 the Scopes trial and the passage of women's suffrage
  3 the Washington Naval Conference and the Kellogg-Briand Pact
  4 the growth of the auto industry and the Teapot Dome affair

Base your answers to questions 27 and 28 on the statements below and on your knowledge of social studies.

Statement A: The best way to economic recovery is to subsidize industry so that it will hire more workers and expand production.

Statement B: If jobs are not available, the government must create jobs for those who are unemployed.

Statement C: According to human nature, the most talented people will always come out on top.

Statement D: Our government is responsible for the nation's economic well-being.

27 Which statement is closest to the philosophy of Social Darwinism?
  (1) *A*   (3) *C*
  (2) *B*   (4) *D*

28 Which statements most strongly support the actions of President Franklin D. Roosevelt?
  (1) *A* and *C*   (3) *C* and *D*
  (2) *B* and *C*   (4) *B* and *D*

29 Which action best illustrates the policy of isolationism followed by the United States before it entered World War II?
  1 signing of a collective security pact with Latin American nations
  2 passage of neutrality legislation forbidding arms sales to warring nations
  3 embargo on the sale of gasoline and steel to Japan
  4 President Franklin D. Roosevelt's exchange of American destroyers for British naval and air bases

30 Deficit spending by the Federal Government as a means of reviving the economy is based on the idea that
  1 purchasing power will increase and economic growth will be stimulated
  2 only the National Government can operate businesses efficiently
  3 the National Government should turn its revenue over to the states
  4 lower interest rates will encourage investment

31 President Harry Truman justified using atomic bombs on Japan in 1945 on the grounds that the
  1 world was ready for a demonstration of nuclear power
  2 Axis powers deserved total destruction
  3 early ending of the war would save many lives
  4 American public demanded that the bombs be used

32 Which precedent was established by the Nuremberg war crimes trials?
  1 National leaders can be held responsible for crimes against humanity.
  2 Only individuals who actually commit murder during a war can be guilty of a crime.
  3 Defeated nations cannot be forced to pay reparations.
  4 Defeated nations can be occupied by the victors.

33 In the years just after World War II, the United States attempted to prevent the spread of communism in Europe mainly by
  1 taking over the governments of several Western European nations
  2 increasing opportunities for political refugees to settle in the United States
  3 holding a series of summit meetings with leaders of the Soviet Union
  4 establishing policies of economic and military aid for European nations

34 Throughout United States history, the most important aim of the country's foreign policy has been
  1 participation in international organizations
  2 advancement of national self-interest
  3 containment of communism
  4 development of military alliances

[OVER]

Base your answers to questions 35 and 36 on the graph below and on your knowledge of social studies.

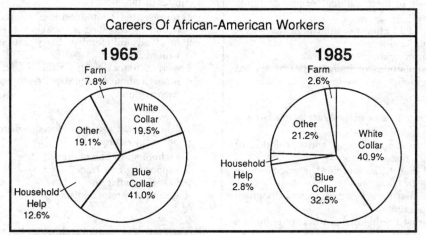

Careers Of African-American Workers

1965

Farm 7.8%

White Collar 19.5%

Other 19.1%

Blue Collar 41.0%

Household Help 12.6%

1985

Farm 2.6%

Other 21.2%

White Collar 40.9%

Household Help 2.8%

Blue Collar 32.5%

Sources: U.S. Bureau of the Census; U.S. Labor Dept.

35 Which statement is best supported by the data in the graph?

1 African Americans are increasingly entering white-collar occupations.
2 Professional opportunities for African Americans were as limited in 1985 as they were in 1965.
3 An increasing percentage of African Americans are unemployed.
4 The United States economy has little need for skilled African-American workers.

36 Which factor best explains the situation shown in the graph?

1 an increase in imports of consumer goods from foreign nations
2 an increase in the wages of agricultural and household service workers
3 an increase in educational opportunities combined with affirmative action programs
4 a growing refusal by blue-collar employers to hire African Americans

37 Under Chief Justice Earl Warren, the Supreme Court was considered "activist" because of its

1 reluctance to overturn state laws
2 insistence on restricting freedom of speech to spoken words
3 expansion of individual rights in criminal cases
4 refusal to reconsider the issues of the *Plessy* v. *Ferguson* case

38 When necessary to achieve justice, which method did Martin Luther King, Jr., urge his followers to employ?

1 using violence to bring about political change
2 engaging in civil disobedience
3 leaving any community in which racism is practiced
4 demanding that Congress pay reparations to African Americans

39 In 1988, Congress voted to pay $20,000 to each of the surviving Americans of Japanese descent who were interned during World War II because

1 the danger of war with Japan no longer existed
2 all of the interned Japanese Americans eventually became American citizens
3 the World Court ordered the United States to pay reparations
4 many Americans believed the internment was unjust and unnecessary

40 A common characteristic of third political parties in the United States is that they

1 tend to focus on one person or one issue
2 come into existence only during periods of corruption
3 have dealt mainly with foreign policy issues
4 have frequently forced Congress to decide Presidential elections

41 The major political parties in the United States obtain most of their national campaign funds from
1 the personal fortunes of the candidates
2 state and local taxes
3 funds appropriated by Congress
4 the contributions of individuals and special interest groups

42 The main significance of the Watergate affair was that it
1 led to the impeachment and conviction of President Richard Nixon
2 showed that the laws of the United States are superior to the actions of a President
3 was the first time a President had disagreed with Congress
4 proved that Presidential powers are unlimited

43 "The great rule of conduct for us in regard to foreign nations is, in extending our commercial relations, to have with them as little political connection as possible."

This quotation supports a foreign policy of
1 imperialism   3 neutrality
2 appeasement   4 economic sanctions

44 The Korean War and the Persian Gulf War were similar in that both
1 represented United Nations efforts to assist nations in repelling aggressors
2 involved unilateral military action by the United States
3 were military defeats for the United Nations
4 brought about lasting solutions to problems in each region

45 Raising import duties on foreign manufactured goods is an example of
1 technological competition
2 supporting free trade
3 lowering inflation
4 economic protectionism

46 The growth of modern technology has resulted in
1 a decrease in the population of the world
2 increasing interdependence among nations
3 a growing need for unskilled labor
4 a sharp decline in the need for oil and coal

☞ GO RIGHT ON TO THE NEXT PAGE.

Base your answer to question 47 on the cartoon below and on your knowledge of social studies.

47 What is the main idea of the cartoon?
  1 Native Americans and Europeans showed a great willingness to share knowledge at their first contact.
  2 Spanish colonization in the Americas preceded British colonization.
  3 American society has failed to recognize the achievements of Native Americans.
  4 The pluralistic heritage of the United States began to receive approval early in the nation's history.

Answers to the following questions are to be written on paper provided by the school.

Students Please Note:

In developing your answers to Parts II and III, be sure to

(1) include specific factual information and evidence whenever possible
(2) keep to the questions asked; do not go off on tangents
(3) avoid overgeneralizations or sweeping statements without sufficient proof; do not overstate your case
(4) keep these general definitions in mind:

    (a) <u>discuss</u> means "to make observations about something using facts, reasoning, and argument; to present in some detail"

    (b) <u>describe</u> means "to illustrate something in words or tell about it"

    (c) <u>show</u> means "to point out; to set forth clearly a position or idea by stating it and giving data which support it"

    (d) <u>explain</u> means "to make plain or understandable; to give reasons for or causes of; to show the logical development or relationships of"

Part II

ANSWER ONE QUESTION FROM THIS PART. [15]

1 In United States history, the system of checks and balances has operated to limit or to strengthen the powers of the branches of the Federal Government.

Examples of Checks and Balances

    Judicial review
    Impeachment process
    Presidential appointment of Supreme Court Justices
    Presidential veto
    —Presidential war powers
    Treaty ratification

Choose *three* of the examples listed and for *each* one chosen:

- Describe its use during a specific historical conflict between two branches of the Federal Government
- Explain how one branch of government either lost or gained power as a result of this conflict   [5,5,5]

2 Many disputes have been brought before the United States Supreme Court. Below are listed Supreme Court cases and the constitutional issue involved in each case.

Cases — Issues

    McCulloch v. *Maryland* (1819) — federalism
    — *Dred Scott* v. *Sanford* (1857) — property rights
    Plessy v. *Ferguson* (1896) — civil rights
    Korematsu v. *United States* (1944) — Presidential power
    Engel v. *Vitale* (1962) — freedom of religion
    Miranda v. *Arizona* (1966) — due process
    Roe v. *Wade* (1973) — right to privacy

Choose *three* cases from the list. For *each* one chosen:

- Show how the constitutional issue listed was involved in the case
- State the Supreme Court's decision in the case
- Discuss an impact of the decision on United States history   [5,5,5]

Part III

ANSWER TWO QUESTIONS FROM THIS PART.   [30]

3 Throughout United States history, opportunities of some groups of people have been limited.

Groups

Hispanics or Haitians
Native Americans
Senior citizens
Persons with disabilities
One religious group of your choice
[Identify the group.]

Choose *three* of the groups listed. For *each* one chosen:

- Show how the opportunities of that group have been limited at some time in United States history [Be sure to include specific historical information in your answer.]

- Describe *one* way that government has attempted to improve the opportunities of that group   [5,5,5]

4 National controversy has frequently occurred in United States history.

National Controversies

Writing of the United States Constitution
Westward expansion
Annexation of the Philippines
Restriction of immigration
Containment of communism in Southeast Asia
National health care policy

Choose *three* of the controversies listed and for *each* one chosen:

- Describe the historical background of the controversy
- Explain the differences of opinion held by two opposing sides regarding the controversy   [5,5,5]

5 Prominent individuals in United States history who have held differing views on the same issue are paired in the list below.

Individuals

Thomas Jefferson — Alexander Hamilton
Theodore Roosevelt — John D. Rockefeller
Booker T. Washington — W.E.B. DuBois
Woodrow Wilson — Henry Cabot Lodge
Herbert Hoover — Franklin D. Roosevelt
Lyndon B. Johnson — Ronald Reagan

Select *three* of the pairs of individuals. For *each* one chosen, identify one issue about which they had differing views. Discuss the point of view held by each individual concerning the issue. Be sure to include specific historical information in your answer.   [5,5,5]

[OVER]

6 Reform movements have sought to solve many problems in American society.

Reform Movements

Radical Republicans during Reconstruction
Populism
– Progressivism
– Women's movement
Prohibition movement
– Civil rights movement after World War II

Choose *three* of the reform movements and for *each* one chosen:

• Describe a problem the movement attempted to solve
• Discuss the extent to which the movement was successful in solving the problem
   [5,5,5]

7 The Great Depression was the most severe economic depression in the history of the United States.

a Describe *two* causes of the Great Depression in the United States.   [6]

b Show how each of *three* New Deal programs attempted to remedy problems that arose during the Great Depression.   [9]

Glossary of Social Studies Terms: What You Need to Know _____

Below is a list of the most important social studies terms that you need to know to pass the Regents Examination. Terms marked with an asterisk (*) are the most frequently tested.

abolitionist   a person seeking the legal end of slavery in the United States

***affirmative action**   steps taken to increase the representation of women and minorities, especially in jobs and higher education

agrarian protest   demands by farmers for improvements in areas affecting agriculture, especially in the late 1800s

alien   a citizen of a foreign country

alliance   group of nations mutually allied by treaty

Allies   nations that fought against the Central Powers during World War I and against the Axis Powers during World War II

***amendment**   a change in or addition to a legal document, motion, bylaw, law, or constitution

American System   a plan offered by Henry Clay for internal improvements

annex   to attach new territory to an existing area, such as a country

Antifederalist   person opposed to the Constitution during the ratification debate in 1787

***anti-Semitism**   prejudice against Jews

antitrust   opposed to trusts, monopolies, price-fixing, and other agreements that restrain trade

***appeasement**   the policy of giving in to an aggressor nation in the hope that this will satisfy it and encourage it to stop being aggressive

appellate jurisdiction   authority of a court to review decisions of inferior (lower) courts

***Articles of Confederation**   the first American constitution

assassination   murder of a public figure

***assembly line**   method of production in which automobiles or other items being manufactured move past workers and machines and are assembled piece by piece until completed

assimilation   process of becoming part of another culture

assumption plan   the taking over of state debts by the federal government after the Revolutionary War

atomic age   term used to describe the period begun by the explosion of the first atomic bomb in 1945

baby boom   the rapid growth in U.S. population between 1945 and 1960

balance of power   a condition, often achieved by alliances, in which two countries or groups of countries are roughly equal in power, and neither can become dominant

balance of terror   a balance of power achieved when opposing sides possess nuclear weapons

balance of trade   the difference in value between a nation's imports and its exports

bankruptcy   court action to release a person or corporation from unpaid debts

belligerents   nations fighting a war, usually after a declaration of war

bicameral legislature   a lawmaking body composed of two houses

*big business corporations or monopolies seen as having too much control over a society and its economy

bill a proposal presented to a legislative body for possible enactment as a law

*Bill of Rights first ten amendments to the Constitution of the United States, dealing mostly with civil rights

bipartisan supported by two political parties

Black Codes laws passed, especially by the Southern states after the Civil War, to control the actions and limit the rights of blacks

blacklist a list, circulated among employers, of people who will not be hired because of their views, beliefs, or actions

blitzkrieg a sudden invasion or "lightning war," first practiced by the Germans in World War II

blockade shutting off a port to keep people or supplies from moving in or out

blue-collar worker someone who holds an industrial or factory job

boycott an organized refusal to buy or use a product, or to deal with a company or group of companies, as a protest or as a means of forcing them to take some action

brinkmanship the policy of being willing to go "to the brink of war" to preserve peace

*Brown v. Board of Education 1954 Supreme Court decision that overturned *Plessy* v. *Ferguson* and declared segregation in public schools unconstitutional

bureaucracy all the men and women, taken as a group, who run the agencies that do the everyday business of government

cabinet group of officials who head government departments and advise the President

capitalism economic system based on private ownership of the means of producing goods and services and upon private initiative, competition, and profit

carpetbagger name for a Northerner who went to the South during Reconstruction

*change alter, make different

*checks and balances system set up by the Constitution in which each branch of the federal government has the power to check, or limit, the actions of the other branches

choice selection, the power to select

citizen a person who by birth or nationalization owes loyalty to, and receives the protection of, a nation's government

citizenship the duties, rights, and privileges of a citizen

*civil disobedience nonviolent protest against unjust laws

civil liberties certain rights guaranteed to the citizens of a nation

civil rights rights guaranteed to U.S. citizens by the Constitution and laws of the nation

*civil service government jobs for which appointments and promotions are based on merit rather than on political patronage

closed shop a workplace where employees must be labor union members in order to be hired

coalition an alliance of political groups

*cold war state of tension between nations without actual warfare, especially the relationship of the United States and the Soviet Union after World War II

collective bargaining process whereby a union negotiates with management for a contract

*collective security system in which member nations agree to take joint action to meet any threat or breach of international peace

colonialism practice under which a parent country takes control of other lands for its economic, military, or other use

colony group of people settled in a distant land who are ruled by the government of their native land

commerce clause Article I, Section 8, Clause 3 of the Constitution, which gives Congress the power to regulate trade

committee system   method under which members of the legislative branch form into smaller groups to facilitate such business as considering proposed legislation and holding investigations

*__communism__   economic and political system based on the collective ownership of property and the means of production, with all individuals expected to contribute to society according to ability and receive from it according to need

*__compromise__   the resolution of conflict in which concessions are made by all parties to achieve a common goal

concentration camp   camp where political opponents or other "enemies" of a nation are confined, especially those established by Nazi Germany before and during World War II

concurrent powers   powers shared by the national and state governments

confederation   an alliance of independent states

conference committee   temporary joint committee of both houses of a legislature, created to reconcile differences between the two houses' versions of a bill

conglomerate   a corporation that owns many different, unrelated businesses

*__Congress__   the legislative, or lawmaking, branch of the United States government, made up of the Senate and the House of Representatives

consent of the governed   principle that says people are the source of the powers of government

conservation   the careful use or preserving of natural resources

conspicuous consumption   public enjoyment of costly possessions done in a way to emphasize the fact that one can afford such possessions

*__constitution__   body of fundamental law, setting out the basic principles, structures, processes, and functions of a government and placing limits on its actions; (Cap.) the supreme law of the United States

*__Constitutional Convention__   formal meeting of state delegates in Philadelphia in 1787 at which the Constitution was written

constitutional   permissible under the Constitution

*__consumer__   person who spends money on goods and services

consumer goods   goods produced for use by individuals as opposed to use by businesses

consumer protection   measures to shield buyers of goods and services from unsafe products and unfair or illegal sales practices

*__containment__   the U.S. policy after World War II of trying to keep the Soviet Union from expanding its area of influence and dominance

corporation   business owned by many investors that raises money by selling stocks or shares to those investors

"court packing"   Franklin Roosevelt's 1937 plan to add justices to the Supreme Court

credit   delayed payment for goods or services

creditor nation   a nation that is owed money by other nations

cultural diversity   many cultures existing in the same society

cultural pluralism   the idea that different cultures can exist side by side in the same society, all contributing to the society without losing their identities

culture   the way of life of a given people

custom   a habit or practice so established it has the force of law

debtor nation   a nation that owes money to another nation or nations

*__Declaration of Independence__   the 1776 document that stated Britain's North American colonies had become free and independent of the parent country

deficit   the amount by which money spent is greater than money received

deficit spending   government practice of spending more money than it takes in from taxes and other revenues

delegated powers powers given by the Constitution to the national government and denied to state governments

demagogue a person who gains political power by rousing the passions of the people

demobilization the process by which a nation reconverts to peacetime status after a war or the threat of war

democracy system of government in which supreme authority rests with the people, either directly or through elected representatives

***Democratic party** one of the two major political parties in the United States

***depression** a long and severe decline in economic activity

détente the easing of tensions between nations

***dictatorship** form of government in which the power to govern is held by one person or a small group

direct democracy system of government in which the people participate directly in decision making through the voting process

***direct election of senators** system put into practice under the 17th Amendment whereby the voters rather than the state legislatures elect members of the U.S. Senate

disarmament reduction of a nation's armed forces or weapons of war

discrimination policy or attitude that denies rights to people based on race, religion, sex, or other characteristic

diversity variety

divestiture a refusal to hold stock in companies that have operations in South Africa

***division of powers** basic principle of federalism; the constitutional provisions by which governmental powers are divided between the national and the state governments

dollar diplomacy President Taft's policy of encouraging United States investment in Latin America

domestic policy everything a nation's government says and does in relation to internal matters

domino theory the idea, prevalent during the Vietnam War, that if one Asian nation became Communist, neighboring nations would as well

Dred Scott v. *Sanford* 1857 Supreme Court case that stated blacks could not be citizens and declared the Missouri Compromise unconstitutional

due process of law constitutional guarantee that government will not deprive any person of life, liberty, or property by any unfair, arbitrary, or unreasonable action

economic pertaining to production, distribution, and use of wealth

economic nationalism policies focused on improving the economy of one's own nation

***economic programs** any policies set forward by a government that relate to the workings of its economy

elastic clause Article I, Section 8, Clause 18 of the Constitution, which is the basis for the implied powers of Congress

***electoral college** an assembly elected by the voters that meets every four years to formally elect the President of the United States

electoral vote the results of the voting by the electoral college

electorate all the persons entitled to vote in a given election

emancipation the act of setting a person or people free

empathy the process of sharing and understanding the feelings or thoughts of another person

entrepreneur a person who organizes, operates, and assumes the risks of a business enterprise

environment natural surroundings and all the things that make them up

equal protection under the law a right guaranteed to American citizens under the 14th Amendment

espionage spying

ethnic group people of foreign birth or descent living in another country

European Economic Community organization, also known as the Common Market, formed in 1957 to ease trade and travel among member European nations

excise tax taxes levied on the production, transportation, sale, or consumption of goods or services

*executive branch part of a government that carries out its laws

executive power the powers of the head of an executive branch of government to carry out the laws

executive privilege the right claimed by Presidents to withhold information from the legislative or judicial branches

expansionism desire to enlarge the territory owned or controlled by one's nation

expatriate a person who gives up her or his homeland to live in another country

expressed powers those delegated powers of the national government that are given to it in so many words by the Constitution

farm output total value of products produced by a nation's farms

fascism political philosophy that calls for glorification of the state, a single party system with a strong ruler, and aggressive nationalism

*federal government the central or national government

federalism a system of government in which authority is divided between national and state governments; the belief in or advocacy of such a system

Federal Reserve System the nation's central bank; a system of 12 regional banks overseen by a central board

Federalist supporter of the Constitution in the ratification debate of 1787, favored a strong national government

feminist movement the struggle of women for equality

1st Amendment Bill of Rights' guarantee of freedom of religion, speech, press, assembly, and petition

fiscal policy policies relating to a nation's finances

flapper nickname for a young woman in the 1920s who declared her independence from traditional rules

*foreign policy the actions and stands that every nation takes in every aspect of its relationships with other countries; everything a nation's government says and does in world affairs

14th Amendment "due process" amendment that gave blacks the right to vote and extended Bill of Rights protections to citizens of the states

free enterprise an economic system based on private ownership, individual enterprise, and competition

*freedom of speech the right of freedom of expression guaranteed to Americans by the 1st Amendment

frontier the border of a country; as defined by the U.S. Bureau of the Census, the edge of settlement beyond which the land was occupied by two or fewer people per square mile

frontier thesis idea set forth by historian Frederick Jackson Turner that the nation's frontier regions shaped its character and institutions

fugitive slave clause Article IV, Section 2, Clause 3 of the Constitution which required states to return runaway slaves to their owners

fundamentalist one who believes that the Bible is the literal word of God

*genocide the systematic destruction of a race of people

Gentlemen's Agreement informal agreement between the United States and Japan in 1907 to limit Japanese immigration to this country

Gilded Age term used to describe the period from 1865 to 1900

glasnost a period of "openness" in relations between the United States and the Soviet Union that began in the late 1980s

*****global interdependence** the idea that the nations of the world must rely on each other in many different ways, including trade, transportation, and communication

gold standard a system in which a nation's currency is based on the value of gold

Good Neighbor Policy Franklin D. Roosevelt's policy toward Latin America intended to strengthen relations with the nations of that region

government that complex of offices, personnel, and processes by which a state is ruled, and by which its public policies are made and enforced

grandfather clause laws passed in some Southern states giving the right to vote only to people who had that right on January 1, 1867, and their descendants; intended to keep blacks from voting

Grangers organization of farmers founded for social reasons in 1867, which later campaigned for state regulation of railroads and other reforms

grass-roots support political backing from ordinary citizens, especially from rural areas

Great Compromise the plan for a two-house legislature adopted at the Constitutional Convention in 1787 that settled differences between large and small states over representation in Congress

*****Great Depression** period of economic hard times from 1929 to 1941

Great Society the name given to President Johnson's domestic program in the 1960s

gross national product (GNP) the total value of all the goods and services produced in a nation in a year

guerrilla warfare fighting by stealth and with small bands, which make surprise raids against stronger forces

*****Harlem Renaissance** name given to the burst of artistic accomplishments by black Americans in the 1920s

hemisphere half of the earth's surface

holding company a company that gains control of other companies by buying their stock

*****Holocaust** name given to Nazi Germany's persecution of Jews before and during World War II; in this time, more than 6 million Jews died

*****House of Representatives** lower house of the U.S. Congress in which states are represented according to the size of their populations

*****human rights** basic rights that should belong to all people including freedom of speech, religion, and the press

humanitarian one who is concerned with the welfare of all people

*****immigration** the movement of people from other countries into a country

*****immigration laws** laws controlling the movement of people into a country

immigration quota limit on immigration allowing only a certain number of people to move into a country during a specified period

impeachment the process by which the House of Representatives makes an accusation of wrongdoing against the President or other high federal officials

*****imperialism** policy by which one country takes control of another either directly or through economic or political dominance

implied powers those delegated powers of the national government implied by (inferred from) the expressed powers; those powers "necessary and proper" to carry out the expressed powers

income tax a tax levied on individual and corporate income

indemnities money paid by a losing nation to a winning nation after a war

independence freedom from the control, influence, or support of other people or nations

*****individual rights** basic rights that belong to each person

*industrialization process by which a nation begins to develop large industries

inflation an economic condition in which prices rise substantially over a significant period of time

injunction a court order prohibiting a given action; used frequently against workers in 19th-century labor-management disputes

*interdependence a condition in which parties are reliant on each other

internal affairs public or business matters within the boundaries of a country

internal improvements roads, bridges, canals, and other similar projects funded by the national government

international law the norms of behavior generally agreed to and followed by the nations of the world in their dealings with each other

internationalism the belief, held by some Americans in the 1930s, that the United States should aid the victims of international aggression

internment camps places of confinement, especially in wartime

*interstate commerce trade among the states

*intervention interference by one nation in the affairs of another

intrastate commerce trade within the borders of a state

Iron Curtain the line between Soviet-dominated Eastern Europe and the West, so-called because the Soviets and their satellite nations prevented the free passage of people, information, and ideas across their borders

*isolationism a policy of avoiding alliances and other types of involvement in the affairs of other nations

isthmus a narrow strip or neck of land running from one larger land area to another

Japanese-American relocation policy under which Americans of Japanese ancestry were confined to internment camps during World War II

"Jim Crow" laws laws in the Southern states in the 19th and 20th centuries that forced the segregation of the races

jingoism aggressive nationalism

joint resolution legislative measure which must be passed by both houses and approved by the chief executive to become effective; similar to a bill, with the force of law, and often used for unusual or temporary purposes

judicial activism broad interpretation of the Constitution leading to court-directed change

judicial branch part of the government that decides if laws are carried out fairly

judicial restraint narrow interpretation of the Constitution

*judicial review power of the Supreme Court to determine the constitutionality of acts of the legislative and executive branches of the government

*judiciary judicial branch of a government, its system of courts

jurisdiction power of a court to hear (to try and decide) a case

jury a group of people who hear evidence in a legal case and give a decision based on that evidence

justice fairness; trial and judgment according to established processes of the law

Know Nothing Party common name for the American Party, a nativist political organization formed in 1849

Ku Klux Klan secret society first formed in the South during Reconstruction to ensure white supremacy over blacks; reformed in the 1920s to express opposition to Jews, Catholics, Bolsheviks, and others considered "un-American"

labor union workers organized as a group to seek higher wages, improved working conditions, and other benefits

*laissez faire noninterference; has come to mean a policy by which the government minimizes its regulation of industry and the economy

landslide election an election in which a victorious candidate gathers an overwhelming percentage of the total votes cast

law rule recognized by a nation, state, or community as binding on its members

*League of Nations association of nations to protect the independence of member nations, proposed by President Wilson in his Fourteen Points and formed after World War I

legislative branch the lawmaking agencies of a government

*legislature group of people with the power of making laws for a nation or state

*less developed nations nations that have not fully industrialized, usually Third World nations

liberal not strict; tolerant; favoring progress and reform

lifespan the lifetime of an individual

limited government basic principle of the American system of government; belief that government is not all-powerful, and may only do those things the people have given it the power to do

literacy the ability to read and write

literacy test test of a potential voter's ability to read and write once used in several states to prevent blacks and other minorities from voting; now outlawed

lobby to attempt to influence legislation; also, groups that attempt to do so

lockout during a labor dispute, the closing of a business (by locking the gates) to keep employees from entering

loose interpretation a belief that the provisions of the Constitution, especially those granting power to the government, are to be construed in broad terms

lynch to execute someone illegally, by hanging, burning, or other means

majority at least one more than half (*e.g.*, over 50 percent of the votes in an election)

Manifest Destiny a commonly held belief in the first half of the 19th century that the United States had a mission to expand its borders to incorporate all land between the Atlantic and Pacific oceans

Marbury v. _Madison_ 1803 case in which John Marshall first asserted the Supreme Court's power of judicial review

margin a small part of the total price of a stock purchase deposited with a broker at the time of purchase with the promise to pay the full sum at a later date

mass circulation reaching a very large audience

mass production rapid manufacture of large numbers of a product

Mayflower Compact agreement signed by Pilgrims before landing at Plymouth

McCulloch v. _Maryland_ 1819 Supreme Court case that asserted supremacy of the federal over the state governments and upheld the doctrine of implied powers

melting pot theory the idea that different immigrant groups in the United States will lose their old identities here and that a new American identity will emerge from the blending of cultures

mercantilism economic theory that a nation's strength came from building up its gold supplies and expanding its trade

merger a combining of two or more companies into a larger company

*militarism policy of building up strong military forces to prepare for war

minimum wage the lowest wage that can be paid to certain workers as set by national or state law

minor party one of the less widely supported political parties in a governmental system

*minority less than half

*minority group group within a nation that differs from most of the population in race, religion, national origin, etc.

missionary one who attempts to spread the religious ideas of a faith in a foreign land

mobilization   a call-up of military forces, usually in preparation for war

monarchy   government headed by a single ruler, usually a king or queen

monetary policy   actions and positions taken by a government in regard to its system of money

*****monopoly**   dominance in or control of a market for certain goods or services by a single company or combination of companies

*****Monroe Doctrine**   policy statement of President James Monroe in 1823 warning nations of western Europe not to interfere with the newly independent nations of Latin America

moral diplomacy   a term describing President Woodrow Wilson's approach to foreign policy, which emphasized the use of negotiation and arbitration rather than force to settle international disputes

*****muckraker**   early 20th-century American journalist who tried to improve society by exposing political corruption, health hazards, and other social problems

multilateral action   joint action taken by three or more nations

municipal government   the government of a city, town, or village

NAACP   the National Association for the Advancement of Colored People, an organization founded in 1909 to fight for the rights of African Americans

*****NATO**   the North Atlantic Treaty Organization, an alliance formed for mutual defense in 1949 under the North Atlantic Treaty, and now made up of 15 nations stretching from Canada to Turkey

national bank   bank chartered by the federal government

*****national government**   in the United States, the federal government

National Organization for Women (NOW)   founded in 1966 to work for equal rights for women

national self interest   aim of all foreign policy

nationalism   pride in or devotion to one's country

nativism   a belief in the superiority of the way of life of one's home country; in the United States, this was often associated with a desire to limit immigration

natural rights   rights that all people are entitled to from birth

naturalization   the process by which a citizen of one country becomes a citizen of another

Nazism   belief in the policies of Adolf Hitler

necessary and proper clause   another name for the elastic clause, which is the basis of the implied powers of Congress

negotiation   talking over an issue by two or more parties with the aim of reaching a mutually agreeable settlement

*****neutrality**   the policy of not taking sides in a dispute or a war

*****New Deal**   name given to the programs of President Franklin D. Roosevelt

New Federalism   name given to the attempt to lessen the federal government role in its dealings with states during the presidencies of Nixon and Reagan

New Freedom   name given to the programs of President Woodrow Wilson

New Frontier   name given to the programs of President John F. Kennedy

New Nationalism   plan under which Theodore Roosevelt ran for President in 1912

nominating convention   political gathering at which a party names its candidates for office

*****noninvolvement**   policy of taking no side in internation disputes, neutrality

nonrecognition   refusal to establish formal diplomatic relations with the new government of a nation

"normalcy"   President Warren G. Harding's term for the return to peace after World War I

nuclear freeze   a halt in the manufacture and deployment of nuclear weapons

nuclear power   energy produced from a controlled atomic reaction

nuclear waste the byproducts of the production of nuclear power

Nuremberg Trials post-World War II trials in which German government and military figures were tried for crimes committed during the war

Open Door Policy policy toward China set out by Secretary of State John Hay allowing any nation to trade in any other nation's sphere of influence

original jurisdiction the court in which a case is heard firsthand

overproduction a condition that exists when the supply of a product exceeds the demand for that product

pacifist a person who is opposed to war and refuses to fight under any circumstances

pardon grant of a release from the punishment or legal consequences of a crime by a President or governor

Parliament the legislature of Great Britain

partnership ownership of a business by two or more individuals

patent and copyright laws laws giving rights to inventions, literary, musical, and artistic works to their creators

patriotism love and support of one's nation

"peaceful coexistence" phrase describing the aim of U.S.–Soviet relations during a time of improved relations between those nations in the 1950s

per capita income income per person

perestroika the restructuring of the Soviet Union's economy under Mikhail Gorbachev that began a move toward free enterprise

plantation large estate farmed by many workers

*Plessy v. Ferguson 1896 case in which the Supreme Court upheld segregation by declaring "separate but equal" public facilities legal

political party organized group that seeks to control government through the winning of elections and the holding of public office

*political system the way a nation is governed

poll tax a tax that must be paid before one can vote, often used in Southern states to discourage or prevent blacks from voting and now banned in national elections by the 24th Amendment

pool method of ending competition used by railroads in the late 1800s in which they divided up business in given areas and fixed prices

popular sovereignty basic principle of the American system of government that the people are the only source of any and all governmental power

popular vote votes cast by the people for the electors representing candidates in presidential elections

*Populist movement political movement begun by farmers and members of labor unions in the late 1800s seeking to limit the power of big businesses and grant greater say in the governmental process to individuals

power control, authority, right

preamble an introduction to a speech or piece of writing

prejudice unfavorable opinion about people who are of different religion, race, or nationality

President the chief executive of a modern republic, especially of the United States

primary election held before a general election in which voters choose their party's candidates for office

*Progressive era the period 1900–1920 that saw the greatest action by Progressive reformers

*Progressive movement reform movement that worked to correct abuses in American society

Prohibition the period 1920–1933 when the making and sale of liquor was illegal in the United States

propaganda spreading of ideas or beliefs that help a particular cause and hurt an opposing cause

protectionism belief in policies that favor the protection of domestically produced goods

*__protective tariff__ tax on imports designed to discourage their sale and to favor the development of domestic industry

protectorate a country under the protection and partial control of a stronger country

public opinion those attitudes held by a significant number of persons on matters of government and politics; expressed group attitudes

"pump-priming" term used to describe an increase in government spending toward the goal of stimulating the nation's economy

purchasing power the ability to buy goods and services; the value of what money could buy at one time compared to what the same amount could buy at another time

racial equality a condition in which people are treated in the same manner by law and society regardless of their race

racism belief that one race is superior to another

Radical Republicans group of Republicans in Congress who wanted to protect the rights of freedmen in the South and keep rich Southern planters from regaining political power

ratification formal approval, final consent to the effectiveness of a constitution, constitutional amendment, or treaty

raw materials natural substances before processing that will in some way increase their value or usefulness

recession a decline in economic activity usually shorter and less severe than a depression

Reconstruction the period 1867–1877 when the federal government or local republican governments ruled the Southern states that had seceded

recovery a restoring to a normal condition; one of the aims of FDR's New Deal

Red Scare term used to describe periods in the 1920s and 1950s when American fear and suspicion of communism was at its height

reform change for the better; one of the goals of FDR's New Deal

regulatory agencies parts of the federal bureaucracy charged with overseeing different aspects of the nation's economy

religious freedom the ability to worship as one chooses, guaranteed in this nation by the 1st Amendment

reparations payments for losses a nation has suffered during a war

*__representation__ condition of being acted and spoken for in government

representative government system of government in which voters elect representatives to make laws for them

republic nation in which voters choose representatives to govern them

*__Republican party__ one of the two major political parties in the United States

reservation limited area set aside for Native Americans by the U.S. government

*__reserved powers__ those powers held by the states in the American federal system

revenue income

"robber baron" term used to describe large-scale entrepreneurs of the late 1800s

Roe v. *Wade* 1973 case in which the Supreme Court affirmed a woman's right to an abortion

Roosevelt Corollary expansion of the Monroe Doctrine announced by President Theodore Roosevelt in 1904 that claimed the United States had the right to intervene in Latin America to preserve law and order

*__rural__ in or of the country

salad bowl theory idea that people of different backgrounds can exist side by side in the United States, maintaining their identities while still contributing to the overall society

salutary neglect manner in which England governed the American colonies in the late 1600s and early 1700s, marked by weak enforcement of laws regulating colonial trade

scalawag   white Southerner who supported Radical Republicans during Reconstruction

scarcity   too small a supply

sectionalism   strong sense of loyalty to a state or section instead of to the whole country

sedition   an attempt to incite a rebellion against a national government

segregation   separation of people of different races

Selective Service   name first given to the military draft during World War I

self-determination   right of national groups to their own territories and their own forms of government

***Senate**   upper house of the U.S. Congress in which each state has two members

***"separate but equal"**   principle upheld in *Plessy* v. *Ferguson*, 1896, in which the Supreme Court ruled that segregation of public facilities was legal

***separation of church and state**   principle set out in the 1st Amendment that the government shall take no actions to establish or interfere with the practice of religion

***separation of powers**   the principle that gives the powers of making, enforcing, and interpreting laws to separate legislative, executive, and judicial branches of government

settlement house   a private center providing social services for the poor in a needy neighborhood

***sharecropper**   farmer who works land owned by another and gives the landowner part of the harvest

sitdown strike   work stoppage in which employees refuse to leave the workplace and occupy it in an attempt to force their employer to come to terms

***slavery**   condition in which one person is the property of another; banned in this country by the 13th Amendment

social contract theory   the idea that people agreed to give up some rights and powers to a government that would provide for their safety and well-being

Social Darwinism   the belief that the evolutionary idea of "survival of the fittest" applied to societies and businesses

social reform   efforts to better conditions within a society

social security   programs of the federal government to provide economic assistance to the disabled, unemployed, poor, and aged

***social welfare**   programs to promote public well being

socialism   economic and political system based on the public ownership of the means by which goods and services are produced, distributed, and exchanged

***sovereignty**   absolute power of a state within its own territory

***soviet**   elected assembly in the Soviet Union; (Cap.) pertaining to the Soviet Union

speculator   person who invests in a risky business venture in hopes of making a large profit

Square Deal   name given to programs of President Theodore Roosevelt

stagflation   an economic condition characterized by both inflation and recession

***states rights**   idea that individual states had the right to limit the power of the federal government

stereotype   a fixed, oversimplified idea about a person or group

stock market   place where shares in corporations are traded

strict interpretation   a literal reading of the Constitution holding that the federal government has only those powers explicitly delegated to it in the Constitution

suburbs   smaller towns surrounding large cities

suffragists   people who campaigned for women's right to vote

summit meetings conferences of the heads of two or more nations

supply-side economics the theory that the government can best stimulate the economy by cutting taxes and encouraging investment in business

supremacy clause Article VI, Section 2 of the Constitution, which makes that document and federal laws and treaties the "supreme law of the land"

Supreme Court the highest federal court and the final interpreter of the Constitution

surplus goods extra goods

tariff tax placed on goods brought into a country

*technology the complete body of ways a society provides itself with material objects

temperance movement campaign against the sale or drinking of alcohol

"territorial integrity" condition in which a nation's borders are guaranteed against disturbance by other nations

territory a political division of the United States before it becomes a state; a large area of land

terrorism the use of violence, intimidation, and coercion to achieve an end, to gain publicity for a cause, or to disrupt the normal functioning of society

*Third World nations in the modern world that profess not to be allied with the Soviet Union and its allies or the United States and its allies, especially the developing nations of Asia, Africa, and Latin America

*three branches of government the division of the powers of government into legislative, executive, and judicial functions

*three-fifths compromise compromise reached at the Constitutional Convention of 1787 whereby three-fifths of a state's slave population would be figured into the state's total population

totalitarian form of government in which the power to rule embraces all matters of human concern

tradition the handing down of beliefs, customs, and practices from generation to generation

treaty a formal agreement concluded between two or more countries

Treaty of Versailles treaty marking the end of World War I that the U.S. Senate refused to ratify

Triple Alliance name of the alliance of Germany, Austria-Hungary, and Italy before World War I

Triple Entente name of the alliance of Great Britain, France, and Russia before World War I

*trust group of corporations run by a single board of directors

trustbuster person who wanted to break up some or all trusts

two-party system political system in which the candidates of only two major parties have a reasonable chance of winning elections

unconstitutional not permitted by the constitution of a nation

unilateral action an action taken by one nation only

unitary government form of government in which all of the powers of government are held in a single agency

*universal suffrage the right to vote is extended to all adults

urban in or of the city

*urbanization process by which more of a nation's population becomes concentrated in its cities

venture capital money invested in a new corporation or other business enterprise

veto chief executive's power to reject a bill passed by a legislature

*__Vietnam War__ nation's longest war, fought in Southeast Asia from the late 1950s to 1973

__void__ without legal force or effect

__War Powers Act__ law passed in 1973 requiring the President to seek congressional approval if troops are sent into action for longer than 60 days

__white-collar worker__ someone holding a job in business or in a profession

__women's rights movement__ the struggle of women for equality

__work ethic__ a belief that hard work was a virtuous end in itself

__World War I__ conflict between Allied Powers and Central Powers from 1914 to 1918

*__World War II__ conflict between Allied and Axis nations between 1939 and 1945

__yellow journalism__ sensational style of reporting used by some newspapers in the late 1800s

__yellow peril__ derogatory term implying that Asian peoples threatened the ways of life of white Americans

Index

BIBLIOGRAPHY

Baker, Richard Allen. "The 'Great Departments': The Origin of the Federal Government's Executive Branch." *this Constitution: A Bicentennial Chronicle*, 17, Winter 1987:11–17

Banning, Lance. "From Confederation to Constitution: The Revolutionary Context of the Great Convention." *this Constitution: A Bicentennial Chronicle*, 6, Spring 1985:12–18

Boorstin, Daniel J. and Brooks Mather Kelley. *A History of the United States*. Englewood Cliffs, N.J.: Prentice Hall, 1986

Burns, James MacGregor and Richard B. Morris. "The Constitution: thirteen crucial questions." *this Constitution: A Bicentennial Chronicle*, 1, September 1983:4–8

Burns, James MacGregor, J.W. Peltason and Thomas E. Cronin. *Government by the People*. Englewood Cliffs, N.J.: Prentice Hall, 1986

Commager, Henry Steele and Milton Centor. *Documents of American History, Vol. 2: Since 1898*. Englewood Cliffs, N.J.: Prentice Hall, 1988

Constitution for the United States of America. CA: Center for Civic Education, 1987

Cortner, Richard C. "The Nationalization of the Bill of Rights: An Overview." *this Constitution: A Bicentennial Chronicle*, 18, Spring 1988:14–19

Davidson, James West and John E. Batchelor. *The American Nation*. Englewood Cliffs, N.J.: Prentice Hall, 1990

Dorsen, Norman. "The Bill of Rights: Protector of Minorities and Dissenters." *this Constitution: A Bicentennial Chronicle*, 18, Spring 1988:20–24

Dubofsky, Melvyn and Athan Theoharis. *Imperial Democracy: The United States Since 1945*. Englewood Cliffs, N.J.: Prentice Hall, 1988

Evans, Sara M. *Born for Liberty: A History of Women in America*. London: Free Press, 1989

Galbraith, John Kenneth. *The Great Crash: 1929*. Boston: Houghton Mifflin, 1988

Greene, Jack P. "The Imperial Roots of American Federalism." *this Constitution: A Bicentennial Chronicle*, 6, Spring 1985:4–11

Graff, Henry E. *America the Glorious Republic*. Boston: Houghton Mifflin, 1988

Harvey, Karen D., Lisa D. Harjo and Jane K. Jackson. *Teaching About Native Americans*. Washington, D.C.: National Council for the Social Studies, 1990

Hirsch, E.D., Jr., Joseph F. Kett and James Trefil. *Dictionary of Cultural Literacy*. Boston: Houghton Mifflin, 1988

Holland, Kenneth M. "The Constitution and the Welfare State." *this Constitution: A Bicentennial Chronicle*, 11, Summer 1986:18–23

Hyman, Harold W. "War Powers in Nineteenth-Century America: Abraham Lincoln and His Heirs." *this Constitution: A Bicentennial Chronicle*, 9, Winter 1985:4–10

Jordan, Winthrop D. and Leon F. Litwack. *The United States: Combined Edition*. Englewood Cliffs, N.J.: Prentice Hall, 1989

Kurland, Philip B. "The Origins of the National Judiciary." *this Constitution: A Bicentennial Chronicle*, 2, Spring 1984:20

Leuchtenburg, William. *Franklin D. Roosevelt and the New Deal, 1932–1940*. New York: Harper and Row, 1963

Lofgren, Charles A. "To Regulate Commerce: Federal Power Under the Constitution." *this Constitution: A Bicentennial Chronicle*, 10, Spring 1986:4–11

Maier, Pauline. "The Philadelphia Convention and the Development of American Government: From the Virginia Plan to the Constitution." *this Constitution: A Bicentennial Chronicle*, 15, Summer 1987:12–19

McCarrick, Earlean M. "The Supreme Court and the Evolution of Women's Rights." *this Constitution: A Bicentennial Chronicle*, 13, Winter 1986:4–11

McClenaghan, William A. *Magruder's American Government*. Englewood Cliffs, N.J.: Prentice Hall, 1990

Morrison, Samuel Eliot, Henry Steels Commager and William E. Leuchtenburg. *A Concise History of the American Republic*. New York: Oxford University Press, 1983

Moss, George. *America in the Twentieth Century*. Englewood Cliffs, N.J.: Prentice Hall, 1989

Nash, Gary B. and Julie R. Jeffrey. *American People: Creating A Nation and a Society*. New York: Harper and Row, 1985

Norton, Mary Beth and Carol Kerkin. *Women of America: A History*. Boston: Houghton Mifflin, 1979

Norton, Mary Beth, David M. Katzman, Paul D. Escott, Howard P. Chudacoff, Thomas G. Paterson and William M. Tuttle, Jr. *A People and a Nation: A History of the United States*. Boston: Houghton Mifflin, 1986

O'Connor, John R. *Exploring American History*. Englewood Cliffs, N.J.: Globe Book Co., 1991

Rakove, Jack N. "James Madison and the Bill of Rights." *this Constitution: A Bicentennial Chronicle*, 18, Spring 1988:4–10

Remy, Richard and John Patrick. *Lessons on the Constitution*. Boulder, CO: Social Science Educations Consortium, Inc., 1985

Silbey, Joel H. " 'Our Successors Will Have an Easier Task': the First Congress Under the Constitution, 1789–1791." *this Constitution: A Bicentennial Chronicle*, 17, Winter 1987:4–10

Wiecek, William M. "Chief Justice Taney and His Court." *this Constitution: A Bicentennial Chronicle*, 6, Spring 1985:19–24

Wood, Gordon S. "Eighteenth-Century American Constitutionalism." *this Constitution: A Bicentennial Chronicle*, 1, September 1983:9–13

Wood, Gordon S. "The Origins of the Constitution." *this Constitution: A Bicentennial Chronicle*, 15, Summer 1987:4–11